The Problem of Evil in the Ancient World

The Problem of Evil in the Ancient World

Homer to Dionysius the Areopagite

Mark Edwards

CASCADE *Books* · Eugene, Oregon

THE PROBLEM OF EVIL IN THE ANCIENT WORLD
Homer to Dionysius the Areopagite

Cascade Books
An Imprint of Wipf and Stock Publishers
199 W. 8th Ave., Suite 3
Eugene, OR 97401

www.wipfandstock.com

PAPERBACK ISBN: 978-1-7252-7163-0
HARDCOVER ISBN: 978-1-7252-7164-7
EBOOK ISBN: 978-1-7252-7165-4

Cataloguing-in-Publication data:

Names: Edwards, M. J. (Mark J.) [author].

Title: The problem of evil in the ancient world : Homer to Dionysius the Areopagite / Mark Edwards.

Description: Eugene, OR: Cascade Books, 2023 | Includes bibliographical references and index.

Identifiers: ISBN 978-1-7252-7163-0 (paperback) | ISBN 978-1-7252-7164-7 (hardcover) | ISBN 978-1-7252-7165-4 (ebook)

Subjects: LCSH: Good & evil. | Philosophy, ancient. | Good and evil—Religious aspects—Judaism—History of doctrines. | Good and evil—Religious aspects—Christianity—History of doctrines. | Theodicy | Devil—History of doctrines. | Platonists. | Neoplatonism.

Classification: BR195.S93 E39 2023 (print) | BR195.S93 (ebook)

06/07/23

For Clement

Contents

Introduction

WHY SHOULD WE STUDY dead philosophies? One answer might be to throw back the question: why should we not be as ready to study authors of the past who happen not to be in fashion as we might be to study some author of our own time who has failed, for some reason, to claim the ear of the public? The seminal effect of rediscovering lost ideas is illustrated by the rise of scholastic philosophy under the influence of the Arabic renovation of Aristotle, and then by the contribution that the recrudescent Platonism of the fifteenth century made to the overthrow of that philosophy. The philosopher whose knowledge is bounded by the modern Anglozone, which no longer remembers even the German origins of its own analytic tradition, will reply that these were all turnings within the same labyrinth, and that nothing is gained by knowing whether in any given epoch it was Plato, Moses, or Aristotle who stifled the exercise of common sense.[1] Or if anything is to be gained, it is that the fly will see the way out of the bottle (to quote the celebrated metaphor of Wittgenstein)[2] when it perceives that some supposed problem of philosophy is a relic of a discarded mode of thinking. The names of past philosophers, on this principle, can serve us best as sobriquets for the fallacies that we have left behind—Cartesian dualism, Platonic essentialism, Kantian solipsism, the Aristotelian distinction of substance and accident. In this assumption that there can be no retracing of steps, the analytic tradition finds an ally in the "Continental philosophy'" that it despises for its refusal to let common sense speak for itself. For, while it is true that French or German philosopher will often commence with the reading of some text whose classic status is held to render it indispensable to any

---

1. On Anglophone philosophy's studious ignorance of its own history see Hankey, "Denys and Aquinas," 141.

2. Wittgenstein, *Philosophical Investigations* no. 309.

modern reflection on the same topic, it often becomes apparent that the text itself is no longer there to be read except through a series of intermediaries, of which only the last can be read without guidance: to Trouillard, the great elucidator of Proclus, it was a truism that Marx can be read only through Althusser and Freud through Lacan.[3]

Neither of these positions offers good auspices to a book on the problem of evil in antiquity, which is written on the assumption that the authors of the past, once we have removed certain obstacles to understanding them, can be as intelligible as our own contemporaries (and more so indeed for those of us who have been contemporaries of Lacan). It will not be the contention of this book that once they become intelligible the voices of the past can be inserted into modern conversations: clarity of understanding is far more likely to reinforce the conviction that Stoics and Platonists, Paul and Augustine, Manichaeans and Gnostics all subscribed to presuppositions and modes of thought that are now irrevocably superannuated. But perhaps, as R. G. Collingwood suggested, it is in its very pastness that the past retains its value for us.[4] Once we see that arguments that now seem merely incompetent or question-begging were in their own time rigorous deductions from the premises that then passed for common sense, we acquire at once a higher regard for dead thinkers than a Hegel or Bertrand Russell would accord to them and a certain diffidence with respect to our own presuppositions, lest they too should prove to be equally transitory. Even if we would no longer grant our ancestors their point of commencement without a long process of justificatory reasoning, we can grant them an equal right to contest the foundations of our own arguments and to be puzzled by the tenacity with which we maintain assumptions that they had no difficulty in contesting, or indeed (as they thought) in proving to be false.

It would be hard to think of a topic that exposes this disparity of perception more clearly than that which we now call the problem of evil. We assume that this a problem only for the classical theist, who may be more properly styled the deist, since he purports to be able to show by reason alone that this world must be the creation of God, who is omnipotent, omniscient, and perfectly good. The God of this philosopher therefore could not be ignorant of the presence of evil in the world, could not be incapable of removing it, and could not be unwilling to do so. And yet, his triumphant adversary declares, it is all too obvious that there is evil, from which it must follow that there is no such God. In response to this challenge, the classical theist has usually replied that the goodness of God prevents him from

---

3. Trouillard, *La Mystagogie de Proclus*, 2.

4. See Collingwood, *An Essay on Metaphysics*.

circumscribing the freedom of his creatures, or at least from circumscribing it more than would be consistent with their free acceptance of the happiness that he intends to bestow upon them. If the atheist refuses to grant that freedom is necessary to happiness, or urges that the freewill defence cannot account for the suffering entailed by famine, pestilence, and natural disasters, the theist may elect to surrender one of the classical tenets. The goodness of God is seldom held to be open to question—for nowadays belief is a choice, and who would choose to believe in a God who is not good?—and the theist will therefore choose to waive either the omnipotence or the omniscience of his deity.[5] He will argue, that is, either that God is capable of no more than a partial remedy for the evils that he deplores or else that he is only partially capable of foreseeing them, and hence only partly capable of knowing, when they occur, whether any remedy that he applies will prevent more evil than it occasions. The atheist can easily retort that unless God is deficient in power or knowledge he is not worth worshipping, for he ought to have been able to accelerate Hitler's death or assuage the violence of a tsunami; it is at this point that the modern theologian brings in his nostrum of divine suffering, an antidote not so much to the suffering of humanity as to "classical theism" itself, which is now deemed to be the principal cause of error in the Christian tradition.[6] If we ask what becomes of the world that Christ came to save, it seems that the best that can be hoped for is that human cooperation, grounded in the assurance that God participates in our universal suffering, will bring about a new order of society, in which the exploitation of the weak by the strong will at last give way to mutual compassion and the habit of treating others as ends in themselves rather than as means to some end of our own.[7]

The problem of evil may therefore drive us either to atheism or to improvised versions of theism that may not sit well with the common associations of the word "God." The existence of a deity being precisely what is in question, no appeal to revelation is permitted. When we turn to the ancient world, the difference is palpable at once, for if there is one fact that is unanimously agreed by ancient thinkers, it is the existence of at least one being to whom the term *theos* or *deus* may be applied. As soon as we go further, there are almost as many opinions as philosophers: the Sceptic, without declaring himself an atheist, may deny the validity of any argument for

5. See e.g. J. V. Taylor, *The Go-Between God*; Stackpole, *The Incarnation*. I am not asserting that the origins of process theology (generally traced to Alfred North Whitehead and Charles Hartshorne) or of kenotic Christology (generally traced to Bishop Charles Gore) lie primarily in a desire to solve the problem of evil.

6. Moltmann, *The Crucified God*.

7. This is what I understand to be the thesis of Moltmann, *The Way of Jesus Christ*.

the existence of the divine beings, while the Platonist may prefer to assign the beings whom he worships to a level below the first principle, perhaps manifesting some diffidence in speaking of that principle as God. Aristotle may be suspected of violating his own definition of being when he postulates a God who is pure actuality; the Stoic may appear to equate the gods with the elements while upholding the cults, which credit them with powers of divination; the Epicurean accepts that there are gods on the basis of popular report, yet ridicules everything that is said of them by the poets. It was indeed the privilege of comic poets and satirists at all times to mock the ancient stories, just as it was the privilege of tragedians to modify them; yet the wise and the simple alike continued to worship not only the old divinities but also those whom they knew to have been created by human fiat. It was permissible to maintain that all gods were in origin human beings who had been deified for their services to humanity, if sometimes for no better reason than their commission of extraordinary crimes. Romans could admit that they had no rationale for their ceremonies other than the example of their fathers, and Cato was said to have wondered how two augurs could meet without laughing. Yet Cicero, who records this quip, built a shrine to his daughter Tullia, and witnessed the most blatant manipulation of sacred rites for political ends without avowing himself an atheist. The existence of persons who not only failed to worship the gods but openly disbelieved in them is assumed in the literature that is designed to refute them; for all that, there are few attested atheists once we eliminate the cases in which the term is used with malice or exaggeration.[8]

The controversies examined in this book would almost always have been framed by those engaged in them as disputes about *pronoia*, or divine forethought, which the Latin equivalent was *providentia*, the source of our word providence. The question therefore was not whether gods existed but whether they *cared* for lesser beings. A negative answer need not trouble the poet or the mythographer, who do not expect the gods to be better than we are; it need not trouble the Epicurean, who holds that because they are better philosophers than we are, the gods care only for their own equanimity. The Stoics are tireless champions of divine providence, but only by representing as acts of solicitude the accidents that those who are not philosophers would call evils. The God of Aristotle would cease to be God

8. See Drachmann, *Atheism in Classical Antiquity*. Drachmann's definition of atheism is the denial of the existence of any deity. Scholars employing the term in a looser sense have found plentiful evidence of atheism in the ancient world, from Cudworth, *The True Intellectual System of the Universe* (1678) to Whitmarsh, *Battling the Gods: Atheism in the Ancient World* (2016). See also Dorival and Pralo (eds.), *Nier Dieu, nier les* dieus.

if he had any object of contemplation but himself. Plato insists that the cosmos must be so regulated as to ensure that all receive their deserts, but he does not maintain consistently that this order is upheld by a benevolent Creator; in the Neoplatonists even the personal Demiurge of the *Timaeus* and the *Statesman* coalesces with the unmoved mover of Aristotle. It is true that more detailed schemes of superintendence are ascribed to the gods by Platonists and Aristotelians of the Roman era, but it seems that this was an age in which the philosophical schools were uncharacteristically willing to make common cause with popular beliefs. For that reason it was also an age propitious to the rise of Christianity, in which *a priori* arguments for the unity and goodness of the divine were blended with notions of God's sleepless love for his people that were derived from the Old Testament. In that book, however, the fickleness and asperity of the Creator, even in his dealings with Israel, seem to be at war with his exclusive claim on the worship of the righteous, and in Gnostic thought he is regularly opposed to a higher God who invades the world to save the elect from his despotism. The Manichaean successors of the Gnostics, by ensnaring the young Augustine, provoked him to write against them in later life, both as a Platonist and as a Christian. In the first guise he maintains that the harmony of the created order entails that that which we call good should be thrown into relief by its contrary; in the second he argues, from a very literal reading of Genesis 2–3, that the one unqualified evil in the world is the evil *will*, which came into being through the misuse of our God-given freedom. These two responses to the problem of evil, which may be said to assume its classic form in Augustine, have become canonical, though the mediaeval exponents of the principle of order are apt to reinforce his authority with that of Dionysius the Areopagite, the subject of the last chapter in this book.

Theologians are fond of affirming, whether in praise or dispraise of the fathers of the church, that they took the Father of Jesus Christ for the god of the philosophers, imposing the *a priori* monotheism of the Greek schools upon the more dynamic and anthropomorphic imagery of the Scriptures. Yet Plato, Plotinus, and Aristotle were all avowed polytheists, inasmuch as they readily spoke of the gods as many, and seldom if ever monotheists if that term signifies one who insists that the noun "god" can be applied to only one being.[9] None of them would have quailed at the problem of evil in its modern formulation, for none affirmed the existence of an omnipotent

---

9. I take this statement, as I have phrased it, to be uncontroversial. It is of course possible to speak of pagan monotheism if "exclusive belief in one God rather than the inclusive acceptance of many gods" is treated as a possible development of monotheism rather than as a definition of the term itself. See Mitchell and van Nuffelen, "Introduction: The Debate about Pagan Monotheism," 4.

guardian who was touched by, or even conscious of, the misfortunes of his creatures. Whether the God of Israel is omnipotent, omnibenevolent, or omniscient is a question on which modern Hebraists are likely to differ from early Christian readers of the Septuagint. We can say that the Old Testament concurs with Plato, Aristotle, and every Christian in espousing at least that minimal doctrine of providence that excludes the mechanical operation of fate. They all agreed, that is, that the order of things must in some general sense be *just*, but it was only in Christianity that God was said to ordain for his own good purpose every accident that befell just and unjust alike.

We shall see none the less that even for early Christians the dilemma of the modern theist was easily evaded: along with the many inherited traditions of Greek thought that might have tempted them to waive the omnibenevolence, the omnipotence, or the omniscience, they inherited the united tradition of Stoic, Pythagorean, Cynic, Peripatetic, Platonic, and Epicurean pedagogy that encouraged them to question the reality of evil. Practitioners of philosophy in the Roman world insisted that it was not so much a speculative exercise as a regimen for body and soul in pursuit of the human good, whether this be defined as happiness, pleasure, autonomy, rectitude, or likeness to God. To be free from pain, from passion, and from coercion was a prerequisite for the enjoyment of the good under any description, and it was evident that this could not be attained by the indulgence of appetites that were destructive to the body or abhorrent to the soul. Hence, even the Epicurean was frugal where the Stoic was austere, the Platonist resilient where the Cynic was indomitable, the Peripatetic steadfast where the Pythagorean was obdurate; and all were agreed that such integrity was achievable only when we perceive that it is not our outward circumstances but our profitable use of them that constitutes the good.

Christianity was born into a world of enemies, and to live without succor or comfort, returning justice for injustice, and counting all tribulation is the rule of life for the saints in every book of the New Testament. Even those whose speculative theology condemned both the law of Moses and the realm of the flesh as works of an inferior god appear to have borne the ills of their earthly pilgrimage with the fortitude that the pagan world expected of its philosophers—and indeed the Christian's claim to be a philosopher was not so much an act of social conformity as an assertion of the right to non-conformity, since philosophers were generally tolerated even where their ways were mocked and their opinions despised. Even Platonism could not offer such a palliative to the sufferings and privations of life as the church could offer with its promises of incalculable rewards in the kingdom of heaven; for those who were not satisfied to be compensated for evils without knowing why they were bound to suffer them, the story of a wrong choice made in paradise (however it was interpreted) shifted the blame from God to the human agent, reinforcing the lesson that the only true evils are our own sins, not the sins of others or the vagaries of nature, which are only as evil as our own fancy makes them. Augustine's position that nothing is evil but the evil will is supported by Platonic reasoning, and adopted in the full knowledge that it was also the position of the Stoics: we shall see that it is at the same time the culmination of centuries of Christian reflection, in the light of both the New Testament and the Old, on the failure of humans to grow in accordance with the design of God.

The response of the early church to our problem of evil would therefore be to give up not the premises relating to God but that which asserts the existence of evil. It is not the intention of this book to persuade modern theologians to adopt the same expedient: that would be to renounce our hope of changing the world and to inculcate an indifference to the sufferings of others which we no longer think consistent with the spirit of Christianity. It may be instructive, for all that, to consider that, knowing hardship as few of us know it, they disdained it with an intrepidity that we cannot emulate—just as we owe the diminution of hardship in the western world to a scientific interrogation of nature that was barely anticipated in ancient thought.

1

From Homer to Plato

IF WE ARE TO judge the world, we must have some reason to expect it to be just. While many civilizations have believed that there is a law that controls our destinies as surely as there are laws that control the motion of natural bodies, we cannot assume that the former is more accountable than the latter to any human calculation of right and wrong. It is only in very modern times, after all, that the abstract justice that inhabits the dreams of philosophers has been more than a figure of rhetoric in parliaments or even in courts of law; it is not surprising, therefore, that when it occurred to the Babylonians, the Egyptians, and the Greeks to imagine the forces that rule the cosmos as magnified copies of themselves, they credited their gods with all the caprice and partiality that they were bound to tolerate in their human masters. The Athenian who opined in the late fifth century BC that "the gods are like us, exercising their might wherever they can,"[1] was not betraying the decadence of Athenians but giving voice to the only theology that was able to compete, in the mind of a typical Greek, with abject fatalism. The wonder is not that Homer's gods are so pitiless or tragedy so amoral but that Greece, in contrast to Babylon or Egypt, should have fathered an enduring tradition of thought that had for its object the vindication of cosmic justice. When Whitehead declared that the history of philosophy was the adding of footnotes to Plato, he was conscious that the most prized bequest of Plato to his fellow Greeks was not the Socratic method of inquiry but his exhortation to "be like God, so far as is in one's power."

1. Thucydides, *Peloponnesian War* 5.105.2.

Homer and His Gods

To speak of moral good and evil in Homer is to risk anachronism. The heroes of the *Iliad* and the *Odyssey* are not for the most part moved by any concern for the common good, but only by the desire to keep what is theirs, however acquired, and to wrest from others what they can by subterfuge or by martial prowess.[2] The runner whose rival is tripped by a goddess is not denied the trophy (*Iliad* 23.782–84); in war the greatest share of spoil accrues to him who shows least mercy in killing. When Menelaus is ready to spare a supplicant, he is rebuked by his brother, the High King Agamemnon (6.55–60). Achilles retires to his tent because a woman whom he counted as part of his plunder has been withheld from him; incurring no blame from anyone in the narrative, he is entreated, cajoled, and bribed at last with a rich array of gifts, including a troupe of compensatory females (9.128–29), while the woman whom he once craved as his prize laments the death of Patroclus (19.348–54). To avenge the death of this friend, whom, rather than help his fellow-Greeks, he had permitted to die in his stead, Achilles not only kills the Trojan champion Hector but also mutilates his corpse. Although he appears to yield to the tears of Hector's father Priam, he is predisposed to do so by divine warning (24.126–40), and does not dismiss the old man without some menaces of his own (24.650–55). The protagonist of the *Odyssey* is equally relentless in his slaughter of the suitors who have laid siege to his wife in Ithaca: their parents attempt to take vengeance only because they are their parents, just as Telemachus and Eumaeus join Odysseus in slaying them only because he is the father of one and the master of the other. The poet leaves us to make what we will of the fact that this same Odysseus had spent seven years in the arms of a nymph before he came back to reclaim his faithful spouse (*Odyssey* 5.148–59).

Homeric man is expected to observe the laws of hospitality and in certain cases to respect a supplicant;[3] otherwise it appears that his only duty is to aggrandize himself at the expense of others, to slay and spoil lest he be slain and spoiled. There appears to be no universal notion of justice: the populist Thersites can be silenced with a blow when he mocks the folly of Agamemnon (*Iliad* 2.265–66), while Achilles too is advised to submit not because Agamemnon is right but simply because he is more of a king (1.280–81). It is not clear that Agamemnon regards himself as what we should now call a moral agent, for when he wishes to reconcile Achilles he explains that he wronged him not by choice but under the influence of an

2. On *arete* (excellence, virtue) in Homer as that which is socially honoured, see Adkins, *Merit and Responsibility*, 31–36.

3. See *Odyssey* 14.283–84; 6.207–8; and 14.57–58; Lloyd-Jones, *Justice of Zeus*, 30.

irresistible madness sent by Zeus (19.86–111). He does not deny that he has a duty to make due restitution in gold and women, but as in a "no fault agreement" of our own day,[4] liability implies no admission of guilt. Some have maintained that Homeric man is not even a physical unity,[5] since the poems have no term for the living body except the plural *merê* or limbs. The soul too is never spoken of as an animating principle, but only as that which forsakes a human at death or in moments of unconsciousness.[6] In the underworld (which may not be clearly distinguished from the grave) the shade lacks *phrenes* or mental powers (*Iliad* 3.104), though these can be restored by the taste of blood (*Odyssey* 11.51 and 96–99). Achilles, who risked his life so often for glory, protests in Hades that he would rather be a landless thrall than king of the dead. Yet the state of the living is hardly to be preferred if it is true, as one of Homer's most famous aphorisms has it, that:[7]

> Each day that mind in earthbound mortals reigns
> That he who sires both gods and men ordains

Who then are these gods, and are they subject to their nominal father Zeus, who is nonetheless styled the son of Cronus? Gods have the advantage of us in being immortal, and their entry into a battle is decisive if no god takes the other side. Far from being superior to us, however, in wisdom and rectitude, they are capriciously obstinate in love and hatred, so that neither fear nor reason can detach Hera and Aphrodite from the Trojans or Apollo and Aphrodite from the Greeks. Zeus, whose favor sways from side to side, may forbid the others to intervene, but he can be foiled in *Iliad* 13 by the wiles of Hera (to whom he is flagrantly and repeatedly unfaithful), while the prayers of Thetis, the mother of Achilles, induce him to help the Trojans against the Greeks at the beginning of the *Iliad*. Thetis reminds him that she once secured the giant Briareus as his bodyguard when the other gods were conspiring to take him prisoner[8]—an episode which makes no sense of his claim to be so much stronger than the rest that he could lift them all with a chain.[9] Sometimes he appears to be not the arbiter but the

4. Dodds, *The Greeks and the Irrational*, 18, perhaps overestimates the difference between the values of Homeric society and our own.

5. For *melê* see *Iliad* 7.131, etc.; for *soma* as corpse *Odyssey* 10.53, etc.; for *demas* adverbially (i.e., in accusative) as living body *Iliad* 5.801, etc.

6. See *Iliad* 16.586 and other passages collected by Snell, *Discovery of the Mind*, 10–11; Clarke, *Flesh and Spirit*, 55–60.

7. *Iliad* 24.525–26. Commenting on this passage, Fränkel, *Early Greek Poetry*, 82, concludes that in the modern sense Homeric man has no soul.

8. *Iliad* 1.503, alluding to 401–5.

9. *Iliad* 8.17–20. On the philosophical interpretation of this as a symbol of cosmic providence, see Lévêque, *Homeri Catena Aurea*.

spectator of a predetermined outcome, as when he waits for the scale to turn after putting in it the fates of Hector and Achilles (*Iliad* 22.209–13; cf. 8.69–71); on the other hand, we may wonder why he should weigh them if the experiment led to nothing.[10] On another occasion it is only the threat of concerted rebellion by his fellow-gods that prevents him from postponing the day appointed for the death of his son Sarpedon (22.177–81). That he should be able to do so is not remarkable when we hear that even Patroclus, had he not been forestalled by Apollo, might have gone so far in his rage as to overthrow Troy before its time (Iliad 16.698–99).[11]

Mortals, it appears, can hope for little after death. The shade of the sage Teiresias may be animated by the taste of blood (*Odyssey* 11.98), but for the majority life in Hades is existence without the *phrenes* or mental faculties, or at least without more intelligence than will enable them to complain of the manner in which they quit this life. Achilles, who daily wagered his life for glory, exclaims that he would rather be a landless thrall in the upper world than King among the dead (11.398–400). Menelaus and Helen are among the few who are promised unending felicity in Elysium, although Menelaus excels the other heroes neither in prowess nor in rectitude, while Helen's infidelity was the cause of the Trojan War (4.561–69). There is no more evidence of divine concern for justice in the realm of the living, unless we count the elliptical comparison of the onset of Patroclus against the Trojan to a rainstorm sent by Zeus to punish those who pronounce false judgments (16.385–86).[12] The *Odyssey* commences with a speech by Zeus deploring the human propensity to blame the gods for their failure to avert the ills that we bring upon ourselves (1.32–43); Athena retorts that so long as her favorite Odysseus is marooned on Calypso's Island by Poseidon he will have a right to complain of divine neglect (1.44–62). It is she and not her father, for all his assurances (1.63–79), who brings the hero safely to Ithaca, Zeus intervening only in the last book to hurl his thunderbolt at the parents of the dead suitors (24.539–40), who are arguably seeking a just revenge.[13]

10. Noting that the *kêres* weighed by Zeus cannot be malignant spirits, as at 23.78. Nótári, "Scales of Justice," suggests that the motif is derived from the weighing of souls in Egyptian depictions of the afterlife.

11. These ambiguities are sensitively discussed by Morrison, "Kerostasia." Cf. *Iliad* 2.155 for the possibility of a return by the Greeks that would be *hypermora*, "outside the bounds of fate."

12. Allan, "Divine Justice and Cosmic Order," 10–12, argues that this episode is not anomalous even in the *Iliad*, though the poet is not so inclined to moral judgment on his characters as the poet of the *Odyssey*.

13. See further Winterbottom, "Speaking of the Gods." On the seeming disparity between the "moral tone" of the Odyssey and the acts of its hero, see Rutherford, "Philosophy of the Odyssey."

Hesiod

In Homer's world, divine action is arbitrary and intermittent; fate, which determines the time of death, may not be insuperable but is never overruled. Even for the dead there is no providential law to ensure that the wicked will suffer while the good receive their due.[14] Where nothing is expected of the gods there is no theodicy, no presumption that any account of the origin of evil is owed to us. The *Works and Days* attributed to Hesiod, and composed (as most scholars opine)[15] a little later than the Homeric poems, admits that life without evils is conceivable when it recounts the successive creation by the gods of five human races, of which our own is the last and worst.[16] The golden race was ageless and godlike, ignorant of strife and the tools that turn strife into warfare, since the soil yielded all that was necessary to life without cultivation (*Works and Days* 110–26). The men of the silver race, which followed the gold, were also peaceable, but not so wise, being granted only a short span of adult life after a century of infantile dependence on their mothers. Because they grew too proud to perform their duties to the gods— which the poet enjoins at all times on those who hope to prosper—Zeus hid them beneath the earth, where they survive as blessed spirits (126–42). He now created the race of bronze, strong in body and harsh in temper, wielding weapons and building houses of the metal from which they were named (143–55). These destroyed one another, and were succeeded by a generation of demigods, no less warlike, whose feats are recorded in legend (156–65). The Trojan War put an end to the last of these, but it seems that, in contrast to Homer, Hesiod believes that all of them were translated after death to the islands of the blest (165–72). They were succeeded by the men of our time, a race of iron, whose internecine strife is not tempered by piety, good faith, or a sense of honor, so that fathers are set against children, friend against friend, and no place remains on earth for Aidos or Nemesis, for shame or the just resentment of injuries (174–201).

In this myth, a memory of the supersession of bronze by iron has been extended to form a schematic account of the degeneration of human society from its primaeval innocence.[17] For all we know, it may be an original creation by the Greek poet, since the use of metals to represent a degenerative succession of empires is not attested before the book of Daniel, written perhaps five centuries later as a commentary on events that had not yet

14. Except, it seems, for egregious sinners at *Odyssey* 11.568–601.

15. For discussion, see West, "Towards a Chronology of Early Greek Epic"; Koning, "The Hesiodic Question."

16. I follow the text of West, ed., *Hesiod: Works and Days*.

17. See further Loney, "Hesiod's Temporaliies," 119.

occurred in the time of Hesiod.[18] The hint that the tools of agriculture are also weapons of war was elaborated, as we shall see, in Roman literature, and may be foreshadowed in Genesis 4, if that is indeed an earlier composition. The intercalation of the age of demigods may be seen as an emollient to patrons who counted the heroes of the waning Bronze Age among their ancestors. The poet's description of the silver race remains a puzzle, which Plutarch solved by equating them with daemons,[19] thus explaining their longevity and their intermediate place between a godlike race and a race of short-lived men. No explanation is offered for the passing of the golden race, and no attempt is made to distinguish the sins for which we are culpable from those that are forced upon us by our natural condition.

The origin of one prevalent evil, the existence of woman, is recounted in the *Theogony*, another poem ascribed to Hesiod. Here the gods are said to have come to power by supplanting the Titans, as they supplanted their father Uranus, by an act of rebellion in their own defence. For this narrative Near Eastern antecedents are easily found,[20] but the Greek departs from them in assigning the creation of human beings not to the victors but to Prometheus, their ally among the Titans. Prometheus nonetheless cheats Zeus into choosing the lesser portion of the first sacrifice by concealing the bones in fat, and Zeus avenges himself by denying humans the gift of fire (*Theogony* 535–60). When Prometheus secretly imparts it to humans, Zeus counteracts his stratagem by the creation of woman, on whom Athena and Aphrodite bestow irresistible but perfidious charms (561–84). The poet of the *Theogony* is content to warn his audience that a woman will deceive him and waste his substance, and that if he desires to be happy he will remain unmarried and bequeath his estate to a distant relative. The *Works and Days*, however, makes the first woman—Pandora, or the All-endowed—the author of a calamity that cannot be escaped by any of her descendants. Again it is Zeus who contrives it, bidding Hermes to visit the house of Epimetheus, the brother of Prometheus, with a sealed jar that they are strictly forbidden to open. Zeus knows, of course, that a woman's curiosity brooks no rein, and when Pandora removes the lid an innumerable multitude of pains and afflictions swarms into the world (*Works and Days* 47–105). Hope alone lingers (96), though whether this means that even hope is denied us or that only hope remains to us, and whether it relieves or embitters our sorrows, the poet has left us to decide.[21]

---

18. See, however, Crabbe, "The Generation of Iron."

19. See chapter 5, but also West, *Works and Days*, 186–87.

20. See West, *East Face of Helicon*, 277–305.

21. See West, *Works and Days*, 169–71, on the illogicality of imprisoning Hope in

Heraclitus

The literature of the archaic era, spanning perhaps three centuries from Hesiod to the heyday of Athens, is almost wholly poetic, except for some pieces of unmetrical writing, often derived from much later witnesses, which we might hesitate to call prose. There was at this time no profession of philosophy, but Greeks of Hellenistic and Roman periods singled out a number of predecessors to Plato and Aristotle and arranged them into schools. In Aristotle himself, an incipient canon has emerged,[22] and while it may seem that speakers in Plato's dialogues attach as much authority to Simonides and Pindar as to Zeno and Protagoras, Socrates shows by his choice of interlocutors that he too distinguishes those who merely opine from those who can argue for their opinions. For all that, we must be wary of assuming a clear distinction in this epoch between philosophical and literary conventions, as though we could know that a defence of the gods against calumny in Pindar was only a trope, whereas Xenophanes's strictures on Hesiod and Homer were inspired by his zeal for truth and his lofty conception of the divine.[23] When we hear that the *Cypria*, an epic describing the Greek expedition to Troy, explains the war as a contrivance of Zeus to curb the earth's population, we do not take this as a serious contribution to theodicy; but have we any more reason to see a transition from myth to philosophy in Anaximander's dictum that the elements make restitution to one another at the bar of time?[24] This is metaphysics because it is quoted by Simplicius, who ignores the use of the same conceit in Solon.[25] Nor do he or the late doxographers quote Theognis, either when he invokes the vengeance of the gods or when he rails against the perfidy of his beloved Cyrnus and other contemporaries.[26] To keep this book within bounds, I too shall pass over the lyric poets, but with the caveat that (as Snell and Fränkel perceived) no

---

a jar of evils, and also on the poet's ascription of Pandora's crime to the will of Zeus. Catevaro, "The Clash of the Sexes."

22. For sources, see Currie, "*Cypria*," 285. On the tradition that the war was provoked by Hera's suborning of Paris to award her the prize for beauty, see Davies, "The Judgment of Paris."

23. Mackenzie, *Poetry and Poetics*, 34–46, observes that Xenophanes wishes to surpass his predecessors, though he does not suggest that this detracts from the sincerity of his strictures.

24. Anaximander, Text 9 Graham; B9 Diels-Kranz. Here and throughout I cite the numeration of Graham, *The Texts of Early Greek Philosophy*, together with that of Diels and Kranz, *Die Fragmente der Vorsokratiker*.

25. See Kirk and Raven, *The Presocratic Philosophers*, 120.

26. On the role that this poet of the sixth century BC played in Greek education, see Jaeger, *Paideia*, 183–204.

strict dichotomy can be drawn between philosophy and other branches of literature in the four centuries between Homer and Aristotle.

Heraclitus is the first philosopher whose thought can be reconstructed from his own words. Although he was a notorious coiner of paradoxes, few of those that survive explain his reputation for obscurity. "The road up is the road down" is an observation that we all make early in life (T61 Graham; Fr 38 DK); "you cannot step into the same river twice" (to paraphrase a dictum that survives in three different versions) has the picturesque banality of a proverb (T62–67 Graham; F39 DK). The inference that he draws from such aphorisms—that everything is in a constant state of flux—was no doubt more contentious in antiquity than in the age of quantum mechanics, but it was never found arcane. Again it is a truism that salt water is life to fish and poison to humans (T79 Graham; Fr. 49 DK) and that asses prefer straw to gold (T126 Graham; Fr. 82 DK). To argue that all good and evil is therefore determined by the percipient and not by the properties of the thing perceived may be a fallacy, and was widely deemed to be so, but the thesis itself was easily understood. There are hints of a relativism that spans more than one order of being when we are told that there are "immortal mortals, mortal immortals, living the death of these, dying the life of those" (T112 Graham; Fr. 69 DK). Is this an intimation that the soul sleeps when the body wakes, or perhaps that the beings who suffer birth and death in the present world have a life elsewhere that is free of vicissitude?[27] Here we approach the subject-matter of theology, and it is generally agreed that if Heraclitus is ever intractably obscure, it is when he is speaking of God or of that which we might suspect to be God by another name.

The Stoics were later to claim him as the father of their theology in which God is the subtlest of elements, a rarefied fire, pervading the world as its logos or hegemonic principle of life and order.[28] Heraclitus does indeed exhort us to listen "not to me, but to the Logos," meaning perhaps to the irresistible cogency of his argument or—what is much the same thing—to the daily evidence of our senses that confirms it (T41 Graham; Fr. 28 DK). He laments that while this logos is common to all, we are apt to live as though we each had a private *logos* (T8 Graham; Frs. 1–2 DK). Neither of these aphorisms, however, implies that the *logos* is that which governs the cosmos, rather than a veridical account or representation of its governance: it may be the ground or content of the knowledge that Heraclitus communicates, rather than the object to be known. Nor is *logos* synonymous with

27. Cf. T109–10 Graham (Frs 68–69 DK) on sleep and waking.

28. For a review of theories, see Miller, "The Logos of Heraclitus." Johnstone, "Logos in Heraclitus," argues that the *logos* is at once common and uncommon, using ordinary speech to sustain a peculiar account of things as "thus and thus."

fire, which is rather the substrate that undergoes the operation of *logos*: all things, we are told, are an exchange for fire (T55 Graham; Fr. 33 DK), the first exchange being water, while half of water is air and the other half an element cryptically named *prêster* or whirlwind (T51 Graham; Frs. 30–31 DK). Fire is the death of air, and water the death of earth (T52–53 Graham; Frs. 32a–b DK): the saying that it is death for souls to become water is of a piece with these, and may not imply that the death of a soul is permanent or evil (T101/105 Graham; Fr. 64/65 DK). Those who have grasped that to be is to perish will not echo Homer's wish that strife could be banished from the world (T60 Graham; cf. *Iliad* 18.107), but will see that war is the father of all (T58–59 Graham; Frs. 38–39 DK), and that the harmony of nature consists, like the tightness of a bow, in mutual tension (T70 Graham; Fr. 41 DK): they will understand, indeed, why *bios*, the name of that deadly instrument, is also the word for life (T72 Graham; Fr. 42 DK).

Who then is God? Is he the one of whom the Delphic oracle speaks in riddles through the mouth of a raving prophetess (T151 Graham; Fr. 106 DK), the one whom the ignorant worship with futile ablutions of mud and gore (T161 Graham; Fr. 115 DK)? If the cosmic is governed, as Heraclitus intimates, by the thunderbolt, (T56 Graham; Fr. 34 DK), is he the one whom we know as Zeus? What is his relation to the Erinys, or Fury, who like the tribunal of justice in Anaximander, forbids the sun to overstep his course (T89 Graham; Fr. 56b DK). The One Only Wise, we are told, "does not choose to be spoken of and chooses the name of Zeus"—or, as some translate, more opaquely than his usual style seems to warrant, "both chooses and does not choose to be called by the name of Zeus" (T147 Graham; Fr. 103 DK). Whatever we call him, this deity is day and night—that is, he is found on either side of all perceived dichotomies, though he is not to be identified, so far as we know, with one or more of the physical elements (T148 Graham; Fr. 104 DK). To such an observer, as Heraclitus declares, it means nothing to say, as we are wont to do, that one of two contraries is evil and the other good (T149 Graham; Fr. 105DK).

Parmenides to Empedocles

Perhaps the first to teach that our deeds in this world will be judged and requited in the life to come were the poets and diviners who purported to have received their knowledge from Orpheus, a Thracian bard who lived centuries before Homer. The majority of surviving Orphic texts are products of late antiquity, as perhaps is the myth that relates that humans are created from the ashes of the Titans or Ciuretes who were destroyed by

Zeus's thunderbolt after he learned that they had killed and devoured the infant Dionysus.[29] This fabulous account of human nature as a diabolic cannibal of the divine does not appear in the Golden Leaves of the archaic age, which are less concerned with the aetiology of the soul's bondage than with the means of its deliverance. The celebrated instructions for the descent to the underworld teach the soul how to refrain from drinking the waters of forgetfulness and what professions of righteousness it will need to recite to be admitted to the lake of memory.[30] In the light of Plato's myths, it has been surmised that forgetfulness is the prelude to reincarnation while the soul that retains its memory is released from the cycle of embodiment.[31]

The theory that Orphics prepared themselves for the afterlife by initiatory ceremonies in the present one rests partly in affinities with the Eleusinian Mysteries and partly on the formula "a kid, I have fallen into the milk," which has the timbre of a ritual utterance.[32] For all that, we have no proof that the Orphics were ever more than a guild of poets,[33] and in any case we must remember that myths and rites do not constitute either a way of life or a system of doctrine. We have also no clear evidence that the Eleusinian Mysteries demanded anything more than initiation as a condition of immortality: it is only in the philosophers that initiation comes to mean the discipline of the soul while the object of the climactic vision, the *epopteia*, proves to be nothing other than the Good.

The first author in whom the soul's fate is unquestionably determined by its merits is Empedocles of Acragas in Sicily, a poet of high ambition who was reputed to be a disciple of Pythagoras. Since Pythagoras set up communities in southern Italy, it is likely enough that Empedocles knew or knew of him, and also that he had perused the Orphic literature, which has left its remains in that region.[34] In Empedocles, however, we find not only a marriage of the soul's moral with its physical itinerary, not only a rationale for abstaining from meat (which Pythagoras may also have enjoined, though without explanation), but also a reconciliation of the subjective and the objective in his definition of evil and an account of the living forces in the cosmos that permits it to be a theatre of vice and virtue without being vicious or virtuous in itself. Ancient testimonies have often been taken to show that his teaching was divided into two books, one on nature (*Peri*

---

29. For an introduction to the early literature, see West, *The Orphic Poems*.

30. Edmonds, "The 'Orphic' Gold Tablets."

31. See Plato, *Gorgias* 493a–c and *Protagoras* 316d; Graf, "Text and Ritual," 57–62.

32. Edmonds, "'Orphic' Gold Tablets," 16; cf. 36–37.

33. See Linforth, *Arts of Orpheus*.

34. See e.g. Furley, *Creationism*, 168–69.

Physeos) and the other entitled *Katharmoi*, or Purifications. Nevertheless, the recent discovery of the long fragment known as the Strasbourg Empedocles has proved that matters conventionally assigned to the *Katharmoi* were treated in the poem *On Nature*, and it thus assures us that, whether or not he wrote two poems, Empedocles did not teach two philosophies.[35] This is not to say that the reconciliation of his cosmology with his hamartiology, or theory of sin, has become a less difficult enterprise.

The cosmos of Heraclitus and that of Empedocles are equally prone to change and decay, but the denizens of the former are mere phenomena of the universal flux, whereas in the latter they are products of two eternal contraries, or if we prefer a fifth and sixth in addition to the four material elements, to which Empedocles gives the names Love and Strife. Love tends to unity, strife to dissolution; love maintains the integrity of bodies, strife the diversity of their components (T41–52 Graham; Frs. 20–29 DK). Each being owes its nature to a certain ratio of elements, ordained by Aphrodite, the mythical representative of love (T46 Graham; Fr. 43 DK). If either the centripetal power of love or the centrifugal power of strife were to prevail unchecked, every organism would lose its distinguishing attributes, and either all or nothing would be one. Empedocles does indeed posit a state of total homogeneity, described in terms befitting a God, which almost satisfies the Parmenidean conditions of oneness (T55–58 Graham; Frs. 30–33 DK). Many scholars believe that this stands at one pole of a cycle of contraction and expansion, in which states of absolute love are succeeded by states of inordinate strife. Others deny any temporal alternation; be that as it may, no existence as we know it would be possible without the reciprocal interplay of both forces. As in the Pythagorean table of opposites,[36] therefore, love and strife are antithetical forces, neither of which can be characterized as good or evil.

Moral judgment enters the narrative when it turns from the periodic to the linear, from endemic patterns in nature to the incremental decline of human society, from an age in which it knew neither war nor sacrifice (T. 189 Graham: Fr. 134 DK) to a carnival of atrocities in which the guilt of murder is aggravated by the father's unwitting slaughter of his son upon the altar (T198 Graham; Fr. 143 DK). The fall of the many is mirrored in the tribulation of the poet himself, who, having once lived in superhuman felicity as a daemon, succumbed to raging strife and incurred the punishment laid down by the pitiless oracle of necessity (T200–201 Graham; Fr.

---

35. See Osborne, "Empedocles Recycled"; Martin and Primavesi, *L'Empédocle de Strasbourg*; papers collected in Pierris, *The Empedoclean Kosmos*.

36. Aristotle, *Metaphysics* 986a22–b2. Empedocles, T192 Graham (Fr. 137DK) is generally taken as an encomium of Pythagoras.

145 DK). Tossed from sea to land, from land to air, and so on, for 10,000 years through the turmoil of the elements, he has been by turns a bush, a fish, a bird, a man, or a maid (T25 Graham; Fr. 8 DK and T178 Graham; Fr. 124 DK). Having come to birth as a sage and undergone the cathartic rites that he at once enjoins and purveys in his own hexameters, he is able to proclaim to his fellow-citizens in Acragas that he stands before them no longer as a man but as a God (T174 Graham; Fr. 120 DK).[37] Thus love and strife, which are necessary and neutral counterparts in the natural order, are moral antitheses in the soul: we may say that good and evil remain subjective, but in this case subjectivity is truth because the good or evil will is a good or evil in itself. In this case, there is no lacuna between my judgment and an external datum that could be differently perceived by another mind.

Tragic Injustice

Empedocles, as we have noticed, is a poet, and it is in the lyric and elegiac verse of the archaic era that scholars have seen the emergence of a private subjectivity, in contrast to the mentality of Homeric man, who is largely a creature of social expectation. At the same time, these authors were shrewd enough to perceive that we do not become self-determining merely because we are free to act on our desires: the passion that impels us against our will may be felt as bondage, sorcery, or assault by some malign power. It is in the tragic drama of classical Athens that unusual intensity of passion collides with a destiny wrought from without—unless (as is often surmised) it is passion itself that drives the protagonist into choices that appear to be fated only when they are fatal. Of course it is impossible here to deal adequately with the most contested topic in classical studies, but we can at least pause to remark that it was not the Greeks who made a rule that a tragedy ought to end with death or discomfiture of the hero as the penalty of a sin or moral defect. Those tragedies that end happily, such as the Ion and the Helen of Euripides, were preferred by Aristotle to those that satisfy our definition of tragedy, and when he wrote that a fall into misfortune should be the consequence of *hamartia*, he does not imply that this term means for him anything but error, its usual sense in classical Greek.[38] For

---

37. On the unity of the Empedoclean daimon, see Darkus, "Daimon Parallels the Holy *Phrên*"; Mackenzie, "Empedocles, Personal Identity."

38. Aristotle, *Poetics* 52b34–53a16. Else, *Aristotle's Poetics*, 379–454, argues that the error is always failure to recognize a blood-relative. Bremer, *Hamartia*. Jones, *On Aristotle and Greek Tragedy*, 48, contends that *hamartia* should be regarded as the mainspring of the tragic action, rather than as a flaw in the tragic hero.

us it is necessary that the victim should in some way deserve his suffering, but when a Greek philosopher denounced a theory as tragic he meant that it showed no concern for justice.[39] As Nietzsche perceives, where God is righteous tragedy becomes impossible.

We may take as our example the *Oedipus Rex* of Sophocles. The drama begins with a plague sent by the gods to punish the city of Thebes for its failure to avenge the murder of Laius, its previous king and former husband of Queen Jocasta. Its present king Oedipus, now Jocasta's husband, believes himself to be the son of King Polybus of Corinth, whose home he fled when warned by an oracle that he was doomed to murder his father. He has secured the throne of Thebes, made vacant by the recent death of Laius, by his victory over the terrible sphinx and his marriage to Jocasta. Although he defeated the sphinx by solving her riddle, it takes him most of the play to divine—what is already known to Teiresias and becomes obvious to Jocasta—that his true father was not Polybus but Laius, who had caused him to be exposed for fear of a prophecy that he would not only slay his father but marry his mother. By the time he learns that a stranger whom he killed in self-defence on the journey to Thebes was none other than Laius, his mother Jocasta has already hanged herself. Nothing is left for him but to sentence himself to blindness and exile, thus expiating his crime and staying the plague in accordance with the mandate of the gods. Scholars have proposed that his tragic flaw was the obstinacy with which he ignored all warnings against unlocking the mystery, or that Laius and his son were fulfilling a curse that has been justly pronounced upon their ancestors.[40] Manifestly, however, he is innocent, as he asseverates shortly before his death in the *Oedipus Coloneus* (257); or rather, he is innocent of everything but the *hamartia*, the bare error, of parricide and maternal incest, which suffice to explain his punishment by his own hand.

The gods who have caused his ruin shepherd the old king to his secret grave in the *Oedipus Coloneus*; elsewhere in Sophocles they are barely present. "Nothing here that is not Zeus" are the last words of the *Trachiniae* (1278), but the poisoned shirt that causes the death of Heracles was given with malicious intent to his wife Deianeira by her expiring lover, the centaur Nessus. Orestes receives no succor from the gods, and is not seen to incur their wrath, when he executes his mother and her lover in retribution for the murder of his father Agamemnon. Athene casts a mist on the eyes of Ajax to prevent his killing the other Greek chieftains; the unconquerable

---

39. See Halliwell, "Plato and Aristotle," 67.

40. Lloyd-Jones, *Justice of Zeus*, 119–23, a somewhat fanciful rejoinder to Dodds, "On Misunderstanding the Oedipus Rex."

chagrin that leads to his suicide, however, is all too human in origin. The epiphany of Heracles at the end of the *Philoctetes* persuades the archer to rejoin the Greeks who abandoned him on Lemnos; it is not clear that it serves the ends of justice, and Heracles is only half a god. In the Antigone, Creon, the successor to Eteocles the son of Oedipus, defies the unwritten laws of the gods by leaving the body of Polyneices, brother and killer of Eteocles, to lie unburied and be devoured by birds. His punishment is to lose his own son Haemon, who commits suicide after Creon imprisons his lover Antigone, sister of Polyneices and daughter of Oedipus, for covering the corpse with dust in lieu of sepulture. Antigone also hangs herself, Creon repents, and the chorus declares that the gods will never fail to chastise the arrogant; but if the gods had any part in the plot, they worked unseen.[41]

In five out of eighteen tragedies by Euripides, the chorus delivers a coda upon the manifold works of the gods who cheat us of much that we once deemed certain and bring about much that we never foresaw. The usual function of his *deus ex machina* is to avert an impending calamity—for example, to prevent the capture of Pylades and Orestes as they escape with Athena's statue from the bloody altar of Tauris, or to ensure that Menelaus escapes from Egypt with the true Helen, having fought for her phantom in Troy for the past ten years. Heracles, as a demigod, can appear on stage before he descends to Hades to rescue Alcestis, who has died to preserve Admetus, her craven husband; it is only by report, on the other hand, that we learn how Artemis snatched Iphigeneia from Aulis when the sacrificial knife was already in her father's hand. Apollo, whose machinations have almost caused his own son Ion to murder his mother, is too abashed to come forward and makes his apology through the mouth of his sister Athena.[42] It has often been maintained that Euripides is unusually disdainful of his gods, or perhaps a skeptic: a speech in the *Madness of Heracles*, denying that the gods invade one another's beds, is said to throw doubt upon the divine paternity of Heracles, and hence to remove any motive for the jealousy of Hera, which is the mainspring of the play (1340–46).

More probably it implies only that the gods do not suffer the woes that they carelessly inflict on mortals.[43] This is surely the terrible lesson of the *Bacchae*, in which Pentheus of Thebes mistakes the demigod Bacchus (or Dionysus) for a charlatan, is induced by the god himself to spy on his maenads, or female votaries, in a ludicrous female costume, and is then torn

41. See Vickers, *Towards Greek Tragedy*, 526–46.

42. The dramas summarized here are the *Iphigeneia in Tauris*, the *Helen*, the *Iphigeneia at Aulis*, the *Alcestis*, and the *Ion*.

43. So Grube, *The Drama of Euripides*, 58–60; contrast Brown, "Wretched Tales of Poets," 23.

14

limb from limb when the women, maddened by Bacchus, mistake him for a bull. There is nothing in the drama, or in anything that we know of Dionysiac religion, to warrant the view that Pentheus is acting as the embodiment of the god.[44] The eating of a deity by his worshippers is a Christian conceit that has been retrojected onto the classical age; the uniform belief of the ancients, as Rene Girard reminds us, is that the god is the one who eats what the priest dispatches, the victim being neither priest nor god.[45]

Aeschylus the Exception?

It is not in the second and third generation of Attic drama, however, that scholars have looked most often for a theodicy or a counterpart to biblical monotheism: it is in the Agamemnon of Aeschylus, oldest by far of the three extant writers of tragedy, that the chorus, conscious of Clytemnestra's plot to kill her returning husband, struggles to weigh her guilt against that which Agamemnon incurred by the sacrifice of their eldest daughter Iphigeneia. Zeus alone, they exclaim, knows the causes of all things, Zeus who decrees that humans will learn by affliction and by the solemn requital of their own wrongdoing. It quickly becomes apparent, however, that Agamemnon, if he did wrong at all, did not do so in perfect freedom, since he was told that the winds that detained his fleet at Aulis could be stilled only by an offering to Artemis. We later hear that Calchas, the seer who proclaimed this, attributed the wrath of Artemis to the killing of a hare by an eagle, a spectacle that the Greeks took as an omen of the destruction of Troy. It is not clear whether Artemis is avenging the hare or the city, and it may also represent the maiden whose death she demands as redress. When Agamemnon performs the rite, he is said to put on the harness of necessity (*Agamemnon* 205): we are not told, and the chorus may not know, whether this implies that he was acting from the outset under necessity or whether he became subject to necessity as a consequence of his act.[46] If his culpability is hard to assess, so is that of Helen and Paris, the adulterous pair whose elopement provoked the Greek expedition: both are blamed with all the devices of poetic eloquence, yet the chorus hints that the irresistible power of Aphrodite was at work in them, anticipating the playful argument of the sophist Gorgias that Helen's responsibility is annulled, both by the passion of love and by the power of words.

44. The thesis of Dodds, ed., *Euripides: Bacchae*.

45. Girard, *Violence and the Sacred*, 119–40.

46. Peradotto, "The Omen of the Eagles," 252–53, argues that the image of "putting on" implies that Agamemnon is culpable, but the words are consistent with his being compelled to don the harness.

Agamemnon has also adopted Cassandra as a mistress—a further crime in the eyes of his wife, and perhaps in those of the poet and his audience if they already knew that the tearing of the virgin prophetess from Athena's altar was one of the manifold offences against the gods to which the messenger alludes. The murder of the king, for all that, is perceived as an atrocity, and when his son Orestes slays his mother and her lover in the *Choephoroe*, he fears that he would otherwise suffer the wrath of his father's spirit. Matricide, however, is at least as great an atrocity as the murder of a husband, and for years to come he is haunted by the Furies until at last his case is judged at the Areopagus in Athens under the presidency of Athena. Apollo pleads for Orestes in a series of bad arguments, the last and worst of which is that the mother is not the true parent of the child but the mere depositary of the father's sperm. The human judges vote for the capital punishment of Orestes by a majority of one, but Athena casts her pebble to make the bites equal, on no better grounds than that she herself is the daughter of Zeus but has no mother. She appears to be alluding to the story that Metis, her mother, was swallowed by Zeus to evade the prophecy that the son whom she had by him would overthrow him. The Furies rage, but are at last reconciled and receive a cult in Athens as the Eumenides or Kindly Ones.[47]

If this is the justice of Zeus it has no analogue that is known as justice in the world of mortals. Still less in the *Prometheus Bound*, if he is indeed its author, does Aeschylus appear to share that faith in the inscrutable wisdom of Zeus that his trembling chorus expresses in the Agamemnon. Prometheus in this drama, as in Hesiod, is chained to a rock to punish him for his theft of fire, and also to extort from him the name of the future offspring of Zeus who is destined to overthrow him. Although his comforters urge him to submit to the power that he cannot resist, he admits no fault and boasts of the numerous blessings that humanity has received from him, or perhaps from the forethought that he personifies. If there was any reconciliation in a subsequent play, it must have required him to give up his secret to Zeus but could not have annulled the injustice that he deplores in his cry at the end of the play, "Behold what I, a god, endure from gods" (1093). In the earliest of his extant works, the *Persians*, Aeschylus no doubt speaks for all his countrymen when he makes Darius return from the grave to reprimand the arrogance of Xerxes; one speaker, however, opines that he was not wholly responsible for his infatuation, since once a man is bent on sin his punishment from the gods is to sin all the more (742). This is a line that Plato

---

47. On the historical context of the performance, see Macleod, "Politics and the *Oresteia.*"

singles out in his *Republic* as a specimen of pernicious teaching about the gods in tragedy (380a), and the rest of the current chapter will be devoted to his endeavors to account for the presence of evil without impugning the divine governance of the world.

Plato on the Captivity of Souls

The vehicle of Plato's philosophy was the dialogue, not the hexameter or the gnomic aphorism. Since, however, he never appears as a character in his own dialogues—since, as the *Second Letter* (itself a forgery) declares, there is and will be no book by Plato—we must regard with diffidence every system of thought that has been constructed in his name. Not least must we be wary of the philosophical handbooks of the Roman era that tell us that the three principles of his philosophy are God, the forms, and matter. In fact, he never employed the term matter (*hylê*), and for the most part is as ready as other Greeks to use the term *theos* in the plural and to call particular deities by their names. In the *Republic*, for instance, God is the contemplator of ideal bed but not the primordial source of being and value (597c); in the *Timaeus, ho theos* (47c, etc.) is not so much God as "the god" who has already been introduced as the Demiurge, superior to the lesser gods but neither the pattern nor the arbiter of his own creation (28c–30a). To judge by *Republic* 509b, the final cause of all things, the measure of all values, and the goal of philosophic endeavor is the Good, and yet his dialogues on love set before us no higher object than beauty.[48] A Neoplatonic reading of the *Parmenides* and the *Philebus* would suggest that the plurality of existence flows from the One, but of this we hear nothing either in the *Timaeus* or the *Republic*, and modern commentators on the *Parmenides* suspect the Neoplatonists of mistaking parody for profundity.

Ancient critics who wished to make a coherent thinker of Plato acknowledged, as we do, that he wrote in diverse modes for different purposes: some works, they thought, were designed to try the reader's intelligence, some to lead him (openly or by stealth) to a new conclusion, some to propound the beliefs of Plato himself in a more assertoric manner.[49] To these formal observations, modern scholarship adds theories of development in the mind of Plato himself, which spare us the duty of resolving all contradictions or looking for surreptitious artifice in a palpable fallacy. It is generally assumed that the earlier writings will be those in which his teacher Socrates challenges sophists and other putative experts to explain

48. See White, "Love and Beauty."
49. See Westerink, trans., *Anonymous Prolegomena.*

their trade, with the object in most cases of eliciting a universal definition of virtue or one of its species. The required definition is frequently styled the *eidos* or form,[50] and it is usual for Socrates, having shown the proposals of others to be untenable or inconsistent with their other convictions, to steer them toward a position that they cannot refute, but without affirming it to be his own.[51] At times the contest of wits will end in nescience or perplexity, as Socrates confesses that his thoughts have come full circle, or suspects that instinctive knowledge may be a better guide than logic. Nevertheless, the premiss of every Socratic interrogation is that if we are to be virtuous we must know what virtue is (*Meno* 72a–73a, etc.). It is never implied that Socrates himself possesses this knowledge, only that knowledge is a precondition of virtue; from which it follows, as Socrates demonstrates in the *Protagoras*, that when we do wrong we are guilty of ignorance rather than wilful turpitude, of error rather than sin (*Protagoras* 354a–358d).[52]

What is the cause of ignorance? The shortness of life, we might answer, were it not that the existence of the soul before embodiment is the premiss for a theory of knowledge in many of Plato's Socratic dialogues. In the *Meno* Socrates purports to show that the principles are innate because they were learned in a previous life, and deduces from the universal kinship of nature that souls are capable of knowing all things (81b–86c). In the great myth of the *Phaedrus* (advanced as an exercise in rhetoric rather than dialectic), the soul is said to be naturally immortal, on the grounds that it is the source of motion, and therefore nothing other than soul could excite the motion that brings it into being (245c–d). It seems to follow, as Socrates maintains at length in the *Phaedo*, that the typical soul will inhabit a series of bodies (79b–88b): we have already noted this as a possible understanding of the sleep of the immortal in Heraclitus. But whereas in Heraclitus every phase in alternation is good, each being in some sense one with its contrary, Socrates appeals near the end of the *Gorgias* to certain Italian and Sicilian muses who declare that the *sôma* or *sêma* is the tomb of the soul, whose hope of deliverance lies in being found blameless at the assize that follows its death (493a and 525b–526b; cf. *Cratylus* 400c; *Phaedo* 61e–62c). On the strength of such pronouncements, Plato is often said to despise the body, yet in the great myth of the *Phaedrus*, his longest reflection on the origin of evil, the body is the place in which the soul has the chance to repeat or reverse the temerity that has robbed it of its wings.

50. It is widely held that for Plato, if not for Socrates, the forms are transcendent archetypes; but cf. Fine, *On Ideas*, 44–65.

51. For diverse evaluations of the *elenchus*, see Scott, ed., *Does Socrates Have a Method?*

52. See further Callard, "Ignorance and Akrasia-Denial."

Plato: The Return of the Soul

The three parts, powers, or aspects of the human soul, delineated by Socrates in the *Republic* (435c–442e), are symbolized in the *Phaedrus* by a winged chariot, in which the driver represents reason, his horses the spirited and appetitive elements (246a–b). The proper abode of all souls is a region above the heavens that cannot be described by any human tongue (247c). Here each soul in its chariot (whatever this signifies) joins the train of the God who contemplates its proper virtue, so that Zeus leads the seekers of justice (246e), Ares the seekers of courage (252c), and other gods the seekers of other forms (although the terms *idea* and *eidos* are not applied to them in the myth). High above all is the plane of truth, which every soul yearns to behold (248c), and all the more intensely as it grows in virtue. Most souls, however, are too weak or impetuous to reach the goal, and when their chariots collide they shed their wings—the corporeal element most akin to the divine (246d), and descend to our world, receiving a life in accordance with their deserts (248d–e). It is hinted at 248c that certain periods are assigned to the fall of souls, while a return to the supercelestial place is not permitted within 10,000 years (248e). In the meantime the soul passes from body to body, and when it enters that of the philosopher it has at first no more memory of its lost abode and its previous incarnations than it has in its other lives. The awakening begins with that stroke of love from without which is so often celebrated by the poets (249a–250c).

The necessity of love as a means to knowledge is suggested by a paradox that is brought to light by Socrates in the *Meno*: how, if we seek an object that is not already known to us, can we know when we have found it (80d–81a)? The doctrine of *anamnesis*, or recollection of previous lives, is the tentative answer in the *Meno*, but it is the *Phaedrus* that explains how recollection is quickened by the sight of beauty in mortal bodies. Beauty in turn awakens love, which, as the seer Diotima tells Socrates in the *Symposium*, is the child of plenty and poverty, a state between having and lacking, which teaches us that we are more than mortal but not yet divine (203b–204a). The genuine lover, Diotima continues, will not be content with a transitory object, but will crave the vision of that which is in all respects beautiful, not at one time but at every time, not from one point of view but from all (211a–c). So too in the *Phaedrus*, the philosopher will cultivate not the body but the intellect of the beloved, in which he sees the ectype of supernal beauty; as he garlands this like the image of a deity (252d–e), the beloved in turn will adorn himself in virtue, using the lover as his mirror (255d), and each will be conscious of the sprouting wings that mark the first stage in the ascent to the supercelestial abode (251b–d; 255c). All too often, however, the intemperate horse proves too strong for his partner, or in plain terms carnal pleasure becomes more dear to the soul than honor. The chariot tumbles, love is shipwrecked in lust, and the wings of the soul contract once more (253c–254e).

Students of Plato have wondered, from antiquity to the present, how literally he intends us to take a doctrine of transmigration that allows souls to pass into animals, where they cannot hope to expiate past transgressions.[53] Again we may wonder why any god should need courage, and how a fall that is predetermined can be imputed at the same time to the incontinence of the soul. In the tenth book of the *Republic*, which purports (though somewhat flippantly) to be based on a fleeting vision of the afterlife (614b), we are told that the soul is wholly responsible for the choice of its life to come in the light of the one that lies behind, and that no blame attaches to God (617e). There is no fall in the *Republic* from the supercelestial place, and little is said of love or beauty except to reproach the *philotheamones*, "lovers of vision," who fail to be true philosophers (lovers of wisdom) because they are still in thrall to the senses. In the simile of the Cave, which depicts the ascent of the soul from the phenomenal to the intelligible[54] and thence to the summit of being, we see the completion of an itinerary that seems not to be quite identical with the one that the soul commences in the *Phaedrus*. Having long been chained in a cave in which he sees nothing but the light thrown onto a screen by the fire behind him, together with the shapes of images carried before that fire (514a–c), the novice emerges into a higher world in which he learns first to distinguish shadows, then real objects, and at last to look with steadfast eyes on the very source of light (515b–516d).

These stages of vision correspond to successive states of knowledge that are attained by tenacious students of philosophy (*Republic* 510b–511e). The subterranean fire remains a riddle to us, but the sun, as the source of all that it renders visible, is the cipher of that which Socrates calls the Good.[55] At *Republic* 509b the Good is placed beyond *ousia* or being, which some take to mean "beyond all other existent things," and some "'beyond existence,'" that is to say, in a state so ineffable that existence cannot be predicated of it.

---

53. See editor's introduction to Partenie, ed., *Plato's Myths*; O'Brien, *The Demiurge in Ancient Thought*, 32–35, on the *Timaeus*; Reed, "Bodily Desires and Afterlife Punishment," responding to the allegorical reading of Plato's eschatology in Dorter, *Plato's Phaedo*.

54. The shadows observed by the prisoners in the cave correspond to *eikasia* in the subsequent delineation of the stages of knowledge. For a defence of the analogy between the eikastic knowledge of sensory objects and the popular apprehension of moral truths by example, see Storey, "What Is *eikasia*?"

55. Often too glibly identified with God (and indeed too glibly styled a form). For a penetrating discussion, see de Vogel, "Who Is God in Plato?"

This positing of the Good as the ultimate object of knowledge is Socrates's rejoinder to Anaxagoras,[56] an older contemporary whom he censured in the *Phaedo* for ascribing all things to mind yet treating the work of mind with reference only to efficient rather than final causes (97d–99a). The fact that it seems to be possible for a philosopher to apprehend the Good in the present world, whereas there is no hint of its presence in the supercelestial realm of the *Phaedrus*, arouses the suspicion that the descent into the body is not in all respects a calamity for the soul.

Plato on the Source of Political Evil

As we shall see, Neoplatonists maintained that the descent of the soul is not in itself an evil but becomes so when the higher soul fails to prevent the lower soul from surrendering to carnal pleasures. In the *Didascalicus*, or introduction to Plato, by Alcinous, a natural affinity for the body is one cause of descent, though not to the exclusion of either wilful incontinence or predestination.[57] Both in the *Republic* and in the *Phaedrus*, the proximate cause of sin in the present life is the subjugation of reason by the lower parts of the soul, most frequently by the appetitive element. The *Republic*, however, also sketches a history of the decline of states, the justice of cities throughout the dialogue being the justice of its citizens writ large. As the just or righteous is one in whom the desire for honor assists the higher or rational faculty in controlling the more vulgar appetites (*Republic* 440e), so the perfect city is one in which wisdom gives laws to temperance with the aid of courage, these virtues being personified respectively in the guardians, the artisans, and the auxiliaries or soldiering class (428a–434d). If the ideal polity were ever to realized, however, it would fall into decadence once an appointed cycle of the cosmos had been completed (546c–547a), and the timocratic, or honor-loving tendency would begin to prevail in its rulers (548a). Because wealth is too often the measure of honor, timocracy will quickly become plutocratic, and then it will not be long before those who ought to rule become panderers to the greed and caprice of the mob (553a).

This epitome of the decline of Athens may be contrasted with the myth told by Protagoras in the dialogue that bears his name, where Athens is to be envied by the barbarians because it has secured itself against the destructive forces of nature by practising *aidôs* and *dike*, the principles of shame and justice (320c–323d). According to the myth told by the Eleatic Stranger in

56. *Phaedo* 97b–c. His criticism that Anaxagoras fails to assign a purpose to *Nous* is challenged by Marmodoro, *Everything in Everything*, 142–43.

57. Dillon, trans., *Alcinous*, 34 and 152–53.

the *Statesman*,[58] the anarchy that preceded the creation of civil society was the result of a withdrawal of the Demiurge, under whose sway (in the period known as the age of Cronus)[59] a race of demigods had acted as stewards to humans and beasts alike (272e). Once the helm had been given to fate and the lesser gods had resigned their functions at the behest of the Demiurge, fate became sovereign until, when sufficient time had elapsed, a degree of serenity returned, with some recollection of divine wisdom (273a–b). Yet this too was lost because the admixture of matter with living creatures brought to life the primordial evil that had been latent in the reign of the Demiurge (273c). Only the return of the Demiurge and his divine retinue, who bestowed the arts of civilization on humans when they were helpless against the attacks of beasts and natural calamities (273e–274d), preserved societies from annihilation. In the third book of the *Laws* we read again of a primitive state of innocence without indigence: as humans multiplied this was succeeded first by the rule of fathers, then of lawgivers, then of kings, who all too often subverted the laws that they were appointed to uphold. The *Phaedrus*, the *Republic, the Laws*, and the *Statesman* agree that both the individual and the collective fall are the predictable, if not inescapable, consequences of natural or numerological laws.[60]

Plato: Evil in the Cosmos

In the *Republic* this is true of the astral configurations that weaken the virtue of a state, but not of the spindle of necessity which in the tenth book assigns to every soul a life in accordance with its own choice. This choice is in turn the fruit and the test of a soul's capacity to learn from its previous lives. In the myth of the *Timaeus*, recounted by the eponymous speaker,[61] the lesser gods, remaining at the posts that they are said to have vacated in the *Statesman*, perform the calculus of merits that determines the next incarnation of the soul. This is the one myth in the Platonic corpus that affirms the operation of divine providence in the world from first to last. Christians prized it above all for its testimony that the world depends on God, or at least a God, for its existence, and that he brought it into being because he was good (*Timaeus* 28c). For the professed disciples of Plato

58. Against the more common view that this myth leaves the world forsaken by God in the present age, see Perone, "Reversing the Myth."

59. Cf. *Gorgias* 524–25.

60. See Inwood, "Plato's Eschatological Myths."

61. Sedley, "The *Timaeus* as Vehicle," 49, maintains that the thought of the dialogue is a "symbiosis of Socratic doctrine and Pythagorean inspiration."

also these became dogmas, yet their interpretation was always in dispute. To say that the cosmos is generated means that is the realm of becoming rather than of being; but is there a coming to be of becoming itself or has this realm existed for ever? And if we hold, with Plato, that the Demiurge is good and what is good can have no particle of jealousy (28c), does it follow that he was bound to create, or as the Neoplatonists put it, to superabound? An affirmative reply to the second question seems to entail an affirmative reply to the first, for if creation were necessary it could not have a temporal origin: nevertheless, there are many scholars today who argue, as ancient readers sometimes did, that Plato would not have adopted the narrative form if he did not believe that the world was created at a certain time.[62]

If that is true, the world is as much a product of divine will as of divine nature; but was the Demiurge free to determine what he would bring into being? In the myth he imitates a paradigm that contains the archetypes of all natural kinds, but we are not told whether he himself shapes the paradigm or whether, if he does, he would been free to conceive any other. Since he himself is *nous* or mind, we cannot ascribe it to any higher intellect; the inference that the contents of the paradigm are thoughts in the mind of the Demiurge was not so readily drawn by pagans as by Jews and Christians, for whom the only possible Demiurge is God. The doxographers who name God, the forms, and matter as Plato's principles[63] identify the first of these with the Demiurge, the second with the paradigm, and the third with the receptacle on which the Demiurge superimposed the image of the paradigm. Plato himself describes the receptacle as a seat of perpetual turbulence, discernible only by a "bastard reasoning" (*Timaeus* 52b); if turbulence signifies motion rather than the mere absence of order[64] it may bespeak the presence of a soul, which if we take it to be the original of the world-soul, affords more evidence of the eternity of the cosmos.[65] On the other hand, we shall see that Plutarch regards it as a perpetual source of resistance to the Demiurge, citing a passage in the *Laws* (896d–897d) that contrasts two souls, one good and one evil, and asks which is the soul of the world. For Plutarch, the good soul is that of the world, the evil one its counterpart in matter; the more usual reading today, however, assumes the

---

62. Furley, *Creationism*, 101, adopts this position.

63. See further, O'Brien, *Demiurge in Ancient Thought*, 21–22.

64. Brisson, "D'où vient le mal?," 18–20, remarks that necessity in the *Timaeus* (48a7) is the source of disorder, which acts as a constraint on the work of intellect, while in the *Phaedrus* the same necessity is the cause of the fall of souls.

65. See further, Cherniss, *Aristotle's Criticism of Plato*, 423–31.

evil soul to be hypothetical,[66] while the receptacle of the *Timaeus* is often understood to be not so much matter in motion as space without form.

Whether it be matter, space, or that which Plato calls elsewhere the unlimited, the receptacle is that which makes it possible for a world to exist that is other than the paradigm or intelligible cosmos. Otherness is the necessary complement to sameness on the creation of the world-soul, which the Demiurge fashions by crossing the same with the other in the shape of the Greek letter X. As the Eleatic Stranger explains in the *Sophist*, every concrete entity must belong to a species, and thus be at once numerically other than its congeners and the same in essence. In the combination of sameness and otherness we see at once the origin of plurality and the precondition of discrete existence for any object in this world. But here too, as Plato repeatedly intimates, is the root of evil, for where there are many members of the same species none is identical with its essence, which is to say that each is in some sense other than that which we predicate if it. In a world of multiplicity we shall not find perfect beauty, perfect duality, perfect justice; wherever we met the theory of forms in Plato, we hear that the just, the equal, and the beautiful are mere copies of, or participants in, the property that they are said to exemplify. Worse still, it is the principle of otherness that permits change, and where there is change there cannot be perfection: the very thought that a God might change would belie his divinity. Therefore, a certain falling away from the best is also implied in the delegation of providential governance to the lesser gods whom the Demiurge has created for this purpose (*Timaeus* 41a). Platonists of the Roman era likened the Demiurge to a human emperor whose eyes and ears are his viceroys;[67] but if we are governed at two removes by a God who is neither omniscient nor omnipotent, we are bound to confess with Socrates in the *Theaetetus* that evils will never vanish from the world (178a).

Our one defence against evil, according to the *Theaetetus*, is to be philosophers, to join that guild of holy fools who are so intent on the higher truths that they barely notice the things that are at their feet (174b). The philosopher is like love in the *Symposium*, who goes unshod and has no permanent lodging (203c); he is one who, if dragged into court, will be convicted for want of eloquence (*Gorgias* 486b–f)—convicted because he would rather suffer any form of injury, death, or ignominy than commit an injustice. Christians thought that they recognized this picture, but in Plato it is a picture of self-sufficiency: the aim of philosophy is "likeness to God so far as is possible" (*Theaetetus* 176b), yet at the end of the *Timaeus* it is not

---

66. See, e.g., Brisson, "D'où vient le mal?"

67. Origen, *Against Celsus* 8.35; [Aristotle], *On the World* 12.6.

the soul but the cosmos that is the sole likeness (*monogenes eikon*) of the intelligible realm (92c).

Conclusion

We may say that the problem of evil, as theologians understand it, begins with Plato; yet we must also say that for Plato it is a metaphysical rather than a theological problem. His metaphysics teaches him that the real is that whose predicates belong to it indefeasibly, while that which is subject to change, or which does not in all respects answer to its predicates, belongs to the realm of becoming rather than being. Since that which is subject to change must change from worse to better or from better to worse, we cannot look for perfection in the realm of becoming; conversely, where being is not subject to change or deficiency, there is the good. It does not, however, follow that the sum of evil would be reduced if there were no realm of becoming, for if being is good it is better for it to be communicated, even imperfectly, than not to be communicated at all. Whether we imagine our labile cosmos as the handiwork of a Demiurge or as a product of spontaneous emanation, the evil, or rather deficit of the good, that seems to mar it is a corollary of that deficit of being which is implied in the term "becoming"—and is thus not an evil at all if we mean by that term that it ought to have been, and could have been, otherwise. By this criterion, vice in the soul is the one true evil, and even this, on Plato's view, is not so much a deliberate choice as a failure to distinguish real from imaginary goods.

Heraclitus had already said that what we suppose to be evil is good in the sight of God; Empedocles had maintained that the present suffering and vicissitude of the soul are ordained by necessity for the expiation of sin. Plato takes up the theory of transmigration with the aim of showing that what we now experience as necessary is the consequence of a choice for which we, and not God, must be held responsible. His theory, as it takes shape in the *Timaeus*, *Republic*, and other works does not require him to posit matter as a recalcitrant substrate, or to endow the receptacle of creation with a turbulent soul. Although both these positions were entertained by some of his followers, both might have seemed to him to savor too much of the tragic fallacy that holds blind fate or capricious gods accountable for misfortunes that are brought upon us by our own vice and folly. We shall have occasion in this book to discuss a number of theories that assume opposing powers of good and evil to be at work in the physical cosmos; none of these, however, will detain us in the next chapter, which will show that neither fatalism nor the denial of providence gave rise to any species of dualism so long as philosophy remained the preserve of the Greeks.

2

Evil and Its Antidotes after
the Classical Era

ALL THE GREAT SCHOOLS of thought that arose in the Greek world after
Plato originated in Athens, and all agreed that the questions of Plato were
questions for every philosopher, however far they departed from his solutions. They differed from him most radically with regard to the nature of
being, for whatever place they were willing to give to the forms in their
ontology, no Peripatetic, Stoic, or Epicurean could admit the real existence
of any entity outside the material cosmos, with the possible exception (for
certain disciples of Aristotle) of an inactive deity and an impersonal soul.
On the other hand, all these schools agreed that a correct ontology was
the prerequisite for a correct understanding of human nature and hence
of the ends that a human being ought to pursue. Because of their disparate
metaphysical premisses, they arrived at disparate views of the relation of
virtue to happiness, though all concurred in holding that neither was likely
to be attained without the other. They were more at one in the practice than
in the theory of conduct, all of them thinking it best to possess and pursue
no more than was necessary to happiness, though the others might think
the Stoics fanciful when they contended that virtue alone, without external
goods, sufficed for the achievement of this goal. It may in fact be true of
all sane societies that the range of ethical choices is much smaller than the
range of metaphysical speculations, and the disputes that will be examined
in this chapter turn primarily on the metaphysical topic (as we would now

say) of divine providence, that is, the role of superhuman agents in causing what seems to us evil or enabling us to see and attain the good.

Aristotle and the Peripatetics

Aristotle had the reputation in antiquity of being, if not an atheist, at least a denier of providence.[1] And yet in the Middle Ages his thought was the cornerstone of philosophic monotheism for Christians, Jews, and Muslims, and even today it furnishes both Protestants and Catholic with a rational vindication of revealed doctrines on the origin of the world and the ends of life. He owes both reputations to his belief in the primacy of final causes, in the realm of being as in that of knowledge. To recognize the operation of natural laws in the cosmos, he contends, is to rule out both automatism and arbitrary causation: *tykhè* or "chance" is a word that we use of events that work out luckily or unluckily for our own ends, and it is of no use in explaining the unvarying operation of the same principle in the growth of plants or the movement of the heavens (*Physics* 196a–197a). Thus, the pupil of Plato reaffirmed his master's principle that to understand a phenomenon we must know not only how but why it occurs; thus he rejected both the fatalism of the Stoics and the lawless cosmos of the Epicureans before either school had come into existence. For all that, he is not a theist whose God creates, like the Demiurge of the *Timaeus*, as a consequence of his superabounding goodness. Indeed, he has little to say of God except in book lambda of the *Metaphysics*, an untypical and perhaps early treatise in which he argues that we must posit a pure actuality as the prime mover of the cosmos, although the moving is not so much efficient causation as the attraction of the lover to the beloved.[2] Whereas in other beings the aspiration to actuality, to the realization of the form or essence, is inhibited by the inalienable substrate that we call matter, God is conceived in *Metaphysics Lambda* as a *nous* or intellect, wholly divorced from matter and hence without the potentially to be other than itself (*Metaphysics* 1071b–1072b). Since intellect thinks, according to Aristotle, by uniting itself to its object, it follows that God, in order to remain God, must be the sole and perpetual object of his own thinking (1074b–1075a).[3] Since he moves the world as the

---

1. On his relation to popular theism see Segev, *Aristotle on Religion*.

2. Because the noun *theos* is employed sporadically, and perhaps in a predicative rather than an appellative manner, some doubt that the unmoved mover is properly God. See Bordy, "Why Aristotle's God Is Not the Unmoved Mover"; but cf. Drozdek, *Greek Philosophers as Theologians*, 176.

3. See Drozdek, *Greek Philosophers as Theologians*, 169–71, on the infinite regress

beloved moves the lover (1072a25–35), it is neither the object of his own love and knowledge nor the product of his will.

In other entities, while the form is the essence or actuality, it does not exist without matter. Since the only characteristic of matter is its potential receptivity to all properties, the conjunction of form and matter in our realm of generation and corruption is always transient: matter is posited, rather than conceived, as the unchanging substrate of that which changes, by virtue of which we can say intelligibly "this is no longer what it was," or "this has been replaced by that" (*Physics* 189b–192a). So far Aristotle concurs with Plato, but he does not embrace the inference that there must be another realm of unchanging forms that furnishes us with a permanent vocabulary for speaking of the ephemeral; for him the forms reside in matter, the actual in the sphere of potentiality. Nor does he postulate one transcendent Good that gives purpose and value to all existence (*Nicomachean Ethics* 1096a–1097a): the good is always specific to a certain order of beings or class of actions, and is realized, so far as it can be realized, under the present conditions of life. If an immaterial Deity to whom all things tend does not sit well with this immanent teleology, neither does a radical disjunction between the body and an incorporeal soul. The soul is the form or *eidos* of a particular body (*On the Soul* 412a17–b24), and the death of the body entails its annihilation; some mystery remains with regard to the *nous poiêtikos*, or active reason,[4] and the passing remark in the treatise *On the Generation of Animals* (736b27) that the intellect seems to come from without, but no case for individual survival after death can be made from Aristotle's writings.

The goal for which we should strive, to be achieved in this world only, is *eudaimonia*, a term that connotes the possession not only of "happiness" in our sense (although this is the standard rendering) but of perfect virtue, a certain measure of wealth, and good report (*Nicomachean Ethics* 1097a, etc.). Virtue lies in a mean between extremes (1106a–1109b), and is acquired by habituation (1103a–b), not by the recollection of the time when we pursued the form allotted to us in the train of a god. Eros is not the unslaked thirst for beauty in the fallen soul, but the tendency of each element to its natural place in the cosmos. The obstacles to virtue are depravity of character, for which there is no remedy but chastisement, and *akrasia*, or failure to consult reason when we are under the sway of pleasure. At no time is it suggested that we can blame the gods or turn to them for succor. Thus

---

that may ensue from positing God as the one whose sole object of thought is the thought of himself;

4. See *On the Soul* 429a–430a with Gerson, "The Unity of Intellect."

we cannot but be startled at the end, when Aristotle recommends contemplation as the noblest and most lasting source of happiness (1177b–1178a), that one of his reasons for doing so should be that this is the ceaseless occupation of the gods.

Aristotle was better known in the Hellenistic and early Roman eras by his exoteric works, which are now known only through later quotations. Among the most widely cited was a treatise *On Philosophy*, in which he declared that there are no beings more worthy of worship than the gods. According to one testimony, he gave the name "god" both to the author of the cosmos and to the cosmos itself; on the other hand, Cicero quotes with approval a variation on Plato's allegory of the cave, in which a subterranean race emerges into the light of day and at first can imagine nothing superior to the sun, but is then instructed by the spectacle of the heavens at night that the source of existence must be still higher than the source of vision.[5] To this protype of the argument from design[6] we may add an early suggestion of apophatic theology in the treatise *On Prayer*, where God is said to be either *nous* or superior to *nous*, as Plato had once opined that the Good is superior to being (*Republic* 509b). Aristotle is thus, to a certain audience at least, a theist, perhaps a monotheist, but with no clear doctrine of providence. His eulogy of the heavens as the chief witness to a creator is mirrored in the arguments of his esoteric treatise *On the Heavens* for the eternity and unceasing rotation of the astral bodies; yet it may have been only those outside his own school who took this to mean that providence rules the celestial but not the sublunar realm.

In contrast to the changelessness of God, there is an alternation in human affairs, and not infrequently from weak to worse, as when democracy becomes tyranny. Since, however, Aristotle believes that the world is eternal and that humans have always dwelt in it, he had little motive to speculate on the origins of society; he neither follows Hesiod in bewailing a fall from innocence; nor joins the sophists in celebrating the progress of the arts. The first Peripatetic historian of culture would appear to have been Dicaearchus, a younger contemporary of Aristotle who, if we may trust our informant Porphyry, entertained strong Pythagorean sympathies.[7] He described the first age as one in which humans resembled the gods not only in being unacquainted with the flesh of beasts, but in having no desires that were evil or

5. Cicero, *On the Nature of the Gods* 2.37.95–97, with Bos, "Aristotle on 'People in a Cave.'"

6. Xenophon, *Memorabilia* 4.3 is perhaps the earliest version of this argument in Greek: Furley, *Creationism*, 74–92.

7. For translation and annotation of the extract from Porphyry, *On Abstinence* 4.2, see Lovejoy and Boas, *Primitivism and Related Ideas*, 93–96.

excessive. The first weapons were forged, and the first bands trained to wield them, not so much to defend the whole population from scarcity or the attacks of beasts as to aggrandize a handful of persons at the expense of the rest, securing for them the authority and honor that accompany the abuse of superfluous wealth. The development of agriculture is the next phase of this concentration in private hands of the wealth once common to all.

The Early Stoa

By the general agreement of ancient authors, the founder of Stoicism was Zeno of Citium, who came to Athens from Phoenicia in 313 BC. He first took as his master the Cynic Crates, who, like the rest of his school, was largely indifferent to metaphysics and doggedly subversive rather than systematic in his ethical conduct. When Zeno set up as a teacher in the *Stoa Poikilê* (painted colonnade) from which the Stoics derived their name, he remained true to the chief principle of the Cynics, that nothing licensed by human societies can be foreign to human nature, and it is said that in his *Republic* he condoned the practice of incest on the argument that it was not forbidden in Persia.[8] In fact, he maintained that the end of all moral striving and intellectual speculation was to live in accordance with nature; but in contrast to the Cynics, who repudiated all systems, he held that it is only through the study of philosophy in all its three branches—logic, ethics, and physics—that we can ascertain what is truly in accordance with nature, that is, with the goal not merely of loving but of living in rational equanimity. Humans being distinguished from the brute world by their capacity for reason, it is not enough that our impulses should be humored, although these impulses are conducive to life, and in that sense good, in both animals and humans. The wise man's quest for equanimity may require him to forgo the satisfaction of certain appetites and to place no value on the material goods that Aristotle had deemed essential to happiness. Such goods being all too often the gifts of fortune, another desideratum of equanimity is to leave to fate those things that we cannot control and to cultivate instead the one good that lies wholly within our power, the extinction of the passions. Fear and desire with respect to the future, exhilaration and grief with respect to the present, are the four tormentors of the untutored soul (Diogenes Laertius, *Lives* 7.116), and to have vanquished them completely is to be one's own master, even if in the world's eyes one is labouring under poverty, pain, captivity, or disgrace.

8. Diogenes Laertius, *Lives* 17.121; Van der Waerdt, "Zeno's *Republic*."

It seems that Zeno's position can be expounded with little reference to supernatural agency. While he is never characterized as an atheist, he has no concept of a transcendent god because he has no concept of the incorporeal. The soul that inhabits our bodies is a body of subtler texture; similarly the Logos or reason that pervades the cosmos, and to which the Greeks give the name of Zeus, is one of the elements, sometimes conceived as a tenuous species of fire, sometimes receiving the special appellation of pneuma or spirit. In its "spermatic character" this Logos sows rational principles of existence, growth, and action in all the beings that populate the universe (Diogenes Laertius, *Lives* 7.135–36). God alone survives the *ekpyrôsis*, or final combustion, of each world, and as each successive world is a replica of the one that went before it, his memory is the source of his foreknowledge (SVF 2.625; Plutarch, *Stoic Contradictions* 1953b).[9] Warm religious sentiment enters the Stoa only with Cleanthes, frequently described as its second founder, and remembered chiefly for his eloquent hymn to Zeus.[10] Here the principles of Zeno's physics are fused with the Heraclitean doctrines that all things are changes of fire: and that these revolutions are governed by a logos to which the logos within us bears witness.[11] Whereas Heraclitus, however, declares that God is indifferent to good and evil, Cleanthes ascribes to Zeus a paternal solicitude for the cosmos, crediting him with a love of that which seems to us unlovable, but denying him any part in the works of those who do evil through ignorance of law. The prayer of the sage will not be for any good of his own imagining, but only to be led at all times by "Zeus and destiny," these two being one inasmuch as nothing ordained by fate can be contrary to nature.

The refinement of Stoic philosophy in response to objections from other schools was not a work for a poet, and the third founder of the school, Chrysippus, was infamous not only for the abundance of his writings but for the ruggedness and obscurity of his style. He believed not only in God, but in gods, so long as it was understood that the myths of the poets are allegories in which the supernatural actors personify physical forces. Against those who denied that a corporeal deity can be omnipresent, he urged that nature furnishes examples of the mutual interpenetration of bodies whenever wine is mixed with water or iron suffused by fire; the same model will account for the presence of soul in body and that of God in the world.[12]

9. The abbreviation SVF denotes Von Arnim, ed., *Stoicorum Veterum Fragmenta*.

10. SVF 1.537; Zuntz, "Zum Cleanthes-Hymnus." Thom, "The Problem of Evil in Cleanthes," argues that the power of Zeus to correct the evil arising from false impressions and desires is the cardinal theme of the hymn.

11. See Long, "Heraclitus and Stoicism."

12. Todd, *Alexander of Aphrodisias on Stoic Physics*, 114–17.

Gods and humans together constitute the cosmos or world, which is the *polis* or commonwealth of the wise man.[13] Against the Cynics and Skeptics who sneered at oracles, Chrysippus argued that if the gods love mortals they will wish to apprise them of impending dangers and tribulations (Cicero, *On Divination* 1.38.82–39.84). Against the Peripatetics, he maintained that definite knowledge of the future is conveyed by prophecy, drawing the corollary that whatever is predicted is predetermined. Against the idle argument—"once the birth of my child is foretold, it will come about even if I abstain from sexual congress"—he urged that the oracle implicitly predicts the required conditions for its fulfillment.[14] It appears, however, that he was unwilling to draw the inference that I am not free if my actions are foreknown. On the contrary, human beings have a special place in the natural order because of their unique capacity for deliberation (*SVF* 2.1152). We are free to determine, not the course of events, but our own response to it; by aligning my reason with the omnipresent logos, I can achieve the goal of living in accordance with nature—or at least of willing to do so, which is the true criterion of virtue (Cicero, *On Ends* 3.31). Every transgression is a falling away from my character as a rational agent, and Chrysippus endorsed the principle already laid down by Zeno, that all sins are of equal weight, and hence all equally unworthy of indulgence (*SVF* 3.529; Cicero, *On Ends* 4.56). The wise man may be only an ideal, but one who propagates that ideal in act and word will have no pity for the infirmities of others, any more than for his own.

Epicurus and His School

Born in Samos in 341 BC, Epicurus settled in Athens in 307 and founded there the community of philosophers known as the Garden. Its principal tenet, foreshadowed in the teachings of Democritus of Abdera, was that nothing exists but atoms and the void. Hence, there are no Platonic ideas or Aristotelian essences; the soul, no less than the world that it beholds, is a transient congeries of atoms, into which tenuous emanations flow from material bodies through pores in our own bodies to stimulate sensory impressions. Since there is no authority to correct them, these impressions are to be trusted when they report that the earth is flat or that the sun is no more than a few feet in diameter (Diogenes Laertius, *Lives of the Philosophers* 10.91). The purpose of such inquiries is not to gratify scientific curiosity but to rid the soul of the fears and superstitions that accrue from false beliefs.

13. Diogenes Laertius, *Lives* 7.129–30; cf. Obbink, "The Stoic Sage," 184.
14. Bobzien, *Determinism and Freedom*, 198–217.

The most pernicious of these are the teachings of religion, which ascribes every freak of nature to invisible agents, pretending that those who offend them in the present world will suffer enduring torment in the next. In fact, the true prerequisite of virtue is to admit that, since nothing exists except the objects of our senses, the end of life should be to enjoy the greatest possible excess of bodily pleasure over bodily pain (Cicero, *On Ends*, book 1). Vicious hedonism will not secure this, as the pleasures that it yields are outweighed by the pains that it entails:[15] the wise will aim for a state of *ataraxia*, or imperturbability, in which the satisfaction of avoiding pain is seasoned by the companionship of others who are intent upon the same goal.

Thus Epicurus, like the Stoics, exhorts us to follow nature; with Plato, he holds that nature's guide to virtue is the calculus of pleasures; for him, as for Aristotle, the ideal is the life that most resembles that of the gods. These too are composed of atoms, with the peculiar (and unexplained) attribute of immortality. Far from acting as efficient, final, or material causes to the physical world they take no part or interest in it, and the wise will honor them not with useless prayers but by imitating their steadfast practice of *ataraxia*.[16] The cosmos, while it exhibits a lawlike harmony so long as it exists, is the result of a fortuitous concourse of atoms. Since the habitual motion of these particles is a vertical fall through the void, Epicurus finds it necessary to posit a "swerve," or aleatory deflection, the origin and operation of which remain obscure.[17] The charge that Epicurus substitutes automatism for divine providence is true only if this word has the sense of chance rather than mechanical necessity. Both are equally antipathetic to reason, the free exercise of which in human agents seems to be guaranteed by the same swerve that has introduced vicissitude into the cosmos. Few would agree that the liberty that we think fundamental to reasoning can be reduced to a kinetic aberration; some at least are grateful to Epicurus for turning the tables on the fatalist with the quip that if he is right he cannot know it, as his argument puts his own mental processes at the mercy of fate.[18]

Lucretius and the Fear of Death

It was a common libel against the Epicureans, assiduously propagated by Cicero, that having no loftier aim in life than freedom from care in the

15. Donas, "Pleasure and Human Good" proposes that pleasure and pain are not so much defining elements of the good in Epicurus as criteria for knowledge of it.

16. See Festugière, *Epicure et ses dieux*.

17. See Englert, *Epicurus on the Swerve*.

18. *Gnomologicum Vaticanum* 40, quoted by Arrighetti, ed., *Epicuro: Opere*, 147.

company of friends, they could form no desire to be useful to the state (*On Ends* 2.76, etc.). As Cicero knew, this was eminently untrue of Rome, where pursuit of civic office was almost a duty if one came of a certain family and the language of friendship was frequently indistinguishable from that of political contracts. Caesar and his murderer Cassius both professed to be Epicureans, as did L. Calpurnius Piso, patron of the innovative teacher and epigrammatist Philodemus, and Lucius Memmius, to whom a much greater poet dedicated his six books in Latin hexameters *On the Nature of Things*. Lucretius contrasts his own tranquility in the midst of troubles with the burdens that cannot be escaped by his patron (*On the Order of Things* 1.42–43); yet he is himself is a less than rigorous pupil of the man who made it an article of his philosophy to shun poetry as Odysseus shunned the sirens.[19] He compounds his unfilial conduct by invoking the goddess Venus in a prologue that far surpasses the hymn to Zeus by the Stoic Cleanthes on which it is modelled;[20] but how can an Epicurean persuade himself that such a being, if she existed, would forfeit her tranquillity to appease the civil strife of the "sons of Aeneas" (1.1), who can hardly be her own progeny, as her votary pretends to believe, any more than she can be the mistress of Mars or the guardian of the daedal earth (1.7; 1.33)?

Internal discord was an endemic distemper in the history, and hence a recurrent motif in the poetry, of the late Republic and the early Principate. According to Catullus, in the coda to his brief epic in the marriage of Thetis and Peleus, it is this crime that accounts for the withdrawal of the gods from human society (64.397–99); elsewhere he reminds his readers, by styling them nephews of Remus rather than sons of Romulus (58.5), that the founder from whom the city takes its name set the example of fratricide. Virgil alludes to scars of an ancient subterfuge that will linger even in the coming age of peace and abundance (*Eclogues* 4.31); an ode by Horace apostrophes the guiltless Roman who expiates the sins of his ancestors (*Odes* 3.6.1). Whether the liar is Romulus, who claimed his brother's omen, or Laomedon, who cheated the gods of their wages for building Troy, both poets imply that maleficence is hereditary and that the present cannot escape the curse of the past. To Lucretius this is chimerical: the cause of evildoing in all generations, the cause of the ubiquitous despondency from which Epicurus delivered us, is the false education that teaches us that death is the worst of evils. The healthier doctrine of Epicurus reveals that nothing can harm us unless it is felt as a perturbation, and that therefore the capital evil is not death itself, which puts an end to all troubles, but the unreasoning fear of death.

19. Arrighetti, ed., *Epicuro Opere*, fr. 89. See now MacCarter, "Lucretius' Didactics of Disgust."

20. On 1.1–40 see Asmis, "Lucretius' Venus."

The appeal to reason in Book 3 of *On the Nature of Things* is a long elaboration of the Master's apophthegm, "While we are, death is not, and when death is, we are not."[21] Our failure to welcome the perfect freedom from pain that death bestows on all is in part the consequence of our inability to imagine our own non-existence. As soon as we try to do so, the absent self is smuggled back as a witness to the loss that will be felt only by the survivors: we range ourselves with the mourners when we shall have neither occasion nor capacity for mourning (*On the Nature of Things* 3.459469). Plutarch's retort to Colotes, that we may fear annihilation more than pain, is not considered, but Lucretius admits that some are sufficiently in love with life to wish it longer. This vain desire can be exorcised by reminding ourselves that time is infinite, and that no conceivable increment to our span of life will spare us one year of oblivion (3.1099–1106). For this reason it is futile to engage in laborious projects for the multiplication of wealth, as though we could hope to purchase some means of avoiding death or even of securing more than a nugatory postponement. When we are foolish enough to stake our fortunes on such ventures, we have permitted our fear of death to rob us of the means of life.

Such are the consolations of philosophy, which would surely prevail if our fancy were not debauched by tales of an afterlife in which horrific punishments are exacted, not so much for moral trespasses as for crimes against religion (*On the Nature of Things* 1.102–35).[22] Fear of capricious penalties drives us to arbitrary expedients, the cruellest of which, although philosophy teaches us that the gods requite no sustenance, is the sacrifice of unoffending beasts. Among the most famous passages in Lucretius are his depiction of a mother cow still wandering with pathetic cries in search of the calf that was stolen for the altar (2.349–70) and his indignant account of Agamemnon's killing of his daughter Iphigeneia to secure a fair wind for his armament against Troy (1.80–101). Such are the wrongs, he exclaims, that religion teaches us to perform. The vigor with which he attacks these superstitions suggests that they exercised an influence on the popular mind of which little record survives. His testimony may be placed against that of a speaker in Cicero's *Tusculan Disputations* that although such tales were current they were ridiculed even by those without education. The same Cicero, we must remember, proposed that his daughter should be worshipped as a goddess and makes Scipio Africanus proclaim, in the sixth book of his *Republic*, that the souls of the noblest citizens will enjoy a place for ever

21. Cf. *Nature of Things* 3.386–89.

22. On the relation of Lucretius to Empedocles, see Sedley, *Lucretius and the Transformation of Greek Wisdom*.

among the stars. It would seem that the notion of posthumous survival is better attested in the higher than in the lower culture of Rome in this era: the publication of Lucretius's poem coincided with that of a work by a certain Sallustius with the title *Empedoclea*, and Virgil was later to represent the underworld as a place in which souls pay a reckoning for the sins of the previous life and are assigned to new bodies according to their deserts.

These speculations have their source in Empedocles and Plato, the latter devising his own myth in *Republic* 10 to counteract both the superstitious fears of his host and the charlatanical promises of the Orpheotelestae (*Republic* 364b–e). Neither of these thinkers, of course, imagined that the gods could be suborned by material offerings, and both substituted transmigration for everlasting torment, except perhaps in the case of a few men so depraved that their vices did not admit of reformation. They are therefore not the chief objects of polemic in Lucretius, who has even been suspected of borrowing from the Pythagoreans when he writes that the pains of hell are experienced here on earth in the conflict of passions and the pangs of conscience.[23] Nevertheless, it is evident that Lucretius saw Empedocles as a rival, whom he would need to surpass if the world was to be convinced that our only hope of peace in this world and release from fear of the next is to be sure of annihilation.[24] If this is his motive for the adoption of verse, some centuries after prose had become the customary vehicle of philosophy, we can give to his prayer for the intervention of Venus a sense that does not contradict his own teaching. It is not by summoning any external power but by the beauty of his poetic overtures that he works upon readers who may be resistant to argument or repelled by the hirsute style of Epicurus. As Socrates dreams in the *Phaedrus* of a rhetoric that is not hostile to philosophy, so the rugged euphony of Lucretius stops his readers's ears to the music of the Sirens—not least of those who sing on the revolving spheres in the tenth book of the *Republic*. The Venus of his prologue stands for the honey that he has mixed with a bitter potion (1.936–50), to quote his own variant of the pharmaceutical metaphor that Plato derived from Empedocles. As a fictitious counterpart to the Uranian Aphrodite of the *Symposium*, she anticipates the denunciation of *venus* in its quotidian (or, as Plato says) pandemic sense of sexual intercourse in the fourth book of the poem. Plato and Lucretius agree in disdaining the aspiration to immortality through one's offspring, but neither was quite immune to the subtler ambition of attaching his name to a deathless work of art.

---

23. See 1.980–1010, with Cumont, "Lucrèce et le symbolisme pythagoricien."
24. 1.716–33, with Edwards, "Lucretius, Empedocles and Epicurean Polemics," 104.

Since Plato it had been a commonplace for both Greeks and Romans that if vicious souls produce a corrupt society, it is equally true that corrupt societies produce vicious souls. It was also a commonplace, again thanks to Plato, that evil has no substance of its own but is a pathology of the good, so that its presence in the cosmos, in society, or in the soul is the result of a want of harmony between parts or powers that, duly tempered, would work together for a common good. The decline of the ideal commonwealth, begins, according to Plato, when desire for honor outstrips the desire to be worthy of it, and becomes more acute when thirst for material gain gets the better of both honor and virtue. At the same time he admits that without the fruits of civilization a society would be more fit for pigs than humans, while both the liberal and the mechanical arts were adduced by sophists of his day as the means and evidence of our superiority to beasts. As Aeschylus traced the origin of all the arts to Prometheus, or Forethought, so the Stoic Posidonius, a contemporary of Lucretius, maintained that philosophers must have been responsible for their invention. Nevertheless, the sketch of human development in the fifth book of On the Nature of Things presents the decay of virtue as an inseparable corollary of progress in the works of mind, the value of which he does not refuse to acknowledge. Since Epicurus supplies no precedent for these reflections, scholars have looked for his source in Democritus, a versatile contemporary of Socrates and founder of atomism;[25] a Roman, however, did not have to look abroad at this time for the argument that refinement of manners weakens the moral faculty, for the collapse of the Roman Republic into a state of perpetual discord was all too obviously the outcome of a period of unobstructed conquest, which had been made possible only by a coalition of martial valor, deep strategy, and mechanical ingenuity. The luxury to which this poor and frugal people had now become accustomed threatened to rob them, as the historian Sallust perceived, of the vigor that was needed to sustain it (*Catiline* 11–13); in Virgil's *Aeneid*, one of the primitive denizens of Italy mocks the Trojans for imagining that they can overcome a race that bathes its infants in cold streams (9.603–5). And yet his death at the hands of his cultured adversary is an omen of defeat for his compatriots (9.621–35), and all Latin writers acknowledge that the hardihood that brings success in battle all too often curdles into rapine and tyranny at home.

Throughout the book, Lucretius plays upon the familiar contrast between the instinctive behavior of animals—which are equipped with all that they need for life by "Nature, the mother of all" (*On the Nature of Things* 5.1362; cf. 2.1171)—with the multitudinous stratagems by which humans

25. Cole, *Democritus and the Sources of Greek Anthropology*, 38–45.

have counteracted their natural impotence and the hazards to which it exposed them. In admiring the fecundity of nature, he all but makes her a second Venus;[26] he contrives nonetheless to forestall any notion of purpose by surmising that in the youth of the world many creatures were spawned that proved to be incapable of survival (5.838–54), so that only an undesigned winnowing of her experiments, not her own foresight, has determined the present complement of species. Nor will Lucretius credit either divine or human prescience with the invention of fire and language, which are the preconditions of every other advance in civilization. Fire, without which we are helpless in winter, blind at night, and at all times a prey to animals, was discovered by accident when some natural object was set ablaze by a bolt of lightning (5.1091–97); speech was not devised by a single human—for how would anyone else have understood him?—but by spontaneous mimicry of the sounds that are still employed for communication by other species (1379–1404). Language made association possible, and the love of glory bred a race of kings until their subjects, weary of despotism, overthrew them and established polities based on laws (5.1136–60). At this time false religion began to thrive, although Lucretius imputes it not so much to priestcraft as to wonder and dread inspired by the spectacle of the revolving heavens, which humans wrongly supposed to be the handiwork of the gods whose images they saw in dreams (5.1161–93). Then followed the discovery of the metals copper and iron, which enabled us to create both weapons for hunting and instruments of agriculture (5.1241–80). Of old, humans lived, as Plato opined, on acorns and other uncultivated fruits; today we cannot eat unless one hunts and another ploughs. Today we wear fabrics woven on iron looms, and we despise the pelts that must have aroused great envy when they were first prized from the carcases of beasts (5.1419–22). With each new artifice[27] humans became at once more effete and more bellicose, from which we infer not so much a history of moral degeneration as an endemic disposition to greed and selfishness, restrained in the past by lack of opportunity rather than natural rectitude (5.1430–47). When we say that it is to nature that we owe the arts of life, we mean to say only that we have made use of our mental and physical resources to eliminate danger and satisfy our needs. If we also enjoy superfluous benefits, for example the pleasure of song in imitation of birds, we may thank our surroundings and our ability to learn from them: we owe nothing either to gods or to godlike men.

26. With the maternal earth as a third at 5.821–22.

27. Compare *natura daedala* at 5.234 with the *daedala signa* created by human artists at 2.1451. The earth is "daedal" (the adjective derived from the name of Daedalus the inventor) at 1.7 and 1.228.

Roman and Stoic Theism

Echoes of Lucretius permeate the *Georgics* of Virgil, ostensibly a versified manual of agriculture, which is also a commentary on the civil discord of its times. Italy is by nature a land of peace and abundance, the fabled realm of Saturn (*Georgics* 2.173), where the "father" (that is Jupiter) has made the task of cultivation arduous enough to stimulate industry and invention (1.121–59), but at the same time requires the farmer to work much less than the soldier at his perpetual trade of killing or the townsman whose seeming wealth is the fruit of unrelenting competition and intrigue (2.458–74). The pastoral life has the virtues of frugality, spontaneity, and simplicity, which are regularly ascribed in Latin sources to the barbarians who oppose Rome's designs of conquest;[28] for all that, the same historians think it the duty of Rome to conquer and assume that the civilized man would never choose to live as a barbarian.[29] Virgil, who wrote the *Georgics* in Naples, is equally conscious that the vigor that tames the natural world can easily take the form of violence against our fellow-humans. The first half of the fourth book is a disquisition on keeping bees, which is often read as a pattern for human society; yet even these cooperative insects cannot give up the custom of forming armies under their kings to wage great battles, which the apiarist can quell by throwing a handful of dust on the combatants (4.66–87). This conceit is so contrary to nature that Virgil seems to be recreating the bees in the image of their keepers, as though to say that the peace that Octavian has brought to the world (3.1.1–48) is doomed to be quickly broken. The second half of the book provides a recipe for breeding bees by a sacrificial rite that was instituted to placate the spirit of Orpheus after his wife Eurydice died of a serpent's bite while fleeing her would-be-rapist, the farmer Aristaeus (4.453.459). Orpheus did indeed win back Eurydice from the underworld, but lost her again by breaching a taboo that would have been waived had her jailers known how to forgive (4.489). In our world death is a stranger to mercy, just as farmers are ignorant of their own happiness: according to Virgil, they were the last of humankind to see the departing footprints of justice (2.474), but that is only another way of saying, after Hesiod, that she now has no home on earth.

In the sixth book of Virgil's *Aeneid* the hero descends to the realm of posthumous judgment and expiation, the very existence of which was denied with ridicule by the Epicureans. Here he learns from his father

28. On the ambiguity of such speeches as the one ascribed to Calgacus in the *Agricola* of Tacitus, see Rutherford, "Voices of Resistance."

29. Virgil's use of the adjective *improbus* (unrighteous) to describe the *farmer's work* at *Georgics* 1.145–46 is much discussed.

that every soul receives its own deserts (*Aeneid* 6.743), and is granted the privilege, not vouchsafed to any of Plato's visionaries, of seeing souls in the guise that they will wear when they become distinguished figures of Roman history. It thus becomes apparent, to the reader at least, that the question of divine justice has not been fully resolved, for no reason is given for the premature death of the future Marcellus, prospective heir to Octavian, whose blameless virtues can move even the dead to tears (6.868–86). The destiny of Aeneas[30] is to satisfy Jupiter—or perhaps his implacable sister, Saturnian Juno (1.23; cf. 1.1.569)—by founding a mingled race of Italians and Trojans, which will exercise dominion without end over other peoples (1.279). This enterprise (at which Lucretius scoffs, as Virgil knows)[31] requires him to abandon his Carthaginian lover Dido, who shuns him in the underworld after dying by her own hand (4.664–65; 6.467–74). If this was a test of his piety (4.393), he seems to lose that virtue when at the end of the poem he butchers—or to use his own word, immolates (12.549)—a young suppliant whom he cannot forgive for the killing of his friend. The way of the Roman is not so much to explain the will of the gods as to endure, and it was no doubt for this reason that so many of them were attracted to the teaching of the Stoics, and that almost every surviving work by a Stoic is written by a Roman or by a Greek under Roman rule.

The Stoics were as notorious for their piety as the Epicureans for their atheism. This might not have been the case had their sole authority been Zeno of Citium, the nominal founder of the school, for Zeus in his theology is not so much a person as the personification of the subtle fire or spirit that pervades the cosmos and acts as the logos, or rational principle, of all natural operations, in the soul no less than in the external realm. In the physical cosmos, all that occurs is fated from the beginning; for the soul a natural end and mode of life are established, but we are free to rebel, in which case our reward will be to be dragged where we might have gone of our own free will. In the hymn to Zeus by Cleanthes, known as the second founder of Stoicism, Zeus is a bountiful monarch who protects mortals from their own ignorance: he is still, for all that, equated with fate or destiny, and it appears that he offers the wretched only the knowledge that their condition is inescapable. The third founder of the school was the subtle dialectician Chrysippus, who is credited by some witnesses with the defence of a provisional, rather than absolute, notion of fate. Oracles, he maintained, do not tell us what must inevitably come to pass, but warn us benevolently what will come to pass if we perform a certain action; even this conditional

30. Already *fato profugus*, a fugitive by or from fate, at *Aeneid* 1.2.
31. Compare *Nature of Things* 5.1130 and *Aeneid* 6.851.

scenario is not ordained by the gods but merely foretold. We may say that this a poor vindication of freedom, for how was it any less capricious of fate to decree that Oedipus, once born, should kill his father than it would have been to decree that he should be born? Whatever Chrysippus taught, his Roman successors were not detained by such conundrums: their aim was to deliver their students from evil, or from the false apprehension of it, by persuading them first to deem nothing good that does not lie within our power, and then to see that nothing lies within our power but the ability to endure what appears to be evil and intend what we know to be good.

Freedom and Fortune in Seneca the Younger

Lucius Annaeus Seneca is the foremost representative, at least in prose, of Roman Stoicism, and we hear the Roman as well as the Stoic in him when he protests in a letter addressed to his friend Lucilius that it is not by words but by conduct that a philosopher shapes the lives of his disciples (*Letters to Lucilius* 16.2–3; cf. 6.6). His own career may strike us as less than exemplary:[32] after coming to Rome from Spain to study rhetoric and philosophy, he was exiled in AD 41 on a charge of adultery with Caligula's sister, but went on to gain honor and wealth as a tutor to Nero, ruthlessly straining the revenues from his estates in Britain, until he was forced to take his own life in AD 65 after being found guilty, with his nephew Lucan, of conspiracy in a plot to assassinate his royal pupil. Defiance of the Emperor was a recognized, and endemic, virtue in Stoics of the imperial age; cupidity was not, but if his tenants had perused his treatise *On Constancy*, they would know that they had no cause to complain, as no injustice can ever befall the just (7.3; 8.1). He will not even concede to Aristotle in his three books *On Anger* that there is any due measure of anger or due occasion for a display of it.[33] In his treatise *On Constancy*, his charm against all mental perturbation is to treat the slights and injuries of the world as we treat the impertinences of children, prizing our fortitude too well even to notice the crimes of women, and reminding ourselves that even Epicureans are capable of restraining passion (11.3; 14.1; 15.3). The goal of the Stoic is to become wholly immune to them, for which purpose he needs to distinguish the things amenable to his will from those that, whether he wills them or not, are decreed by fate.

Seneca's *Natural Questions* is the longest surviving treatise by a Stoic on the causes of physical phenomena. Yet, as he himself says in the third

---

32. In his defence see Griffin, "*Imago Vitae Suae*."

33. *On Anger* 1.9.1, 1.10.1, 1.17.1, etc. Cf. Aristotle, *Nicomachean Ethics* and Ephesians 4:26.

book, it is always more profitable to discuss the *faciendum* than the *factum*, the thing to be done than the thing already done (*Natural Questions* 3, preface 7). Although, therefore, he draws his scientific hypotheses freely from philosophers who were not Stoics, he seldom fails to derive a moral lesson that will make a better Stoic of his friend Lucilius. In his preface he asserts that the first stage in understanding the cosmos is to grasp the relation between the divine and human, which (as he says in book 2) is the same thing as to grasp the meaning of fate and providence (1, preface 2; 2.45.2). Whatever we style it, the power that superintends this world is subject to no constraint from without, and hence to no appeal or revolt on our part, but is *necessitas sua*, its own necessity, infallibly decreeing that which it judges infallibly to be the best (1, preface 3). It is futile for us to resent the lot or post to which we are assigned, or to rail against natural vicissitudes and changes of worldly fortune. Omens and prophecies are indeed vouchsafed to us in abundance, but since the predictions of augurs and astrologers would not be true unless everything, including the prediction itself, were ordained, they cannot create new duties or give us power to alter anything but the inward disposition with which we meet the inevitable (2.35–40). We need no heavenly sign to inform us that our task as humans is to transcend humanity and become like God, not in the sense of being immortal but in the sense of willing only that which is in accordance with nature. In a letter to Lucilius, he opines that the man who acquires by will the serenity that the gods possess by nature may even be said to have surpassed them (53.11). Where Lucretius assures us that we need not fear death because we shall suffer no pain from it, the Stoic condemns the futility of grieving over that which we cannot change.

The question put to Seneca by Lucilius to elicit the treatise *On Providence* is, as Seneca hints in the preface, far from new. Doubters have always asked why, if the world is governed by a benign divinity, we see the wicked prospering while the good go unrewarded. The antidote to atheism, as ever, is to contemplate the harmony of the world, the regularity of its laws, and the adaptation of all phenomena to the needs if its inhabitants. Having proved to ourselves that nothing is undetermined, we may be confident that an earthquake or the eruption of a volcano has its own causes (*On Providence* 1.3–4) and affords no more of an argument against providence than the hot springs and other rarities for which we are wont to give thanks (1.3). To the sage all things are equally products of fate, which for him is providence, as no evil can befall us when we do not perceive it as evil. We think the world unjustly harsh to the good because we forget that a father has purposes for his own children that he does not entertain for his slaves and therefore imposes a stricter discipline on the former (2.5–6).

The austerities that athletes undergo before they compete at the Olympic Games exemplify the principle that higher goods are secured at greater cost (2.3–4). If fortune seems to lay the rod more heavily on us, we should not be aggrieved but proud, remembering that the most able soldier will be the one whom the general assigns to the most demanding mission (4.4–5). This martial simile lays the ground for Seneca's appeal to the fears of those whom he cannot influence through their vanity: consider, he says, the poverty of the Germans, their indifference to all that we think essential to happiness, and the success with which they match their arms against ours (4.14). They are formidable because they have been tried by adversity, as we have not, and have not suffered the hardship of never encountering hardship, which the Cynic Demetrius held to be the worst of all misfortunes, and indeed the only one (3.3; 5.5).

The Cynic was a man (less often, if ever, a woman) who lived in calculated defiance of common norms and bonds. He could demonstrate his autonomy by licentious sexual conduct or shameless opulence, but the classic type, as Epictetus was later to portray him, was one who had learned to live without those products of labor and skill that are commonly deemed inseparable from our humanity. Seneca was not such a man—he could not even persevere as a vegetarian[34]—but he firmly rejected the thesis of Posidonius that philosophy was responsible for the arts of civilization (*Letters to Lucilius* 90.7). He concedes that his fellow-Stoic was right to surmise that the first communities were ruled by the wise, as nature ordains, and that want was unknown until certain men, through avarice and by artifice, made themselves lords of the persons and property of others (90.5–6). In consequence of this tyranny, societies were dissolved and their inhabitants scattered, as Posidonius argues; it was not, however, the arts that redressed this calamity, for they are products of mere sagacity rather than wisdom (90.11). Philosophy teaches us not to live comfortably but to live well; it teaches us to revere the gods and bring peace to our fellow-humans (90.26), but we do not win peace by humoring desire. It was human ingenuity that erected houses of marble, where true wisdom was content with a thatch to keep away the rain (90.11). It is reason of a kind, but not right reason, that clothes us in delicate fabrics, whereas philosophy reminds us that the Scythians have survived to this day without knowledge of the loom (90.16). The tools of agriculture and the chase are incentives to decadence;[35] locks

34. *Letters to Lucilius* 108.22, where some surmise that the foreign cult from which he wished to dissociate himself was Christianity.

35. At 90.37 he quotes *Georgics* 1.125 on the absence of agriculture in the Saturnian age, without the Virgilian coda that Jove, by making nature more hostile, stimulated the invention of agriculture.

and keys are not required by those who are content with the means of life (90.8). The only source of concord is the philosophy that banishes all desires save that of living in accord with nature and reason (90.29). With these as our guides we shall easily perceive that there is no good for one that is not the good of all (90.38).

Scholars have expressed surprise that a man who scorns the amenities of life, as Seneca does, or professes to do, should be not only an accomplished rhetorician but a tragedian whose plots are even bloodier than their Greek prototypes, as his characters are even more intemperate in lust and anger, in grief and in the appetite for revenge. Is the arousal of pity and fear—the proper effect of tragedy, according to Aristotle—a lawful intention for the Stoic? One answer might be that he wished to hold up to his audience—an audience of readers rather than spectators—a mirror of the false and unreasoning passions that philosophers of his school were accustomed to stigmatize as tragic. Thus explanation, however, implies, if carried no further, that the protagonist is no more than a foil to the philosopher when in fact he or she is more often his caricature. It is when emotion has dethroned humanity and reason that a character is most likely to make a boast of mental fortitude, pertinacity in enterprise, and indifference to any common estimate of vice and virtue.[36] Heracles, the nonpareil of benevolent courage for Cynics, Stoics, and Epicureans, is still a true son of Zeus and the strongest of mortals, even in madness; Medea, while she complains of the numerous snares that fortune throws between her and her object, is also confident that fortune fears the brave and daunts only those of weaker spirit. Her error, like that of Phaedra, Agamemnon, Oedipus, and those who counsel them, is not to see fate behind the mask of fortune, and thus to imagine that there may be profit or honor in defiance. Whenever a character (typically the chorus) speaks of fate, it is with a sense of inexorability that is absent from the use of the name *fortuna*,[37] even if no one in the drama has enough philosophy to distinguish them. References to fate are especially frequent, as might be foreseen, in *Oedipus*;[38] in other works we are left to guess whether the whole concatenation of events was inescapable, or whether a person more capable of mastering passion might have avoided

36. Staley, *Seneca and the Idea of Tragedy*, 124, writes: "literary tragedy is by definition about characters who are not Stoic."

37. On the inevitability of fate see *Medea* 431, 452, 462; on the vagaries of fortune 159, 176, 219, 242, 287, 520.

38. *Oedipus* 19, 28, 72, 75, 125, 206, 293, 297, 411, 711, 751, 780, 787, 792, 832, 60, 882, 915, 926, 980, 993–94, 1019, 1043, 1046, 1059, See also *fatidica* at 269, 302 and 1042, implying that that which the gods foretell is fated and hence ineluctable.

the tragedy of a Phaedra or a Thyestes.[39] Since Zeno there had always been Stoics who suspected that even our choices may be fated. If Seneca's cursory disavowals of this tenet do not sit well with some of his pronouncements as a dramatist, it is possible that, like Lucretius and many later poets, he thought of verse as a medium for the airing, if not the stilling, of intellectual vacillations that could not be confessed in prose.

The Philosophy of a Slave

The typical philosopher in antiquity was a free man of more than common wealth and leisure, and this was true of those who preached frugality and who practised it with more zeal than Seneca. The most austere of Stoic prescriptions for happiness, however, were dictated to young men of wealth and leisure by one who had no temptation to regard these as desirable concomitant to virtue. As a slave in constant peril of death and physical injury, Epictetus had only the choice of accepting his lot or bewailing it: the lesson of his *Discourses*, which were transcribed in four books by Arrian, the biographer of Alexander the Great, is that this is in fact the only choice that rests with *any* of us, with the Caesars and Alexanders or with the meanest of their subjects. The world opines that no one can afford an education unless he is free; the philosopher says that no one is free without an education. The only learning that is of use to us—and here he follows Epicurus rather than Chrysippus[40]—is that which enables us to discern the good from the bad in the sphere of action. Once we know what it means to live according to nature,[41] we know that it is against nature, and therefore futile, to harbor any inclination to change or escape that which cannot be changed. We shall thus not join the multitude in fearing death (*Discourses* 1.2.15, etc.) or in hoping for prosperity (1.4.1–4, etc.): our fear will be rather that we might fail to govern these inclinations, and thus fall short of nature in that one thing that lies in our power, the exercise of the will (1.29.1, etc.). Where common wisdom teaches us to be wary of the future and to indemnify ourselves against loss and suffering by the accumulation of wealth and constant visits to physicians, the philosopher has need of two things only—*tharsos* or courage to bear the assaults of fate and *eulabeia* or circumspection with respect to his private instincts and desires.[42]

39. On Seneca's aim of tearing the mask from passion, see Sciesaro, *The Passions in Play*.

40. On the inutility of merely reading Chrysippus, see 1.4.6, 1.10.10, etc.

41. *Discourses* 1.4.14, 1.21.1; 2.5.24, etc.

42. *Discourses* 2.1.3 and 2.1.5; 2.13.3 (*tharsos*); 2.14.3 (*eulabeia*), etc.

Epictetus the Stoic and Lucretius the Epicurean are at one in holding the greatest of human ills to be not death but the *fear* of death (*Discourses* 1.17.25, etc.). The Epicurean remedy is to rid ourselves of religion with its fables of the afterlife and its recipes for the appeasement of imaginary gods. Epictetus adopts the opposite line of reasoning, that if we are children of God (1.9.5–6), and, as it were, members and portions of him (1.14.6), we must accept the conditions on which he vouchsafes existence to us (2.6.16–18). As Epicurus had urged that pain, "if lasting is not severe, and if severe not lasting," so Epictetus suggests that it is better to suffer a quick death at a tyrant's hands than a lingering death from fever (1.19.6; 2.6.19). Just as God—corporeal though he is, as all things are—is not flesh but intellect, knowledge, and spirit, so the philosopher knows himself to be spirit and not the flesh to which it is transiently united (3.7.25). He knows himself also to be but a part of a whole, whose functions is realized when he serves God as an honorable vessel,[43] when he is ready to undergo what a foot undergoes for the sake of the body,[44] when he lives as a citizen not of Rome or any man-made city but of a commonwealth peopled by both gods and mortals (2.5.26). While he repeatedly commends the fortitude of Socrates,[45] Epictetus endorses neither the theory of forms that his pupil Plato ascribes to him nor the hylomorphism of Plato's rebellious student Aristotle. By the *ousia* or essence of the good he understands "intellect, knowledge and right reason," which is also the essence of God (2.8.1–5); by *hyle* or matter he understands not the stuff of the world nor the substrate of a form but the unrefined mass, the raw data, of perception, into which we introduce moral rather than ontological difference when we judge one course of action to be right and another wrong (2.5.1–5).

Epictetus on Providence

Those who knew nothing else about the Stoics in antiquity knew that they attributed all things to fate. Epictetus, however, not only denies that the cosmos is ruled by mechanical necessity (*to automaton*)[46] but will not admit that anything falls outside the purview of that which he calls God or "the divine."[47] In the preface to his discourse he lists the competing theories

43. *Discourses* 2.4.6; cf. Romans 9:22–23.

44. *Discourses* 2.5.24 and 2.10.4–5. Cf. 1 Corinthians 12:15.

45. *Discourses* 1.29.16–19; 2.16.25; 3.18.4; *Enchiridion* 5.1, etc.

46. *Discourses* 1.6.11.

47. For *theos*, see *Discourses* 1.16; 3.136; 4.4.29, etc.; for *theoi*, see 1.12.4; 2.20.3, etc.; for *to theion*, 1.12.1; 2.14.13; 4.1.61, etc.

of providence, commencing with those who hold that since there are no gods there is no tutelage of the world for good or ill. Although he barely pauses here to reject this view, he proves his familiarity with the arguments of Plato, Cleanthes, and Aristotle in *Discourses* 1.6, where he urges that the indestructible harmony of the world and the exquisite adaptation of its laws to the needs of its denizens afford sufficient evidence of design.[48] The same considerations would no doubt suffice to refute the Epicurean view that the gods do not care for the world and the Aristotelian limitation of providence to the heavens beyond the moon, both of which are pronounced in *Discourse* 1.8.1–3 to be inconsistent with the character of God. Even to say (as Plato appears to say with regard to the present life) that providence regulates only the general order and does not concern itself with the individual is to be ignorant of the special rank to which we have been assigned by the Creator, and of the duties which this honor imposes upon us. He has granted to human beings not only the faculties of perception and appetition but also the power to act or to refrain from acting upon the impulses arising from these faculties (*Enchiridion* 1). Where a perception may be true or false, the action based on it may be fitting or unfitting, that is, it may either conform or fail to conform to nature. The capacity for deliberative reasoning which enables us to make this choice is not only a compensation for our natural infirmities but a property that we share with the author of nature, so that we alone of his creatures have the right to call him our father and to proclaim that each of us is the *idios huios*, the true son, of God (*Discourses* 1.9.5–6).

But if this is special providence, what is providence? Stoics before Epictetus had maintained that the peculiar love of God or the gods for humanity is revealed in their disclosure of the future (to those who are able to decipher it) through omens, oracles, and astral portents. The soothsayer tells us at most what will come to pass, not how to align with fortune, though this is all that is in our power (*Discourses* 2.7.3–5). In his own exhortations, however, any reference to oracles is perfunctory[49] and astrology plays no role; having almost no interest in divine condescension to humanity, he seldom names any deity other than Zeus.[50] "The gods" is merely his synonym for the divine, and it is a maxim of his that they send us all that is needful, both for happiness and for virtue (which he, like all Stoics, assumes to be coextensive). Yet this consists in nothing more than the power to apply

48. See above all 1.6 on the harmonization of phenomena to our needs and those of animals.

49. See *Discourses* 2.1718, etc.

50. For Zeus, see *Discourses* 1.3.2–3; 2.8.18 (statue by Phidias); 2.17.22 (in accusative with other unnamed gods); 4.6.5; *Enchiridion* 53.1 (quoting Cleanthes), etc.

prohairesis, or choice, to our impressions.[51] While Epictetus grants that we possess this power in varying degrees, he does not ascribe these inequalities to any sin on our part or to the policy of the gods (3.17); on the other hand, the gods do not work any miracles to redress these inequalities, and those who excel in virtue cannot look for any material reward, but only for adversities and afflictions, which are vouchsafed to us as tests of our moral strength. What athlete, Epictetus asks, would not wish to advance from an easy victory to a more difficult competition, and at last, if he has the capacity, to an Olympic triumph (1.18.21–22)? Another maxim is that the gods ensure that the better will always subdue the worse (1.29.13–14), but this signifies only that a sage will maintain his rectitude in defiance of all tribulation, not that he will be repaid in wealth or honor or any other external benefit.

"External benefit" is of course a misnomer for the rigid Stoic, who holds that the secret of happiness is to care only for that which lies within our power. Even without a concept of the separable soul, Epictetus can urge us to show as much indifference in surrendering the body to a tyrant as in yielding a coat to a thief. All wrongdoing is the consequence of the same error, the error of thinking that because a thing appears to us to be so we must act as though it were really so. Agamemnon fears for his sovereignty if he is the only king without a prize; Achilles in turn will not allow Agamemnon to snatch the booty by which he has come to measure his own worth as a man (*Discourses* 1.22.5–6). Philosophy sets before us the means of escaping these delusions, first by study and then by practice. Both are necessary, for if detachment cannot be achieved by reading the precepts of Chrysippus, there is no more hope of surmounting all the obstacles to the practice of detachment without having mastered the comparatively simple elucidation of the theory. All too often life mimics art and we resemble the figures of tragedy in all but masks and buskins, deploring the injustice of all that befalls us though it were our part and not God's to define our lot (1.28 *passim*).[52]

In summary then, divine providence is shown in the testing of our capacity for resignation. Conversely Epictetus understands by divine

51. On its divine origin, see *Discourses* 4.12.12; on its immunity to external compulsion, see 1.1.23; 2.15.1; 3.19.2; 3.26.24; 4.5.23. Reale, *Epitteto: Tutte le opere*, 14–23, distinguishes *prohairesis* from will. By contrast Long, *Epictetus*, 28–34, defends the translation of *prohairesis* as "volition," arguing that volition in Epictetus is the self.

52. See also at *Discourses* 1.29.49, "the calling to which we are called," as at Ephesians 4:1. *Discourses* 1.2.25–29 is often adduced to prove that Epictetus favored suicide on grounds that we would now consider trivial, but he speaks here only of readiness to endure death to preserve one's character, not of inflicting death one oneself. His argument at *Discourses* 2.15.7–12 (which uses metaphors reminiscent of 1 Corinthians 3:15) implies that one should not take one's own life unless one is a felon.

retribution nothing more than the ferment of a disordered conscience, the pains of unconsummated desire, the fear of losing what we had no right to possess. The antidote to these distempers is to sift our impressions, reserving *prohairesis* or choice for those that we find to be true.[53] Our sole, but ubiquitous, organ of discernment between impressions is *logos* or reason, which we alone of all animals share with the gods; since the soul has a natural bent to shun falsehood and to seek truth, the cause of wrongdoing is not any positive will to evil but ignorance (*agnoia*), by which Epictetus means not so much a failure to calculate the true balance of pleasure as the mistaken pursuit of pleasure, rather than life in accord with nature, as an end.[54] While he is less of a hedonist than Plato or Aristotle, he concurs with them in holding that human beings do not habitually do what they know to be wrong. He differs from them, however, in assuming that our choice of rational ends is almost always at odds with the impulses engendered by the weakness of the body and the follies of those around us. If the soul is permitted to relax it will succumb to *orexis* or appetite, and therefore the precondition of equanimity is to put to death all our passions and desires.[55]

The Stoic, so far as his temper and condition permit, will live without the external goods that the Peripatetic deems intrinsic to happiness; the Platonist may be equally austere, but only because he has weaned his desire from transient to eternal objects. The *Phaedrus*, like Epictetus, credits the soul with a natural appetite for truth, but the resumption on earth of its quest for the plain of truth is stimulated by a sudden recollection of the beauty that drew it toward that goal in the supercelestial heaven. The appetitive and desiderative tendencies are thus to be redirected rather than suppressed. The sublimation of this thirst for beauty is the theme of the *Symposium*, while in the *Republic* the vision of the Good is the consummation of philosophy.[56] The Stoic account of moral deliberation, by contrast, accords no role to beauty or the love that it inspires: *pistis* or fidelity must be added to the soul's natural inclination if knowledge of truth is to inform our moral conduct.[57] Goodness, as we have noted, is for Epictetus a property of actions, not an object of desire. Thus, while reason is sovereign, inclination is rebellious, and Medea, tragic heroine though she is, is a mouthpiece for all when she confesses that she sees and approves the better but does the worse.

53. *Discourses* 1.17.36, 1.30.4, etc.

54. *Discourses* 1.26.7; 2.22.22, etc.

55. *Discourses* 1.1.4.1; 2,13.7, 2.14.22; 3.12.4, 3.22.36; 4.1.1; *Enchiridion* 2.1, etc.

56. See Sorabji, *Emotion and Peace of Mind*, 181–210; Weissner, "Why Does Philo Criticise the Stoic Ideal?"

57. *Discourses* 2.8.23; 3.14.13–14, with Morgan, *Roman Faith and Faith and Christian Faith*, 41–45.

To be unable to do as one wills is not only the plight of the unphilosophical man when he yields to passion against his conscience, but also—indeed, pre-eminently—of the Stoic who is constantly finding that he is too much a man of the world to maintain the character of a sage.[58]

Conclusion

None of the authors examined in this chapter gives a radical account of the cause of evil that can be compared with Plato's; most have little use for the term itself, although they are liberal with their nostrums for pain and adversity. They may say that our bodily passions are at war with the intellect, but they do not explain the infirmity of the body by drawing a contrast between true being and its shadow in the realm of generation. They look for the seeds of political injustice in the cupidity and belligerence of our ancestors, but cannot tell us how these vices were born or why we have not outgrown them. They argue that by wrestling with misfortune we become stronger, and that the enmity of the natural world compels us to develop skills and virtues that would otherwise have lain dormant; yet even when they add that gods have placed us in harsh conditions for this very purpose, this is said by way of exhortation rather than to satisfy our desire for an aetiology of evil.

That desire arises when we believe it possible for the world to be otherwise, and that belief is unlikely to be held where there is no concept of a Creator whose purpose is good and his power commensurate with his purpose. Once we accept this premiss, the only evils that are natural to the world are those entailed by finitude, which in their proper place (we might argue) are not evils. Those that were avoidable must be imputed, as Plato asserts, to the creature rather than the creator; but the source of the evil will in the creature is a riddle, to which Plato's answer is that it is caused by the ignorance that accompanies finitude, and therefore once again is not truly evil. Whereas Plato and Aristotle assume that we customarily do as we will except in pathological cases, we have seen that Epictetus regards the frustration of the will as a habitual phenomenon. Yet even he would have been perplexed to hear to hear one of his older contemporaries lamenting that the typical condition of humanity is to fail in the good that we will

---

58. Frede, *A Free Will*, 76–85, maintains that we see in Epictetus the emergence of a concept of free will, which was to color the thought of Augustine (p. 266). The chief attributes of a free will, on this theory, are its immunity to coercion from without and its alignment with the will of God, because that will is perceived to be rational. Frede does not claim to find in Epictetus the notion of either an evil or a debilitated will, both of which we shall also encounter in Augustine.

and to do the evil that we do not will. This plight of Paul the Christian is revealed to him by meditation on texts that were unknown to the majority of Greeks; and even the perusal of these, as the next two chapters show, was not sufficient without a further revelation to sustain his new understanding of the relation between embodiment and sin.

3

God and Evil in the
Jewish Tradition

To be a Greek in the Hellenistic and the Roman era was not merely to speak the Greek language but to take a pride in the literature that was written in that language, and to feel oneself to be in some sense the heir of the poets, philosophers, and statesmen of the ancient Greek cities and their colonies. How far the classical culture of Greece had been nourished by the more ancient civilizations of western Asia and Egypt was a topic of debate in this time, as in ours, but the universal diffusion of the Greek language among the educated classes of the eastern Mediterranean world in the wake of Alexander's conquests was to be followed by its diffusion among the educated classes of the western Mediterranean world in the wake of the Roman conquest of Greece itself. It was not true, however, that everyone became Greek, for one result of this linguistic hegemony was the translation of a barbarian scripture into Greek in order that those for whom it was made would not become Greek but retain their ancestral patrimony as Jews. Thanks to the Christian appropriation of it, this putative work of seventy scholars that replicated in Greek the idiom of the Hebrew Torah was to eclipse the culture of Greece as Greece herself, in Horace's conceit, had captured Rome (*Epistles* 2.1.156). To pagans it was a curiosity rather than a classic, and sometimes an object of derision. Nevertheless, the third verse of Genesis, in which God creates by his word alone, was cited by the eminent critic Longinus as an instance of sublimity,[1] while Numenius, who is able to cite the preceding verse, was so impressed by the likeness between the Demiurge of Plato and the "imparticipable" God of the Hebrews (Fr. 56 Des Places) that he exclaimed, "What is Plato but Moses in Attic dress?"[2]

This comment suggests, however, that he had yet to take the measure of the gulf that divides the biblical from the Greek conception of God. In Greek thought it is always assumed that the Good is an object of a priori knowledge and definition, which is either superior to the divine or to be identified with it. The biblical Creator, on the other hand, is the source of all law because he is the one source of the world itself and of every finite being: the Good in Greek thought may coexist with evils that it is unable to eliminate, but if a biblical author admits the presence of any evil in the world, he must also admit that God is in some sense the author of it. To speak of opposing philosophies would be incongruous so long as we think of the Torah as a miscellany of books composed over half a millennium in a culture that excelled in poetry, prophecy, and narrative, but not in the arts of ratiocination. The Greek translation, however, was completed at the end of the Hellenistic age, when Jews were no longer strangers to philosophy and some of them liked to imagine that the seventy (or seventy-two) translators had been selected for their proficiency in that discipline. If we approach this text in a philosophical spirit, at least three inchoate arguments against the justice of God invite our attention. The first we may call the argument of a wronged people: why does God, having chosen Israel for his own, permit her to be repeatedly defeated and oppressed by the impious nations? The second is the argument of the wronged saint: why are the wicked allowed to prosper in all their doings while the righteous enjoy neither wealth nor honor? The third, and some would say, the most philosophical, is the argument from the mere existence of wrong in a world that its omnipotent Creator pronounced to be good. Having examined the emergence of these three themes in the biblical canon, we shall end with Philo's attempt to extract a theodicy from the patriarchal narratives and the legislation of Moses, and we shall see that in his treatise on providence even pagan narratives bear witness to the divine ordering of the cosmos for the good of each and all.

---

1. See [Longinus], *On Sublimity* 9.9, with the comments of D. A. Russell, ed., *Longinus: On the Sublime*, 92.

2. Clement of Alexandria, *Stromateis* 1.22.150; Eusebius, *Preparation for the Gospel* 9.6.9. Edwards, "Atticizing Moses?," 67, observes that Eusebius entertains doubts that Clement does not appear to share.

God, Evil, and Israel

In the Old Testament God has many names, of which the most frequent are *Elohim*, a plural of the generic term for deity in many Semitic languages, and YHWH (Yahweh, Jehovah), which is supposed to mean "I am what I am," or more accurately, "I shall be what I shall be."[3] *Elohim* is represented in the Greek Bible by the term *theos*, Yahweh by *kyrios*, "lord," because it is customary, when the text is read aloud in Hebrew, to substitute the equivalent term Adonai for the sacred appellation. *Elohim* is used of God as Creator in the opening chapter of Genesis, and, while it is generally treated as a singular, its morphological history is remembered in the famous pronouncement, "Let *us* make humanity in *our* own image and likeness" (Genesis 1:26). Both the provenance and the etymology of the name Yahweh remain obscure, and there is no surviving text in which another people lays claim to him: to Israel he is Yahweh Sabaoth, the LORD of hosts, and the nation itself is personified in the second Isaiah as *ebed Yahweh*, the servant of the LORD.[4] There are numerous passages in which the two names are combined, and the statement at Exodus 6, that the patriarchs Abraham, Isaac, and Jacob were ignorant of the name Yahweh, is repeatedly contradicted in the Book of Genesis. This is one among many indices of a long and perhaps irrecoverable history of redaction, which is elucidated only in part, if at all, by assigning different segments of the first five books in the canon to a Yahwist, an Elohist, a Priestly writer, and the author of Deuteronomy.[5] To Philo of Alexandria, the Scripture was an indivisible text in which *theos* signifies the goodness and *kyrios* the lordship of the Creator who is also the peculiar God of Israel. No doubt, to the common Israelite it was enough that the Lord God who had said "you shall have no other God beside me" at Exodus 20:3 was also he who had told the overweening kings of Babylon and Egypt that *"I"*—not you—"am God and beside me there is no other."[6] Whether the beings worshipped on other territories were idols, fallen angels, or appointed viceroys, Yahweh had chosen Israel for his portion, and she could boast with a confidence not vouchsafed to humankind in general that "the LORD our God is one" (Deuteronomy 6:4).

We need not wonder that the princes of Babylon and Tyre were overthrown so easily when the world itself had been created at no cost by their conqueror. There is no dragon Tiamat to be slain before there can be land,

---

3. See Exodus 3:14.

4. Isaiah 42:1–4; 49:1–7; 50:4–11; 52:13—53:12.

5. On the history of this scholarly hypothesis, see Nicholson, *Pentateuch in the Twentieth Century*.

6. Isaiah 43:11; 45:2, 5; 46:6, in contrast to Babylon at 47:10.

as in the Babylonian cosmogony.[7] When we hear in other writings of God's victories over Rahab and Leviathan,[8] these monsters are not said to have lived before the creation or to have menaced his life as the life of Baal is menaced in a Phoenician myth. At most, he has to contend with the anarchy of the *tohu-bohu*, the earth "without form and void" of Genesis 1:2. This, however, is easily mastered, as God first brings forth light by his word and divides it from darkness (Genesis 1:3–4), and then by a second fiat creates a firmament to separate the upper and lower waters (1:6–8). Only on this second day, perhaps by oversight, are we not told that his work was good; even if we grant some allusion here to the recalcitrance of matter, it does not impair the goodness of God's design as he successively creates the dry land (1:9), populates both sea and land with living creatures (1:11–23), and finally makes humanity in his own image, male and female, to exercise rule over all the rest (1:26–28). Posterity was left to guess whether the image of God resides in our physical form, in our capacity for reason, or in our dominion over the beasts.[9] Again we are not told why, when he promised both image and likeness, God created us only in his image: are the two terms synonymous, is the likeness deferred, or does our being male and female somehow constitute the likeness rather than dimming it, as most suppose? At Ezekiel 1:28 God is seen in the similitude of the likeness of a man, and when Israel is brought before his throne as "one like a son of man" at Daniel 7:13, she is given dominion over the beasts, who symbolise the consecutive empires under which she has groaned. Since Egypt appears in prophecy as a dragon (Ezekiel 32:2) it is possible that every beast who contends with Yahweh represents an enemy of his people: the placing of humanity at the summit of creation thus prefigures the subjection of the world to Israel, the chosen race to whom God says, as he also says to its king at his enthronement, "You are my son; this day you are born to me."[10]

But if the might of God is so irresistible, why is it that Israel not only fails to conquer, except in the days of David and Solomon, but cannot even maintain her independence against her sinful neighbors and their impotent monarchs? The responses of all her prophets may be condensed into one: "your iniquities have come between you and your God."[11] He has not only

7. See Clifford, "*Creatio ex nihilo* in the Old Testament."

8. Psalm 89:11; Isaiah 51:9–10; Job 26:12; 41:1. Before we reduce this monster to the natural dimensions of a crocodile or hippopotamus, we must ask why God would boast at Job 41:1–2 of a feat that has been emulated by many humans.

9. Whitney, *Two Strange Beasts*, 168–80.

10. See Psalm 2:7, with Petersen, *Royal God*.

11. Isaiah 59:2. On sin in the Old Testament as apostasy, see Konstan, *Origin of Sin*, 33–60.

chosen Israel from the nations (Amos 3:2), but has made a covenant with her,[12] sealed by sacrifices (Exodus 24:8), in which he undertakes to protect her borders and to bless her abundance, but only so long as she continues to perform what is commanded and to "love the LORD [her] God with all [her] heart" (Deuteronomy 6:5). The bond is represented as a marriage, in which Israel is perpetually unfaithful and God implacably forgiving. He has signed no divorce (Isaiah 50:1), he has taken Israel back as Hosea took back his repentant wife (Hosea 2:23), he can pardon repeated acts of prostitution—that is, the courtship of foreign enemies—by both the northern and the southern kingdoms (Ezekiel 23). But with love comes a proviso, "those whom the LORD loves he chastises" (Proverbs 3:12), and if his bride will not learn from his tenderness she must learn from his severity. The God who can overthrow Nineveh can also bring the Philistines from Crete;[13] he can drive away Sennacherib or raise up Nebuchadnezzar to impose the final reckoning, and then summon Cyrus as his instrument of restoration.

Israel's perennial sin is to go whoring after false gods, under which description the prophets and historians include not only the worship of Ashtaroth, the Queen of heaven,[14] but the performance of infant sacrifice and the erection of high places, which, since the dedicated is a nameless king or lord (that is, Moloch or Baal), may have been intended as offerings to God himself.[15] Religious infidelity is compounded by alliances with idolatrous powers, some of which entail the licensing of cults that are clearly proscribed by the laws of the Pentateuch. The vengeance of Yahweh on such delinquents is inexorable: 450 priests of "Baal" are slaughtered in a day when their rites have been proved inefficacious (1 Kings 18:40), while in the Book of Joshua whole tribes are massacred lest their survival imperil the purity of the cult.[16] There is also a sin of a second order, against one's fellow-Israelite, which is denounced with equal vehemence by the prophets and the psalmists. "Woe to those," says Isaiah, "who join house to house and field to field" (5:8). The psalmists, always convinced that they are the wronged, predict with relish the vengeance of God upon the wrongdoer and declare that one never sees the just forsaken or their children begging for bread (Psalm 37:25). In contrast to the political sphere, in which God may

---

12. See above all Deuteronomy 29:1, with Nicholson, *God and His People*. The dates at which the covenants with Noah, Abraham, Israel, Mount Zion, and the house of David were first promulgated need not be determined for the purpose of the present study.

13. Amos 9:7. Cf. Deuteronomy 2:23 and Jeremiah 47:4. On God's care for the nations in Amos, see Barton, *Amos's Oracles*.

14. 1 Kings 11:5; 11:33; 2 Kings 23:13; cf. Jeremiah 44:17–18.

15. Leviticus 18:21; Leviticus 20:2–25; 2 Kings 23:10; Jeremiah 32:3.

16. See further, Hofreiter, *Making Sense of Old Testament Genocide*.

authorize acts that would otherwise be atrociously wicked, the everyday sphere, at least since the time of Moses, is one in which good and evil appear in their customary dress. God no longer prefers the crafty Jacob to his unsuspecting brother or requires an Abraham to offer up his remaining son.[17]

It was all too clear, nonetheless, that the moral economy by which the world was administered was not the one that God had revealed through his prophets or inculcated in his own law. It was not the one that the Book of Proverbs reduced to the experimental precept that as thrift leads to plenty so idleness leads to want (Proverbs 6:6–11). The omnipotence that was claimed for God seemed to leave him without apology: "can there be evil in the city," Amos exclaims, "and the LORD has not done it?" (Amos 3:6), while second Isaiah reasons, like Heraclitus, that the God who creates both night and day is the author of evil no less than of good (Isaiah 45:7). There was reason to fear that his punishments and rewards were bestowed capriciously, for why should David, the murderer of Uriah, be a man after God's own heart (1 Samuel 13:14), while the pious Hezekiah was sick to death before his time and even Josiah, restorer of the law, was killed by the heathen at Megiddo?[18] Even David, we read, had been prompted by God to hold a census, for which he had then been capriciously punished (2 Samuel 24:1); but for that matter it was not easy to discover what his predecessor Saul had done to earn his deposition but for his failure to butcher the Amalekites (1 Samuel 15:11–35). After the return of the Jews from exile, to occasional independence but much less than Davidic splendor, the man or men whom we know as the Chronicler substituted Satan for God as the tempter of David (1 Chronicles 21:1) and rewrote the Books of Kings to ensure that those who died by violence would be understood as guilty of flouting the ceremonial, if not the moral, law. Where history could not be amended it was invented, as in the tale of Judith's decapitation of the fictitious Holofernes or the miraculous inscription foretelling the ruin of King Belshazzar, which was accomplished by the equally fictitious Darius the Mede.[19]

Good and Evil in Wisdom Literature: Job

Outside the Psalms, it is in the books that make up the wisdom literature of the Septuagint (or seventy translators) that God is most called to account for his dealings with the righteous and the wicked. Whether they consist of

17. See Genesis 22 on the uncompleted sacrifice of Isaac; Genesis 25:19–34 on Jacob's beguilement of Esau.

18. 2 Samuel 11; 2 Kings 20:1; 23:29.

19. Daniel 5:31. See further, Rowley, *Darius the Mede*.

precepts for worldly success through piety, thrift, and industry, as in Proverbs, or of precepts against these precepts, as in Job and Ecclesiastes, such writings admit of no confident dating because they refer to no historical transactions and are subject to continual augmentation. While it is often assumed that the interrogation of God by the individual must have followed a loss of faith in collective providence, collections of proverbial lore already existed in Egypt, and we possess the remains of a Babylonian diatribe that bears some resemblance to the Book of Job.[20] For our purpose it is sufficient to know that all the texts that now compose the Torah existed in Hebrew and in Greek by the end of the Hellenistic era:[21] my reason for considering Job before Ecclesiastes in this chapter is that the former seems to me to be written as much for Israel as for the individual believer, who is certainly the sole addressee of the latter. My third text, the Wisdom of Solomon, is undeniably later than both and has no Hebrew prototype. Its morality may be of universal application, but Wisdom is not a Greek goddess and the recapitulation of her acts, which are those of Israel's Lord of Hosts, is as much an admonition to the triumphant pagan as a consolation to the uprooted Jew.

While the dramatic structure of the Book of Job is commonly acknowledged, the crisis of the plot and its resolution are often buried by commentators in their efforts to extract a theodicy from its antiphonal speeches. No doubt we are still too inclined to assume that all tragedies turn on an error, if not a sin, which precipitates the hero from happiness into misery; perhaps we also think it necessary that there should be action and not only the strife of words. Yet Aristotle and his beloved Euripides refute the first claim, and Aeschylus the second: Job's ululations and the replies of his comforters serve to deepen pity and heighten expectation between the scenario, which is a wager between God and Satan, and the denouement, which is the testing of that wager.[22] There is no vindication of God because the person accused is not God but Job, whose steadfastness ensures not only God's victory but the mending of his own fortunes, and the overall lesson is therefore the one that is constantly impressed on us by the prophetic oracles, psalms, and proverbs of the Old Testament, that those who put their trust in the Lord will prevail against all odds. Satan, the defeated party, is not the universal author of sin in this or in any other book of the Hebrew canon. As his name and the Greek equivalent *diabolos* imply, he is the adversary, the slanderer,

---

20. Annas and Lenzi, *Ludlul bēl nēmegi*.

21. For an introduction to modern debates concerning the date and purpose of the Greek translation, see Law, *When God Spoke Greek*, 33–42.

22. Frye, *The Great Code*, 195, observes that the plot turns on the outcome of the wager, but asserts that God has already won by chapter 29.

who accuses God's people of sin.[23] His charge is that Job loves God only for his gifts (1:9) and he predicts that if these gifts are withdrawn he will curse God to his face (1:11). God accepts the challenge and appears to win at once, for when Job is robbed of his cattle, his property, and his children, he not only rejects his wife's injunction to curse God but reminds her that what God has given God has the right to take away (1:21–22). Now, however, God permits his opponent to go further, and Job is afflicted with sores from head to foot with sores (2:7–8). At first he defies his wife's incitement to curse God (2:9–10), but when his friends gather round in commiseration he no longer blesses God but denounces him as his adversary, demanding yet fearing that which is necessary for the testing of the wager—that he and God should come together in judgment (9:32–34; 23:3).

The role of Job's comforters is to prevent this encounter, not only by persuading Job of his guilt but also by admonishing him that even if his cause were just, it could not prevail against the judge and creator of all.[24] Can a mortal be righteous before God, asks Eliphaz the Temanite, trembling at his own memory of the formless spirit that passed before his face (4:15). No one, says Zophar the Naamathite, can sound the depths of his wisdom (11:7–9), certainly not the man whose days, as Bildad the Shuhite declares, are a fleeting shadow (8:8–19). And yet these savants assure Job that the righteous will infallibly be rewarded, that the wicked will be scattered like chaff, and that justice in God is tempered only by mercy, so that if Job suffers his punishment must be less than he deserves (4:7; 8:20; 11:11; 15:20; 18:5; 20:5; 22:4–11). Job's reply is to throw their reasoning back at them, to exclaim that if mortals have a short time to live there is all the less hope for them when they fall into adversity (14:1–12), and that God's ways are indeed unfathomable because no one can say why one man dies in bitterness and another in prosperity (21:22–26). It is unjust that a man who was eyes to the blind and feet to the lame should now be mocked by young men whose fathers he once held in derision (30:1). Invincible as his adversary may be—Job never suspects that this is Satan—he cannot rob the just man of his conviction that he is just (13:19), or of his appeal to the heavenly advocate who, after his death, will enable him to see God (19:26). At last his friends fall silent, but the confrontation with God is delayed by a young man named Elihu, who taunts Job's professions of innocence, reasserted the inscrutability of God, and in short has so little to add to his predecessors

---

23. On the evolution of this figure, see Breytenbach and Day, "Satan."

24. On Job as scapegoat, see Girard, *Job, the Victim of his People*, 86–90. On the difficulty of finding a theodicy in Job, see Barr, "The Book of Job," 42–44.

that his speech is often dismissed as an obtuse interpolation.[25] If he thinks of himself as the arbiter for whom Job has prayed, he satisfies neither party, for God's first question when he speaks unannounced[26] from the whirlwind is "Who is this that darkens counsel by words without wisdom?" (38:1).

God proceeds to address Job in the taunting manner foreshadowed by Elihu.[27] Was Job present when he laid the foundations of the earth, when the morning stars sang together and the sons of God shouted for joy (38:7)? Can Job master Behemoth (40:15) or draw up the scaly Leviathan with a hook (41:1)? These are surely mythical creatures, not the hippopotamus and the crocodile, which even human beings gave been known to subdue; their prompt submission proves that God is greater than his Phoenician and Babylonian counterparts, greater than the kings and gods of the nations that they symbolize.[28] Yet no explanation is given to Job of his suffering and no promise of deliverance; the wager cannot be disclosed until Job has been given the opportunity to curse God to his face. Although his plea remains unanswered, Job does no such thing, but meekly confesses that he has spoken without understanding (42:1–3); he has now learned that all is possible for God and rejoices to see at last the one whom hitherto he knew only by hearing (42:5). Reprimanding the comforters for their failure to give him the honor that he had received from his servant Job (42:7–9), God bestows on him more than he had lost (42:10–11). While Job himself is a legendary figure, inhabiting the fictitious land of Uz, the title "servant of God" is one that God had conferred through his prophets on Israel herself, and the promise of future prosperity if Israel endures her present tribulation is as close as the prophets come to a theodicy. For Israel there would have been no problem of evil had she been willing to imitate the patience of Job.

Good and Evil in Wisdom Literature: Ecclesiastes

The book of the Preacher (Hebrew Qohelet; Greek Ecclesiastes) announces itself as the work of a son of David (1:1), who goes on to recall that he has been king in Jerusalem (1:12). Whoever the author is, therefore, his persona is that of Solomon, whose populous harem and commercial affluence sat

25. For recent scholarship on chapters 32–37, see Andersen, "The Elihu Speeches."

26. Except by inadvertence at 36:29 when Elihu asks who can understand God when he thunders from his pavilion? Cf. 37:5.

27. And indeed by Job himself, e.g., at 26:5–14. Arcturus is cited as a specimen of God's handiwork by Job at 9:9 and by God at 38:32.

28. On the caricature of Pharaoh as a dragon at Ezekiel 29:3 and 32:2 see Yoder, "Ezekiel 29.3."

uneasily with his reputation for wisdom. The bleak exordium—"vanity of vanities, says the preacher; all is vanity" (1:2) is the epitaph of one who has drained all pleasures, including even the pleasure of despising everything that was wont to please him. The preacher recalls his former life as a buyer and seller of slaves (2:7), a connoisseur of the world's luxuries (2:8), a practitioner in diverse arts (2:4–6), all of which gave satisfaction for a time (2:10). Yet now he has come to see that all our work will perish as that which was before us has perished (2:11, 17), that birth and death, love and enmity, labor and leisure all have their seasons, that none of us can determine by our efforts and merits what the next day will bring (3:1–8). With the spectacle of perpetual vicissitude comes also the knowledge of that which we cannot change, that we cannot make straight that which is crooked (7:13), divorce authority from oppression (4:1–3), or prevent the same end from coming upon the righteous and the unrighteous, the wise man and the fool (9:2; 2:14). For all that, the preacher enjoins the pursuit of wisdom (7:11–12) and the practice of honesty, frequently commending these as our duties to God our Creator, of whom we can say, as of no other agent, that what he does will endure for ever (3:14). It seems that the book is written in two keys, for we sometimes read that it is God himself who allots our trade to each of us, God himself who has made that crooked which cannot be made straight, God himself who has set the day of prosperity against that of adversity, so that the future will always be hidden (7:14). But does he do this merely to remind us that we are not gods, or rather to test us, as one text implies (3:18)? And if test there is, for what purpose are we tested, and what does it mean to succeed or fail?

Perfect obedience to God, with fear and reverence, is the preacher's counsel at all times. We must enter the temple in the submissive spirit that befits the house of God; our words in prayer should be few, for we are on earth while he is in heaven; it is better that we should make no vows at all to him than our vows should go unfulfilled (5:1–6). We are not told, however, that those who break their vows to God will be punished. The living have one advantage over the dead, that they still remember that they will die (9:5). And thus they can see that while there is nothing more honorable than the quest for wisdom, there is nothing more profitable than to eat, drink, and be merry (2:24; 8:15). The injunction to cast our bread upon the waters (11:1) has been taken by some to mean that we should invest in foreign trade and by others to mean that we ought to be liberal in the giving of alms; in either case we are promised no return, but only that we do not know what good or evil may ensue. The book ends with a sonorous exhortation to remember the Creator in the days of youth before the decay of our inward and outward faculties (12:1–5). Yet whether we remember him or not, the spirit "returns to him who gave it" (12:7), and perhaps his having given it is the sole ground of our obligation to "love God and fear his commandments," which is said to be the entire duty of humanity (12:13).

No wonder that this putative work of Solomon is often seen as a hybrid composition, in which an inept redactor has tried to counteract the pessimism of the original. One commentator suggests that God is not so much a figure of awe to the author as a "completely amoral being," a "gigantic spider" who draws us into his web for his own amusement.[29] This is not so absurd a conjecture when we recall the text in which circumcision is improvised by the wife of Moses, not as the seal of a covenant but as an apotropaic response to Yahweh's murderous assault upon her husband (Exodus 4:24–26). No doubt we owe something to God as our Creator and the donor of all that he will one day take from us; we cannot, however, trust him to be the guarantor of justice, and we have no reason to serve him other than that he is God. According to the prophets, there is no other reason for his loving Israel, and Solomon's answer to Satan's jibe, "Does Job serve God for nought?" could only have been the first response of Job himself: "The LORD has given, the LORD has taken away; blessed be the name of the LORD" (Job 1:21).

Evil and Good in Creation

"God made humans upright in the beginning, but they have found out many inventions (Ecclesiastes 7:29). Reflection on the universality of human wickedness necessarily carries the authors of the wisdom literature back to the creation, to which no evil or imperfection could be imputed. The Wisdom of God is personified in the Book of Proverbs as his coadjutor in creation, whom he created (or possessed) in the beginning, having brought her forth before the hills were formed (Proverbs 8:22–25). In the Wisdom of Solomon, she is the breath of God's power, the image of his goodness in whom there no blemish is to be found (7:25–26). But if it is true that all things are made in wisdom (Psalm 104:20), or as the Gospel of John construes this, that all things were made by and through the Logos (John 1:3), how is the presence of suffering and iniquity in the world to be explained, and why should the creature that is most often both the agent and the victim of iniquity be the one who was fashioned in the image of God (Genesis 1:26–28)?[30]

---

29. Macdonald, *The Hebrew Philosophical Genius*, 86 and 137.

30. On the controversies surrounding the meaning of this expression, see Jónsson, *The Image of God*.

Although the verb *bara* at Genesis 1:1 would normally signify the fashioning of an object from some antecedent matter,[31] it is only at Genesis 2:1 that we hear of God taking a substrate and molding it, rather than creating by his word. The being whom he produces from the red clay is Adam, whose name can denote humanity in general. The plants, which at Genesis 1:11–12 appear by God's command on the third day, are now said to have sprung up—for all we know spontaneously—after the fashioning of Adam (2:5). Again, it is only at Genesis 2:19–20 that the animals are presented to him so that each can receive a name. This is therefore a second narrative of creation, seemingly inconsistent with the one that is crowned on the sixth day by the making of humans, male and female, in the image of God. Ancient readers perceived this clearly enough, as they also perceived that the lofty style of Genesis 1 had been succeeded by a more anthropomorphic representation of divine activity. Since it was not open to them to assign the two texts to different authors, let alone to distinguish a more advanced from a more primitive sensibility, Philo surmised that there had indeed been two creations, one of the inner and one of the outer man (*Allegorical Interpretation* 1.2.12–13). In this, he was followed, with qualifications, by Origen and Gregory of Nyssa; the kneading of the outer man from clay could be read as a metaphor of his special love for those who bear his image, and perhaps as the adumbration of a Trinity in which the Son and Spirit play the role of the Father's hands.[32]

In contrast to the one whom God proposed to make "in our image," the clay-born Adam is man without woman. He is still alone when God places him in a garden, or to use its Persian name a *paradeisos*, which is encircled by four rivers (2:10–14). Since these have the names of earthly rivers, few ancient readers doubted that paradise, or Eden, was in some sense a place in this world, though now inaccessible to us: in a paraphrase of Genesis entitled the Book of Jubilees, Enoch is translated to this asylum to save him from death, yet it is still so much a part of earth that a miracle is necessary to shield it from the great flood.[33] It was widely agreed, on the other hand, that the trees that God planted in Eden were symbolic,[34] and that some esoteric sense should be attached to the command to abstain from the tree of knowledge which stood in the midst of it (2:16–17). The prohibition, so far as we know, was heard by Adam alone, though it was also

31. See O'Neill, "How Early Is the Doctrine?," 453.

32. See Irenaeus, *Against Heresies* 4.20.1. On Origen and Gregory, see later chapters in this volume.

33. Jubilees 21–26, translated in Sparks, ed., *The Apocryphal Old Testament*, 23–24.

34. See the papers collected in Estes, ed., *The Tree of Life*, and, on the author's intention in Genesis 3, Heard, "The Tree of Life in Genesis."

imparted in some way (3:2) to the woman who was subsequently created as his helpmate (2:18–19). Some commentators reasoned therefore that, while it was the woman who allowed a snake to dupe her into eating the fruit (3:4–6), the greater blame attached to Adam, who ate it at her prompting but in *conscious defiance* of God (3:6–7).[35] To Philo of Alexandria she is an emblem of the weak and appetitive element in the soul, which is prone to error when divorced from reason; Adam, in permitting her to beguile him, personifies the surrender of reason to passion, which is the true cause of sin (*On the Making of the World* 150–56).

In the biblical myth the seducer is merely a reptile: his motives are not explained, and he has not yet received the name Satan in the periphrases of Philo, Jubilees, or Josephus. The Wisdom of Solomon, echoing Plato, ascribes the fall to the *phthonos* or jealousy of the devil (Wisdom 2:27), but the Book of Revelation is the first text to unmask this adversary as "Satan, that old serpent who tempted Eve" (12:9). All Christians have concurred, but Jews were more circumspect, even in late antiquity: The Life of Adam and Eve, with its circumstantial accounts of Satan's occupation of the serpent and his subsequent assaults on Eve in the same guise, is agreed to have profited heavily from Christian redaction. Nor did Jewish students of this narrative invoke it to explain anything but the mortality of the human race, the difficulty of extracting fruits from the soil, and the pains of childbirth.[36] These—together, it seems, with the amputation on the serpent's legs (3:14)—are the curses pronounced by God in the biblical narrative (3:15–20). The notion that a propensity to sin was bequeathed by Adam to all his offspring originates with Paul of Tarsus. The first text not purporting to be Christian in which Adam is denounced as the cause of sin in his descendants is 2 Ezra, and it is widely held to have suffered interpolation and does not even pretend to have been composed within thirty years of the destruction of Jerusalem in AD 70. The teaching that seems most typical of the rabbis is that each of us has as companions both a good and an evil spirit, together with the freedom to choose between them.[37] There is no one spirit that fathers the impulse to sin in all children of Adam, and no universal corruption of human nature by his fall that can be deemed to render our own sins either more or less culpable.

---

35. On the appraisal of Eve in modern commentary, see Stratton, *Out of Eden*, 41–50 and 85–99.

36. For a review of this question, with a warning not to underrate the significance of this narrative, see Smith, "Before Human Sin and Evil."

37. See Aitken, Patmore, and Rosen-Zvi, eds., *The Evil Inclination*.

The Enochian Tradition

In fact, there is no one sin in the Book of Genesis that causes the world to sin. The rebellion in Eden is only the first in an incremental catalogue of disorders that is not arrested even by the flood, but culminates in chapter 11 with a project for scaling heaven. Since God averts this by destroying the Tower of Babel (Genesis 11:1–8), which is evidently a caricature of Babylon's pretensions to world dominion, the inference that progress in the manual arts estranges us from the Maker is easily drawn. Corroborative arguments could be drawn not only from Greek and Roman authors (as we shall see in the following chapter) but from the acts ascribed to Cain's posterity in the fourth chapter of Genesis. Having murdered his brother Abel, he is sentenced to exile (4:8–10) and founds a city (4:12), peopling it (as Josephus conjectures) by incest with his sister (*Antiquities of the Jews* 1.2.1). It is their descendants who, as befits the first city-dwellers, invent the tools of music and metallurgy (4:20–22), which, according to Josephus, they employed in war and plunder, as Cain had taught them. Philo impugns Cain's choice of a wife and assumes that all the artefacts of Tubal Cain, the smith descended from him in the sixth generation, were martial weapons (*Antiquities* 1.2.2). The biblical narrative passes no judgments either on Cain's marriage or on his descendants, but hints at a new cause for the increase of wickedness on the eve of the flood, when the sons of God made wives of human women, and giants appeared upon the earth (6:1–3). For Augustine, this was the mating of the progeny of Seth with that of Cain,[38] but when Philo cites the Greek text in *On the Giants*, "sons of God" is replaced by "angels" (*On the Giants* 1). Although this is not the reading of the Septuagint, the same sense is accorded to the passage by Josephus (*Antiquities* 1.3.73) and by many Christian authors before Augustine. They are surely correct—for who are the sons of God who shouted for joy at the creation (Job 38:7) if not the angels?—but they were following another source than Genesis 6 when they added that this union of the mortal and the immortal produced not only monstrous offspring but estrangement from God and strife throughout the earth as the weapons of husbandry and smithcraft were turned into instruments of death.[39]

The elliptical text that now survives in Hebrew in Genesis 6:1–4 would appear to be an abridgement of a lost narrative. Nevertheless, 1 Enoch, the oldest surviving account of the fall of the angels, perhaps the only one with which early Christians were familiar, was composed in the first half of the

38. *City of God* 15.22–23, citing the translation of Aquila against the common identification of the sons of God with angels.

39. So also Barr, *The Garden of Eden*, 70.

second century BC, either in Greek or in Aramaic, although in ascribing itself to Enoch it purports to be much more ancient.[40] The sixth chapter of the Ethiopic version (the one complete, though adulterated, form that remains to us) relates that two hundred angels swore an oath that they would beget children in the daughters of men, thus sparing their leader Semyasa the opprobrium of having suggested the crime. It is nonetheless Semyasa who sows the world with charms and spells, while the manufacture of swords and shields is attributed to Azazel, together with the creation of meretricious adornments for women. In chapter 11 God intimates that he caused or allowed the seduction of the angels by mortal women as a punishment for descending from a realm in which reproduction and death were unknown. Once their gigantic progeny have murdered each other, the renegades are to be imprisoned for seventy generations and liberated only when the world comes to an end.

Azazel, who in this book is either Semyaza in altered guise or one of his retainers, appears to owe his name to Leviticus 16:26, where the goat on whom the sins of the people have been laid is said to have been set free "to Azazel" when the priest releases it into the wilderness. Some take Azazel to be a precipice, others a demon; in either case, the absolution of the people depends upon the goat's failure to return. Azazel returns in a more malign role in the Apocalypse of Abraham, another Jewish text of uncertain date that has undergone Christian redaction. For now he is the male figure whom the visionary sees embracing Eve and persuading her to eat the fruit of the tree of knowledge. The angelic tempter appears still to be distinct from the snake, and in this work his own fall is not described or invoked to explain the abuse of mechanical arts. Both in Enoch and in the Apocalypse, however, this fallen angel is the chief progenitor of sin and thus the counterpart of Satan as he appears in Christian thought.

Resurrection and Judgment

As we have found, neither Job nor Ecclesiastes offers any guarantee of the vindication of the just or of retribution for the wicked. One's hope is at best that if one is true to God one has done one's duty and that if Israel can remain blameless under affliction, she will at last inherit more than she has lost. When this comes to pass, the reward of the righteous who are already dead will be to have foreseen it, not to see it for themselves. The psalmist knows well enough that in Sheol the dead can no longer praise God (Psalm 115:17; cf. Isaiah 38:18). Indeed, the term Sheol, translated as Hades in

40. See Nickelsburg, trans., *1 Enoch*.

Greek, seems often to be no more than a synonym for the grave:[41] it is only by a poetic conceit that Isaiah can imagine the king of Babylon descending to the underworld to be welcomed with mockery by his fellow tyrants (Isaiah 14:9–20). The verb "to raise up" means always to exalt a living person or ordain them for a divine purpose; in Greek the same verb signifies resurrection, but only in the New Testament, where prophecies that had hitherto been interpreted metaphorically are literally fulfilled in the person of Christ. If the suffering servant of Isaiah 53 were an individual rather than a type of Israel, there might be a presage of life after death in the prophecy that he will look on his descendants;[42] if Job 19:26 does indeed say "in my flesh I shall see God" rather than "not in my flesh," it will be the earliest testimony in Hebrew to the hope of resurrection. By the common assent of scholars, however, the only certain promise of return from the grave in the Hebrew Bible occurs at Daniel 12:2—that is, in the latest chapter of the latest book—where we read that on the day of judgment the wicked will rise again to everlasting reprobation and the righteous (that is, the children of Israel) to everlasting life.

The Book of Daniel is a product of the Macedonian era, or more precisely of the Maccabean revolt in 167 BC against Antiochus Epiphanes, a descendant of Alexander's successor Seleucus. By this time large communities of Jews had formed throughout the Mediterranean world, most prominently in Egypt's new metropolis, Alexandria, which was also an opulent center of Greek learning. We distinguish such expatriates, who relied on Greek translations of the scriptures, from their Judean coreligionists who continued to speak and think in Aramaic, if not in Hebrew; in fact, however, no part of the Jewish world was untouched by Greek manners and intellectual culture, just as no part of it was entirely severed from its ancestral traditions.[43] The diffusion of Greek thought cannot be irrelevant to the emergence among Palestinian Jews of a widespread belief in a personal assize for all the dead, but when we encounter this in the Second Book of Maccabees it differs in three ways from the Hellenic, or rather Platonic, doctrine. It anticipates *a bodily resurrection*, not the survival of an incorporeal soul; it rests not on natural properties but in *the will of God*, who has made all that is from that which is not (7:28); and it is *the privilege of Israel*, in which the nations who now oppress her will have no share.[44] According

41. For some semantic theories and criticisms of these, see Johnston, *Shades of Sheol*, 73–74.

42. Isaiah 53:10. At 53:11 it is foretold that he will see the light of life, though not in the version preserved at Qumran.

43. See the classic work by Hengel, *Judaism and Hellenism*.

44. At 2 Maccabees 7:14 one of the martyrs declares that "God will raise us from death but for you there shall be no resurrection."

to Josephus, the first proviso was waived by the Pharisees and Essenes, two Jewish sects of the first century AD, who taught the immortality of the soul.[45] The New Testament, however, credits the Pharisees with belief in the resurrection of the dead,[46] and modern scholars have generally agreed, in this one instance, to prefer a Christian to a Jewish witness. If the Essenes may be judged by the Dead Sea Scrolls, they looked forward not so much to a personal reckoning as to the day that would see the overthrow of the sons of darkness by the sons of light.

Solomon in Greek

Among the books in the Septuagint that have no Hebrew antecedent, the one whose depiction of justice in the next world bears the closest resemblance to pagan teachings is the self-styled Wisdom of Solomon.[47] After the usual exhortations to virtue, with the warning that the spirit of discipline cannot coexist with deception and blasphemy (Wisdom 1:5), the author imagines the wicked saying, almost in the words of Ecclesiastes, that one end comes to the pious and the impious, that thought and feeling perish with the body, and that no remembrance of us survives our death (2:1–5). Their inference is not the one drawn by Solomon at the end of Ecclesiastes, that we must love God and fear his commandments, but the one that tempted him after his disenchantment, that there is nothing better for mortals than to eat, drink, and be merry (2:6–8). They carry the argument further than the Preacher when they resolve to profit by robbing the innocent man, and when they find such a man censorious in his demeanor towards them, they avenge themselves by ambushing and killing him, imagining that the courts of heaven are as blind as ours (2:13–20). But they have forgotten that humans were created by God for perfection and immortality, according to his image, the loss of which this author is the first to impute to the envy of the devil (2:24). Again, the wicked are unaware that "the souls of the righteous are in the hand of God" (3:1), who preserves them from death and sets them in judgment against their adversaries. The kings of the world, who thought themselves judges, will find that they are the judged, and will be scattered like chaff in the wind while their accusers live for ever (6:1–6).

---

45. *Antiquities* 18.1.3 and 5. J. Bremmer, *The Rise and Fall of the Afterlife*, 44–46, suggests that we take Josephus at his word.

46. Acts 23:6. Cf. Mark 12:18, where the Sadducees are distinguished by their denial of resurrection, and the belief in resurrection professed by Martha at John 11:24.

47. On the Book of Wisdom as a response to calumny and persecution in the first century AD, see Cheon, *The Exodus Story*, 125–49.

It will be observed that, just as there is no resurrection in Maccabees for the persecutor of Israel, so the end of the wicked in Wisdom is neither hell nor reincarnation, but evanescence into nothing, in accordance with his own prophecy and desire (2:3; 5:13–14).

Although there is no explicit mention of Israel in these early chapters, and Solomon's recollection of his helplessness as an infant could have been put in the mouth of any other mortal (7:3–6), the author's personification of Wisdom as the daughter of God is clearly modelled on her encomium of herself in the Book of Proverbs (8:22–30). She is not a second deity,[48] and in chapter 13 the author roundly castigates the folly of the Greeks, who not only overlooked the marvelous unity of the cosmos when they postulated a multitude of deities, but failed to perceive that the power that regulates the visible elements must be greater than any of them and hence invisible (13:2–4). Thus, while it is the devil who prompts us to sin, the firstfruits of his prompting are polytheism and idolatry, as Paul was to urge in chapter 1 of his letter to the Romans (1:18–23). Wisdom is the executor of God's wrath against the nations who beset Israel as the wicked beset the righteous, and the plagues that she sent upon Egypt are recited with jubilation (18:4–6). At the same time she is also the preserver of mortals from the just wrath of God. Thus, when he drowns the world in the flood (in vengeance, as it appears, for Cain's murder of Abel), she is the one who rescues Noah by means of a wooden wall (10:3–4), as she also causes Lot to quit Sodom before the conflagration (10:6–7). It would be absurd to surmise that she is working against her father, as Ea or Enki in Mesopotamian myth works against his fellow-gods by rescuing one human from the deluge;[49] in the book of Wisdom, as in that of Genesis, the same God wills the destruction of the many and the salvation of a few. It may nonetheless be in this book that we can trace the opposition in Gnostic texts between the penitent Sophia and the incorrigible Creator of all things seen.

Philo of Alexandria

The doctrine of transmigration, though later associated with the Kabbalah, appears to have been unknown to Jews of the Early Roman era whose first language was not Greek. It may indeed be a logical implication of the question put to Jesus by his disciples, "Who sinned, this man or his parents, that he was born blind?" (John 9:2). The inference, however, was not drawn

---

48. On the possibility that Wisdom in this text is a prototype of the Valentinian Sophia, see Edwards, "Pauline Platonism," 214.

49. *Epic of Gilgamesh*, Tablet XI, translated by George, *The Epic of Gilgamesh*, 89.

in antiquity, and even the Jewish writer of this epoch who owes most to Greek sources, Philo of Alexandria,[50] does not speak of the descent and re-embodiment of souls in more than a handful of passages. Of these the most expansive is *On the Cherubim* 113, where Philo surmises, as in his treatise *On the Making of the World*, that Adam stands for reason and Eve for the carnal desires to which reason surrenders (53.151). It is not implied that souls fall from an incorporeal heaven or that incarnation is in itself an evil.[51] Nor does the fall of one historical character named Adam impair the capacity of those who come after him to resist temptation. On the contrary, it lies in the power of every soul to choose between surrender to its base companion, in which case the sequel to death will be a new embodiment, or else to raise its gaze to the immaterial world of which God himself is the *topos* or place and to raise itself to his presence by renouncing the allurements of honor, pleasure, and all that vulgar minds imagine to be good. Philo does not conceal his acquaintance with the Stoics, the Pythagoreans, and other Greeks who have followed this path of abnegation; at the same time, he regards the profane or encyclopaedic disciplines as mere ancillaries to the higher science of seeking God through the scriptures of Israel (*On Mating with Preliminary Sciences* 3.10, etc.), and in his work *On Rewards and Punishments*, the three patriarchs of Genesis are held up as exemplars of virtues that the Stoics could not even name.

In *On Rewards and Punishments* laws are divided into three classes. The first are those that annex rewards and honors to acts that are deemed to be just and penalties to those that are deemed unjust, the rule of justice being the common good (*On Rewards and Punishments* 2.7). These the Jews have in common with the Greeks, whereas the laws of the second class, prescribing acts to be performed in penance for sin, bespeak a consciousness of God as Lawgiver and of our filial duty to obey him (3.15). The laws of the third class set before us the actions that conduce to the vision of God (4.22).[52] These too, although the image and likeness are present in all human beings, have been vouchsafed to one nation alone through the words of Moses. A rough correspondence holds between the three kinds of legislation in this treatise and the three patriarchs in the treatise on Abraham, where Abraham is the type of the soul that receives a moral education, while

50. Classified as a Middle Platonist in Dillon, *The Middle Platonists*. His affinities with rabbinic thought are demonstrated by Wolfson, *Philo*, who also notes that he is often the first, if not the sole, proponent of doctrines that he is supposed to have imbibed from the Middle Platonists. On his desire to "make Greek culture Jewish," and thus resist the "Hellenization of scripture," see Dawson, *Allegorical Readers*, 74.

51. This is regarded as a late work by de Luca, "Providence and Cosmology."

52. For Jacob as the image of God, see *On Flight* 13.67.

Isaac his son represents the soul whose virtue is spontaneous, and his son Jacob stands for the soul that has advanced in virtue by its own exertions (*On Abraham* 11.52).[53] The gentiles, being ignorant of the true source of morality, do not possess either the faith of Abraham, which is the foundation of obedience, or the joy that is connoted by the very name of Isaac (*On Rewards* 5.31). They know something of the resolute separation of the soul from its carnal envelope, which is allegorically signified by the flight of Jacob (19.117),[54] but the symbolical understanding of the law must be combined with perfection in the outward practice of it before the soul can be worthy of the name Israel ("the man who has seen God"), which Jacob received after wrestling with the angel (7.43). Philo does not seem to doubt that the promised rewards of keeping the law, protection from enemies and prosperity in worldly enterprises, will be fulfilled in their literal sense; on the other hand, since observance means for him nothing less than total detachment from the corporeal appetites, if not from the body itself, there are not many even in Israel who have put this divine assurance to the test.

Philo also appears to hold, with the Stoics, that if one does reach the acme of virtue, no external goods will be necessary to happiness. This is the burden of two treatises whose titles have a classical ring, *That Every Good Man Is Free* and *On the Contemplative Life*. The first describes the regimen of the Essenes, a Jewish sect extolled by Joseph's and admired by such Greeks as Porphyry and Pliny, who may have mistaken their enmity to the temple in Jerusalem as a sign of indifference to outward forms and rites. The second portrays an otherwise unknown and perhaps fictitious society of male and female celibates, whose daily routine of study, prayer, and abstinence is designed to awaken the faculty of seeing—or, more properly, of entering into ineffable communion with—the God who is so far above all sensation and perception that even the intellect grasps only a rumor of him (*On the Contemplative Life* 11–12 and 68). Philo's conception of God in *On Rewards and Punishments* may not be quite so sublime, but it unambiguously precludes all responsibility for evils, even as accidental corollaries of a general law. He grants that the existence of noxious animals might be thought to betray the imperfection of providence; but he answers with the prophets (and, as it seems, without allegory) that a day will come when predators lose their natural ferocity and all animals are at peace.[55] In any case, their

---

53. Cf. *On Rewards and Punishments* 4.27; *On Change of Names* 2.12; *On Rewards and Punishments* 4.27 on Abraham and 5.31 on Isaac.

54. Cf. *On Flight and Finding* 7.43.

55. *On Rewards and Punishments* 15.89. Cf. Isaiah 11:6.

ferocity is nothing to that of humans, whose sins are the consequence not of some inescapable proclivity but of their own free will.

Nowhere in the works of Philo are humans said to be endowed at birth with their vices and virtues. Even in the treatise *On the Giants*, where the earthborn giants represent the carnally minded multitude and the angels stand for those who belong to heaven (13.60), we are not given to understand that any of us is by nature an angel or a giant. In *On Rewards and Punishments* the ills of human society are declared to be intractable even when they are ruled with justice, but that is because there can never be a law, however salutary, that brings benefits to all and loss to none. Injustice, which is more endemic than justice, is the result of the conquest of reason by the appetites, and we have seen above that Philo regards the seduction of Adam by Eve as a parable of this quotidian fall (*On the Making of the World* 53.151). The biblical story illustrates our weakness but does not reveal the cause of it: the first sin in recorded history is that of Cain, who may thus be said to have corrupted the entire race by his example. This notion of Cain as the archetypal sinner is carried over to the New Testament, where he is represented as a chattel of Satan, who conversely is declared to have been a murderer from the beginning (1 John 3:12). As we noted, little was made of Adam in Jewish thought on the causes of evil; for those who were not Jews or who, being Jews, were also philosophers, the sin of Cain was more intelligible than that of Adam, since the former was a violation of natural law and the latter a breach of an unexplained command.

Philo on Providence[56]

Philo, disciple of Moses though he was, appears to have defended the eternity of the world in an experimental treatise.[57] On the other hand, Eusebius preserves a fragment of a lost disquisition *On Providence* in which Philo appears to make God the creator of matter, affirming that God took care to ensure that neither more nor less of this substrate existed—if indeed it existed at all—than was required for the perfection of the cosmos.[58] In a second

56. I have confined myself here to the Greek remains of this treatise; on the Armenian fragments, which it lies outside my competence to discuss, see Runia, "From Stoicism to Platonism." Runia's title will be easily intelligible to anyone who compares Philo's treatise on providence with Plutarch's *On the Delays in Divine Punishment*, which is discussed below in chapter 6.

57. See Runia, "Philo's *De Aeternitate Mundi*."

58. Eusebius, *Preparation for the Gospel* 7.21.2–4. Matter is here considered as an *ousia*, and the suggestion that it may not exist is one of a number of Jewish and Christian anticipations of Bishop Berkeley that have bene overlooked in such discussions as

fragment he seems to adopt the pose of a Greek philosopher confronted by the venerable argument that no benevolent guardian of the world would permit the righteous to live in poverty and disgrace while the wicked profit by their misdeeds (*Preparation for the Gospel* 8.14.1). His first reply, which shows some originality, is that if God is a father (as both Greeks and Jews suppose) he will cherish his erring children more than the righteous, since the parent is the one who must go on being a friend and protector when all good will has been lost in other quarters (8.14.3–5). He next invokes the platitude that a true philosopher cannot envy the wicked because he knows that the sole and sufficient grounds of happiness lie within us (8.14.7–10). Lamenting that the philosophers of his day exhibit none of that zeal in the therapy of souls that doctors exhibit in their courtship of wealthy patients, he holds up the tyrant as the stock example of the man who is rich in all and happy in nothing (8.14.12–23). Did not Polycrates of Samos confess that, having seemed to tread the air, he had now discovered that he was burnt by the sun and washed by the rain like any other mortal (8.14.24–25)? Did not Dionysius of Syracuse, a man who lived in terror of his own wife, declare that to be a tyrant is to live at all times under a dangling sword(8.14.26–30)? Conscious perhaps, that neither his native scriptures nor the world at large was content to entrust the work of providence wholly to inward monitors, he relates the story of three men who committed a sacrilege for which three penalties were prescribed by law. That each then died by the natural equivalent of one of these modes—the first by a fall from a cliff, the second by drowning, the third by a fever that raged like fire—could not, he insists, be the work of chance (814.33–34). He seems not to foresee the retort that if there were more such tales there would be no need of an essay to explain why providence does not punish sin.

From this point—or perhaps we ought to say, from the beginning of the next excerpt by Eusebius—the treatise assumes that every great transgressor will be subject to retribution, which is all the more certain if it befalls them in God's time and by God's will rather than ours. While they live, he continues in a vein that reminds us of his ancestral prophets, he may employ a tyrant for the chastisement of a city or a nation, abandoning him to death when his work is done, as fire expires when its substrate is consumed (*Preparation for the Gospel* 8.14.39–40). God is not always bound to use intermediaries, and may choose to destroy an entire population by famine, plague, or natural disaster (8.14.41). This too is the teaching of the prophets, but the argument that ensues is not so consonant with the general belief of Jews in the age

---

Sorabji, *Time, Creation and the Continuum*, 287–94. See Origen, *First Principles* 4.4.7 with Edwards, "Christians against Matter."

of Philo. Rather than ascribe every death from natural phenomena to the will of God, he maintains that hail and lightning may be unavoidable consequences of the rains that are sent to purify the air or the winds that fertilise the crops (8.14.43). Taking from Greek philosophy the image of the gymnasium, which Jews of a stricter persuasion would have avoided, Philo observes that no one pupil will always enjoy the attention of the trainer or occupy the firm ground in the center rather than the adjacent mud (8.14.44–46). Just as the needs of the one must yield to those of the many in a well-governed city or a well-directed army, so even the Ruler of the physical cosmos cannot ensure that the good of all is invariably the good of each.

Animals furnish numerous examples of the rule that the goodness or badness of a creature depends on its use (*Preparation for the Gospel* 8.14.60). Physicians have discovered medicinal properties in venom, while God makes use of noxious beasts to punish those who have been condemned by the law of nature (8.14.61). We should not forget that most noxious animals, if they are left alone, will shun the society of humans, just as birds, if they are not hunted, will become tame (8.14.62–63). The honor paid by Egyptians to the crocodile no longer seems incongruous when we observe that in places where it receives most honor it permits the inhabitants to swim unharmed (8.14.65). There follows an encomium of Greece as a nursery of rational beings because the people do not enjoy the natural luxuries that tempt barbarians to value the body more than the intellect (8.14.66–68). The causes of illness never reside in the nature of the food but in the intemperance of our diet (8.14.69–70), and there are many plants that are useless alone but salutary in combination, just as neither man nor woman alone can procreate without sexual congress (8.14.71). The Eusebian extract ends with this pronouncement, perhaps the only one that might have occurred with equal readiness to a Jew who could not read Greek.[59]

Conclusion

Is there, then, such a thing as a biblical or a Jewish theodicy? No doubt, if it is enough to say with Job that we have received good from the Lord, and shall we not receive evil?, proverbial wisdom also taught that thrift and fear of the Lord will always prosper, while one fortunate psalmist had never seen the righteous forsaken or their children begging for bread. Yet only in later accounts of Israel's history, composed at a time when the influence

---

59. Without impugning the authenticity of *On Providence*, Sterling, "'The Most Perfect Work'" notes the difficulty of reconciling its doctrine of creation with that of other works by Philo.

of Greek thought cannot be excluded, is every misfortune that befalls her kings shown to be commensurate with their deserts. Nor is there any conceivable revision of this history that consistently allots a happier reign to the righteous monarch than to the wicked. At some date wisdom literature became wise enough not to pretend that God keeps a tariff of debts and credits with his subjects, but it offers no theoretical justification of his indifference: the problem of evil is the problem of bearing it, and the solution is to love God and fear his commandments, resigning ourselves to his will in the hope (if Daniel and Job can be trusted) of recompense at a time known only to him. The one text that undertakes to prove in detail that apparent evils are goods, or at least are always offset by equivalent goods, is written in Greek, makes use of Greek examples, and is not even a characteristic work of the Greek-speaking philosopher to whom it is ascribed.

The Roman sack of Jerusalem was followed in 135 by the Emperor Hadrian's expulsion of the Jews from their homeland. After this date Greek ceased to be a language of instruction or speculation for the Jews of the Roman Empire. By this time, however, it had become both the everyday language and the language of scripture for the main body of Christians, who were no longer a Jewish sect but had subverted the prevailing definitions of good and evil by teaching that all are born in sin, that death and pain are at once the wages of sin and the means of curing it, and that the kingdom foreseen by Daniel is reserved for penitent sinners (not for those who deplore the suffering of the righteous but confine this term to persons like themselves).

4

Dualism and the Beginnings of Christianity

EPICTETUS THE STOIC, WITH whom I ended chapter 2 of this book, is the earliest pagan writer to allude, under the name of Galileans, to the sect of fools and fanatics who will occupy the present chapter and most of those that follow. As many scholars have pointed out, the first Christians were not only contemporaries of the most celebrated Stoics, but neighbors in thought and sensibility. The notes on the previous chapter have drawn parallels between sayings of Epictetus and the injunctions of the New Testament to give up one's coat to a robber and to be content with the calling to which one is called. There is, however, a deeper likeness in literary style and in self-perception between Epictetus and Paul of Tarsus, whom an early Latin Christian imagined to be not only (as Luke informs us) an acquaintance of Seneca's brother but a correspondent of Seneca himself.[1] The correspondence is evidently forged because it makes Seneca write Latin no better than Paul's, which has all the ineptitude of his Greek; in the genuine writings of Epictetus, by contrast, we see a more elevated version of Paul's elliptical manner with its demotic use of questions and interjections—"What then?,"[2] "God forbid!"[3]—and the same concomitant inversion of Roman values.[4] Epictetus was a domestic slave

1. Acts 18:12; Ramelli, "Pseudepigraphical Correspondence."

2. Romans 6:15 and 11:7; Epictetus, *Discourses* 1.10.7; 2.24.12, etc.

3. Romans 3:4–6 and 7:12, etc.; Epictetus, *Discourses* 1,10.7, etc.

4. On the shift from "I" to "we" by the rededication of the self either to God (in Paul) or to reason (as in the Stoics), see Engberg-Pedersen, *Paul and the Stoics*, 33–35.

who accepted his condition, Paul a free man who willingly became a slave to Christ. Paul contrasts spirit with flesh[5] and employs the metaphors of the vessel, the foot, and the city;[6] for him, as for Epictetus, nature informs the conscience of the tutored and the untutored alike, and never more clearly than in the demarcation of male and female, by length of hair and by the rules governing sexual behavior.[7] Each proclaims and practices extreme austerity, one of them styling his outward frame a corpse and the other a body of death,[8] and both maintain that the real slaves are not the afflicted and despised but those who are considered great in the eyes of the world. Each nonetheless makes a policy of tempering his demands to the capacity of his interlocutor, each being proudly aware that he is commonly thought to be mad.[9] Each, since he holds adversity to be no evil in itself but rather a trial of our capacity to suffer without doing evil, refrains from suicide only because he believes that he holds his life as a trust from God.

But as we shall see (and as the wisest critics are quick to warn us), Stoics and Christians do not build on the same foundation. Both are theists and champions of divine providence, but providence for the Stoics assists the righteous only by signs and admonitions, whereas the God of the church has been a worker of miracles since he formed all things from nothing. Both regard the body as a burden that may be lightly shed, but whereas the Stoics assume that it was created as it is for the probation of virtue, Christians contrast its present corruption, for which we must hold ourselves accountable, with its purity at the beginning, when God fashioned it as the vehicle of immortality. Both the Stoic sage and the Abraham of their Jewish admirer Philo are *kosmopolitai*, or citizen of the world.[10] Christians were taught that God chose a single people, Israel, as trustees of his law and confidants of his purpose until such time as his gospel of love could be preached without distinction to Jew and Greek. The condition of peace is deliverance from the prison of sin and incorporation into the body of Christ as we await the incorruptible body of the resurrection. And the necessary prelude to resurrection is a miracle that transcends and completes all miracles, subsuming all the prophecies of the Old Testament and inverting the act of creation by clothing God in the detritus of his world.

5. Galatians 5:17; Romans 7:14; *Discourses* 2.8.2 and 3.7.3.

6. Romans 9:22 and *Discourses* 2.4.6; 1 Corinthians 12:21 and *Discourses* 2.5.24; Philippians 3:20 and *Discourses* 2.8.27–28.

7. Romans 1:26; 1 Corinthians 11:13; *Discourses* 1.5.9–10, 1.16.9–12; 3.1.28–29.

8. Romans 7:24; *Discourses* 2.19.27.

9. 2 Corinthians 5:13; *Discourses* 1.22.17.

10. Philo, *On the Making of the World* 1; Diogenes Laertius 6.63.

The Christian Inversion of Values

As we have seen, the Old Testament does not offer a theodicy for the world because the question "Why do sinners prosper and the righteous perish?" is seldom asked without some personal sense of unrequited worth. The psalmist seeks his own vindication, the tribulations of God's servant Job mirror those of Israel, the prophets are mortified when they have falsely predicted the ruin of some other nation,[11] and the Preacher is content to be at peace with the Creator without demanding that the swift or the strong should always reap their laurels (Ecclesiastes 9:11). God, who has mercy on whom he will have mercy (Exodus 33:19), hardens the heart of Israel's oppressors in order that he may punish them (9:12), alternately chastising and forgiving his people even as he prompts their kings to do evil. Although the law is given as a way of life, with assurances that the righteous will never be forsaken, those who witness the breaking of these promises can say only "we have received good from the Lord; shall we not receive evil?" (Job 2:10). When we turn to the New Testament, it seems at times that its Jewish authors have imbibed the mentality of the Greeks whose language they have borrowed. Jesus has to correct those who imagine that every death is a visitation by adducing the fall of a tower on eighteen victims and an indiscriminate massacre of Samaritans (Luke 13:1–5), much as the Skeptics asked whether everyone who fell at Cannae could have been born under the same star. When his disciples surmise that even congenital sickness must be a token of sin, they seem willing to countenance the notion of a pre-existent soul, since it would otherwise be absurd to suggest that the victim was as likely as his parents to be responsible for his own blindness (John 9:2–3). Once again, however, Jesus warns them not to imagine any such calculus of demerits, and the evangelists advance no general theory regarding the origin of sin.

Yet sin is rife, not only in the tax-collector Zacchaeus, whom he induces to repent (Luke 19:10), and in the adulteress whom he exhorts to sin no more (John 8:11), but also, and indeed especially, in those whose business it is to keep others from sinning. Jesus reserves his harshest censure for those who make a show of themselves in religion by encumbering the common folk with precept upon precept, and those who make themselves rich in the goods of this world while the beggar starves at the gate (Luke 16:20–21) and the prisoner chokes for want of water (Matthew 25:34–35; cf. 10:42). He does nothing to subvert the political order—Herod Antipas may be a fox (Luke 13:32) but Pontius Pilate receives the power to crucify

---

11. Jeremiah 1:7; Jonah 4:2–3; cf. Ezekiel 29:18.

him from above (19:11)—and he does not intimate that either keeping the law or owning property are evil in themselves. Nor, though the price of following him is to hate one's father and mother (14:26), does he make light of the commandment that requires us to honor our parents (Matthew 15:3–6). There is no simple tariff of sins and rewards: the Pharisee may be pardoned along with the son who wastes his patrimony (Luke 18:14; 15:20), so long as neither is guilty of the mysterious sin against the Holy Spirit.[12] The greater delinquent suffers the greater penalty (Luke 12:47), yet the Lord feels no duty either to allot the same means to everyone or to reward us according to our hours of labor (Matthew 20:1–16). There is more joy in heaven over the penitent sinner than over ninety-nine who are righteous (Luke 15:7), and in the world to come the blessed will be those who are now hungry, poor, and meek (Matthew 5:13; Luke 6:20–21). Are they blessed because they suffer these privation, as the pure in heart and those who hunger for righteousness are blessed because they exhibit these dispositions? Or are they merely beneficiaries of the divine Saturnalia, like the lost sheep of the house of Israel (Matthew 10:6; 15:24)?[13] Gentiles will be admitted to the kingdom at the expense of some who thought themselves chosen, but is this because the whole world is reconciled—"if I am lifted up, I shall draw all people to me" (John 12:32)—or because there are a few among so many sinners whose faith goes proxy for obedience to the law?[14]

We are at least assured that sin can be pardoned on condition of repentance, and where possible of reparation, in the present life.[15] There are certain verses in all the Gospels, however, that intimate that sin is not merely a habit to be broken but a state from which we must be rescued, and that the means of this rescue is a sin that hitherto not even the most depraved could imagine—the murder of the Son of God. This is at once a predestined good for humanity—"the Son of Man goes as is written of him"—and an act of the basest perfidy—"woe to him by whom the Son of Man is betrayed" (Mark 14:21). Judas confesses his guilt by hanging himself (Matthew 27:5), yet it was Satan who caused him to sin (Luke 22:3; John 13:8) and Jesus himself who emboldened him with words—"What you are doing, do quickly" (John 13:27). The priest who laid the snare was unwittingly acting as God's

12. For a review of theories and reconstructions of the supposed original form of the saying, see Boring, "The Unforgivable Sin Logion."

13. On the fulfillment of Isaiah 61 and other promises of the Old Testament in the beatitudes, see Beasley-Murray, *Jesus and the Kingdom*, 157–68.

14. See further Romans 2:15.

15. Mark 1:15; Matthew 4:17; Luke 15:7, etc. Nevertheless, Sanders, *Jesus and Judaism*, 204–5, endorses the view that Jesus did not make repentance a condition of entering the kingdom.

mouthpiece when he deemed it "fitting that one man should die for the people" (John 11:50)—which is no more than Jesus himself said when he professed to be giving his life as a ransom for many (Mark 10:45), or when he said in the Upper Room that the bread and wine represented the breaking of his body and the new covenant in his blood (Luke 22:20). If he does not save everyone, the reason in one place is that he has estranged them by his own preaching—"had I not preached to them, they would have no sin" (John 15:22)—and in another that they are children of the devil, who was a liar from the beginning (8:44). Since Judas too is a devil (6:70), and temptation by the devil would appear to have prepared Jesus for his ministry (Matthew 4; Luke 4), we are left to wonder whether there is any work of Satan's that is not also a work of God. And from this we are led to wonder whether there is any deed of ours that is not predestined, and how, if there is none, we are held accountable for doing right or wrong.

Paul against Adam

The doctrines of original sin and predestination are commonly traced to Paul, a Jew of Tarsus in Cilicia, whose training as a Pharisee had taught him to perceive sin in the smallest infractions of the Mosaic law. He will also have learned, as the general opinion of the Jewish teachers of his day, that Israel's covenant with God is indissoluble, and that no one who belongs to this community by birth will be excluded from it, in this world or the next, on account of occasional transgressions. The contradiction between this view and the curse on those who break the law at Deuteronomy 27:26[16] may not have troubled him so long as he had no consciousness of his own sin (Philippians 3:6). In the wake of his encounter with the unseen "Lord" on the road to Damascus, however, he came to believe that sin consisted not so much in discrete acts of transgression as in clinging to the life of the flesh in ignorance of the new life that has been opened to us by the death and resurrection of Jesus Christ. And since this Christ had died under the curse of the law (Galatians 3:13), being "made sin for us," although he was the one human being since Adam who had no acquaintance with sin (2 Corinthians 5:21), it became clear to Paul that the law of Moses was not only an insufficient means of salvation, but even an impediment to salvation if it were permitted to occlude the true source of deliverance, which is the covenant made 430 years before Moses with Abraham, the father of all the elect (Galatians 4:17). This covenant was a reward for the *faith* of Abraham, not for his works (Genesis 15:6; Romans 3:2), and the object of his faith was the

16. Cf James 2:10 and also Matthew 5:19.

promise of the birth of a son from his superannuated loins (Romans 4:19). Today, says Paul, it has become possible for Jew and gentile alike to recapture this faith by trusting that Jesus Christ has risen from the dead, and that through the ceremony of baptism we *all* may share both his death to sin and his rising to life (Galatians 3:27; Colossians 2:10–12; Romans 6:1–6). Those who have yet to discern that Christ is the end of the law, inasmuch as he is at once it fulfillment and its abolition (Roman 10:4), have not understood that the law was given to multiply transgression (5:20), and that a gentile may be less subject to divine judgment than a Jew (2:15) because "without law no sin is reckoned" (5:13). The dichotomy between righteous Jews and sinners of the gentiles (Galatians 2:15) is therefore obsolete; this is not to say, however, that the gentiles are not sinners, but that the term "sin" must be understood in a sense that comprehends *all* human beings—or to use a more biblical phrase, all descendants of Adam—whatever instruction they may have received by way of positive law.

The history of humanity's estrangement from God and reconciliation is condensed by the apostle into a terse antithesis: "As in Adam all died, so in Christ shall all be made alive" (1 Corinthians 15:22). The doctrine that Adam's trespass was the cause of both his own and our mortality is, of course, biblical; the notion that the curse can be lifted is new, and all the more so when the means is said at Romans 4:25 to be faith in the resurrection of Christ, mirroring Abraham's faith that a son will issue from his dead loins. Since Christ on the cross is said to have become sin for us, since baptism is our dying to sin by immersion in his death, since Paul can say that had Christ not been resurrected we should still be in our sins, it is clear that for him the association of sin with death is inextricable. If all have sinned and fallen short of the glory of God (Romans 3:23), it follows that all receive death as the wages of sin (6:23): does it also follow that, since it was Adam who sentenced all humanity to death, it was also Adam who sired our universal tendency to sin? Paul has often been understood to say so in a lingering sentence riddled with parentheses, which declares that "sin came into the world through one man, and through sin death" (5:12). This may mean no more than that Adam was the first to sin and hence to incur death as a penalty: yet in the succeeding clause—"so that death has come upon all, ἐφ' ᾧ all have sinned"—an association is made between Adam's death, which is the consequence of his sin, and the death that all other humans suffer as a consequence of their own sins. Are we to infer that his sin is the cause of our sin? The syntactic construction linking sin with death—ἐφ' ᾧ—is difficult to construe, but scholarly conjectures include "on the basis of which," "in which circumstances," "through which,"[17] "because of which,"[18] and "with the result that."[19] Yet these explain neither why sin is universal nor why the universality of sin is also said to be a consequence of the sin and death of Adam. It might be better construed as "on which condition all have sinned," that is, that from Adam we inherit the law that sin entails death so that neither Jews nor gentiles have any right to expect a more merciful outcome of their sins than the one ordained from the beginning.

It may be that mortality provides the conditions, if not the cause, of sin, for Paul speaks of our present state as one of *phthora* or corruption (1 Corinthians 15:50); he seems barely to distinguish moral from physical dissolution. Thus the man in whom the law itself has awoken sin exclaims at Romans 7:24 "who will deliver me from this body of death?" It is often alleged that the speaker in Romans 7, who complains that he finds a law in his members intractably opposed to the law of God and compelling him to sin against his will, cannot be Paul himself, who even before he turned to Christ had been perfect according to the Mosaic law (Philippians 3:6). It is argued, therefore, that Paul has adopted the voice of a gentile, perhaps a neophyte in Christianity, who has taken the yoke of the law upon himself, to his own undoing.[20] This argument gains some force from Paul's pronouncements in the same letter that where there is no law sin is not imputed (Romans 5:13), and that gentiles may be deemed innocent if, without knowing the law of Moses, they are a law unto themselves (Romans 2:14–15). Nevertheless, it is difficult for those who hold this position to explain (a) why Paul gives no sign of his shift to another voice or the identity of the new speaker, (b) why he should be sure that a gentile could not obey the law in which he was perfect, and (c) why the speaker should throw himself gratefully on the mercy of Christ at Romans 7:25, but then confess that while in his mind he observes the law of Christ, in his flesh he observes the law of sin.

The gentiles sinned when, ignoring the visible evidence of the invisible Creator, they represented gods under the likeness of beasts, whereupon he abandoned them to customs that were not only illicit but contrary to nature (Romans 1:18–32). The Jews who defied their own law were all concluded under sin, though only in order that God might have mercy on all (Romans 11:32). The Christian is dispensed from the Mosaic law to live by that of the Spirit, of which the one article is love (13:10). Where Jesus declare that the

17. For these three, see Käsemann, *Commentary on Romans*, 148.

18. Ziesler, *Paul's Letter to the Romans*, 146–47.

19. Fitzmeyer, "The Consecutive Meaning."

20. See Timmins, *Romans 7 and Christian Identity*. Dryden, "Revisiting Romans 7," argues that Paul's "I" includes himself, his purpose being "to connect the Law to the eschatological life-giving work of the Spirit."

entire law of Moses rests on the two commandments to love the Lord with a one's heart and to love one's neighbor as oneself,[21] Paul reduces it to the second of these injunctions at Galatians 5:14. If this is the law that the speaker in Romans 7 cannot fulfil because he cannot renounce the desires of the flesh, he can stand for every gentile, for every Jew, and even for Paul, the unblemished Pharisee. At the same time, because he is walking in the Spirit of Jesus Christ, he can dissociate his true self from the "body of death," from the law in his members, which is no longer "I, but sin in me" (Romans 7:17).

Although faith works by love (Galatians 5:6), the life of faith in the present world is one of continuing warfare between the flesh and the Spirit (5:17), even if there is now no condemnation for the believer (Romans 8:1) and we have the assurance that our mortal bodies will be quickened by the same God who raised Christ Jesus from the dead (8:11). All Christians of Paul's time were schooled to accept affliction in this world as a foretaste of beatitude in the next. "Blessed are you when all persecute you and revile you," says the Master at Matthew 5:11, and the disciple echoes, "Count it pure joy, my brothers, when you meet tribulation" (James 1:2). The Christian, like the Stoic, could bless ill fortune, and sometimes for the same reasons. Paul of Tarsus, rejoicing in his three shipwrecks, his five beatings, and his alienation from all that was held in honor by his brethren after the flesh (2 Corinthians 11:24–26), was not only content to remain unmarried (1 Corinthians 9:5) but urged his correspondents to do the same, on the grounds that those with a mind to serve the Lord should not be burdened by the obligation of ministry to a partner (7:8–9 and 32–38). But neither this argument nor his supplementary advice that those with wives should live as though they have none (7:29) are prompted only by contempt for the present world and its distractions: he also believes that the reign of God on earth will commence before his own death, with an instantaneous transfiguration of that which he calls elsewhere his body of death (1 Corinthians 15:51–52; 1 Thessalonians 4:13–16). Yet both his disgust and his hope are grounded not in a Stoic indifference or Platonic animosity to embodiment but, on the contrary, in his conviction that the body is, in origin and destiny, more glorious than it appears. Behind this lies a doctrine of creation and corruption that has no precedent in Jewish thought and supplies what the Gospels lack—an explanation of the origin of sin and the necessity of Christ's death as its antidote.

21. Matthew 22:37–39, citing Deuteronomy 6:5 and Leviticus 19:18. Cf. Mark 12:30–31 and Luke 10:27.

The Dualism of Paul

To be in the flesh is to have no share in the Spirit, to be as Paul or his imitator declares a "child of wrath."[22] At the same time there is a danger that those who attempt to rise above the human standard of virtue, exclaiming "let us do evil that good may come" (Romans 3:8), and will commit misdeeds that are not even spoken of among the gentiles (1 Corinthians 5:10). When Paul enjoins that such offenders be handed over to Satan (5:5), he implies that the world outside the church lies under the jurisdiction of God's enemy (cf. 1 Timothy 1:20). Not all his vassals are pagans, for Paul can say of the Jews who do not believe that their eyes have been blinded by the God of this world (2 Corinthians 4:40). Some may protest that this is not Satan but, as it were, the Creator with his left hand, for in Romans 9 Paul seems to aver not only that the elect are foreknown and foreordained, but that (as the Old Testament teaches) the Lord makes even the wicked for the day of evil (Proverbs 6:4). He loved Jacob and hated Esau before either showed proof of merit or demerit (Romans 9:13; cf. Malachi 1:2); he has made one vessel fir honor and one for dishonor (Romans 9:22; cf. Jeremiah 18:6 and 19:10–11); he has mercy on whom he will have mercy, and none can tell him how to treat his own (Romans 9:13; Exodus 33:19). The majority of ancient commentators construed these verses to mean that God elects to have mercy on those whose acceptance of this mercy he foresees; and this reading is consistent with the many texts in letters ascribed to Paul that attest the desire of God that all should be saved, his determination to reward us for our works, and our own capacity to avoid those sins that exclude us from the kingdom. All this being said, a reader of Paul who concluded that the body that we now have is irredeemable, that the destiny of the soul is already fixed when it enters the world, and that its usual place is not in the hands of God but in those of Satan could not be accused of perverting the obvious meaning of the text.[23]

There are modern theologians who assure us that the New Testament knows nothing of dualism, and that otherworldliness and supernaturalism are ancient heresies born of a strange liaison between Platonic intellectualism and pre-scientific credulity.[24] At its worst this is a facile attempt to purge the gospel of elements that offend our reason because they take away our present comforts; at its best it is an acknowledgment that the two worlds of early Christian thought are not time and eternity but the transitory present

22. Ephesians 2:3. Cf. 1 Thessalonians 1:10; Matthew 3:7; John 3:36; Romans 3:5.

23. Engberg-Pedersen, "Stoic Freedom," compares Pauline freedom to serve God in the Spirit with Stoic freedom to live in accordance with nature.

24. See, e.g., Robinson, *In the End, God. . . .*

and he everlasting future. When Paul writes that the things that are seen are transient whereas things unseen are eternal (2 Corinthians 4:18), he is speaking not of incorporeal forms but of a time not far off when the transfigured bodies of those who are still on earth and the spiritual bodies of those who must rise from the grave will be conformed to the glorious body of Christ (Philippians 3:21). So too when we read at Hebrews 11:1 that faith is "the evidence of things not seen," we should take this to mean "of things not *yet* seen," though the author also intimates that sacred things on earth are copies of their archetypes in the mind of God (Hebrews 8:5; cf. Exodus 25:40). When Jesus in the fourth Gospel declares, "I have overcome the world" (John 16:33), his enemy is not the entire creation, for the Creator loved this world so much that he gave his only Son for its salvation (3:16). "World" here signifies rather those who idolise that which was given for a season—the Herodian temple,[25] the Jewish remnant of Israel, the letter of the law. Paul, when he accused the Galatians of returning to the weak and beggarly elements (*stoikheia*), subtly conflates the stuff of which idols are made with the Hebrew characters that the Jews spell out in vain. While he himself has no vivid conception of the wrath that will fall upon unbelievers, the Book of Revelation divides humanity into the few who will reunite the twelve tribes in the everlasting city (7:5–8) and the multitude who will drown for ever in the burning lake (20:14). Thus, while the New Testament does not maintain that creation is evil or that the incorporeal is superior to the corporeal, it does teach that the present world is doomed and that those who follow its ways will lose the prospect of eternal life.

Who Were the Gnostics?

We must bear in mind this world-denying strain in the primitive literature of the church if we are to understand why so many Christians of the second century maintained, in their speculations on the genesis of evil and the conditions of redemption, that the fault lay in the creation itself, not in our perception of it nor in some local aberration. The tradition that we now regard as catholic enjoins celibacy on its clergy and commends degrees of abstinence in the laity, but denounces as heresy any ascetic movement that denies the goodness of the material object, be it wine, meat, or sexual congress, that it has chosen to eschew. It has set its own norms of unworldliness, only to be upbraided throughout its history by its own children, both for setting these norms and for not having set them with more rigor.[26] And

25. Compare Jeremiah 7:4 and John 2:19.
26. See further, Brown, *The Body and Society*.

notwithstanding our disposition to celebrate the body and all that it loves, it is liberal theologians of the modern age who protest that the corpse of flesh and blood that decays in the grave cannot be the spiritual body whose resurrection is promised by the apostle.[27] All these tenets, wittingly or unwittingly, echo those of early Christian groups who are apt to fall under the rubric of Gnosticism in modern scholarship. The term is an eighteenth-century formation from the epithet *gnôstikos*, the meaning of which in antiquity we cannot define with confidence, though we can be sure that it was applied more sparingly then than now.[28]

It derives, of course, from *gnôsis*, the noun for knowledge; but while all philosophers, prophets, and theologians claimed knowledge in late antiquity, the term *gnôstikos* before the second century was applied to the cognitive faculties rather than to those who exercised them. The parsimonious use of it by the first heresiologists, together with their frequent qualification, "the so-called *gnôstikoi*," indicates that it was, or was thought to be, a self-designation.[29] All authors who employ it, including the Neoplatonist Porphyry, assume that those to whom they apply it thought of themselves as Christians. Neither of these adjectives occurs in texts that we now describe as Gnostic, but few would deny the term "Christian" to Paul or the evangelists on the ground that it is absent from their writings, and those who maintain that the authors of the New Testament regarded themselves as Jews are seldom on firmer ground. We have no ancient evidence for a sect or school of Gnostic thought outside the Christian sphere; even if we follow the common practice of modern scholarship in extending the term to all who held, in Porphyry's phrase, that "the author of the cosmos is malign," the only thinkers of this guild whom we can name were all professing Christians. It need hardly be said that the notion of an evil creator cannot be elicited from Plato, from the Old Testament, or from popular religions of the Roman world without intellectual violence: it is not even a tenet of Persian dualism, which taught in this period that the world was brought into being by a benevolent deity but marred by his evil twin.

The oldest texts attributed by their ancient readers to self-styled Gnostics are the Naassene Sermon and the Apocryphon of John. The former,

27. For the body as the Christian community, but with no expectation of personal immortality, see Robinson, *The Body*. For a review of twentieth-century theories, see Pittenger, *After Death*, chapter 5. On the cogency of Gnostic exegesis of 1 Corinthians 15, see Pagels, *The Gnostic Paul*, 81–86. For the argument that a spiritual body need not be of a different texture from the present one, see Thiselton, *Life after Death*, 87–98.

28. See Brakke, *The Gnostics*; Edwards, "The Gnostic Myth."

29. See above all [Hippolytus], *Refutation of all Heresies* 5.6.4: "they styled themselves Gnostics professing a gnosis of deep mysteries."

preserved in the original Greek but only in excerpts, has been dated to the first quarter of the second century; the latter may be of similar age, but survives in a number of Coptic versions, the variations in which attest its widespread use and lingering popularity. Both texts adapt biblical symbolism, drawn predominantly from the Old Testament, to account for the soul's perambulations in the realm of matter. In the Naassene Sermon it seems that spirit and matter constitute two worlds with a common root, the lower being fashioned by a fiery Demiurge named Esaldaios. The immortal soul meanders between the two, and its sojourn under the Demiurge is allegorical portrayed in the diverse cults of the Roman world, the key to interpreting which is the typological contrast between the first and the second Adam. This appellation, derived from adamas (*adamas*), signifies the obduracy of the carnal nature; in Christ, however, the sense of the metaphor shifts, and the stone that the builders rejected becomes the palladium of a new life in the spirit.[30] The *gnosis* professed by the authors of this document would seem to be the discernment of an esoteric sense in cultic texts. In stigmatizing this sect as Naassene or serpent-worshippers, Hippolytus insinuates that, like other Gnostic innovators, they made a trope of inverting biblical imagery; of this, however, he gives no evidence in his long quotation, and there is little more than the name to link the Naassenes to the Ophites, who gave the name Tartarus to the lower universe, described the Demiurge as an accursed God, and held that the serpent, far from seducing Adam and Eve, had unveiled the mysteries to which flesh is blind.[31]

The derivation of Adam's name from *adamas* is one of a number of features in the Naassene discourse that suggest an association with alchemy.[32] The most celebrated practitioner of this science in late antiquity was Zosimus of Panopolis, whose recipes for the deliverance of the soul are based on the works of Hermes, Zoroaster, and a certain Nicotheus, "the hidden one," who also figures in Porphyry's list of writers adduced by the Gnostics of Plotinus.[33] The dissolution and reconstitution of the soul is recounted in a series of visions, the most notorious being the self-immolation of a homunculus who casts his dismembered flesh into a bowl shaped like a chalice (*Authentic Memoirs* 10). To Jung, this was a nightmare of the unconscious;

---

30. [Hippolytus], *Refutation of all Heresies* 5.6.4–5.9.8, with the notes of Litwa, 197–263.

31. Origen, *Against Celsus* 6.22–31; Casey, "Naassenes and Ophites"; Rasimus, *Paradise Reconsidered*, 80–82.

32. Reitzenstein, *Poimandres*, 98–106.

33. See Porphyry, *Life of Plotinus* 16, with Jackson, "The Seer Nikotheus."

others may see it as a meditation on the Eucharist.[34] Jung and Campbell[35] are right at least to argue that Gnostic tropes survived in alchemy when they had been excluded from Christian literature; the tradition reaches its climax in the viscous meditations of Jacob Boehme, which represent the material creation as a precipitate of spiritual tension within the Godhead, and offer circumlocutory prescriptions for the deliverance of the inner light from its filthy robe of flesh.[36]

Primitive Gnosticism: The Apocryphon of John and Its Derivatives

These conjectures owe their plausibility to the absence of any marks in Naassene or alchemical literature that point to a date or place of composition. Even our date of c. AD 300 for Zosimus of Panopolis is conventional, and some would trace the beginnings of his craft to Empedocles.[37] His readiness to learn from all peoples might be thought symptomatic of an age in which the barbarian had been levelled with the Greek under Roman dominion; it was in the Hellenistic era, however, that the Stoics had defined the wise man as a citizen of the world (*kosmopolites*), to be imitated by Philo and outdone by the church with its proclamation that the veil that severed Israel from the nations had been torn away on the cross.[38] The authors of these works regard the body as a dungeon to the soul, but say nothing to indicate that they saw their own age as one of unprecedented misery, disorder, or injustice. The Apocryphon of John, on the other hand, is often felt to breathe the spirit of insurrection,[39] as it burlesques the figure of Wisdom and endorses Plato's axiom that no being who deserves the name God is capable of jealousy.[40] Some have inferred that the author was a Jew, disowning the God who had broken his oath to Zion in AD 70 and his covenant with the whole people of Israel after Bar-Kochba's revolt.[41] Records of Jewish Gnosticism,

34. Jung, *Alchemical Studies*, 67.

35. Campbell, *The Masks of God*, vol. 4, 262–97.

36. Boehme, *Signatura Rerum*, 12–30.

37. Kingsley, *Ancient Philosophy, Mystery and Magic*, 61–68.

38. Mark 15:38; Hebrews 10:20.

39. The texts are collated by Waldstein and. Wisse in Robinson, ed., *Coptic Gnostic Library*, vol. 2, 14–177.

40. NHC II.1.25.41; cf. Wisdom 2.23; *Timaeus* 28c. On the distinctively Christian theology of the *Apocryphon*, however, see now McCashen, "The *Apocryphon of John's* Father Discourse."

41. Grant, *Gnosticism and Early Christianity*.

however, are sparse at best, and if the intended audience were not Christian, and thus not predisposed to revere or even to read the apostles, what would be conveyed by the title Apocryphon of John?

The text survives in four divergent editions, all in Coptic, together with a summary by Irenaeus (c. AD 180), now extant only in Latin. It was evidently the most popular of the texts that modern scholarship calls "Gnostic," and the only one that would certainly have received this epithet from Irenaeus, who believes it to be a prototype of the Valentinian myth (*Against Heresies* 1.29 and 1.31). The shorter versions (Berlin Codex and NHC III.1) appear to be independent renderings of a Greek original, while the longer texts (NHC II.1 and IV.1) have undergone heavy redaction. All four agree in presenting it as a supernatural revelation to John the apostle within a few days of Christ's ascension, after the Pharisee Arimanius has challenged him to say what has become of his teacher. This name recalls that of the evil twin of Ormuzd, the creator in the Zoroastrian scriptures. The being who communicates the secrets of cosmogony and salvation to the apostle, however, describes himself as Father, Mother, and Child, and is identified at the end of the text as the Savior.[42] His appearance is accompanied by an opening of the heavens, and in aspect he is first an old man then a youth (II.1.2.1–19). Love undergoes a similar metamorphosis in some classical writers, and analogues can be found in the depiction of both Christ and the church in early Christian texts.[43]

The cosmogony begins with a celebration of the Father, who is also known as the One and the Invisible Virginal Spirit. Illimitable, unfathomable, invisible, and eternal, the source of knowledge, blessedness, goodness, mercy, and grace, he is unconfined by space or time, transcending all that tongue can utter or mind conceive, and even the logical antitheses between the great and small, the corporeal and the incorporeal, which are inseparable form the world of our experience. Reflecting upon his own image in the light that surrounds him, he brings forth a virgin thought under the name of Barbelo, though in Greek she is also styled his Pronoia, or forethought (NHC II.1.5.13, etc.). At her own request she receives the attributes of foreknowledge, incorruptibility, eternity, and truth. Quickened by the Father's gaze, she brings forth a child as his luminous image, and the child asks for mind in order that he may glorify the paternal spirit and his maternal forethought (II.1.6.33–34). Mind conceives a desire to create, which is realized as Will, and through the Word that supervenes on Will a supernal realm

42. NHC 2.1.2.12–14, Waldstein and Wisse, *Apocryphon of John*, 19 (Not in IV.1); NHC 2.1.31.32, Waldstein and Wisse, 175.

43. Longus, Daphnis and Chloe 2,3,5; *Poimandres* 4: Acts of John 29; *Shepherd of Hermas* vision 3.10.5.

comes into being under the monarchy of the Child, who is also acclaimed as the Autogenes (Self-Begotten) and the bearer of the name above all names.[44] From him spring four new luminaries, bearing the appellations Harmozel, Oroiael, Daveithai, and Eleleth (II.1.9.1–23). These correspond to the powers of grace, perception, understanding, and thoughtfulness, though in a longer enumeration we discover that each of these powers is one member of a triad, and in the triad appertaining to Eleleth, thoughtfulness is replaced by Sophia, the Greek term denoting wisdom (II.1).

What are we to make of this strange recital? The etymology of the name Barbelo remains a "mystery of scholarship,"[45] but the name above all names is the one bestowed on Christ at Philippians 2:9. The names of the luminaries do not lend themselves to a plausible etymology, but the terminations suggest that they were intended to pass for Hebrew. Sophia is not a goddess in Greek mythology, and the creative role assigned to her in the Apocryphon is prefigured only in works of the Jewish canon—Proverbs, Sirach, and above all the Wisdom of Solomon. In this text, however, her rash desire for motherhood belies her name, for she brings forth without the approval of her male consort (NHC II.1.10.1–5). Her offspring is a monster with the body of a serpent and the head of a lion (II.1.10.8); in shame and consternation, she enthrones him in a bright cloud, impenetrable to all but the Virgin Spirit, and gives him the name Yaldabaoth (II.1.10.19). This first of the archons, mating with his own mindlessness, creates seven others and sets them over the planets that govern the days of the week (II.1.11.27–35). Yaldabaoth—whose name is most probably a "condensation" of divine appellatives in the Jewish scriptures[46]—proclaims himself a jealous God, beside whom there is no other (II.1.13.9).

Sophia—who has been reasonably explained as a personification of erring human wisdom[47]—repents of her misjudgment, and is restored by the Virginal Spirit, receiving a portion of his fullness and a special heaven, the ninth, as her abode (NHC II.1.33–14.12). A voice informs Yaldabaoth that he is not the sole deity, for man exists and the son of man.[48] A radiant shape shines forth upon the nether waters, embodying both the masculine and the feminine aspects of the transcendent deity (II.1.14.27–34). As

44. For the name, see, e.g. NHC II.2.7.20. See further Whittaker, "Self-Generating Principles."

45. Thomassen, *The Coherence of Gnosticism*, 14; yet the derivation form *bara elohim* "God created") at Genesis 1:1 has not lost its allure.

46. Rasimus, *Paradise Reconsidered*, 105.

47. Burkitt, *Church and Gnosis*, 45.

48. NHC II.1.13.14–15. Cf. Psalm 8:4, cited at Hebrews 1:6, and the worship of Man and the Son of man by the Naassenes at Hippolytus, *Refutation* 5.6.5.

dismay begets emulation, the archons create a facsimile of this image in flesh and bone. Here follows, in the longest version, the allocation of 365 parts of the body to their respective angels, which purports to be drawn from the Book of Zoroaster (II.1.15.27–19.10). The body, however, cannot be animated until Yaldabaoth is induced to breathe what he takes to be his own spirit into Adam's face, though in fact this is the spirit of his mother.[49] Perceiving that Adam is more enlightened than they, the archons are jealous and confine him to the lowest realm of matter, making him captive to the four elements (II.1.20.35–21.9) and conspiring to hide from him the tree of knowledge which would reveal his nakedness.[50] The Savior, however, persuades him to eat and enlightenment grows within him (II.1.22.9–15). Yaldabaoth fashions a female counterpart to Adam in the hope of capturing his insight, but once again it is Sophia who imbues her with life (II.1.22.259–23.25). Yaldabaoth, trying to master her by force, sires Yaveand Elohim, the two proper names of god in the Hebrew scriptures (II.1.24.15–24); in the meantime Adam begets Seth, the progenitor of the elect (II.1.25.1–2). Yaldabaoth induces his angels to mate with Wisdom, and the bonds of fate, which imprison the majority of mortals, spring from this union (II.1,28.–31); yet neither this rape nor the subsequent inundation (II.1.28.35) can prevent the Savior's summoning of the elect from darkness and the chains of sleep (II.1.31.4–6).

All this is manifestly a parody of the Book of Genesis, which is contradicted four times in this part of the treatise.[51] It is likely enough that, as in the New Testament, the supernatural archons coalesce in imagination with the false rulers of the world, among whom the Gnostics may have numbered their enemies in the church.[52] Motifs derived from other religious traditions are also detectable—for example, the commonplace of Greek mythology that parthenogenesis always produces monsters. Lion-headed statues, some of them dedicated to Arimanius, have been found in shrines of Mithras, another figure whose pretensions to a Persian origin have been contested.[53] Affinities between the Adam, or primal man, of the Gnostics and the Zoroastrian Gayomart have also been posited by a number of scholars.[54] Nevertheless the title of the Apocryphon of John, like the bulk of its contents, seems to

49. NHC II.1.19.22–33; cf. Genesis 2:7.

50. NHC II.1.22.3–8; cf. Genesis 2:16–17.

51. NHC II.1.13.20; II.1.22.2; II.1,23.3; II.1.29.6.

52. Pagels, "The Demiurge and His Archons."

53. Bianchi, "Mithraism and Gnosticism."

54. Kraeling, *Anthropos and Son of Man*, 85–127.

be calculated to deter any readers who did not feel that the confrontation between the old and the new in Israel was any concern of theirs.

The Valentinian Sophia

While the Apocryphon seems to have been much the most popular manifesto of Gnostic thought, the teacher who acquired the largest following was Marcion of Pontus, who was wise enough to disclaim the role of prophet, relying only on the inspiration of Luke and Paul. Rather than amplify them with his own revelations, he pruned them, Tertullian avers, of every text that failed to uphold his own antithesis between justice and goodness, matter and spirit.[55] Where Philo regarded the sovereignty denoted by the noun *kyrios* as a complement to the goodness denoted by the noun *theos*, the Christian Cerdo had posited two antagonistic deities, one just and one good, the former judging us by his own law while the latter redeems us from its impositions.[56] Marcion is said by some witnesses to have adopted this polarity, by others to have added a third who corrupts the world that the just God has created.[57] Even on this second view, which seems to acquit the Demiurge of malice, there is no salvation for the material realm, in which the soul is doomed to stray from body to body until the good God sends his own Son to preach the gospel of emancipation.[58] This Son appeared in a spectral robe of flesh, but in reality suffered nothing even when the minions of the Demiurge condemned him to die on the cross. How the lesser divinities came into being, how the Savior won the right to invade a world that he had not made, why he waited so long to do so, and how the Demiurge, not being good, is nonetheless trusted to act as a judge of souls are questions to which the heresiologists professed to have found no answer in his writings; nor was he able to tell them why the body was created, why the Savior should need to counterfeit his own death, or how the soul, which has neither died nor fallen, can be said to have undergone a resurrection. The provenance of evil may not be adequately accounted for

55. Tertullian, *Against Marcion* 4.4–5, 4.21, etc. For the contrary thesis that Luke, as we now know it, is an amplification of Marcion, see Vinzent, *Marcion and the Synoptic Gospels*.

56. Irenaeus, *Against Heresies* 1.27.1; Tertullian, *Against Marcion* 1.2.3, 1.22.10. See Löhr, "Did Marcion Distinguish?"

57. [Hippolytus], *Refutation* 7.29.25–30.2. See Osborne, *Rethinking Early Greek Philosophy*, 130 on the assimilation of Marcion to Empedocles in Hippolytus.

58. Tertullian, *Against Marcion* 3.22; 3.4.1, etc. Transmigration in Marcion is implied by *Refutation* 7.29.7.

in this simplification of the Gnostic myth, but the remedy is, clearly enough, the emancipation of the soul from all traffic with matter.

It is thus not a tenet of every Gnostic system that the Demiurge is evil.[59] In the teachings attributed to the disciples of Valentinus, even matter is a concretion of the penitent tears of Wisdom, and hence not wholly irredeemable (Irenaeus, *Against Heresies* 1.2.3). The flesh survives, though transfigured, in the aeon, not only for spiritual Christians, who are children of Wisdom, but even for the psychic progeny of the Demiurge, who have the capacity, once they have heard the gospel, to turn from flesh to spirit.[60] In this tradition, as in certain expositions of Marcion, there is a third power in heaven, the Cosmocrator, who is Paul's God of this world.[61] His tribe, the hylics or people of matter, cannot receive the salvation that is offered to the psychics and predestined for the spiritual; the fatalism implied by this taxonomy offends our ancient witnesses, who did not consider that it might be as figurative as the parable of the origin of humanity from three metals in Plato's *Republic*.[62] We need not doubt that when they differed among themselves as to whether Christ had a psychic or a spiritual body, the Valentinian understood both these terms to signify a real body, as they do in Paul's first letter to the Corinthians.[63] When the so-called Gospel of Truth styles Christ on the cross the firstfruits of the pleroma,[64] it says nothing that we would find obscure in Paul, and when it blames this crime on the rage of Plane or Error, we see at once that this allegory personifies the universal sinfulness of which the priests, the governor, and the mob were unwitting tools.

The attempt to fathom the highest principle may be as dangerous for the soul as the contemplation of matter. In a new adaptation of the Gnostic myth by Ptolemaeus, reportedly a pupil of the Alexandrian teacher Valentinus, the Father is the abyss of ineffability and his consort is Sige, or Silence (Irenaeus, *Against Heresies* 1.1–4). The name may be an allusion to the Greek mysteries, or to the picturesque image of the newborn Christ as the Word proceeding from the silence of the ages in a letter by the martyr Ignatius of Antioch (*Magnesians* 8.3).[65] The first progeny of the Abyss and

---

59. Indeed, Ptolemaeus, allegedly a disciple of Valentinus, rejects this as the tenet of unnamed antagonists in his letter to Flora: see Markschies, "New Research on Ptolemaeus Gnosticus."

60. *Epistle to Rheginos (Treatise on the Resurrection)* 47.4–10, trans. M. L. Peel in NHC I, 153.

61. Irenaeus, *Against Heresies* 1.5.4 and 1.27.2. Cf 2 Corinthians 4:4 and John 12:31.

62. Irenaeus, *Against Heresies* 1.8.3; 2.14.4; 2.29.3; Plato, *Republic* 415a–c.

63. See Thomassen, *The Spiritual Seed*, 83–85.

64. Gospel of Truth 18.30, trans. H. Attridge and G. Macrae in NHC I, 85.

65. On Ignatius as a precursor of the Valentinians, see Edwards, "Ignatius and the Second Century."

Silence is a couple or syzygy named *Nous* and *Aletheia*, Mind and Truth. Philosophers would applaud, but the second pairing, *Logos* and *Zoe*, or Reason and Life, is manifestly taken from the prologue to John's Gospel, while the source of the third, Anthropos and Ecclesia or Man and Church, is possibly Ephesians 4:9. Sophia's fall is occasioned by a premature desire to know the Father in his fullness—a presumption that mirrors the sin of Eve in one way, as her temerity in the Apocryphon of John does in another.[66] Some thirty or thirty-two aeons or emanations now make up the Pleroma, or Fullness of the Godhead; when Sophia repents the agents of her redemption are the Holy Spirit and Christ, the collective offspring or first-fruits of the Pleroma. She continues to be excluded from the Godhead by a boundary (Horos), which also bears the name Stauros, or Cross. Allusions to Pauline themes—the fullness of aeons before the coming of Christ, the fullness of the Godhead that dwelt in him bodily, the cross as a stumbling-block to worldly wisdom—are palpable enough to betoken the presence of an allegory, if not to furnish us with a key to its elucidation.[67]

Both the Valentinians and the Gnostics style the child of Sophia the Demiurge (Irenaeus, *Against Heresies* 1.5), adopting Plato's nomenclature without his belief that the Demiurge created because he was good. The Valentinians also employed the Pauline term *ektrôma* or abortion (Irenaeus, *Against Heresies* 1.6; 1 Corinthians 15:8). Like Plato, they can entertain a variety of myths: in the so-called Tripartite Tractate, for example, Sophia gives way to the Logos or Word, who does not so much fall as suffer an inevitable severance from the Father.[68] The allegory of the Gospel of Truth, in which the Savior is nailed to the cross by Error,[69] requires no commentary and no demonstration of its Christian provenance.

Basilides and the Seed of Being

Our evidence for the doctrine of Basilides is mere flotsam, sufficient nonetheless to show that he must have been one of the most remarkable thinkers of late antiquity.[70] An allusion in Irenaeus to "Basilides and other gnostics" should not be pressed as evidence that he styled himself, or was commonly styled, a Gnostic, and he escapes that designation in our chief informant,

66. Macrae, "Jewish Background."

67. Edwards, "Pauline Platonism."

68. On the adoption of a less mythical and more philosophical idiom in this Valentinian treatise, see Berno, "Rethinking Valentinianism."

69. Gospel of Truth 18.22, trans. H. Attridge and G. Macrae in NHC I, 85.

70. See Quispel, "Gnostic Man."

Hippolytus of Rome. Even in that author's *Refutation of All Heresies* he is almost without antecedents or posterity, a fitting apostle of his own God whom he raises so far above all thought and speech as to divest him even of *ousia* or being. Hippolytus lampoons him as a disciple of Aristotle, to whom he ascribes the doctrine that a first *ousia*, or concrete individual, is a constellation of things that do not exist.[71] But of course the Greek precursor of this superexistent principle is the "Good beyond being" of Plato's *Republic* 509b. Perhaps this is already fused, as in Plotinus, with the One of the *Parmenides*, for as the first antinomy in that dialogue states "if the One is, nothing is," so Basilides proclaims that when God was alone there was neither effable nor ineffable, neither entity nor matter (*Refutation* 7.20.3; 7.21.1). He is thus the earliest Christian proponent, not only of apophatic theology, but of creation out of nothing; for this, his text is the prologue to the Fourth Gospel, in which, as he understands it, the only substrate of creation is that procession from himself whereby the Ineffable takes the form of a light to the intellect, a word to the understanding, a Son to himself, and a seed to all that comes into existence (7.21.3; 7.22.3–4; 22.7.1).

The germination of this seed appears to follow some principle of necessity, yet it is equally necessary that the cosmos that results from it should be inferior to the Father. The Sonship, or rather the highest form of it, reascends instantaneously to the Father, (7.22.8), leaving behind a lower form of Sonship which must strive, like the embodied soul in Plato's *Phaedrus*, to grow wings that will enable it to rise (7.22.10). This it achieves with the assistance of the Holy Spirit, which continues to inform the residual elements of the cosmos when both Sonships have returned to the higher realm (7.22.13–15). The two realms are now divided by a firmament, and an archon is set over the lower cosmos (7.23.1–3). In the characteristic style of the Gnostic Demiurge, he believes this to be the only world and himself the one God, beside whom there is no other (7.23.4). He also sets an archon over the hebdomad, or system of seven planets, to act as a jailer to the soul (7.23.6, 7.25.4). Basilides clearly shares the ubiquitous belief that the planets are instruments of fate, but he asserts that their despotism is counteracted by a new descent of the Sonship, the light of which is communicated through their own sons to the Archon and the Lord of the Hebdomad (7.25.7, 7.26.1, 7.26.8). This double Incarnation, which explains how pagan astrologers learned the date of the nativity (7.27.5), culminates in the Passion, whereby Jesus becomes the firstfruits of discrimination as the

71. Hippolytus, *Refutation of All Heresies* 7.17. On the possible sources of this caricature, see Litwa, ed. and trans., *Refutation of All Heresies*, 493n11.

natures that can be redeemed are winnowed from those that are doomed to perdition (7.27.8–10).

We are told by other witnesses that Basilides thought the Passion illusory, and since we can scarcely doubt that his myth has some allegorical import, it is probable that the efficacy of Christ's death consisted for him not so much in the mere fact of its occurrence as in its recapitulation in the believer. We are also told that he was a determinist who asserted that we are saved or damned at birth; since we have abundant testimony in Clement and Origen that he maintained the transmigration of souls in accordance with their merits, the truth would appear to be that he followed Plato in holding our lot in the present life to be dictated by our choice at the end of the last. He was even alleged to have taught that souls may pass from humans to beasts and that death by martyrdom is an expiation for sin in a previous life.[72] Nevertheless, he demonstrates his allegiance to Christianity, at a time when the evangelists were seldom quoted as scripture, by reading creation and revelation alike through a Johannine prism: indeed, he is reported to have written a commentary in twenty-four books on a gospel that may have been that of John.[73] I have suggested elsewhere[74] that his three sonships represent the work of the Logos in creating, of the incarnate Christ in redeeming, and of the Spirit in adopting the elect. Be that as it may, he concurs with John in seeing the world at once as a product of light and as a seminary of darkness, and if he equates salvation with enlightenment, the Fourth Gospel too represents the Messiah as the embodied Word of revelation. Again, he can find some warrant for his own fatalism in Jesus's retort to the children of Abraham, that in denying him they prove themselves children of Satan. Of course, there is no intimation in the Fourth Gospel that the planets are our jailers or that ignorance is the result of our incarceration in matter, but whatever we make of the riotous imagery of Basilides, it is clearly more a fugue than a literal gloss on a text that already contains its share of symbolism.

Eros and Gnosis

No reader of Gnostic myth will be unaware that it is peppered with motifs that we ordinarily call Platonic. The fall of Wisdom resembles, and in

72. Clement of Alexandria, *Stromateis* 4.81.1–8.3.1, with Löhr, *Basilides und seine Schüle*, 125–38.

73. Eusebius, *Church History* 4.7.7. For evidence of his knowledge of John, see Hill, *The Johannine Corpus*, 224–27.

74. Edwards, *Origen against Plato*, 26–28.

many Gnostic texts entails, the descent of individual souls to bodies as in the *Phaedrus*; even in Basilides, for whom the world is a consequence of an emanation rather than a fall, the doctrine of transmigration is retained, together with the conceit of the soul's growing wings to escape her prison.[75] Even the seduction of Wisdom by her own image in matter is a collation of two Platonic images, one of the lover as a looking-glass to the ideal self of the beloved, the other of the charlatanical artist who professes to create all things by catching their reflections in his mirror (*Republic* 596b–d). For Plato, these mirrors exemplify higher and lower modes of knowledge, corresponding to higher and lower objects of eros. In Orphic myth, where the mirror represents the distracting influence of the senses on the intellect, the Author of the cosmos is depicted as an ithyphallic figure who, although some call him eros, would have been construed by Plato as a symbol of the desire for procreation, which prevents the vulgar soul from "begetting in the beautiful." A Christian may have been the first to say that God is love, but the Greek is agape; the Gnostics may have preempted the substitution of eros for agape in Origen and Gregory of Nyssa, but with corollaries for the soul and its Creator that neither of these authors could have entertained.

Sexual transgression is a recurrent motif in the Apocryphon; in other Gnostic texts the iconography of the divine is blatantly phallic, and not only in the lower planes of being. In the Book of Baruch by a certain Justin, known to us only from the hostile testimony of Hippolytus (c. AD 230), the authors of the material world are Elohim, who plainly represents the God of the Old Testament, and his consort Edem, who represents the material principle (Hippolytus, *Refutation* 5.23–28). The cosmos that they jointly bring forth is subjected to the dominion of twelve archons, who can be plausibly equated with the signs of the zodiac. The denizens of this world are impregnated by the spirit of Elohim; he himself, however, now ascends to a higher sphere, where he repents of his work and labors to free his spirit from captivity (cf. Genesis 6:3). The unredeemed Edem works against him, creating the serpent Naas to commit lewd sin with Adam and Eve and entice them into eating from the forbidden tree of knowledge. Elohim sends Heracles to do battle with the twelve archons, and he overcomes them in the same order as he achieves his labors in the more familiar tales. Unfortunately, he loses his manhood to Omphale (the queen at whose court he wore women's clothes, according to an older Greek myth), and Jesus is now commissioned as savior by the angel Baruch. Naas contrives his death, but the consequence is that Jesus ascends to the Father of all, the good one, who has already admitted Elohim to his mysteries. To the surprise of the Christian reader,

75. [Hippolytus], *Refutation of All Heresies* 7.22.9, etc.

the Father is identified with Priapus, a figure who was always depicted in a state of erection (*Refutation* 5.26.32). The name is here etymologized to mean "the one who created before all things," but the ithyphallic demiurge is a regular apparition in myths ascribed to Orpheus.[76]

In contrast to the Orphics, Gnostics are apt to portray creative deities either as syzygies of male and female or as hermaphroditic individuals. In another variation of the myth of Sophia, entitled *On the Origin of the World* (NHC II.5), the stimulus to sexual desire is the generation of Eros or Love from the blood of Pronoia, the providential aspect of the supernal mind. Enamoured, of the light that shines forth from the eighth or highest heaven, this masculofeminine power remains unsatisfied and pours out her desire in the form of a luminous man of light to the nether regions. From this blood springs Eros, another is an androgynous figure, whose masculine side is Himereris (Greek *himeros*, "desire"), while his feminine side is a soul of blood from the stuff of the virgin Pronoia. He is clearly a mythical adumbration of Christ, whom the author may have supposed (with Origen) to be the subject of the dictum "my eros is crucified" in Ignatius of Antioch's letter to the Romans.[77] The gods and the angels become enamored of Eros, who sets them afire, as many lamps are lit from one. Although this also was a simile for the generation of the second person of the Trinity from the first without division of substance, the *Origin of the World* relates that, on the contrary, Eros was disseminated through all crated beings, inspiring all sexual unions, including that between angels and human beings, which, according to Genesis 6:1–6, engendered the giants and provoked the flood. In spite of his divine pedigree, therefore, Eros is the cause of our bondage in the material realm under the sway of the seven planetary archons: salvation, as the arcane sequel relates, is the work of Sophia, working through the disobedience of Eve.[78]

Conclusion

Many scholars quote, as the essence of Gnostic thought, a question from the *Excerpts from Theodotus*, a text ascribed by Clement of Alexandria to the Valentinian school of the late second century:[79]

76. Marcovich, *Studies in Greco-Roman Myth and Gnosticism*, 89–92.

77. Ignatius, *Romans* 7.2, quoted by Origen, *Commentary on the Song of Songs*, prologue 36.

78. See further Crislip, "Envy and Anger."

79. On the classification of Theodotus, see Pearson, *Ancient Gnosticism*, 164–67.

> It is not the baptism alone that liberates, but also the knowledge,
> who we were, why we came into being; where we were or where
> we have been cast; whither we are bound, whence comes our
> baptism; what is generation, what regeneration. (Clement of
> Alexandria, *Excerpts from Theodotus* 79).

If the Gnostics, Basilideans, Marcionitrs, and Valentinians truly regarded
the present world as the handiwork of an evil God, or at best as a poor
simulacrum of the divine realm, they must take the credit not only for having given an unprecedented answer to this question, but for making it the
linchpin of their cosmogony. For the Greek philosophers, as for the Old
Testament, the question is rather whether the world is governed by a just
providence: the recognition of evil does not entail a negative reply, and
providence can be denied without asserting a preponderance of evil over
good. For this reason alone, it does not seem that Gnosticism can be fairly
characterized as the acute Hellenization, or even the acute Hellenisticiza-
tion, of Christianity;[80] nor as we have seen, is the dualism to which it testifies
born of the teaching of Zoroaster. If there is a theology in the ancient world
that is radically inimical to the cosmos, it is that of Christianity, and the
proliferation of Gnostic systems in the second century is somewhat more
intelligible because it follows the promulgation of the gospel. At the same
time the faith of the Gnostics, for all their attested professions of Christianity, is not that of the New Testament, which assumes the intrinsic goodness
of the creation and justifies its repudiation of the Mosaic law as a means to
salvation with a new aetiology, not of natural evil, but of sin.

If the Gnostics nonetheless passed for Christians, was it because they
camouflaged their true beliefs, as the Manichaeans were later reputed to do,
or because, in the absence of a creed or canon, it was easy for them to draw
the faithful into their unduly literal reading of a few dualistic expressions in
Paul and John? Or was it, on the contrary, because the faithful understood
the Gnostics well enough not to take them as literally as their ancient Cen-
sors and some modern critics? The reader of 2 Corinthians knows that the
god of this world is not divine except in the estimation of his votaries; the
reader of the Fourth Gospel does not infer, when Jesus speaks to the Jews
of what is written in "your law," that he subscribed to a different law; the
zealots who were once accustomed to say that the God of the Christians was
not the God of the Jews were never under suspicion of believing in more
than one God, though the charge could be levelled without belief in any.
It is possible, though it cannot be proved, that the Valentinian Demiurge

---

80. Nock, review of Lewy, *Sobria Ebrietas*, 309, adapting the famous dictum of Ad-
olf von Harnack.

merely personifies an idolatrous conception of the deity, and that Marcion labors the weaknesses and vices of the Creator only to illustrate the false conclusions that would follow if the church clung to an obsolete religion. Such an assumption would at least explain why the bishops feared for their flocks, as the following chapter will demonstrate. Whether or not they were misconstrued, the Gnostics acted as whetstones to these pioneers of credal theology, furnishing them not only with a motive but at times with the materials for speculations that, however dimly foreshadowed in the New Testament, have come to define the faith and expectation of the church.

5

Providence, Fate, and Fortune in the Second Century

THE HIGH IMPERIAL PERIOD of Rome has often been represented as a neurasthenic sequel to the principate, the beginning of a "failure of nerve" that resulted in the collapse of philosophy into superstition and the irresistible triumph of Christianity. The adoption of the cults of Mithras, Isis, and other Oriental deities by the Roman aristocracy was compared to the vogue for the wisdom of the east that accompanied, and perhaps helped to precipitate, the decline of the European churches in the modern era.[1] The rise of the sophists, a peripatetic class of Greek men of letters who took no part in the government of the empire or their own cities, was found to be mirrored by a privatization of religion, the cultivation of an internal faith that, when not tempered, became pathological, even if the "madness" of the fourth century was impossible for a pagan of the second.[2] Economic histories of the Roman world suggested that the seeds of fissiparation were present in the second century, while the third was notoriously an epoch of military, political, and financial decadence, punctuated by devastating plagues. The emergence of Gnosticism, an unprecedented denial of the goodness of the cosmos and the validity of human institutions, was attributed to a general loss of faith

---

1. Cumont, *Oriental Religions*. For the opposing argument that "Oriental" religions followed the migrations of their native adherents, see Macmullen, *Paganism in the Roman Empire*, 112–30.

2. Dodds, *Pagan and Christian*, 34.

in the capacity of mind or soul to act upon a world in which the best and the worst, the richest and the poorest, wore the same fetters.[3] Dodds borrowed the description "age of anxiety" from Auden, who was commenting on the unease of Europe in the late twentieth century.[4] Thirty years earlier he might have said "age of absolutism," and thirty years later "age of globalization." Whatever name was used, it was easy for western eyes to see in the ferment of the second century and the crisis of the third a perspicuous omen of our own decline and fall.

There had always been a countervailing opinion, much of it taking the form of a different commentary on the same facts. Gibbon opined that humanity had never enjoyed such a period of tranquillity and prosperity as the Mediterranean world enjoyed in the age of the Antonines; Michael Grant went so far as to see the "climax of Rome" in the turbulent third century,[5] and others have doubted whether this was more an age of crisis than any other. We may regard the sophists as dull and prolix imitators of greater authors, but they show little consciousness of their own insolvency, and the Byzantine scribes cannot have found it as tedious to copy the works of Aristides as we now find it to read them.[6] Like the other sophists he bows to Rome but retains a defiant belief in the supremacy of Greek culture, while Latin authors for their part become increasingly independent of Greek models. No orator, Greek or Latin, shows any sense that the cities who paid him for his eloquence were mere graveyards of past glory; many had increased in size and wealth and Roman rule, and archaeologists of the twentieth-first century report that at all times up to the collapse of the western empire the impoverishment of one site tends to be balanced by new affluence in another. Quacks and hypochondriacs are more numerous in the literature of late antiquity than in that of classical age, but the literature of the later epoch is also more voluminous. The growth of elective cults and private devotion cannot be cited to prove the decay of religious belief unless we also had clear evidence of more widespread skepticism in the age of Lucian than in that of Plato and Aristophanes. And if there is a rising cult of the great man as a mediator, by temporal power or spiritual capacity, between this world and a higher one,[7] this might signify not so much a loss

3. Jonas, *The Gnostic Religion*.

4. On the influence and continuing value of Dodds, see Athanassiadi, "Antiquité Tardive"; Morgan, *"Pagans and Christians."*

5. Grant, *The Climax of Rome*.

6. In Festugière, *Personal Religion*, Aristides is represented by his uncharacteristic sacred tales and not his voluminous orations, the effusions of a man who is entirely at home in his world.

7. Brown, *Making of Late Antiquity*.

of nerve as a high estimation of the human faculties, just as the increasing religiosity of philosophers[8] may betoken not a loss of faith in reason but a willingness to extend its tools to phenomena that had once been beneath the notice of the learned.

When philosophy becomes more demotic in its interests, it may gain in potency more than it loses in rigor. Most of the authors who make up the present chapter believed in the gods, and all assume that if gods exist they have a duty to attend minutely to the affairs of humans. This presupposition is foreign to Aristotle, at least in his esoteric works, and is far from prominent in the works of Plato. Although, therefore, their touchstones are always classical, it is reasonable to surmise that Plutarch, Alexander, Lucian, and Apuleius were addressing a popular question of the day. Whether the typical reader approached the question as a believer or as a skeptic we cannot say, but there is little evidence in our surviving texts that it became more urgent because of some perceived deterioration in society or in nature. That charge was made in polemics against the Christians from the middle of the third century, and it will be revisited in later chapters of this volume. So long, however, as they came only from the ancestral shrines of the eastern provinces, new gods were not the putative cause of any new malaise.

Plutarch as Platonist

Plutarch regards himself as an Academic, though not of the skeptical persuasion.[9] Those who are wont to say of every dogma that it is no more true than its contrary, for all that they may claim descent from Socrates by way of the New Academy, are in his eyes no better than the Epicureans, who are constantly upbraided in his writings for their equation of the good with sensual pleasure and their consequent denial that there is any higher part of us that can be brought before a tribunal after death. In common with other Platonists who opposed the New Academy, he draws freely on Stoic recipes for virtue, and in his defence of providence he displays a religiosity that is more redolent of Chrysippus than of Plato.[10] His attachment to oracles and celestial signs is characteristic of his age, as is the eclectic spirit that leads him, as it led Seneca before him, to recognize merit even in some sayings

8. See King, "Ancient Philosophy Transformed."

9. Dillon, "'Orthodoxy' and 'Eclecticism,'" 106, argues that his intelligent eclecticism extended to the sue of skepticism as a weapon against the Stoics.

10. On his espousal of the Stoic belief in a tradition of ancient wisdom, see Boys-Stones, *Post-Hellenic Philosophy*, 107–12.

of Epicurus.[11] This hospitality is the concomitant of his polymathy, which enabled him to write forty-eight biographies of noble Greeks and Romans, together with a corpus of essays ranging from the most homely to the most abstruse of topics, not all of which are by any definition philosophical. These may have impaired his credit as a philosopher, notwithstanding the logical acumen and the minute criticism of his interlocutors that distinguish his occasional polemics; but as the examples of David Hume and Bertrand Russell remind us, it is often those who cultivate other interests who are able to engage in their philosophical works with the topics of most profound concern to their readers, and in a style that is all the more penetrating because it is more humane.

His principal contribution—the most important before Plotinus—to the exegesis of Plato is his treatise *On the Generation of Soul in the Timaeus*.[12] In Plato's myth the Demiurge frames the world-soul in the form of the Greek letter X from the Same and the Other: the consensus of all speakers that the world is *genêtos* ("generated") suggests that by this action we are to understand, if not a strict creation out of nothing, the production of that which had not hitherto existed. Plutarch himself, in common with almost every Christian reader of Plato, takes him to mean that the cosmos has a temporal beginning, which is also the beginning of time itself. He observes, however, that even before the Demiurge adopted it as his receptacle, the space that now contains the world was already in an unruly state of motion (1014b–c). Reasoning perhaps more closely than Plato himself, he argues that, as the cause of motion is soul, the receptacle must have been animated by its own soul, which was not created by the Demiurge. Whereas his younger contemporary Alcinous surmised that the Demiurge did not so much create a new soul for the world as waken it from a restive slumber,[13] Plutarch couples this passage with one in the *Laws* where it is conceded that souls are of two kinds, good and malign.[14] At the same time he notes that there is evil in the world, which Plato declares in the *Theaetetus* to be indelible: against the Pythagorean Eudemus he urges that, since matter is inert, it can effect neither good nor evil, and concludes that it is the restless opposition of this primordial, and irrational, soul that prevents the world-soul from perfectly executing the design of its creator (*Generation* 1015d–e).

---

11. See *On the Saying, "Live Unknown."* He is as hostile to the Stoics as any Epicurean in *Stoic Refutations* and *On the Principle of Cold*.

12. For extensive commentary, see Cherniss, ed., *Moralia*, vol. XIII.1, 133–57.

13. Alcinous, *Didascalicus* 14.3, on which see Dillon, *Alcinous*, 125–26.

14. *Generation* 1014d–e, with Plato, *Laws* 896c–898c and Cherniss, *Moralia*, 187, note f. Note also the citation of *Statesman* 272e–273b at 1015a.

This dualism returns in a more exotic guise in Plutarch's treatise *On Isis and Osiris*, the only work of his, and perhaps the first by any Platonist, that takes up allegoresis as a palliative for the superficial obscenities of myth.[15] Neither he nor Plato applies the same remedy to Homer, but Plutarch reads this narrative of divine fratricide as the Egyptian cipher for a truth that has been believed by both the wise and the multitude of every nation. Another example of the mythical form that it assumes among the multitude is the Persian tale of the purposeful corruption of the world by Arimanius, brother of Ormuzd the creator;[16] the Greeks have received from Plato both a mythical rendering of it, in the conceit that the soul is formed from the Same and the Other, and a clear asseveration in his last work that the world is the theatre of two contending souls. Osiris, the counterpart of Greek Dionysus (*On Isis and Osiris* 364d–f), represents both the fertilizing waters of the Nile and the activity of Logos, or divine reason,[17] in sustaining the natural and the moral order of the universe (372b–c). Seth or Typhon, his brother and murderer, stands for the arid desert that encroaches upon the irrigated land, and for the appetites and passions that move the soul in defiance of reason. Again, matter is blameless, but it appears to be no longer passive, for the union of form and substrate to produce the visible word is symbolized by the marriage of Osiris to his sister Isis, whose love for him can be construed as the salutary yearning of the inchoate for actuality and perfection.[18] Plutarch compares the Platonic myth of the birth of Love from Poverty and Plenty, where it is Poverty, the weaker and female principle, who initiates the union (374c–d; *Symposium* 203b). Neoplatonists subsequently cited a Phoenician myth in which the movement that results in creation is initiated by Pothos or Desire.[19] The closest analogue to this notion of matter seeking form was to be found, however, a century after Plutarch in Mani's fable of the incursion of the kingdom of darkness into the kingdom of light: in this case, however, the union is resisted because the

---

15. Contrast *On Isis and Osiris* 354b–c and 362a–b with *How a Young Man Should Read the Poets* 19e–f.

16. *On Isis and Osiris* 46–46 (369d–370c). On the related practice of symbolism in Plutarch, see Roslem, "Apollon, est-il vraiment le dieu du soleil?," 178–85. On his sources and his value as a witness to Egyptian myth and exegesis, see Plutarch, *De iside et Osiride*, 470–82.

17. Dillon, *Middle Platonists*, 200–202, assimilates Logos in Plutarch both to Eros and to the realm of ideas.

18. *On Isis and Osiris* 372e–f, citing *Timaaeus* 49a and 51a on the receptacle.

19. Damascius, *First Principles* 3.3.2.

Lord of darkness combines the natures of Isis and Seth, the craving for good with the predisposition to destroy.[20]

The irrational soul in matter is the counterpart of the Pythagorean dyad, which is the source of multiplicity, and consequently of evil. God is the monad, transcending all things, identified in myth with both Apollo and Zeus,[21] but best represented, as the E which surmounts the door to Apollo's shrine at Delphi indicates, by the shortest of Greek verbs, *ei*, which means "Thou art" (*E at Delphi* 392a). Since he is to be identified both with being and with the good, he cannot be the cause of evil; Plutarch indeed is scarcely willing to grant that there is such a thing as evil, except as an aberration of the human will. If the highest deity cannot enter the world himself, he can impose the forms upon it through the world-soul, which is mythically represented as the Logos in *On Isis and Osiris*.[22] Below the moon the ministers of providence are the daemons of whom a seeress of Delphi says in the *Symposium* that they occupy a place between gods and mortals. These are the beings who receive our offerings and divulge the future in oracles.[23] Although they are of a nature closer to ours, they are not responsible for evils, even for those perpetrated in the name of piety, and while there is a race of maleficent daemons, their only function is to punish the wicked in the afterlife, thus serving the object of divine justice.[24] The souls of the blessed dead constitute a second race of daemons who, as Hesiod testifies, extend their help to those who are striving to make a virtuous end of the present life.[25] The *daimonion* of Socrates belongs to a third class, equated in the *Timaeus* with the rational intellect.[26] This divine element, though universal in human beings, is inaudible to the mass of us who remain in thrall to our sensual appetites.

Plutarch is offering not an aetiology for the evil in the word but a justification of the popular custom of prayer and sacrifice to beings who, if

20. At the same time, Bianchi, "Plutarch und der dualismus," 363, correctly observes that Plutarch practices "keine Mythologisierung der Ontologie, sondern eine Ontologisierung des Mythos."

21. On the E at Delphi 388f.

22. See 372b–c, 381b and Plutarch, *De iside et Osiride*, 557.

23. *Decline of the Oracles* 418e–f. On the difficulty of ascertaining Plutarch's own convictions in this sportive dialogue, see Schröder, "Plutarch on Oracles," 156–58.

24. See *Tardiness of Divine Punishment* 567c, and on the coherence of this with his other myths, see Deuse, "Plutarch's Eschatological Myths," 191–93.

25. *Decline of the Oracles* 431e–432a, citing Hesiod, *Works and Days* 123, on the silver generation. Cf. *On the Daemon of Socrates* 593d–f.

26. Plato, *Timaeus* 90a, is cited at *Daemon of Socrates* 591d.

they are moved by such oblations, cannot be true divinities.[27] He was not alone in holding that this lower realm is administered on God's behalf by beings who are more akin in nature to its denizens: both Celsus, the first philosophical assailant of Christianity, and a tract *On the World* attributed to Aristotle urge that it would be no more fitting for God to respond to all our importunities than for an emperor to act directly, rather than through the agency of governors or satraps in every portion of his realm.[28] Apuleius recognizes the same three orders of daemons, identifying the souls of the dead with the Manes and Lares of the Roman household and the *daimonion* of Socrates with the Genius whom Romans believed to be set over each of us from the time of birth (*God of Socrates* 15). His function is to convey by dreams and other private signs the divine admonitions that the daemons of the air communicate through portents and oracles (7). While gods and humans have antithetical properties, the daemons are able to act as mediators because they are subject to passion as we are, yet immortal (4–6). Animals as we are, they dwell in an element closer to heaven (11–13), and they share with us and the gods a rational faculty that is given to no other creature. For Apuleius, no less than for Plutarch,[29] daemons are essential instruments of the divine economy, injuring us not by any malice of their own but through our own improvidence and delinquency.

On the Tardiness of Divine Punishments

The speakers in the dialogue *On the Tardiness of Divine Punishment* are Olympichus, Patrocleas, Timon, and Plutarch himself, who narrates the conversation in the first person. We may assume that the others are historical, but we are never introduced to them, as the text begins abruptly with the departure of their Epicurean friend, who assumes, as Epicureans do, that his own harangue refutes in advance any notion of divine rewards or penalties according to our deserts. No lacuna need be suspected, for Plato's *Timaeus* commences with a report of a conversation that had not been preserved, while Cicero gives the first speech to the Epicurean in his treatises *On Ends* and *On the Nature of the Gods*, in order that the weakest argument may be one most quickly superseded. The absentee shows the characteristic arrogance of his tribe, and since he remains anonymous we can reconstruct

27. On his desire to harmonize the speculations of Plato and the testimonies of popular religion, see Brenk, "An Imperial Heritage," 286–94.

28. Origen, *Against Celsus* 8.35; [Aristotle], *On the World* 6.30.

29. A further debt to Maximus of Tyre or to a source of his *Orations* 8 and 9 is indicated by Harrison, "Introduction," 187.

his argument from Plutarch's writings against the Epicurean Colotes. He will have railed against every philosopher in turn, recited the aphorisms of Epicurus as though they were oracles, denounced the supposed impositions of religion without acknowledging either its pleasures or its usefulness to society, and scoffed at the fear of death as though the only cause of this were the expectation of posthumous suffering and not the intellect's natural antipathy to the thought of annihilation.[30] This venom, and its equally humdrum antidotes, all philosophical readers can mix for themselves. The question that exercises the four companions, however, is one that is most acute for the most devout: how is it, if the gods are just and mindful of us, that the punishment of the wicked so often lingers, so that even when it falls we are barely conscious of a link between the reckoning and the crime?

Patrocleas, the first to take up the argument, quotes a dictum of Euripides on divine procrastination, and retorts that suffering ought to be assuaged by immediate retribution, of which Thucydides records at least one true instance.[31] The worst result of delay is that the wronged gain no satisfaction, least of all if they do not even live to witness the elegant requital that the gods are said to reserve for notorious sinners (*Tardiness* 548f). Olympichus now takes up the complaint, observing that if a punishment is too long deferred, the relation of cause and effect will be obscure, and the wrongdoer is more likely to blame his misfortune on chance or fate than on providence (549d). The slow foot of justice, to borrow another saying from Euripides, serves the cause of reformation no better than that of retribution: why should the gods be any less prompt in chastisement than a trainer would be in breaking in a horse? The case against heaven is already so persuasive that Plutarch asks Timon to postpone the "third wave" while he replies to the other two (549e). His first response is to challenge the question itself: how can we, his frail and benighted creatures, question the ordinances of the master-artificer (550a)? If even the laws of the Spartans and the Romans seem absurd to other nations (550b), how can we hope to sift every judgment that matures in the mind of God?

Seeing that this appeal to human nescience is not sufficient, Plutarch suggests that—taking up a word from Plato, though not in its original application[32]—we ought to regard the deferral of divine justice as a paradigm for our own conduct. The wisest have always been reluctant to strike a blow in anger, and Archytas went so far as to spare his slaves when he could not bear

---

30. *That One Cannot Live Pleasantly as an Epicurean* 1102a–b; 1104b–c; 1106f.

31. *Tardiness* 548d, citing Euripides, *Orestes* 420, and Thucydides, *Peloponnesian War* 3.38.1.

32. *Tardiness* 550e, citing *Timaeus* 29e–30a.

them with equanimity (*Tardiness* 551b). Let us consider also, he continues, that the retaliation of suffering on the criminals is the only human expedient for reform or retribution; the gods, being wiser than we, discriminate between the incorrigible sinner, whom they remove from the world at once, and those whose loss would be a greater ill to society than their survival (551d–e). The Athenians were wise enough not to cut short the careers of the offenders who went on to secure their victories over Persia at Marathon, Artemisium, and the Eurymedon (552b–c). The Egyptian law that forbids the execution of a pregnant woman until she has borne her child (552d) is vindicated by the emergence of such men as Pompey and Pericles from a vicious ancestry (553b). Nor should we forget that the crimes of a tyrant may be used as a chastisement for the wrongs committed by those whom they oppress (553a). Furthermore, divine retribution often takes a peculiarly memorable and exemplary form, as when it is decreed that the sword of a murderer should later become the instrument of his own death (553d).

On the one hand, then, the temporary impunity of the malefactor may be of service to others; on the other hand, it is frequently more vexatious to him than the punishment that in any case he is bound to suffer at last. In the meantime, he is distracted by the anticipation of inescapable vengeance (*Tardiness* 554c–556a); it was not only the legendary Clytemnestra who lived her last day repeatedly in dreams (555a). We ought not to be like children at a play who admire the tyrant in his pomp and cannot foresee the end of the story (554b); instead we should compare the life of the unpunished sinner to the hours that a convict spends in prison before his execution or the slow approach of hemlock to the heart (554c). A man who agreed to live among the Getae as the price of a drink of water exclaimed that for an instant of relief he had sold a kingdom (555d): such is the condition of the villain who lives in daily torment long before the posthumous assize.

The picture of the tyrant living in daily apprehension of betrayal, exposure, or assassination was familiar to every student of Plato's *Republic*.[33] Now, however, comes the third wave of Timon. Let us concede, he says, that the gods await their opportunity: with what pretence of justice do they postpone that opportunity to the second or third generations, visiting on the descendants the iniquities of those who, as individuals, go scot-free (*Tardiness* 556f–557e)? Shall we compare divine providence to a river that plunges underground to reappear in a distant region under another name (557e)? In response, Plutarch continues to beg the question of the afterlife,[34] since he implies that there is some sense in which the wrongdoer suffers the penalties

---

33. *Republic* 544c–d, etc.
34. As Olympichus notices at 560a–b.

that are visited on his descendants. Moreover, he argues, it would be as false to deny the unity of a man with his descendants as to deny that the child is the seed of the adult man (559e–560a) and that, whatever Heraclitus says to the contrary, I am accountable in my prime for all the delinquencies of my youth (559a–b). We think it right and reasonable to stigmatise the wrongdoer by destroying his statues (559d): why should not the gods inflict a similar indignity on his descendants, who are organically more of a piece with him than his manufactured image? And again, if Athens transgressed in one generation we think it right that she should be punished in another, because we recognize that bonds of common blood and common action give the city a continuing identity that is as real and integral as that of an individual man (558f–559c). The viciousness that we inherit is more ingrained than that which results from our own indiscretions, and must therefore be purged with more abrasive salts (562a–563b).

We are now at some distance from the thought of Plato, for the burden of all his myths of the afterlife is that every soul is judged for its own deeds at the heavenly tribunal, and that in the next life it will pay the price for no choices but its own. "The blame lies with the chooser: God is blameless." Hereditary taints and vicarious expiations are plot-devices of the tragedians, whom Plato (in contrast to Plutarch) seldom quotes except to deplore their blasphemous representation of the gods. Plutarch's reversion to a belief that Plato thought superstitious is in two ways characteristic of his age. Firstly, as we have noted, it was common for Roman adherents of the Stoa, the Lyceum, and the Academy to pay more respect to popular religion than their founders had done, and Plutarch himself, as a priest of Delphi, had all the more reason to imitate the residual piety rather than the pervasive skepticism of Socrates. Secondly, although he does not share it himself, he must have been acquainted with the suspicion that the transmigration of souls was only a metaphor even for Plato. The Pythagoreans, as we have noted, may have been the first to maintain that the only transmigration into a beast that the soul can suffer is to fall into bestial passions; this conceit was echoed by Platonists of the second century, and we shall see that it recurs in Origen. Plutarch does not reject the doctrine in its literal form, but provides an alternative that may be more credible to certain readers, without entailing that we are conscious and accountable only for one brief span of life.

Nevertheless, the dialogue *On the Tardiness of Divine Punishment* concludes with one of the longest of his embellishments of Plato's myths of the afterlife, and as ever it leaves little doubt that he thought survival after death an essential element in theodicy. The protagonist is a man of dissolute life who falls into a deathlike trance (*Tardiness* 563d). Like Plato's mouthpiece Er in the final book of the *Republic*, he finds himself transported to the afterword, where the first souls that he encounters are as speechless as those of the unfed ghosts in *Odyssey* 11 (564b–c). The soul that comes to guide him—that of a relative who died as a boy—addresses him as Thespesius, although his original name was Aridaeus (564c). Thus he does not need to await a new incarnation before he acquires a new identity. He learns that souls undergo three orders of punishments, the mildest being that of those who have made some redress already by a premature death or bodily tribulation (564e). Those who have enjoyed more licence here must undergo a more exacting purification in the next world (564f; 565a–b), while those who are depraved beyond redemption are sentenced to everlasting torment (564f). Those who can be purged of every imperfection ascend to the plane of Apollo, to which an earthbound soul like that of Thespesius cannot follow them (566d). Those who are bound to return to the present world are prepared by amputation and cautery to inhabit the body assigned to them in accordance with their deserts (567f).

Plutarch on Chance

The Epicurean having departed, opposition is raised in *On the Tardiness of Divine Punishment* to the theses that the gods act in the world with infallible prescience, and that where they refrain from action it is to throw the malefactor upon his own terror and remorse. Yet one of the most common idioms in Greek ascribed prosperity and adversity alike, not to any of the Olympian deities, but to Fortune, who was credited with power and personal agency sufficient to warrant the dedication of temples to her throughout the Roman world. Plutarch himself wrote an essay *On the Fortune of the Romans*, in which he inquires, without reference to other deities, whether Rome's prolonged ascendancy was the gift of fortune, of virtue or of both. Virtue, according to popular report, is noble but useless, fortune bountiful but capricious; yet if Rome owes her empire to one or the other, virtue must be more profitable or fortune more trustworthy than we suppose (*Fortune of the Romans* 316c). The solution, which precedes and informs the review of Roman history, is that just as the world itself was once a cauldron of jarring elements until each prevailed in its proper sphere, so kingdom has striven with kingdom for pre-eminence until there arose a race that had learned to pass on, from generation to generation, the wisdom and fortitude that enabled it to take advantage of doubtful opportunities and accidents of birth (317a–c). Plato had quoted the rejoinder of Themistocles to the Seriphian—"not I had I been from Seriphos, nor you had you been from Athens" (*Republic* 1, 330a)—and Plutarch strikes the same balance when he observes, in a longer essay *On the Fortune of Alexander*, that greatness resides not in the possession of goods but in the use that is made of them. The marble supplies the material of the statue but not the art that gives it form (334f–335e); similarly, after all allowance is made for the occasional luck that rescued Alexander from his own rashness (343e–f), it was his combination of the austere and the philanthropic virtues that enabled him to outdo the philosophers in teaching Hellenic arts and customs to those who were not yet Greeks (329a–c).

Nevertheless, the personification of fortune in these disquisitions is patently rhetorical, for when Plutarch is at his most rigorous he allows neither chance nor fate to contest the sovereignty of the gods. He repudiates what he takes to be the doctrine of the Stoics, that God himself is subject to fate, and argues, in his tract *On Stoic Contradictions*, that in spite of their pretensions to moral freedom, their determinism leaves nothing in our power. That which is fated is that which God himself wills, be it good or evil (*On Stoic Contradictions* 1049e–1051a); what we call chance is a by-product of the irrational activity of the world-soul, and is therefore not independent of all divine agency. Whatever is not determined by these causes lies with us. Plutarch has an Aristotelian horror of *to automaton*, of that which merely happens of itself without any design on the part of either mundane or supramundane agents. This presupposition of divine supremacy was shared by the author of a treatise *On Fate*, preserved in the corpus of Plutarch's works but generally held to be by another hand.[35]

The author's aim, whoever he may be, is to find a place in the sphere of providence for both the apparent determinism of the natural order and the manifest freedom of the human will. It is evident from the conclusion of the treatise that the author's interlocutors are the Stoics, who (as he understands them)[36] base their doctrine that everything is governed by fate on the *a priori* argument that nothing can be without a cause, the empirical observation of regularity in nature, the success of oracles in foretelling the future, the voluntary submission of the wise to that which they see to be unalterable, and the logical point that if we make a statement about the future it must already be either true or false (*On Fate* 574e–f). The author makes no allusion to the decadence of the oracles (the subject of a long dialogue by Plutarch) or to Aristotle's contention that no statement can be definitely true or false that concerns the future choices of a free agent. Plato

35. Valgiglio, ed., *Plutarco: Il fato*, 34–42, surmises that he is one of the writers on fate who are listed by Proclus at *Commentary on the Republic* II, 96.11–13, ed. W. Kroll.

36. Opsomer, "Is Plutarch Really Hostile?," argues that the real Plutarch does not reject Stoic philosophy root and branch, but subordinates to Platonism those elements that he endorses.

alone is his lodestar, as is clear from the introduction, which distinguishes two senses of the *heimarmene* (fate), one signifying an *energeia* or operation and the other an *ousia* or entity (568c). The operation of fate is described in Plato as the dictum of necessity, the legislation of God and the decree of Adrasteia, which acts as an acolyte to God (568c–d). The *ousia* of Fate is none other than the world-soul of the *Timaeus*, which governs with equal benevolence the unwandering heavens, the planetary orbits, and the sublunar realm (568e). But whereas there is no possibility in the two higher domains of any deviation from the natural order, the place below the moon is peopled by agents who are not only free but capable of defying nature in that which is *eph' hêmin*, or in our power.[37]

That which is germane to us encompasses both our reasoning and our appetites. It is also divisible into that which is present and that which is *endekhomenon*, capable of coming to pass or of not coming to pass (*On Fate* 570e–f). Where both these outcomes are consistent with the natural order, it will be our own *prohairesis*, our voluntary decision, that determines which comes to pass (571d). Fate embraces all that is possible, where the possible is that genus that contains both the *endekhomenon* and that which exists or obtains because it is necessary (572e). Under this term the author appears to subsume whatever belongs to the unvarying course of nature, and which therefore cannot be otherwise as a consequence of any choice on our part, though there might not be any logical contradiction in imagining it to be other than it is (571b). The fact that we inhabit this realm of natural necessity, in which certain causes are bound—or, if we will, fated—to bring about certain effects does not rob human agents of their freedom to act as causes. To say that all that exists is subject to fate does not entail that everything happens according to fate, any more than to say that all human acts are subject to law entails that all humans act according to law (570c–e). As the law defines and punishes actions that are not lawful, so fate prescribes the consequences of actions that in themselves are free and therefore cannot be laid at the door of fate (569d–e). The prescriptions of fate, like those of the civic law, are universal, dictating only what will follow from a certain class of actions, but not which or how many actions will be of that class.

Since only that which is definite can be an object of perfect knowledge, the author asserts that only the universal can be a proper object of knowledge for a divine being (*On Fate* 570a). Here again he tacitly, and perhaps unwittingly, follows Aristotle, and his argument for the subordination of fate to

---

37. At this point, pseudo-Plutarch invokes the notion of a preordained return of all things to their original state, for which both Stoic and Platonic antecedents can be offered. On its history, and the apparent inconcinnity in the argument of the treatise, see Burns, *Did God Care?*, 49–50; Opsomer, "The Middle Platonic Doctrine," 159.

divine *pronoia* or providence rests on a maxim that was as dear to Aristotle as to Plato, namely that every efficient cause acts for the sake of a final cause. To complete his demonstration, he posits three orders of providence, the highest of which, the ordinance of the Demiurge, is determined only by his essential goodness and the consequent necessity of imparting his goodness to the whole domain of possibility (572f–573d). Fate, as the manifestation of his benign will, circumscribes the administration of the natural world by the lesser gods, which constitutes the second tier of providence (573e–f).[38] The third is the provision of laws by which the gods are absolved of all blame for our actions, since the soul that perceives the true nature of the world would conform to them even if they had never been promulgated (574a–b). Insofar as it is true, therefore, the doctrine that our world is governed by fate does not so much circumscribe our freedom as explain how the realm of matter can be a theatre for the free choices of the soul.

Alexander of Aphrodisias on Fate

Plutarch as we have seen, opposes the Stoic position on fate, which he understands (perhaps unjustly) to be a strict determinism, allowing no possibility that fate can be frustrated either by accident or by rational agency. Of the Stoics themselves there is little to say in this chapter, for both the slave Epictetus and the Emperor Marcus Aurelius write homiletically rather than analytically, making no advance on the typical Stoic positions that only good can proceed from God, that in themselves prosperity and adversity are indifferent, and that therefore we have only to maintain our inward rectitude to be proof against all evil from without.[39] It is nonetheless to one of their antagonists in this period—not a Platonist but the Peripatetic Alexander of Aphrodisias—that we owe our longest vindication of human liberty against fatalism.[40] This is one of his treatises that is not a commentary on Aristotle, and he breaks with his master by not commencing with the *koinai ennoiai* (common notions), which in this case he believes to be too discordant (*On Fate* 165.25–27). Some who maintain that fate is a cause believe nonetheless, with Homer, that things can happen in spite of fate, while others impute to it

38. The authority for the first is Plato, *Timaeus* 29d–30a, and for the second *Timaeus* 42d–e. On similar taxonomies in Apuleius, *On Plato* 12 and others, see Sharples, "Threefold Providence."

39. On the religious elements in Marcus and his unusual devaluation of the body, see Rutherford, *The Meditations of Marcus Aurelius*.

40. For text, translation, and commentary, see Sharples, *Alexander of Aphrodisias on Fate*. On the significance of Alexander's appeal to the agent's power of doing otherwise, see Bobzien, "The Late Conception."

all that disappoints them, while ascribing to their own merits all that prospers (166.6–13). Instead, we must begin by assigning fate to its place among the four causes—efficient, final, formal, and material (166.22–167.16). It is evidently conceived as an efficient cause, but does it bring about its effects with a purpose or with none. All usage associates fate with a final end: is it therefore a function of nature or of art? If it were a function of art, it would be capable of acting otherwise, for reason is free to decide its own objects (168.11–19). It is nature who pursues her own ends infallibly, yet it is possible to act contrary to nature. It follows that, if fate is equated with nature (169.20), it is not incoherent to speak of action contrary to fate. Hence, it is that prophecies sometimes fail and that Socrates was able to refrain from the vices to which he was predisposed.

The proponents of necessity (whom we may take to be the Stoics, although they are not named)[41] are guilty of a number of confusions. For example, they assert that what happens by chance is fated, but by chance we mean the unintended result of intended actions (*On Fate* 172.21–28), which like everything that we do by intent could have been done otherwise. This distinction between the contingent (that which could be otherwise) and the necessary (that which could not be otherwise) is persistently occluded in their reasoning; yet observation tells us that, whereas fire cannot fail to be hot, it is possible for water both to be heated and to be cooled (175.19–22). It is equally nonsensical to argue that an event may be contingent, because it is logically preventable, and at the same time fated because the means of prevention is fated not to occur (176.14–177.5). Against this sophistry, Alexander upholds the standard Peripatetic view that nothing can be foreknown with certainty unless it is predetermined. Aristotle was therefore right to argue, in the celebrated example of the sea-battle,[42] that I cannot today be certain whether or not such an event will occur tomorrow, and hence that if I predict that "there will be a sea-battle tomorrow," this proposition has neither definite truth nor definite falsehood at the time when I utter it (177.22–178.1).

Alexander echoes Aristotle when he charges necessitarians with denying us any power of deliberation—the faculty that sets us above all animals (*On Fate* 186.6–189.21)[43]—and any accountability for our choices, which would make us amenable to reward or punishment. He shows himself a man of the second century, however, when he turns this into a question

41. Bobzien, *Determinism and Freedom*, 368–96, proposes Philopator as the chief interlocutor.

42. See Aristotle, *On Interpetation* 18b–19b, with Gaskin, *The Sea Battle*.

43. Sorabji, "A Neglected Chapter," 248, suspects that this is inconsistent with Aristotle, *Nicomachean Ethics* 1111b8–9.

about divine providence: how could rewards and punishments be allotted after death to mere automata who could not have chosen to act but as they did (188.12–17; 191.1). After further expatiations on the difference between effects that are inevitable and those that are not inevitable but contingent (as, for instance, when a man elects to become the cause of a child), Alexander returns to the gods, forestalling the argument that if they exercise providence through their oracles, it must follow that they can predict the future, and therefore that the future is ineluctable. If they have foreknowledge at all, he rejoins, it is foreknowledge of the contingent as contingent (201.17–19);[44] it remains to be shown, however, that they have even this (201.27–29), and if the price of certainty is to make the god himself bring about the misfortune that he prophesies, all religion is at an end (202.27–203.12).

Whereas Aristotle was commonly thought to have banished providence from the sublunar realm,[45] Alexander appears to maintain the contrary view in his *Problems and Solutions*.[46] Here he admits two definitions of providence: according to one, which encompasses both the eternal and the mutable, all that is moved by its proper object is subject to providence, while according to the other, the object of providence is that for the sake of which the rest are moved. In this second sense, providence governs only the bodily realm below the moon (*Problems and Solutions* 41.4–15). Alexander appears to know nothing of the doctrine that only things above the moon are subject to providence, which was commonly ascribed to Aristotle outside the Lyceum. In the second book of his *Problems and Solutions*, the twenty-first question is whether the world is a primary or an accidental object of divine governance. The notion of an accidental providence is dismissed at once as a contradiction in terms (65.25–29); on the other hand, it is also agreed that if it were the function of "the divine" to exercise providence in this world, it would exist for the sake of the world—a patently impious conclusion—and would be obliged to trouble itself with a host of matters that fall below the dignity of a supernal intellect (69.28–70.6).

---

44. With Alcinous, *Didascalicus* 26.2, Alexander seems willing to concede to Apollo the knowledge that if Laius has a son the son will kill him. On "conditional fate" in the Middle Platonists, see Sharples, "The Stoic Background."

45. See, e.g., Diogenes Laertius, *Lives of the Philosophers* 5.32.

46. See further Edwards, *Aristotle and Early Christian Thought*, 29–30; Sharples, "Alexander of Aphrodisias on Providence," 199–200, adds the caveat that the *Problems and Solutions* may have been compiled by Alexander's pupils.

Lucian: Scoffer or Skirmisher?

Lucian of Samosata has been called the Voltaire of antiquity, a comparison that does less than justice to the moral ardor of the French deist or to the sulphurous blend of bigotry and hypocrisy that characterized the religion of his age. While he scoffs at Christianity as a new and superstitious cult that harmed its votaries more than it harmed society, he can seldom be accused of writing a book in anger except when his proficiency in Greek was called into question. A Syrian of modest birth, he made his fortune as an itinerant sophist or public speaker, then settled in Athens to write the saline masterpieces to which he owes his fame.[47] Ridicule was the art in which he excelled, whether his butt was the ignorant sophist, the literary charlatan, the insincere philosopher, or the ubiquitous vanity of human wishes. Above all he is remembered for his satires on poetic and mythological depictions of the gods. Since the tradition of laughing at the Olympians is as old as the tradition of worshipping them, we must not be too quick to call him an atheist;[48] on the other hand, he speaks well of Epicurus and puts some eloquent barbs into the mouths of the Cynics Demonax, Lycinus, and Menippus, even if the joke seems sometimes to be at their expense.[49] While, therefore, his own convictions remain unfathomable, the two works in which Zeus is visibly worsted, *Zeus Cross-Examined* and *Zeus the Tragedian*, present the case against providence with a trenchancy that puts all belief on trial.

Zeus the Tragedian opens with an exchange of iambic trimeters between Zeus and the other Olympians, which is followed an assembly of all the gods to hear the next round of an unconcluded debate between the Stoic Timocles and the Epicurean Damis (*Zeus the Tragedian*, chapter 4).[50] The proceedings are delayed by a confusion of tongues, since gods speak only the language of their own worshippers (13), and by the refusal of those who are cast in gold or marble to sit beside deities of a less precious mold (9–10). Zeus, eschewing the verse that is his customary idiom, delivers a prolix allocution (15–18), but is quickly discomfited, however, by the satirical Momus, who reminds him that humans seldom see any evidence of divine justice (19), but are well acquainted with the scandals of Olympus (20–21). Apollo

---

47. On the chronology of his life and his intellectual formation, see Jones, *Culture and Society*, 6–23 and 167–59.

48. See Edwards, "Was Lucian a Despiser of Religion?"

49. See further Helm, *Lucian und Menipp*.

50. Coenen, ed., *Lukian: Zeus Tragodos*, 46, identifies this Damis with a rich Corinthian at Lucian, *Dialogues of the Dead* 27.7. Anderson, *Philostratus*, 240–57, suggests that he is remembered in Arabic literature under the name of the atheist Dini.

predicts the outcome of the debate in a thunderous oracle, which Momus pronounces hopelessly obscure (31)

When the human protagonists join issue, Timocles urges that we cannot account for the harmony of the cosmos and its regular operations unless we postulate an intelligent designer (*Zeus the Tragedian* 38). Damis simply refuses to draw the inference, and Timocles cites Homer as a witness to the providential activity of the gods (39). Damis demands to know which of the crimes imputed to them by Homer has convinced him of their benevolence. While Momus chuckles, Timocles appeals to the tragedians but Damis retorts that only a fool would imagine a stage-performer to be a true representative of divinity (41). Timocles at first can only bluster that if there are shrines there must be gods who receive our offerings (42); Damis rejoins that no two nations agree as to what will please them, and when Timocles reminds him that there are oracles, he asks why beings who know so much speak only to deceive (43). Timocles now brings out his sovereign proof, a synthesis of Plato and Aristotle: if even a ship cannot steer without a pilot, how can the world maintain its course with no god at the helm (46)? Zeus is enraptured, but Damis observes that many a ship is piloted by the worst blackguard among the crew (47). To this the champion of providence has no answer but to chase him from the stage (52).

In *Zeus Cross-Examined* there are only two characters, Zeus and his human petitioner Cyniscus. The latter, a Cynic, seeks no material blessing but a resolution of a Homeric dilemma: how can it be that Zeus is at once the unassailable tyrant of the gods and yet the meek executioner of the decrees of fate (*Zeus Cross-Examined*, chapter 1)? Undeterred by Zeus's threats against those who would put an end to prayer and sacrifice (6), he exacts from him an admission that the fates are inexorable (7). That being so, Cyniscus opines, the gods themselves are not secure, as the sufferings of Prometheus, Cronus, and Hephaestus testify (8); either the gods themselves are slaves to destiny, or a providence must be imagined that is superior to gods and fate alike (9–10). Zeus pleads that the gods are allowed to prophesy: Cyniscus replies that oracles are futile, firstly because whatever is truly predicted cannot be altered (12–13), and secondly because they can be interpreted in contradictory senses (15). Zeus now claims for the gods the office of punishing and rewarding the dead (16o17), but again the Cynic is prompt with his rebuttal: it is patently inequitable to punish those who had no power to do otherwise, and if fate is the mistress of all it is not in our power either to sin or not to sin (18).

Literary Reflections

Maximus of Tyre is the author of forty-one tracts in which the stock topics of public debate are varnished with a mixture of Stoic and Platonic commonplaces. The forty-first is entitled "Since God Does Good, What Is the Source of Evil?"[51] Alexander the Great, he begins, desired to learn nothing from his father Ammon but the source of the Nile ("Since God Does Good," 41.1a–c); the benefit to the world would have been incalculably greater had his question concerned the origin of evil (41.3a). God, the Creator and Father of all, can no more intend to cause evil instead of good than the sun can fail to dispense its light to every part of the cosmos (41,2c–d). Such evil as proceeds from his actions therefore must be either incidental or illusory. The sculptor cannot work without some attrition of his material; we cannot expect the blacksmith's hammer to strike without a spark (41.4e). By the same token, so long as vicissitude is the law of nature, nothing can come to life if nothing dies, and the equilibrium of the elements cannot be maintained unless there is sometimes plague in Athens, an earthquake in Sparta, a flame from the bowels of Etna (41.4g–h). We have at least the security of knowing in what region each phenomenon occurs (41.4h–i). We are less disposed to perceive a more immediate source of evil in our own vices (41.5a). In accordance with the same principle that we see in the revolution of the seasons, God has created two living races: animals, resourceful in body but destitute of reason, and humans, more feeble in body but endowed with a rational soul that is capable of surviving death (41.5c–d). The body is a burden and a reproach to us, in cold and heat and in every stage of life; still more pernicious (as Maximus argues at length in *Oration* 7) are the maladies of the soul as it revolves from grief to fear, from fear to wrath, from wrath to envy. Maximus, platitudinous to the last, reminds us that the chariot of reason has two horses, and that it lies with us to ensure that the spirit is not outrun by lust (41.5.i–l).[52]

The same optimism pervades a Latin translation, dubiously attributed to Apuleius,[53] of a work with the title *Asclepius*, of which fragments also survive in Coptic and in the original Greek. Although the Coptic is found among the Nag Hammadi Codices[54] and the Latin is generally treated as

51. For commentary, see Trapp, *Maximus of Tyre*, 321–30.

52. Despite the allusion to Plato's *Phaedrus*, Reydams-Schils, "Maximus of Tyre," 137 observes that Maximus seems to incline to the Stoic position that "nothing is, strictly speaking, evil."

53. See Hunink, "Apuleius and the *Asclepius*."

54. The Coptic text of Nag Hammadi Codices VI.7 is judged more primitive than the Latin by Mahé, "Remarques d'un latiniste."

part of the Hermetic Corpus,[55] it has none of the Gnostic features that appear in other texts from both collections. In its present form the argument is poorly arranged and the teacher's replies to the questions of his pupil are often elliptical or obscure. There is no doubt that he holds all things to be directly or indirectly created by an omnipotent deity, who transcends all sensory apprehension, all distinction of sex, and all our powers of imagination (*Asclepius* 20). His first creation is the visible cosmos, a second God,[56] and his next is the human soul, which is to be capable of apprehending the beauty of the cosmos (*Asclepius* 6). The matter that he employs is coeval with him, but whereas God neither comes into being nor changes, matter is the universal precondition of change and generation, without being itself subject to either.[57] Heaven, the lesser deities, and the daemons are all said to act as intermediate causes, although their functions are not clearly delineated. In a moment of lucidity the teacher distinguishes three tiers of agency: *Heimarmenê*, or fate, is identical with the will of the supreme God, while necessity determines the consequences of *Heimarmene*, and order ensures that the things produced by necessity are consistent with the harmony of the cosmos (39).

When the pupil is bold enough to ask why there is evil in the world, he receives little more than a hint that evil resides not so much in things as in our false perception and use of them (*Asclepius* 16). Souls that excel in virtue attain the condition of the gods (23), while those that carry their imperfections into the next life will either undergo purification or be thrown into the abyss if the presiding daemon finds them incorrigible (28). The author's picture of Hades is borrowed largely from the *Phaedo*, but he also echoes the *Statesman* when he prophesies that as the world grows old the shrines and statues of the gods will fall and that Egypt, which is an image of heaven itself, will be disfigured by superstition (24–25).[58] By the bounty of God, however, a new world will arise in which true worship will be restored (26).

---

55. For commentary, see Copenhaver, *Hermetica*, 213–60.

56. *Asclepius* 3. Cf. Lactantius, *Epitome of Divine Institutes* 37.5. His borrowings from the *Asclepius* and other Hermetic writings are collected by Scott, *Hermetica*, vol. 4, 9–27.

57. Though matter is imbued with spirit from the outset: see *Asclepius* 14, with Genesis 1:2. For a more Platonic account of matter, see *Asclepius* 34.

58. On this adaptation of the much older Potter's Oracle, see Copenhaver, *Hermetica*, 238–46. Both the Coptic text and the version known to Lactantius antedate the destruction of the last pagan temples in Egypt in the late fourth century.

Epilogue: Fiction as Philosophy

There is no philosophy that hands the reins of life entirely to chance or fortune, but without this fickle agent there would be no plot for the Greek or Latin novel. Her customary stratagems are encounters with travelling strangers, kidnap by pirates, deaths that prove to be counterfeit—in short, a catalogue of accidents that would never be replicated in ordinary life. The most fantastic is the *Golden Ass* of Apuleius, also known as the *Metamorphoses*, the main plot of which begins with his transformation of the hero (another Lucius, and also from Madaura)[59] into an ass as a result of a rash experiment with magic. He is informed that he can recover his human shape by eating roses dedicated to Isis; his asinine form, however, makes him an easy quarry for thieves and a legitimate object of purchase, thus enabling fortune to pass him from hand to hand with repeated indignities, until Isis at last appears to him in a dream (*Golden Ass* 11.3–6). She instructs him to join a procession in her honor and to snatch the roses from the hand of a priest. Restored to his human form, he becomes an initiate into the mysteries of Isis (11.23) and the narrative ends with his ordination into the greater mysteries of Osiris (11.30). If Apuleius were not a known philosopher, we might suspect that all these vicissitudes were invented only to furnish occasions for undetected eavesdropping on the part of Lucius; one of the stories that he overhears as an ass, however, is the tale of Cupid and Psyche, in which the character whose name means soul falls victim to her own curiosity.[60] Banished from the presence of love, she makes her way back only after a subterranean journey resembling that which the ass will undergo in the course of his initiation. All agree that this tale invites an allegory, and Mithras, the priest of Isis (11.22), seems to supply one in the last book when he tells Lucius that his fall into the body of an ass was both the consequence and the cure of the moral decadence of his soul (11.15).[61]

Should the whole of the *Golden Ass* be read, then, as a Platonic allegory?[62] Or should we maintain, on the contrary, that even the few solemn passages should be understood in accordance with the pervasively ludic character of the book? If Lucius, as a character, was convinced by the

59. The protagonist of the novel is also said to be from Madaura at 11.27. Nevertheless, some allegorical readings of the words *patrium larem* (paternal hearth) at 11.26 are noted by Griffiths, *Apuleius of Madauros*, 326.

60. For differing opinions, see Dowden, "Cupid and Psyche" and O'Brien, "'For every tatter.'"

61. His reliability is questioned by Winkler, *Auctor and Actor*, 210–15.

62. See the seminal discussions of C. Schlam, "Platonica in the Metamorphoses" and *The Metamorphoses of Apuleius*, 12–14.

interpretation of Mithras, why does Lucius the narrator continue to speak of his asinine self as the sport of fortune rather than as a patient of divine justice?[63] In all he offers us three ways of construing his adventures: as a chance concatenation of improbabilities, as an odyssey from the magical to the miraculous, and as a pilgrimage, under invisible guidance, from darkness to light. None of these readings can be proved to be closer than the others to the intention of Lucius Apuleius the author, even when it is agreed that the author's intention is what the reader should be seeking. The *Golden Ass* is a suitably ambiguous microcosm of its time, which, as we noted at the beginning of this chapter, has been characterized by modern scholars both as an age of anxiety, in which the sense of human autonomy withered, and as an age of appetition, which had ceased to be conscious of an unbridged gulf between the human and the divine.

---

63. Fortune is hostile at *Golden Ass* 8.24, benign at 7.20 and 11.15, perhaps calumniated at 7.2. See Harrison, *Apuleius: A Latin Sophist*, 248–59, for a "satirical" reading.

6

Early Christian Reflections on Evil

THE GOSPELS, WHILE THEY offer no general explanation either for sin or for sickness except for the evil of the human heart, attribute certain instances of both moral and mental infirmity to malign agents known collectively as demons, and individually by such names as Beelzebub, Satan, and Belial. As Satan is said to have fallen from heaven and shares with his angels the fire that has been prepared for him, it seems likely that the evangelists would recognize in him the dragon of Revelation 12, who led a third of the heavenly host in an insurrection against its maker, tempted Eve in the guise of a serpent, and continues to harry the church with persecution. Jesus encounters the devil and his legions chiefly as occupants of the bodies of lunatics, all of whom he cures with a word, and with the threefold purpose of concealing his own identity, fulfilling his mission as servant of God, and demonstrating that the kingdom of God is now not merely "at hand" but "upon you" (Matthew 12:28).[1] There is little if any precedent for either possession or exorcism in pagan or Jewish sources before the New Testament, and the expulsion of demons was regarded by early evangelists

---

1. Dodd, *Parables of the Kingdom*, 36–37, contends that because the verbs *eggizein* (draw near) and *phthanein* (arrive) can be used to translate the same Hebrew verb, the translators must regard them as synonyms. But surely this rather implies that the verb was felt to exceed the semantic range of either (just as "do" and "make" are both required to translate the Greek verb *poiein*). If Matthew uses *phthanein* of the kingdom of God (12:28) and *eggizein* of the kingdom of heaven (4:17), it may be to hint at the contrast that he draws clearly enough at 13:41–43 between the Son of Man's kingdom in this world and that of the Father in heaven.

as a self-interpreting miracle. The devil is the prince of this world at John 12:31 and the god of this world for Paul, who (in contrast to John) does not proclaim that he is cast out (2 Corinthians 4:4). On the contrary, Paul hands delinquent Christians over to Satan, who appears to play a role comparable to that of the daemons who punish the most flagitious sinners after death in Plato.[2] Satan does not always wait for his prey, and if he fails to tempt Jesus into disobedience, it is he who precipitates the death of Jesus by entering into the heart of Judas (Luke 22.:3; John 13:27). But for the prayers of Jesus, he would have sifted Peter like wheat (Luke 22:31); no such protection is extended to the saints of the late second century, who could not account for the massacres at Lyons and Vienne except by supposing that God for a season had chosen to let the devil reign unchecked.

It is, of course, men who inflict the tortures on Christians, Satan being only the instigator. In the Old Testament Satan is given power to destroy the property of Job and to disfigure his body with sores; this, however, is fable, and in passages purporting to be historical he is capable only of putting the thought of sin into other minds. Even Job, insofar as he is a cipher for God's servant Israel, raises no universal problem of evil, but only the question why God tarries so long in the vindication of his elect. Gentile Christians, schooled in philosophy, as the apologists were, were predisposed to read the Old Testament with other eyes, and to ask why the God who had sent his Son as the Savior for all should have allowed all the nations, not only Israel, to fall into such a state of abjection. The Gnostics, as we gave seen, had answered in a manner that put God himself on trial: the apologists, who had abandoned the religion of their compatriots for that of the Jews, could not transfer the blame from the Demiurge to the pagan gods, for the latter had no claim to be the authors of creation. Even to mar creation was more than the prophets and psalmists appeared to grant to the unseeing idols whom their worshippers carved and carried about at will.

The only active maleficence in the world that does not proceed from human beings proceeds from the fallen angels, and the stratagem by which they defy their Creator is suggested by Paul's teaching that, on the one hand, an idol is "nothing in the world" (1 Corinthians 8:4), while on the other those who honor an idol are entering into fellowship with demons (10:21). In other words, it is *not the idol itself* that causes evil but the soul that forsakes the true God for this delusive object of reverence. The demons take advantage of our folly, but have otherwise little capacity to injure us: the apologists never go further than to credit them with some power to

---

2. 1 Corinthians 5:5; 1 Timothy 1:20. For a recent discussion, see Moses, "Physical and/or Spiritual Exclusion?"

inflict disease, for which warrant could be found in Job.[3] The evidence that demons were not only the putative objects but the real disseminators of false religion was furnished by the Book of Enoch, which was shown by at least two allusions in the New Testament to be authoritative if not canonical (Jude 14; 1 Peter 3:19–20). Here it is related that the angels who descended to mate with mortal women also became the inventors of those demiurgic arts by which men shape not only weapons against the earth and one another but counterfeit images of the divine, translating the invisible God, as Paul said, into the likeness of four-footed beings (Romans 1:22–23). In thus unmasking the origins of pagan cult, however, the apologists did not allege that the angels had merely diverted to themselves the veneration that we owed to our Creator; to explain the absence of any cult of Satan under his own name, they advanced a theory consistent with their own scriptures, but with a supplement that pagans could not deny without disavowing a widespread tradition of their own.

Apologetic Theories of False Religion

Christian apologists of the second century zealously embraced the Lucretian doctrine that the chief cause of the evils that religion purports to assuage is religion itself: in Greek there is no generic term for what we now call religion,[4] but Christianity was sufficiently distinguished from the objects of attack by the designation *philosophia*. Eclectic in all that was not already thought to have been determined by the scriptures, this philosophy could avail itself of insights that had escaped the Epicureans, unmasking vice at its origins where they suspected only vanity, and proving it to be a more chronic distemper than either Lucretius or Plutarch imagined when they held up human sacrifice as the worst atrocity of superstition. The argument that human wickedness was as much the cause as the consequence of false religion could be demonstrated easily from Greek myth, if one followed Plato in assuming that the self-declared sons of the gods had spoken reliably of their own fathers (*Timaeus* 40d). No doubt this is playful, and so too, we presume, was the travelogue of Euhemerus of Messene, in which this Hellenistic romancer purports to have come to an unknown island and to have found there a stele, or pillar, on which the deeds that poets ascribe to the gods were narrated instead as those of human kings and adventurers

---

3. Tatian, *Oration* 16; Minucius Felix, *Octavius* 26. Both imply that the demon affects the body through the mind.

4. *Thrêskeia* is conventionally translated as "cult" and *eusebeia* as "piety."

in a forgotten age.[5] Nevertheless, our chief source of information on Euhemerus, the *Universal History* of Diodorus Siculus, commences its account of each nation in turn with a summary of its myths, in which the gods are portrayed as ancestors rather than immortal overseers of human affairs. Nor can we be certain that any satire was intended by Philo of Byblos when he translated or fabricated an ancient text in which the same trope is applied to the Phoenician pantheon.[6] Theophilus of Antioch, however, reckons Euhemerus among the notorious atheists of antiquity (*To Autolycus* 7), asserting for his own part that this name cannot be justly applied to one who has merely exposed the true identity of impostors. Athenagoras informs his pagan readers that they have been duped into worshipping their fellow-mortals (*Embassy* 25–26, 28, 30); like Tatian, who is conscious that the same indictment has been brought against Christians, he demands to know what thaumaturge other than Christ has performed any work of healing after his death (*Embassy* 26). He and Clement of Alexandria cite with pleasure the hymn in which Callimachus alludes to the grave of Zeus, and Clement also opines that mysteries began as games in honor of the dead.[7]

Religion is thus the worship not of imaginary deities but of real men, and one of the manifest ills that it breeds (as Plato divined)[8] is the direct imitation of their crimes. Fear of death, on the other hand, is not the root of superstition, as Epicurus imagined, but an incentive to piety once the false myths of the afterlife are exploded. For of course, on the Christian view, there is a hell, since we can be neither our own saviors nor our own torturers, and even a cult of the dead is less pernicious than one in which they are only the ostensible beneficiaries, while those who haunt the altars and consume our oblations are beings of deeper and more inveterate malice. The argument that the gods of shrines and oracles were demons masquerading as higher deities appeared to be corroborated by Platonists such as Plutarch and Apuleius,[9] who held that, while the true gods are inaccessible to our petitions, they delegate the exercise of special providence to lesser beings, subtler in body and more percipient in intellect than humans, though neither omniscient nor eternal. The term *daimon*, which was thought to imply sagacity, becomes pejorative only when Porphyry writes, in his treatise *On Abstinence*, that the daemons who require sacrifice are usurpers rather than

---

5. See now Winiarczyk, *The "Sacred History."*

6. See Baumgarten, *Phoenician History.*

7. Callimachus, *Hymn to Zeus* 8; Titus 1:12.

8. Plato, *Republic* 396c–398b. See further Nadaff, *Exiling the Poets.*

9. On these authors as unwitting precursors of Christian thought, see Rankin, *Athenagoras*, 63–66.

intermediaries, falsely assuming the names of their superiors and sending plague and famine upon whole peoples who refuse to stain their altars with innocent blood.[10] Christians were wary of ascribing such power to demons, except by occasional permission of God,[11] but they had seen abundant evidence of their thirst for incense and the blood of martyrs. They also possessed, in the Book of Enoch, the record of an ancient fall of angels who descended to earth for love of mortal women. Banished from their celestial home, Justin tells us, they avenged themselves by sowing idolatry and polytheism among the nations. In this machination they had at least four objects to enslave the soul by superstition (*First Apology* 14.1), to substitute their own images for those of God (9.1), to wrest for themselves the offices and honors that we owe to God alone (12.5) and to make sexual prey of women and young boys (5.2). Their trumpery includes the sending of nocturnal images and the transmission of deceitful oracles through the souls of the dead (18.3). The allusion to fornication seems to bespeak an acquaintance with the Book of Enoch, or at least with Philo's reading of Genesis 6:1, according to which the defection of the wicked angels was prompted by their desire to copulate with mortal women.[12] The account of demonic imposture at oracles purposely conflates the souls of the dead (who were believed in certain cases to have become tutelary spirits) with the denizens of the air whom both Apuleius and Plutarch, in their treatises *On the God of Socrates*, recognized as intermediaries between gods and mortals.

Justin therefore ascribes some prescience to the demons, in order to explain the concoction of rituals and myths that anticipated the work of Christ. His pupil Tatian speaks of an evil spirit dwelling in matter (*Oration* 12), and it is likely that both these Christian philosophers, when they read Plato, agreed with Plutarch[13] in ascribing an evil soul to the receptacle or substrate of creation as the cause of its mobility and resistance to the imposition of form. The African Tertullian follows Enoch in holding that the pagan gods are angels, creatures only a little higher than ourselves, who abandoned heaven to cull the pleasures of the flesh.[14] Both he and Minucius Felix believe, with Justin, that these demons were imprisoned in the

10. See chapter 8. For comparison of Greek and Christian demonologies, see Edwards, "Greeks and Demons."

11. See, e.g., Origen, *Against Celsus* 8.23, overlooked in Edwards, "Greeks and Demons."

12. On the versatility of demons in Justin, see Proctor, *Demonic Bodies*, 91–100. Reed, *Fallen Angels*, 137–39 observes that at *Trypho* 79 the belief in the fall of the angels is stigmatized as a Christian error.

13. *On Isis and Osiris* 369e, a tendentious reading of Plato, *Laws* 896a–897b.

14. Tertullian, *Apology* 35.2; *On idolatry* 5; *Veiling of Virgins* 7.4.

lower realm, and took their revenge by imposing themselves as gods upon the nations (Minucius Felix, *Octavius* 26; Tertullian, *Apology* 23). Neither appears to have heard of the dereliction of the oracles; neither admits the distinction that some pagans drew between denizens of these shrines and the deities who are worshipped in their own temples.[15] Both hold that a demon may enthral a human body, that his presence may engender disease, and that only the name of Jesus Christ has the power to exorcise him.[16] Neither, therefore, can permit an act of deference to an idol. Whereas, however, Minucius denounces only the absurdity of such genuflections, the fiery Tertullian warns that to bow to wood and stone is to flatter the powers who rule the world through human puppets, and hence to become their accomplices in persecution.[17] He repeatedly forbids Christians to hold a magistracy or even to join the legions, because no service to the Roman state can be *sine pompa diaboli*.[18] The Christian will be always a private figure, obedient to the emperor (*Apology* 30.1), but immune to the overtures of his unseen masters, whether they operate by force or subterfuge.

Tatian and Athenagoras

Tatian, said to have been a pupil of Justin, concurs in identifying the gods of the nations with the retinue of the "firstborn" angel (*Oration* 7), who, having been transformed into a demon by his own ignorance and contumacy, set about the creation of a fraudulent pantheon with Zeus at its head (8). Because they have now assumed bodies that are visible to eyes illumined by the Spirit (15), the demons have imbibed the malevolent spirit that dwells in matter (12).[19] They are therefore all the more eager to propagate the doctrine of fate, which subjects the mind to the same implacable laws that coerce the body (9). It is through our members that they achieve their purposes,

15. See, e.g., Apuleius, *On the God of Socrates* 13–14.

16. See especially Minucius Felix, *Octavius* 27; Tertullian, *Apology* 22.4.

17. Demons are fattened by incense at *On Idolatry* 11.2; the Christian may be a spectator at a sacrifice but may not assists (ibid. 16–17).

18. See Tertullian, *On Spectacles* 24.2, with Danièlou, *Origins of Latin Christianity*, 412–18. Some understand this *pompa* to be the host that fell with Satan, others that the word denotes the apparatus of prayer and ceremony that invariably accompanied the exercise of public office.

19. Matter is wholly other than God because it depends on him for its existence, not because it is an equipollent principle: see *Oration* 5.3, with Torchia, *Creation and Contingency*, 151–53. As Trelenberg argues in *Tatianos. Oratio ad Graecos*, 33, matter is baneful because we misconceive it as an independent principle (*Oration* 11.4, 17.6 and 19); by the same principle, while we have nothing to fear from fate, we may be betrayed by demons into fatalism (*Oration* 8.1, cited on p. 47).

colluding with those whose bodily or mental ailments predispose them to evil (17). While they are not human souls (16), they are capable both of perverting minds and of troubling the body, though not, as they pretend, of effecting a cure (17). They are not to be believed when they take the credit for any naturally caused convulsion (16), nor when they teach that souls are naturally immortal (16). The true doctrine is that souls are sustained by God for reward and punishment: the demons will suffer greater woes than those whom they have misled (14), while souls who resist their intrigues will be rewarded in due measure (13). As they were driven from heaven, so we have been driven by sin from a higher earth to a lower one (20), but the wings of the fallen soul may sprout again if, like Tatian himself (29), we perceive the vanity of the festivals held in honor of the demons (22). Reason tells us that if the ancient myths are true the demons deserve no homage (21), and that since the books of Moses are older than any of the poets, we ought to give more credence to his revelations than to theirs (40).

Where Tatian embellishes his master's claims, it is Athenagoras who gives philosophical cogency to Justin's aetiology of religion.[20] We do not have to choose between a cult of the dead and a cult of demons because the latter was surreptitiously achieved by the promotion of the former, it being obvious to the demons that they would not be worshipped under their proper forms. The critique of polytheism in Athenagoras is a logical catena of all four arguments that had been urged against it in previous apologies. He is not content to argue episodically (1) that pagans are serving demons, (2) that their cults originate in the worship of elements, (3) that idols are not proper objects of reverence, and (4) that the beings commemorated in religious effigies were as short-lived as the worshippers. Instead, he undertakes to demonstrate (1) that because the captain of the demons is also the prince of matter he will naturally (2) desire to make us thralls of matter,[21] his method of doing so being (3) to introduce material objects of worship, which will be seductive (4) because they represent not the demons themselves, who are obviously entitled to no honors, but beings who are entitled to all the esteem that a creature can owe to another instrument of the Creator.

1. Matter, for Athenagoras, is a creation of God, but the stewardship of the material world was entrusted to a being who—though not by nature evil, as Tatian may have held—has now become hostile to everything that is good in his Creator (*Embassy* 24.3–6). If he and his

20. This discussion is taken from my "From Justin to Athenagoras."

21. We cannot say that matter is the proper home of Satan because, as Torchia observes (*Creation and Contingency*, 134), Athenagoras considers it not so much evil as "non-existent in the absence of God's creative fiat" (cf. *Embassy* 15.1).

myrmidons cling to the blood and carcases of slain beasts, it is because they have succumbed to the lure of matter: we may turn to their votaries, the pagan poets, for illustrations of the sins that accrue from this infatuation (26.2; 29.2–3, etc.).

2. It appears to have been widely held in the time of Athenagoras that only a soul could account for the animation and indocility of the receptacle on which the Demiurge superimposed the forms.[22] He himself construes *Timaeus* 30a as a paradigmatic description of the human soul in chapter 27, where he writes that it is typical of all souls to be propelled by diverse currents, giving birth to specious images.[23] The last notion may owe something to his contemporary Numenius, who had imagined the fall of a "second god" into the matter that contained his own reflection. The turbulence of the soul is a sign of its natural affinity to the medium that has now been colonized by the rebellious demons; contumacy within and temptation without of causes of kindred origin, which conspire to make apostasy the usual, though never the inevitable, corollary of the soul's embodiment.

3. One of Paul's best-known sayings is that the nations have paid to the creature the honors due to the Creator (Romans 1:25). Another, addressed to Israel, is that the pot has no right to ask the potter "Why hast thou made me thus?" (9:21) This is his refashioning of a conceit that had been employed for a different purpose at Jeremiah 18:2, where it meant that God may choose to inflict a season of affliction on his people before he redeems them; for Paul it appears to mean that God determines for himself who is of his people and who is not. When Athenagoras reclaims the simile at *Embassy* 15.2, the potter is still God but the pot now signifies the creation, in itself neither good nor reprobate. The gentile is no longer the vessel that God has destined for glory in place of Israel, but the fool who admires the pot so inordinately that he forgets to commend the potter. Athenagoras's fusion of Romans 1:25 with Romans 9:21 suggests a cause for the ubiquitous diversion of pagan worship from the Creator to the creature, which Paul had been more ready to mock than to explain.[24]

---

22. See Köckert, *Christliche Kosmologie*, 38–47.

23. For his contemporary Numenius, Fr. 16 Des Places, matter is a beguiling mirror of which the demiurgic mind becomes enamored when it turns its gaze from the eternal forms and looks below. More will be said of Numenius in the chapter on Neoplatonism.

24. Ginunchi, "*Dunamis* et *taxis*," 124–26, concludes that Athenagoras outdoes the other apologists in his asseverations of divine unity.

4. While he does not openly espouse the Euhemeristic theory, the objects of false worship that Athenagoras enumerates in the first chapter of the *Embassy* are almost all, by common admission, deified mortals rather than gods by birth. At 26.1 he expressly states that the idols set up by demons represent the dead, and at 28.1ff he purports to demonstrate from Herodotus that the gods of Egypt not only behaved like men but were as mortal as those (like Alexander) who claim descent from them. His demons therefore work upon the piety of their devotees more subtly than those of Justin, who populate the shrines with images representing themselves, though none is in fact a true facsimile of its supposed original. Noting that the statues of three charlatans,[25] lately deceased, are alleged to work miracles, Athenagoras retorts that in this case too it is demons who advantage of the soul's natural propensity to produce delusive images, a consequence (as we have seen) of the protean character that it shares with matter (*Embassy* 27). The true image of God is Christ, who was the incorporeal offspring and Word of his Father before he took on a material body for our salvation;[26] as this body was proved immortal by his resurrection, he is worshipped without the mediation of any sublunar image, and bestows a foretaste of the life to come by his action in the regenerate soul.

Irenaeus

For Irenaeus, history begins not with an impossible convulsion in the Godhead, nor with the accidental creation of a sick world, but with God's decision to make a being capable of bearing his image and likeness. Neither of these biblical terms implies for him that the Godhead has corporeal properties, nor conversely that humans are by nature incorporeal. He does not take the position—soon to become a Christian commonplace—that the image is constituted only by such invisible properties as the capacity for reasoning or the freedom to exercise virtue. He was further still from imagining, with the Gnostics, that the outer man is a clay facsimile of a supernal archetype, bereft of life until he receives the insufflations of the Holy Spirit. It is one God who fashions Adam from the soil and who breathes life into his nostrils,[27] and the consequence is that the body participates in the image, though its

25. Neryllinus the healer, Alexander the counterfeit prophet and Peregrinus Proteus the self-immolating Cynic (*Embassy* 21.3; 26).

26. On the incorporeality and invisibility of the divine in Athenagoras, see Rankin, *Athenagoras*, 117–19.

27. Genesis 2:7, quoted at *Against Heresies* 5.7.1.

natural properties are not those of God (*Against Heresies* 5.6.1). Irenaeus asserts that it will also share the likeness of God, recalling no doubt Paul's promise that Christ will "make the body of our lowliness conformable to the body of his glory" (Philippians 3:21). A few lines later we learn that there are many who, notwithstanding their possession of a body, have not the likeness because they lack the Spirit.[28] It is Paul again who explains how this can be, with his exhortation to let our mortal bodies be quickened by the Spirit of him who raised Christ Jesus from the dead (Romans 8:11).

It is not clear whether the presence of the Spirit in the saints is a restoration of that which Adam received when God breathed into his nostrils, or a higher gift that had not yet been vouchsafed to him at the time of his transgression.[29] At *Against Heresies* 5.16.2 we read that Adam "easily lost the likeness" because the image and likeness had not yet been revealed in their perfection. This implies, on the one hand, that the likeness had already been imparted, and on the other that Adam possessed it only inchoately, as an earnest of things to come. Elsewhere we are given to understand that much must come to pass before either the image or the likeness can be realized in humanity:

> It had been necessary first that nature should appear, then that the mortal should be vanquished and absorbed by the immortal, and the corruptible by the incorruptible [1 Cor 15:54], and that humanity should come to be according to the image and likeness of God, having received the knowledge of good and evil. (*Against Heresies* 4.38.3)

Here the image and likeness supervene upon the knowledge of good and evil, which, according to God's first design, was not to have been acquired until the corruptible had put on incorruption. In the chapter that follows, however, we are reminded that human beings have already acquired this knowledge, and Irenaeus does not seem to think that we suffer greatly from our precocity (*Against Heresies* 4.39.1). Whatever God's original design, it is now through the use of our rational freedom, after having experienced both good and evil, that we are able to choose the good. The inference that God intended Adam to sin has been derived by some modern readers from a poor translation of the Latin of *Against Heresies* 4.38.2, where God's plan for human growth includes the verb *convalescere*. If this word had its

---

28. On the dynamic character of the likeness and the role of the Spirit in conferring it, see Orbe, *Antroplogia di S. Ireneo*, 121–26.

29. Behr, *Asceticism and Anthropology*, 104–5, persuasively argues that Irenaeus distinguishes two infusions, one to all humanity as the "spirit of creation," the other to the elect alone as the adoptive "spirit of the Father."

English meaning, "to recover," one could infer that if we were intended to recover then we were intended to fall sick, that is, to sin; but *convalescere* means "to grow strong," as does the Greek *iskhusai*, of which it is a translation in this passage. Sin is more than "epistemic error" for Irenaeus, but some importance should be attached to his choice of the term *parekbasis*, ("trespass"), rather than *ptôma* ("fall") to characterize the act of disobedience.[30] Whether or not the offence was inevitable,[31] it was certainly venial, for our parents in Eden, innocent as they were, were far from perfect in understanding: "God did indeed have the power to bestow perfection on humanity from the beginning, but humanity had not the power to receive it, because of its infantile condition" (*Against Heresies* 4.38.1).

Are we to understand that Adam and Eve were children not only in mind but in body? Theophilus of Antioch, a contemporary of Irenaeus, says that Adam and Eve were children in age (*hêlikia*),[32] and one of the best of recent studies on Irenaeus argues that, in the light of previous usage it would have been unnatural to take the word *nêpios* in a metaphorical sense.[33] Yet Homer applies it at *Odyssey* 22.32 and 22.370 to the ghosts of Penelope's suitors and Philo also shows a partiality for the metaphorical usage.[34] But more familiar to Irenaeus than either Homer or Philo was Ephesians 4:13–14, where Paul exhorts his converts not to be *nêpioi*, buffeted by every wind of doctrine, but to grow under his instruction into the form of a perfect man (*teleion andra*). If he is purposely echoing Paul, the unfallen condition of Adam in Irenaeus will be a paradigm for that of immature Christian at Ephesians 4:14, who errs, and is permitted to err, because he is not yet perfect; it will also be a parable for the Gnostics, who err and persist in error because they aspire to knowledge without the mediation of the Word whose body in this world is the church.

Here there may be more common ground between Irenaeus and his interlocutors than he imagines. It has been for some decades a common belief among scholars that Sophia, who defies her consort to grasp at

---

30. First employed, perhaps, by Hippolytus, *Antichrist* 64; cf. Methodius, *Symposium* 3.6.

31. That it was inevitable has been most recently and most cogently argued by Behr, "'Since the Saviour Exists.'"

32. Theophilus, *To Autolycus* 2.5. The translation "stature" would imply the same thing.

33. Steenberg, "Children in Paradise."

34. Francis, *Adults as Children*, 139 cites metaphorical uses of *nêpios* at Philo, *Migration of Abraham* 26–31, *On Sobriety* 9, *Confusion of Tongues* 19, with *teleios* at *Confusion of Tongues* 145.

knowledge hidden from finite creatures, is the Valentinian Eve.[35] It can be argued that she also epitomizes the false pretensions of philosophy, and that her son the Demiurge personifies the idolatrous worship of both matter and the law. Irenaeus cannot agree with the Gnostics as to the origin of our ignorance, which for him is no privation but a natural concomitant of Adam's mental infancy. He is, however, of one mind with the heretics in maintaining that this ignorance could not have been dispelled without the apparition of a divine redeemer:

> Hitherto the Word, in whose image humanity had been made, was invisible, and for that reason humanity easily lost the likeness. When, however, the Word of God had been made flesh, he realised both. For on the one hand, he revealed the true image, himself becoming that which was his own image; on the other hand, by realising the likeness he restored it, making humanity similar to the invisible Father through the visible Word. (*Against Heresies* 5.16.1)

In God's eternal plan for the education of humanity it was necessary that the Son should take on a visible body, disclosing the image and likeness in their fullness to those who had hitherto possessed only the rudiments of them.[36] The revelation could not be understood without a preliminary exercise of intelligence and virtue; on the other hand, intelligence and virtue could not have been perfected without the revelation. The incarnation is not for him, as for most theologians after him—for Athanasius, Augustine, Thomas, and Calvin, for example—a purely remedial measure, foreseen but not willed, and necessitated only by the fall.

That Christ has to die for Adam is an indispensable element, yet never the whole, of Irenaeus's theory of salvation. It is true, as Gustav Aulen has urged,[37] that in common with Paul he can acclaim Christ's victory over our jailer, the devil; but for him the scene of victory is the wilderness, and he never quotes Colossians 1:14, where Christ is said the apostle to have humbled the principalities and powers. Again we should not deny that Irenaeus speaks as clearly as any Latin author of a propitiation of the Father (*Against Heresies* 5.17.1); he does not assert, however, that the means of propitiation was his death rather than the obedience of which death was the predestined culmination.[38] When he employs the noun *apolytrôsis* we cannot be sure that it has its etymological sense of ransom rather than the more

35. See the classic study by Macrae, "Jewish Background."
36. See further Steenberg, *Of God and Man*, 34–38.
37. Aulen, *Christus Victor*, 32–51.
38. Cf. Romans 3:25, with Deissman, *Bible Studies*, 129–35.

generic meaning of deliverance; we should therefore hesitate to construe God's "persuasion" at *Against Heresies* 5.1.1 as an act of purchase, given that Christ has no reason to haggle in death with one whom he has already vanquished in the course of his ministry, and that the object of persuasion is our personified apostasy, not the apostate angel himself. We need not fear that this is too nice a distinction for Irenaeus, since it forms the corollary to a famous assault on the ransom theory by Adamantius, whose rejection of dualism in various guises will be examined at greater length in chapter 9.

It was nonetheless in the letter to the Ephesians that Irenaeus found the coping-stone of his theology. At Ephesians 1:10, as we have seen, the author speaks of a recapitulation of all things in heaven and earth, which will succeed the growth of the neophyte into a "perfect man," and the gathering of the elect into the ecclesiastical body. Irenaeus is the first author to quote this passage, anticipating at *Against Heresies* 5.20.2 the "paradise into which God leads those who obey his proclamation, recapitulating in himself all that is in heaven and all that is in earth." When the term occurs elsewhere in his work, the events and phenomena that it signifies are not eternal, eschatological, or even recurrent, but circumscribed by the thirty years of Christ's sojourn on earth. Thus we read that by taking a body from earth he "recapitulated" his handiwork (*Against Heresies* 3.22.1), that in being born of a virgin he recapitulated the birth of Adam from the virgin soil (3.21.10; 3.30.1), that on the tree of life he recapitulated the disobedience that has been occasioned by another tree (5.19.1), that the travail of his soul and the wounds of his side bore witness to the earthly provenance of the flesh that he had "recapitulated in himself" (3.22.2). Because he is the Word through whom all humanity was created, he recapitulated the whole posterity of Adam (3.18.2; 3.18.7), and his sacrifice recapitulated the blood of all the prophets (5.14.1). Because he recapitulates in himself the entire history of our enmity to the serpent, he can be the Son of no God but the Creator (3.21.2); it is the Father's handiwork that he recapitulates, as he comes to seek those who were lost (5.14.3). Salvation means for us the restoration of the image that was present in the first man who is now recapitulated in Christ (5.12.4); an inevitable consequence of this recapitulation of God's comprehensive economy is the salvation of Adam himself (3.23.1), and it is because the creation of Adam took place on the sixth day of creation that the recapitulation of his disobedience took place on the sixth day of the week (5.23.2). In the sentence that follows his gloss on Ephesians 1:10, Irenaeus declares that all things have been recapitulated by Christ's war against sin on our behalf and his debellation of the one who had taken the whole race captive in Adam (5.20.2).

Fate in Bardesanes of Edessa

If Gnostics were fatalists, or reputed to be so, it was only to be expected that other heretics would surrender their Christian freedom to astrology or the kindred superstition of numerology. Adherents of the latter held that the arithmetic value of the letters in one's name foretold the day of one's death and the outcome of a duel with an antagonist whose name was of a higher or lower value. Astrologers—or, to be more precise, the professional *genethlealogoi* or casters of horoscopes—maintained that the position of the stars at the time of birth dictated not only the day of a person's death (which is already fixed in Homer for cities and heroes) and not only the rank and station of that person (which Plato held to be chosen by the soul before entering Lethe) but every external accident, leaving nothing in our own power but to endure whatever befalls us without demur. Many Stoics regarded the calculations of these "mathematicians" as a scientific validation of their own cosmology; the poet Manilius, far from inferring that God is any less God if we call him fate, proclaims that it is our liberty to be virtuous in defiance of all vicissitude that proves the soul itself to be divine.[39] Skeptics wondered how everyone who fell on the same day at the battle of Cannae could have been undone by the same conjunction of stars (Cicero, *On Divination* 2.33.70); dogmatic Platonists could not be so scornful, since according to the *Timaeus* every soul is allotted to a natal daemon that has its seat in a certain star.[40] For Christians, however, the rule of fate could not be reconciled with divine providence, and the justice of God could not permit this blind force to determine whether a free and rational being is damned or saved.

The most popular Christian novel of antiquity, the prototype of which is generally thought to have been composed in the second century, survives in Latin under the title *Clementine Recognitions*.[41] Like the cognate Greek text, the *Clementine Homilies*, it reaches its narrative and didactic climax when an astrologer, who believes that his wife and twin sons have been torn from him by the irresistible violence of the stars, is reunited with his whole family; as they have now become Christians, they are able to inform him that the cause of their deliverance is not fortune or fate but God. This episode is preceded by a logical refutation of the premisses of astrology, which we now know to have been derived largely from Bardesanes of Edessa.

---

39. See MacGregor, "Was Manilius Really a Stoic?"

40. *Timaeus* 41e–42b, with *Timaeus* 90a and Plotinus, *Enneads* 3.4, as in chapter 8.

41. On *Clementine Recognitions* 9.19–29 and Bardesanes, see Kelley, "Astrology in the Pseudo-Clementine Recognitions," where she argues that the *Recognitions* evolved from its Greek original to meet a variety of polemical needs in the Syrian region.

Bardesanes—or Bar Daisan in his native Syriac[42]—is said by other witnesses to have been half a Gnostic himself, and there are modern scholars who prefer to classify him as a pagan. Be that as it may, all Syriac writing belongs by default to the Christian tradition, and the Greek translation of this treatise may have influenced authors more illustrious than those who produced the *Clementine Recognitions*.

It seems that Bardesanes had acquired some reputation as an astrologer,[43] calculating the periods of revolution round the central earth for a number of planets, before he figured as the principal speaker in a dialogue on *the Laws*, the complete text of which survives only in Syriac. Here, abjuring the errors, though by no means the entire science, of the Chaldaeans,[44] he gives the response of a Christian to the question, "why did God not create humans capable only of doing good and thereby spare us the pains and penalties of sin?" He reminds his interlocutors that humans were created in the image of God, and hence with that authority over their actions that is denied to all other creatures (Drijvers, *Bardaisan*, 25). As we are appointed to rule, so they are appointed to be our ministers: if we too were ministers, who would receive our ministrations? Animals are governed entirely by nature, and every species has its diet, its patterns of growth, and its habits of mating, which every member observes without variation (p. 23). Among human beings, by contrast, one nation lives almost wholly on flesh, another eats only vegetables, while some, to the disgust of the rest, consume their fellow-humans (p. 43). Some abhor marital unions between kinsfolk, while others enjoin them (p. 53); moreover, any particular human being may elect to forgo the customs of his own nation for those of another. Every nation has its own laws, prohibiting such crimes as theft and murder; the uniform practice of punishing those who violate such ordinances shows that to obey or not to obey is held to be within our power, whereas no society thinks of calling anyone to account for being short or tall, ill-favored or handsome, healthy or deformed.

As animals we are subject to natural principles, which determine for us, as a species, how we are born, how we grow, and what foods are nutritious or harmful. The astrologers are also correct, against the extreme proponents of free will, to maintain that even as individuals we are subject to influences from without that determine whether we are born with sound or defective faculties, whether we grow up to be rich or poor (Drijvers, *Bardaisan*, 31),

42. For a collection and review of the evidence relating to Bardesanes or Bar Daisan, see Drijvers, *Bardaisan of Edessa*. For the thesis that he was a forerunner of Origen, see Ramelli, *Bardaisan of Edessa*.

43. See further Jones, "The Astrological Trajectory."

44. See Drijvers, ed. and trans., *Book of the Laws of Countries*, 27.

and whether our death comes to us in one way or another (p. 35). How we dispose of our wealth, however, whether we overcome or are overcome by our misfortunes, whether we bear ourselves viciously or virtuously in the face of danger or temptation, are matters of choice which the very stars cannot snatch from our volition. The making of laws too is as much the collective choice of a people as obeying them is the choice of the individual: only if all Gauls were born under one star, all Britons under another, and all Indians under another could astrology explain why the first permit unions between men and men, the second permit many men to marry one women, and the third permit many women to marry one man (p. 49). The history of legislation tells us that the laws of a people may change while the stars under which it lives remain constant. Moreover religions impose their own rules of conduct which are honoured by those who profess them in every locality, with no interference or assistance from the constellations. Brahmins eschew the idolatry that is permitted in India to other castes (p. 43); Jews, wherever they dwell, will keep the sabbath and abstain from forbidden foods (p. 37); Christians live in Britain, Gaul, and India, but never with bedfellows of their own sex, or with more than one (p. 43).

Tertullian on Matter and Evil

If fate is not the cause of evil, is matter its precondition, as some readings of Plato imply? It is all too common to read that the principal error of the Gnostics, in the eyes of their first assailants, was their devaluation of matter, with its consequent elevation of the Creator to an immeasurable distance from his creatures. In fact, it is Irenaeus who accuses his Valentinian adversaries of confusing matter with spirit and compressing the infinite gulf between God and the world.[45] Their teaching, as he interprets it, is not that God is an incorporeal and transcendent intellect, antipathetic to any commerce with the body, but that the realm that he inhabits is a theatre of perpetual change and passion, resulting first in a proliferation of aeons, then in a rupture that severs wisdom from divinity, entailing first the birth of an ignorant Demiurge as the offspring of her temerity and then the secretion of matter as the fruit of her repentance. The imperfections of the physical cosmos are to be traced not to its substrate but to its creator. The chief concern of Irenaeus, therefore, is not so much to exonerate matter as to demonstrate that change and passion have no place in God. For this purpose, philosophical reasoning is of more utility than any scriptural text.

45. See, e.g., *Against Heresies* 13.2–4 and 17.3, with Brigmann, *God and Christ in Irenaeus*, 99, and Stead, *Divine Substance*, 190–202.

Granting that at the beginning there was nothing but God, what lay outside him, he asks, that would give any latitude for expansion? And why, if there has eternally been nothing but God, should the will to expansion suddenly overtake him, and what new factor would precipitate a fall? By contrast, the ecclesiastical doctrine of creation out of nothing forestall any question as to the provenance of matter; and if this action is voluntary rather than pathological, his omnipotence is not challenged by our ignorance of his reason for creating at one time rather than another.

The doctrine of creation out of nothing is not explicitly maintained in the Hebrew scriptures, where the earth "without form and void" is often taken to represent the amorphous chaos from which God fashioned heaven and earth. The Greek translation is equally ambiguous, and the reference at 2 Maccabees 7:28 to God's creation of all things "from that which is not" does not preclude a material substrate.[46] When Justin Martyr asserts that Plato's doctrine of creation out pre-existent matter was derived from Moses, he reads prophecy as philosophy and applies a Middle Platonic or Peripatetic interpretation to the receptacle of the *Timaeus*. This concession did not please Athenagoras or Tatian, both of whom aver that the matter from which the world is made was itself the first creation of God.[47] No polemic against the Gnostics is discernible here: their aim is rather to defend the power and benevolence of God against philosophers who deny that a material world can be exempt from sin. They do not, in so many words, affirm creation out of nothing: the first to use the locution *ex oudenos* rather than *ex ouk ontôn* was Theophilus of Antioch, in the course of his demonstration that sin is the product of an abuse of freedom by rational creatures on whom this freedom had been conferred as a blessing.[48] In another of his works, now lost,[49] Theophilus had attributed the contrary position to one Hermogenes, who is clearly more of a Platonist than a Gnostic. Our fullest account of his theory (which, as we shall see, is not free of tendentious elements) is the treatise written against him by Tertullian, the first Latin Christian author of note, and, for all his studied intemperance and injustice, one of the subtlest reasoners of the early church.[50]

According to Tertullian the problem addressed by his adversary is "What is the source of evil?" and his answer is that, since it is too substantial to come from nothing and could not have come from God, it must come

---

46. In the Latin rendering, however, *creatio ex nihilo* is already a biblical doctrine.

47. Athenagoras, *Embassy* 4; Tatian, *Oration* 5.

48. *To Autolycus* 2.4 and 2.10.

49. See May, *Creatio ex Nihilo*, 156–59.

50. See Evans, ed. and trans., *Adversus Marcionem*.

from matter (*Against Hermogenes* 14.3; 15.1). Yet his own polemic betrays the inadequacy of this paraphrase, for after much polemic against the notion that matter is evil, he makes a great show of perplexity on finding that his opponent in fact holds matter to differ from God not so much in its moral properties as in being eternally mobile whereas God is eternally changeless (*Against Hermogenes* 26 and 42). Matter thus has for Hermogenes the attribute of the receptacle in Plato's *Timaeus*; he also appears to know Plato's dictum at *Theaetetus* 176c that evil will never be banished from the world. He is not accused of saying that the motion is caused, as in Plutarch, by a malevolent soul: on the contrary, he declares that it has no tendency either to good or to evil (41.1), thus laying himself open to the invidious and clearly unintended deduction that good and evil have their own places and therefore must be substantial (41.3). The conclusion that he himself invites us to draw is surely that matter is the potentiality to do good or evil, which is absent from God because (as the church and Plato agree) his nature is such as to be capable only of good. Another of the heresies imputed to him, that matter is spatially infinite (38.2–3), is admittedly a hostile inference on Tertullian's part, and if in fact he equated matter with bare potentiality, we may guess that he meant by "infinite" what a Platonist of this epoch would have meant by it, namely "without any definite form."

If so much can be granted to Hermogenes, there is little to the purpose on Tertullian's attempts to rebut his teaching. He makes his own contribution to the history of Christian thought by formulating what is now the standard "problem of evil": a God who is good would not wilfully create from an evil medium without converting it to his own purpose, while if he were forced to employ it but unable to improve it he would not be omnipotent (*Against Hermogenes* 8.2; 12.1). Hermogenes can accept both limbs of the argument without renouncing either the omnipotence or the goodness of the Creator; if "infinite," as I proposed, is his word for "indefinite," he would be equally unperturbed by the objection that infinite matter would exclude God from the realm of being, or that some part of the infinite would always remain unconsumed.[51] The objection that it is better not to create than to create in a labile medium (9.5) is strong if matter is evil, but not so strong if it has only potentiality for evil: all Christians must admit that the Creator has knowingly permitted evil, whatever they take to be its source. Tertullian may be on stronger ground when he urges that if two principles are coeternal neither can be subject to the other (11.1–3), and again when he says that if God needs any substrate that he has not created, he will be

---

51. Although I put this question hypothetically, Hermogenes appears to have conceded that God used only parts of matter (*Against Hermogenes* 38.3).

in debt to that substrate, and in that respect at least inferior to it (8.1). Hermogenes may have replied that both these arguments assume matter to be a substance as well as a substrate; Tertullian can rejoin that in opposing it to God we are already making it a substance, and that if we ascribe eternity to this substance we are investing it with an attribute peculiar to God and therefore falling into ditheism (16.2).

The philosophical reasoning of Hermogenes was supported by exegesis of the opening verses of Genesis: matter, he declared, was the "beginning" in which God created the heaven and earth, and the second verse, which relates that the earth was invisible and rude or imperfect, reveals its inchoate character (*Against Hermogenes* 23.1). Tertullian's retort is that the beginning, as other scriptures demonstrate, is God's own wisdom, which is not external to him but of his own substance (18.2; 20.2): it may be a sign of dependence on Theophilus that he styles this Wisdom Sophia, not *Sapientia*, and equates it not with the Son but with the Spirit (18.1). The term "beginning" also has a temporal connotation, and Tertullian, in response to Hermogenes's plea that if God is Lord there must always be matter for him to govern, contends that Lord is not an eternal title, but one that accrues to God when he fashions the world from nothing (3.1–3). He is also willing, more candidly than in other works, to surmise that "Father" is also a supervenient title (3.4), and thus postpones for a century the difficulty of reconciling the eternal Sonship with the temporal creation (cf. 18.3). The argument that the earth of Genesis 1:2 is matter is not persuasive, according to Tertullian, because it requires us to take the word earth in a different sense from that which it bears in the preceding verse (25.2). It is the earth of Genesis 1:2 that is said to be good, and since it is from this earth that all discrete beings proceed, it cannot have been devoid of form, as Hermogenes opines (38.1; 40.2). Rather, it contained all forms in potential (30.2–3), and the statement that it was invisible signifies only that it was buried under the waters (29.5). Even its imperfection implies a measure of formation, since we use the compound *in-per-fectum* of things that are *facta* or made (28.2) and which will one day be *perfecta* (29.2). It is the absolute sovereignty of God, as implied in the doctrine of creation out of nothing, that gives us the assurance of his power to confer perfection on the sinful creatures to whom he has proclaimed at Psalm 82.6 "I have said ye are gods" (5.4).

Tertullian, in his treatise *Against Hermogenes* as in others, has not been entirely just in the criticisms of his opponent's views or temperate in the expression of his own. If the true position of Hermogenes was that matter is not by nature good or evil, but a mere potentiality for being, it was not given to his adversary to anticipate the objection of Adamantius in the fourth century, that potentiality cannot exist without form. For all that, we must not allow the shortcomings of Tertullian's polemic to blind us to its historical significance, for it lays down rules of engagement that were to govern Christian disputation for centuries after him. The trichotomy "from matter, from God, or from nothing" was applied by Arius to the origin of the second person of the Trinity;[52] the atheist's dilemma that God must either be lacking in goodness or lacking in power if he permits evil seems to have grown more formidable with every attempt at a new solution. And there is one corollary of Tertullian's reasoning that, though seldom observed, seems to put him at the head of a striking trend in Christian thought on which we shall have more than one occasion to reflect in the course of this study.[53] Because his purpose is only to gainsay the theory that evil owes his origin to matter, he does not feel obliged to pronounce on either the nature or the origin of matter; he does not conclude, with Tatian and Theophilus, that God first created matter and then created all things from it. His last word in the subject indeed is *nullam materiam fuisse* (*Against Hermogenes* 45.4), as though he had surmised, long before Bishop Berkeley and even a little earlier than Origen, Methodius, and Adamantius, that matter is not a substance, a substrate, or even a mere potential for existence, but an otiose postulate of Greek philosophers who had failed to perceive that nothing is required to make a thing possible for God but his own decree that it should be so.

Tertullian against Marcion

In bulk at least, *Against Marcion* is Tertullian's *magnum opus*, and modern discussions of Marcion lean heavily on the close examination in Books 2–5 of his strictures on the Old Testament and his alleged truncation of early Christian writings. If Tertullian's veracity even on these points is contested in recent scholarship, it would be rash to look for a perfect transcript of his opponent's arguments in the first book, which draws on generic refutation of polytheism in answer to positions attributed not so often to Marcion himself as to contemporary, though anonymous, patrons of his heresy. We need not assume therefore that he really arrived at his antithesis between the justice of one God and the goodness of another by collating two biblical texts, one of which makes God describe himself as the author of evil while the other asserts, on Christ's authority, that a good tree cannot bring forth evil fruit.[54] On such weak grounds, and also under the influence of

52. See *Against Hermogoenes* 14.3 and 15.1 above; and cf. Athanasius, *On the Synods* 16 for Arius's letter to Bishop Alexander.

53. See further Edwards, "Christians against Matter."

54. *Against Marcion* 1.2., citing Matthew 7:18 and Isaiah 45:7.

Cerdo, says Tertullian (*Against Marcion* 1.2.3), Marcion reasoned that the Creator who gave the law to Israel is just but not good, while the Savior who redeems our souls exhibits a goodness superior to justice, at least as the present world conceives it (1.6.1; 1.25.1). Some will suspect that this is fact the theology of Cerdo rather than Marcion.[55] Tertullian himself is less concerned to authenticate the teaching than to convict it of absurdity, insofar as it bestows the name God, which properly designates the *summum magnum*, on two distinct beings, thus making a plural of that which is logically unique (1.6.1, etc.). Between two supreme gods, he avers, there could be neither parity, since the first brooks no equal, nor disparity, since supremacy admits of no degrees (1.7.6). If both are gods, they are equally worthy of worship, yet it would be as impious to worship both as it would be invidious to worship only one. I might worship both in one, but if that is possible, why are there two (1.5.3–5)?

Marcion's solution is to subordinate one to the other, but that is to say that only one is truly God (*Against Marcion* 1.7.4–5). Moreover, it would appear that he is bound to allot to the higher god his own heaven and his own matter from which to create it: if all three are eternal, there are three entities superior to the creator which share with him the cardinal attribute of divinity (1.15.1–4). By the same logic, it seems, the heaven and earth, which the creator himself inhabits, must be eternal, as must the matter from which he creates: thus we have reached a total of seven deities before Christ even enters the reckoning (1.15.4–5). According to Marcion, Christ is the revelation of a hitherto unknown God; since, however, all the apostles took him for the Son of the Creator (1.20.6), the true revelation tarried until Marcion published it, over a century later (19.1–2). Since that time, the Higher God has left us without any evidence of himself, as he did for centuries before. The Creator,[56] by contrast, is known through his works, as Paul declares,[57] and those who disparage these works not only fail to appreciate the exquisite fashioning of the cosmos and every creature that it contains, but are forced to admit that the higher God had no other means of redeeming us than those that the Creator had furnished for him. Why should we believe in such a God at all, when he offers no visible artefact as evidence of his invisible sovereignty (1.17.2)? If he is eternally good, while the physical cosmos is evil from its inception, why did he not intervene at once to forestall sin or to deliver us from its penalties (1.17.4)? If his power exceeds that

55. See Irenaeus, *Against Heresies* 3.4.2, with Deakle, "Harnack and Cerdo."

56. On the likelihood that Tertullian derived the term Creator from Marcion, see Braun, *Deus Christianorum*, 372–76.

57. *Against Marcion* 1.16.2, citing Romans 1:18–20.

of the Creator, why does he leave the body unredeemed, when it is evident that sin proceeds from the will, and that it is therefore not the body that beguiles the soul but the soul that suborns the body as its agent of theft and murder (1.24.3–4)? What is a human being but flesh (1.24.5), and what was the purpose of Christ's assuming the semblance of a body if the flesh is to be excluded from salvation? A sinner who is but partially saved is punished, not reprieved (1.24.6). And what right, in any case, had this idle divinity to steal from the Creator that which he alone had made (1.23.7–9)?[58]

Many of these objections were republished, as we shall see, in Christian refutation of the Manichaeans. Mani too was said to have appealed to the saying that good trees cannot yield good fruit, and was challenged to explain how two hundred years had elapsed between the promise of the Holy Spirit and its coming in his own person. As we shall see, the inference from two gods to two creations of matter was also deployed against dualistic theologies of the fourth century, and it was regularly assumed that those who sever grace from law have also denied that justice is part of goodness or that matter can be saved. Tertullian represents the God of Marcion as a negligent father who fails to instil in his children the fear that engenders moral rectitude (*Against Marcion* 1.27.3), and as an injudicious magistrate who in his zeal to forgive the unworthy forgets what is due to the righteous (1.26.1–2). Marcion's error is to suppose that because the gospel extends the law it condemns the law, whereas on the contrary it is to reveal the purpose for which the law was given (1.21–21.2): his hero Paul did not denounce Peter for having been circumcised but for paying more honor to this sign than to the inward circumcision of the heart that it signified (1.20.2–5). As Tertullian demonstrates in the next four books, the charges that Marcion brings against the Lawgiver of the Old Testament arise from his obstinate misconstruction of allegory and his mutilation of the fourfold Gospel in which the new covenant fulfils and deciphers the old.

Tertullian on the Fall

Tertullian yields to none in his horror of demons. The daily traffic of Rome and its pagan subjects, he exclaims, is *pompa diaboli*, a pageant of the devil (*On the Shows* 12.5);[59] when he asserts that barely any human is unaccom-

---

58. I have restricted myself, for convenience, to the first book of *Against Marcion*: on the iteration and refinement of his philosophical principles in the other books, see Lieu, *Marcion and the Making of a Heretic*, 63–85.

59. Examples of this diabolic suzerainty are collected from Tertullian by Daniélou, *Origins of Latin Christianity*, 412–19.

panied in this world by a demon (*On the Soul* 57.4), he does not exempt, and indeed is addressing, children of Christian parents. The Jewish notion that everyone has a good and an evil angel will have been less familiar to him than the Roman belief that destiny and character are shaped by a personal genius, or the astrological teaching that the individual's destiny is shaped by a natal demon, of which more will be said in chapter 8. In contrast to both superstitions, however, Tertullian knows that the demon is neither a god nor a part of the self, that it is exorcised in baptism, and therefore that we not naturally bound to obey its promptings. In common with Alexander of Aphrodisias, and with all Christians of his epoch, he held that God cannot justly reward or punish us if we do not have the freedom to sin or not to sin. And hence although, in common with the heretics, he divides the human race into pneumatics and psychics, he cannot hold, as they were supposed to do, that we are unalterably assigned to one of these categories at birth. We acquire the status of a pneumatic by discipline and service, not by nature, and while he concedes to Marcion that we have a second, diabolic nature in addition to the one that God created, that too is the product of a voluntary transgression.[60] It would seem that all human flesh save that of Christ is tainted by the *vitium*, or infirmity, of Adam (*On the Flesh of Christ* 16.3), but neither this nor the natal daemon renders a person guilty or incapable of good actions. Those theses belong to Augustine, who favored the baptism of infants, whereas Tertullian rejects this practice on the grounds that an infant has no sins to forgive.

Adam sinned at the instigation, but not yet under the tyranny, of the devil, bequeathing to his descendants a propensity, but not an irresistible predisposition, to go on sinning. Since both Adam and his tempter acted in accordance with their creaturely freedom, there are no grounds for Marcion's charge that the Creator must have been deficient in power, in benevolence, or in foreknowledge (*Against Marcion* 2.5.2). On the contrary, his power and benevolence are manifest in the creation of a being in his own image, which is to say a being endowed with rational freedom (2.6.3). Tertullian forestalls the objection that a free and rational being may be incapable of sin by explaining the whereas God is good by nature Adam was good by *institutio* or design (2.6.4). It is in the nature of God, as archetype, to do the good freely on all occasions, while it is in the nature of his human image to do good freely when it does not, with equal freedom, choose to do evil. Wrongly deducing from Genesis 2:7 that the spirit of Adam was also the Spirit of God, Marcion commits the Valentinian error of involving

60. Steenberg, *Of God and Man*, 79–88, argues from *On the Soul* 20 and other texts that the supervenient nature should be understood economically rather than ontologically.

the Creator in the error of his creature. Tertullian replies by distinguishing created spirit from the creating Spirit, urging that the property of being uncreated cannot logically be imparted to a creature (2.8–9). God foresees but does not participate in the rebellion of the soul that he brought into being by the infusion of his spirit. Nor can it be alleged that his foreknowledge makes him complicit in the transgression: it lay within his omnipotence to pre-empt it by annulling Adam's liberty, but only at the cost of giving up his design, which Marcion knows well enough to be inconsistent with the perfection of the true God (1.7.3).

Conclusion

In pagan theodicies of the second century, the gods were above and mortals below, while daemons (if their existence was acknowledged) were intermediate powers, never purposely doing evil, though inferior to the gods in wisdom and virtue. In Gnostic thought the world itself was the product of malign and ignorant powers, who are no longer conscious either of their inferiority to a higher realm or of their own origin within it. The demiurge and his archons no longer act as executors of the divine will, as ambassadors to mortals or as pilots to the soul in its ascent: they are intermediate beings but not mediators, less akin to the daemons of Plutarch and Apuleius than to the prince of this world and his archons in the New Testament. The writings of the New Testament differs, however, in assigning the creation of the physical world to God and in treating the devil and his angels as usurpers who will rule only so long as they enjoy God's forbearance. Christian authors of the second century are therefore at pains to show that, while they are skilful in the propagation of evil, the demons are not the ultimate cause of it: they set up idolatrous cults with the complicity of mortals who glorify their unworthy ancestors, they pervert the use of matter among the materially minded, who ignore the proofs of divine invisibility, and their captain initiated the general ruin of humanity by tempting Adam and Eve into a misuse of their free will. In this phase of Christian thought, it is rare to address, let alone to resolve, the paradox of God's foreseeing the fall but incurring no blame for it or to ask how a being that is created good could conceive a desire to sin. As we shall see in the following chapter, these questions were pursued with more tenacity, and with subtler tools, by the Alexandrian masters of the third century, who, notwithstanding their use of Greek philosophy, were as determined as their predecessors not to let either Platonists or Gnostics shake their faith in the omnipotence of God, the malice of demons, and the freedom of created minds to choose both good and ill.

7

Alexandrian Theodicy

CLEMENT AND ORIGEN ARE by convention the "Christian Platonists of Alexandria," although Clement is alleged to have come from Athens and Origen was ordained in Caesarea.[1] The locution Christian Platonist seems to imply that they were a variety of an intellectual species, but if that is so the species has left little trace in the metropolis of Egypt, for the Platonists of whom we know most in the early Roman era taught in Attica, Rome, Apamea, Gerasa, and Carthage. Moreover, while it was almost a scholarly platitude in the last century that Alexandrian Christians superimposed an extraneous system of thought on the scriptures that they were interpreting, the most detailed and careful studies of the present day concur in taking Origen and Clement at their own word when they declare that for them the scriptures are the one sure source of knowledge, to which philosophy can act at most as a tool of exegesis and discernment.[2] Thus they are Platonists not in regarding Plato as an authority or an independent depository of knowledge, but in turning to him more often for the elucidation of their own difficulties or for corroborative testimony that would outweigh that of scripture in the eyes of a pagan reader. Plato was a witness, after all, to the creation of the cosmos and to the posthumous judgment of souls by God's

---

1. Epiphanius, *Panarion* 32.6. Bigg, *Christian Platonists of Alexandria*, 72–73, argues that *Stromateis* 1.1.11 is barely consistent either with this tradition or with the intimation of Eusebius at *Preparation for the Gospel* 2.2.64 that Clement was brought up in a pagan household.

2. See Osborn, "Arguments for Faith."

executors; of all the Greek philosophers, Plato was the one who most clearly held a doctrine of providence, which did not teach (with the Stoics) that all seeming evil is illusory, but that we each receive what is due to us in this life and the next.

Yet hitherto only those who were known as Gnostics had endorsed the daring premiss that gives coherence to this theodicy—that souls pass through innumerable lives in the present world, each of which may be seen as a recompense or expiation for the acts of the previous life inasmuch as the choice made by the soul reveals how much it has learned from that sojourn and the assize that followed. Tertullian had ridiculed the notion of transmigration into beasts on the grounds that the soul in such a state is deprived of reason and will remain ignorant both of the cause of its captivity and of the means of emancipation.[3] Clement, as we shall find in the present chapter, is prepared to weigh the arguments, though he remains opposed to the doctrine; Origen owes his notoriety chiefly to his assertion of the pre-existence of souls, although he severs this from the doctrine of transmigration and combines it with a belief in the fall of Adam. For him, both are mystical teachings in which history is checkered by allegory, and it has been a fault of both ancient and modern critics to ignore the studied vagueness of his pronouncements. The one fixed presupposition of his theodicy is that all human beings are of one nature, and therefore equally free to accept or reject the felicity that God, for his part, has denied to none.

The Origin and Defeat of Evil in Clement of Alexandria

No change either of residence or of religion is attested in the extant works of Clement, though all display an erudition in every branch of literature that exceeds that of anyone known to have been born of Christian parents before Nicaea, and is surely the fruit of reading for pleasure rather than under a sense of obligation. It is for this reason that his works survive, while his expositions and vindications of scripture have met the fate of almost all Greek works of their kind before Nicaea, except for those of Origen.[4] Doctrine evolves, but scholarship is perennial; we must consequently be wary of assuming that those texts by Clement that proved to be the most durable were also the most representative of his theology. The purpose of his *Stromateis* is to bring to light the numerous homologies between Greek

---

3. See *On the Soul* 24 and 32–33, with further animadversions on Simona Magus and the Carpocratians at 34–35.

4. On the misreading of Clement in the Byzantine era, see Ashwin-Siejkowski, *Clement of Alexandria on Trial*.

philosophy and Christian teaching; to infer, however, that he was at heart a philosopher, for whom Christ was a teacher rather than a savior, is not only to overlook the titles of his unpreserved writings but to ignore the allusions in his surviving works to the death of Christ and the crown of thorns.[5] Even in the *Stromateis*, he does not accord any independent authority to the philosophers, whom he charges with plagiarism, while allowing direct inspiration only to prophets, whose effusions are now perceived to be Jewish or Christian forgeries. In his *Paedagogus*, or manual of Christian living, liberal use is made of philosophical exhortations to frugality and spiritual fortitude, but he is too austere for any of the four chief schools when he writes that men should abstain from laughter and the wearing of shoes.[6] That he writes for women at all, enjoining a slightly less painful regimen, is a mark of his Christianity, while his argument that the rich may retain their wealth so long as they put it the disposal of the church is more exacting than Paul's precepts to the Corinthians. His modern detractors are right to object that Christ's command to "sell all your goods" was intended literally, but they seldom come nearer than Clement to executing the command in its literal sense.

The Christian can be more rigorous than the philosopher because he knows that the world was created by God to reward the righteous and educate the sinner. For example, it was God's will that gold should be rare and pearls too deep to be mined by any but criminals in chains:[7] by this we are to learn that the wealth that all can enjoy consists not in precious stones but, as Plato says, in the beauty of that which eludes our carnal senses. Plato, however, fails to dissociate beauty in virtue from beauty of person, treating both beauty and goodness as objects analogous to those that we covet in this world; Christ, himself distinguished by no outward beauty of form, holds up another ideal of beauty as a self-emptying love for others with no admixture of selfish desire.[8] This godlike state cannot be attained without divine assistance, which often comes to us in the disguise of evil (*Stromateis* 7.56.3–4, etc.): the enlightened soul, however, will see that the pains imposed on us are corrective and therefore salutary, just as it will yield itself with thanks to the admonitions, upbraidings, censures, invectives, and reproofs of Holy Writ (*Paedagogus* 1.9.76–77). The philosophers, who understand the world but not its Creator, are not such pernicious enemies to the true faith as the

5. On the ubiquitous but creative use of scripture in Clement, see Ward, *Clement and Scriptural Exegesis*, 5–8.

6. *Paedagogus* 2.5.46.4, citing Ecclesiasticus 21:20 on laughter; *Paedagous* 1.11.117 (shoes). See further Halliwell, *Greek Laughter*, 83–195.

7. *Paedagogus* 2.13.120.

8. *Paedagous* 1.26.1–3, 1.98.3; 3.2.1, with Russell, *Doctrine of Deification*, 127–29.

Gnostics, who disparage the creation, deny that justice is the corollary of goodness, and advertise their freedom from the material realm by indulging every sin that pollutes the flesh.[9]

The heretics have at least divined the presence in the world of a radical wickedness that the philosophers disguise by their connivance. Clement subscribes to the prevalent Christian teaching that the gods of the pagan cults are fallen angels who wish to involve other creatures in their ruin, and that since their medium in this world is matter they betray us into superstition through sacrifices and idols.[10] Few authors, pagan or Christian, have furnished more vivid accounts of the atrocities that have been performed to appease these suppositious overlords, or more detailed recitations of the salacious rites and senseless incantations that disgrace their most solemn mysteries. The only effect of these cults of the dead is to turn us into beasts by stirring up the appetitive element of the soul (*Protrepticus* 1.7.4; *Paedagogus* 2.1.7), and at worst we ourselves fall into a demonic state of vanity and unbridled appetition (*Stromateis* 6.12.98.1). The worship of demons is all the more absurd because we know that they wear gross bodies that are fattened by unclean vapors (*Protrepticus* 4.55.5); at the same time, they are capable of penetrating the bodies of their votaries, though their presence is revealed not so much by physical maladies as by psychic disorders (*Protrepticus* 10.99.1). Clement says of a certain demon, whose special office is to excite gluttony, that it is even more deadly than the spirit of prophecy which possessed the witch of Endor and continues to haunt the bellies of pagan soothsayers.[11] Their power is bounded, however, by our capacity for resistance. Our bodies, as God created them, are so far from being evil that they serve to conceal the virtues of the soul from its demonic assailants, and if the soul remembers the end for which it was created, it will know that its proper food is the flesh and blood of the Son of Man (*Paedagogus* 2.1.9; *Stromateis* 7.3.13.1–3).

Eating and drinking are metaphors in Clement's soteriology, but they are metaphors that he pursues with uncommon tenacity. The serpent in Eden, who crawls on his belly, symbolizes the blandishments of carnal pleasure (*Paedagogus* 2.1.7); Adam, instead of feeding on the word of God, fell prey to his sophistry (or rather to that of Satan) because he had been

9. On Clement against the Gnostics, see Ashwin-Siejkowski, *Project of Christian Perfection*.

10. *Protrepticus* 2.38.1; 3.42.7, 3.44.1. These citations, with most of those that follow, are taken from Proctor, *Demonic Bodies*, 129–37.

11. *Paedagogus* 2.1.15. On the Witch of Endor (1 Samuel 28) in Christian literature, see Greer and Mitchell, eds., *Belly-Myther of Endor*. On Origen's use of Plato to build a philosophy form the scriptures, see Osborn, *Clement of Alexandria*, 56–106.

equipped with the image but not the likeness of his Maker, which is to say that he had reason enough to choose but not yet virtue enough to choose well. As in Theophilus and Irenaeus,[12] Adam and Eve are described in Clement as *nêpioi* or juvenile in discernment and therefore guilty of aberration rather than deliberate sin (*Protrepticus* 11.111). While Adam enjoyed an immortal life in paradise, he was not yet perfect in virtue,[13] and he abused the freedom that God imparted to him to exchange an immortal life for a mortal one (*Stromateis* 2.19.98). It is not because God is jealous (as the Gnostics suppose) but because he is free from jealousy that he has granted us the capacity to will both good and evil, so that by our own free choice we may grow into the divine likeness that has been revealed in Christ.[14] Our present state differs so little from the initial state of innocence that we can scarcely speak of a fall, and may feel that we have as much licence in Clement as in Philo to regard Adam and Eve as universal emblems of the human condition rather than as historical figures whose sins have fathered ours.

Origen and the Pre-existence of Souls

Origen was reputedly the successor to Clement as head of the Catechetical School in Alexandria. Although his biblical commentaries were voluminous and have never ceased to be read, it was the almost the universal opinion of twentieth-century scholars that he was "not a biblical scholar . . . but a philosopher who used biblical exegesis as a vehicle for views not derived from the sacred text but read into it."[15] Today he is taken more at his own estimation, at least in the Anglophone world, where it is generally acknowledged that philosophy played a supplementary role to his hermeneutic labors, enabling him to fill lacunae and harmonize apparent contradictions in the scriptures and to eke out exegesis by his own speculations where the mind of the church was not yet clear. Continuing disagreement as to whether he was a philosopher, and if so whether he adhered to any one school, have now become questions of nomenclature: is one a philosopher if one appropriates the tenets of an existing school without canvassing the reasons for which they were held, and does one become a Platonist by consistently finding Plato's tenets superior to those of other philosophers, even if one accords no authority to him and pronounces all philosophical methods

12. See further Tennant, *Sources of the Doctrines*, 182–96.

13. *Stromateis* 6.12.96 and 3.17.103.

14. *Protrepticus* 10.98; *Paedagogus* 1.12.98; *Stromateis* 6.12.96. See Behr, *Asceticism and Anthropology*, 135–40.

15. Barnes, *Constantine and Eusebius*, 93.

inferior to the acceptance of revealed truth? However one answers these questions, the point that is no longer in doubt is that Origen in all his extant writings turns to Plato to resolve difficulties arising from his own study of texts that he takes to be the infallible word of God.[16] His axioms were those of Justin, Irenaeus, and Tertullian, and his enemies among professing Christians were their enemies: as we shall see, a desire to uphold the justice and omnipotence of the Creator is at the root of his desultory conjectures on the pre-existence of souls, as it is evidently at the root of his insistence that even the subterfuge of demons never compromises the freedom of the will.

Because he holds that every soul is created from nothing by God, and that it is subject to no evil from without except the penalties brought upon it by its own sin, Origen had little choice but to trace the unequal lots of souls in the present world to some antecedent mystery, which is never fully elucidated in his extant writings. It plainly implied some mode of pre-existence for the soul, for which he found evidence in Paul's use of the noun *katabole* at Ephesians 1:4, which he takes in its literal sense of "sending down."[17] It is equally clear that the sending down is from God and that the destination of those who undergo it is determined by their merits, though we are not told clearly when or in what way merit and demerit are acquired.[18] Far more lucid accounts of Origen's teaching are to be found in the many indictments that were drawn up after his death. Most lucid of all is the amalgam of Byzantine testimonia which Paul Koetschau inserted into his edition of the *First Principles*, commonly known as Fragment 15.[19]

The gist of it is already ascribed to Origen by Augustine, who justly remarks that it falls short of uniting the moral with the metaphysical, since if bodily weight were determined by the gravity of one's sin the demons would not inhabit the air between us and heaven. This is one reason to doubt whether the Greek deserves to be called a fragment of Origen, and in the twenty-first century it is generally agreed that Koetschau's additions to the *First Principles* should be treated (as he intended) as aids to scholarship rather than as correctives to the Latin of Rufinus. Nevertheless, the

---

16. I can see no disagreement on this point between Edwards, "Origen's Platonism" and Martens, "Embodiment, Heresy and the Hellenization of Christianity."

17. Origen, *First Principles* 13.5.4, commenting on Ephesians 1:4.

18. For a balanced view of the evidence on Origen's theory of creation, see Heine, *Origen: An Introduction*, 101–15.

19. On the influence of this and other insertions in Koetschau's edition, see Rombs, "A Note on the Status of Origen's *De Principiis*"; Origen, *First Principles*, ed. J. Behr, vol. 1, xxvi–xxvii; Ramelli, "Gregory of Nyssa's Purported Criticism," 279. Arruzza, "Le refus du bonheur," maintains that both the doctrine and its Philonic provenance can be inferred from other passages in Origen's works.

influence of the old habit of reading Koetschau as though he were Origen can be detected in two continuing trends, the ascription of the soul's descent to *koros* or satiety and the assumption that one law governs the descent of all rational beings in the theodicy of Origen, be they angels or human souls.

The one passage of the *First Principles* in which the word *koros* (2.3.8–2.4.1) occurs is also the one most frequently adduced to prove that he held the descent of souls from the presence of God to be a consequence of satiety. Yet the text says nothing of a descent from heaven, and when it compares the fatigue that breaks the soul's contemplation of God to a lapse of attention in a geometer, it echoes Aristotle's explanation of those instances in which the embodied reason fails to will what it knows to be right. At the end of his own discussion, Origen speaks of a recovery of virtue in the embodied soul, without any allusion to its return to heaven or even to its deliverance from the body. The common interpretation of it therefore seems to rest on the posthumous indictment quoted above; and this in turn, as I have suggested elsewhere, would seem to rest on the false assumption that *koros* has the same meaning in Origen as in Philo or Plotinus.[20]

At *First Principles* 1.7.1, Origen contends that if the foetus were not ensouled we could not explain the adoration of Jesus by John the Baptist when both were in the womb. This may be a covert argument against abortion, but it does not imply the pre-existence of souls before conception: his interlocutors here are the unnamed precursors of Porphyry who maintained that the rational soul is infused at birth. Elsewhere indeed he deduces from John's recognition of Jesus that he had known him before his descent to this world; but this is a unique privilege, which others have already explained by surmising that the Baptist was an angel or that he came from paradise— meaning by the latter theory, of course, that he was Elijah, who had been carried up *bodily* to a higher sphere.

It is far too common a habit among modern scholars to conflate the fall of angels with the fall of souls, and to cite texts that affirm the one as though they affirmed the other. At *Against Celsus* 4.40 Origen declares that the church has a teaching that surpasses the myth in Plato of the fall of the soul and the shedding of its wings. From the one recurrence of the participle *pterroruesasa* at *Against Celsus* 6.43, we learn that the better teaching is Ezekiel's lament for the expulsion of Satan from paradise under the guise of the Prince of Tyre (cf. *First Principles* 1.5.4 on Ezekiel 28:1–19). Being a defence of Christianity as it was publicly taught, this treatise never affirms the preexistence of the soul. In the *Commentary on John* the verse "I have said ye are gods and children of the most high, but ye shall fall as men" is said to betoken

20. See Edwards, *Origen against Plato*, 92–93.

a human fall analogous to that of the angels, but this fall is not equated with a descent of souls to bodies.[21] At *First Principles* 2.9.1 we are told that in the beginning God created a sufficient number of rational intelligences to govern the world, but some who had turned away were relegated to a distance from him in proportion to their deserts. These beings are plainly angels, possessed of *animos*, or intellects rather than *animas* or souls, and the fall of humans is introduced once again by way of similitude at 2.9.3.

In this discussion of the human lottery Origen takes it as an axiom that our fortunes in the present world are apportioned to our merits. Since he opines that God rewards and punishes not only deeds foredone but deeds foreseen,[22] some of his statements in *First Principles* 2.9 may be open to more than one construction: have we been placed in a certain station on account of our merits or in order that we may acquire them? There is no such ambiguity, yet not a little obscurity, in his argument that a just God would not have loved Jacob and hated Esau, while the two were still in the womb, unless some title to favor or disfavor had been earned in a "former life" (*First Principles* 2.9.7). In Plato, or in any disciple of Plato, this would signify a sojourn in another body, animal or human; Origen, however, says repeatedly that those who entertain such doctrines do not belong to the church. He rebukes Basilides for holding that the time when Paul was "alive without the law" was the time when his soul dwelt in the body of a beast.[23] He confesses at *First Principles* 1.8.4 that the injunction in Leviticus 20:16 to stone an ass that has lain with a woman might warrant this inference, but intimates by his silence that it is not to be pursued. In his *Commentary on John* he declares explicitly that, whatever truth underlies the speculation that John the Baptist was Elijah, the man of the church cannot believe in transmigration even from one human body to another.[24] The former life must therefore either be that of the foetus (as Jews of the time may have argued)[25] or (as most modern scholars assume) a phase in the history of the soul preceding all embodiment in the present world.

While most proponents of the latter view purport to be upholding Origen's Platonism, no Platonist of his era could have held it. The doctrine of perpetual transmigration from body to body was not contested because it rested on two premises that were assumed to be incontrovertible—that

21. See *Commentary on John* 32.198.233–34.

22. *First Principles* 3.1.21; *Commentary on Romans* 7.15–16 = Origen, *Römerbriefkommentar*, ed. C. Bammel, 627–30.

23. *Commentary on Romans* 6.8 = Origen, *Römerbriefkommentar*, ed. C. Bammel, 502–3, commenting on Romans 7:9.

24. *Commentary on John* 6.11.66, with reference to John 1:21.

25. Edwards, "Origen's Platonism," 36.

the soul is by nature immortal and that its function is to animate a body. The only dissenters from the plain text of Plato were those who held that the passage of rational souls into beasts is an allegory of the subjugation of intellect by the passions. Origen himself was aware of this theory,[26] and we may therefore be sure that when he insists on assigning a single embodiment to every soul, he was declaring his freedom from Plato and devising his own theodicy to reconcile a difficult text in scripture with his conviction of divine justice. The same must be said of his commendation of Christ's soul as the one soul that has adhered to God since the beginning of creation: if this means the creation of the world and not merely (as I have suggested elsewhere) its own creation, Origen must have held that it is possible for a soul to escape embodiment in this world for any period of its own choosing.[27] And that, as Plotinus observes, is not the teaching of the *Phaedrus*, where it is hinted that the soul's shedding of its wings is subject to periods determined by the gods.[28]

The novelty of Origen's views will be all the more striking if we follow those witnesses who credit him with the thesis of a perpetual recreation of matter in order that other souls than that of Christ may be tested again. This is not a Platonic notion, even in the *Statesman*; it bears a closer resemblance to the Stoic doctrine of the eternal recurrence of worlds, which is repudiated at *Against Celsus* 4.65. The perplexities of Origen's commentators are compounded by his statements on the fall of Adam in paradise, for while these seldom if ever imply that the Garden and its inmates were incorporeal, they also lend no countenance to a naive equation of the historical with the literal sense of the biblical narrative. Only to his adversaries, in the treatise *On Prayer*, does Origen impute the belief in an asomatic paradise (*On Prayer* 23.3–4); when he scoffs in his own person at those who take the trees of paradise for earthly plants, he says no more than Chrysostom or Augustine, and does not offend the pious editors of the *Philokalia*. Elsewhere he seems to hesitate, like Plato in the *Phaedo*, between locating paradise on our own earth and assigning it to another earth; nevertheless, against at least one contemporary exegete of Plato, he denies that the paradise to which the saints go is an incorporeal realm subsisting only in *phantasia* or imagination.[29] He does indeed ask, in a fragment preserved in a catena on Genesis, what kind of body Adam could have had before he was clad in coats of skin; it is only his ancient critics, however, who say that his answer

---

26. *First Principles* 1.8.4.

27. See Edwards, *Origen against Plato*, 94 on *First Principles* 2.6.4.

28. Plotinus, *Enneads* 4.8.1.38, alluding to *Phaedrus* 247d5.

29. On *First Principles* 2.3.6 see Edwards, "Origen, Plato and the Afterlife."

was "none." In this fragment he has already deduced from Genesis 2 that Adam was created with a body, and his own response to his question, here as elsewhere, is that this body differed from ours in being free of the weakness that we now associate with the flesh.[30]

Nothing is proved by texts that speak of a paradise in the soul,[31] since Origen repeatedly asserts that the historical truth of a narrative is not belied by its figurative application. Texts in which he extols Christ's love of the church before the ages are merely testimonies to divine omniscience in imitation of St. Paul. There is no need to construe the one text that speaks of "all the souls that have existed since the creation" as though it meant more than it would mean in any other Christian author, namely "every soul that has come into being at any point since the creation" (*Commentary on the Song* 2.8.4). In short, we have no reason to suppose that Origen's teaching on the pre-existence of souls infringed his own rule of asserting nothing that the church denied. Whether his own speculations on unsettled points took the form of a systematic theology is a more difficult question: he was not by temperament a philosopher but a scriptural exegete, or at most (as in the *First Principles*) a harmonizer of scripture.[32] For the purpose of construing a given text in accordance with his own moral axioms and his reading of cognate passages, he was ready to avail himself of any tool that philosophy or philology could afford him (*Philokalia* 1). Just as it does not follow that he embraced the whole of any such philosophy, so it does not follow that he had any clear conception of the "former life" in which Esau incurred God's punishment or of the paradise that is neither place on a map nor a figment of the imagination. His principal object at all times was that his reading should be faithful to the content of his text, to the explicit proclamations of the church, and to the known character of God.

Demonology *versus* Demonolatry

From this review of the fragmentary and heterogenous evidence, it is clear that Origen entertained a belief in the pre-existence of the soul that was motivated not by Plato's arguments for its immortality but by his own

---

30. Simonetti, "Alcune osservazioni," 373–74; Edwards, "Origen in Paradise." On the orthodoxy of Origen's reading of the coasts of skin, see Tzamalikos, *Origen and Hellenism*, 124–56. In the *Commentary on John*, however, creation in the divine image is directly opposed to the fashioning of the body, with no reference to the coats of skin: Pinizivalli, "L'uomo e il suo destino," 374–77.

31. Industriously collected by Martens, "Response to Edwards," 195–99.

32. On his reticence, see Tzamalikos, *Origen: Philosophy of History*, 47–49.

conviction that God would never fail to deal with his creatures according to their deserts. It is difficult to pursue his application of this premiss in any more detail, not only because we are often dependent on lacunose remnants of Greek or Latin translations, but because he himself is generally reluctant to say more than is necessary for the vindication of a particular text, without taking pains to reconcile his conjectures in one place with his positive affirmations in another. Thus, as we have seen, his allusions to the former life of Esau, which acquit God of injustice at Romans 9:6, are not reconciled with his vigorous disavowals of Platonic and Gnostic doctrines of transmigration. Some of his glosses are studiously economic, as when he is content to infer that if Jesus claims to be from God there must be other souls that are not in the same way from God.[33] This is not so much an assertion of a Platonic fall of souls as a refusal to convert the language of scripture into that of Platonism. Allowance must be made for the possibility—the likelihood, we should say—that he was not always certain of his own opinion, that his thoughts may have developed (or for that matter, grown more tentative) in the course of his long career, and that his fixed resolution at all times was to say nothing inconsistent with the teaching of the church. The content of that teaching, or his perception of it, may have been subject to change in the course of his life, but he will always have been aware that the most abundant writing on the pre-existence of souls by professing Christians was produced in circles that he and his coreligionists deemed heretical. We know that he was often prepared to consider the speculations of such teachers and the evidence that they supplied for them, before endorsing the judgment of the church, and we should therefore take him seriously when he intimates—as, for example, in his comment on Matthew's parable of the labourers in the vineyard—that he is passing on an opinion held by others, which he does not choose to make his own.

Some scholars opine that Origen's theories regarding the pre-existence of the soul are not only speculative and occasional but figurative, and perhaps mythical, in whatever sense he might use that term of Plato.[34] Thus it is suggested that before its one embodiment it exists only in the foresight of the Creator, or else that the unfallen soul should be understood to precede the fallen soul only in the sense that the ideal is said to precede its adumbrations. To this we may reply that it is Plato himself who opposes myth

33. *Commentary on John* 20.162. Lettieri, "Il νοῦς mistico," 273–74, contends that Origen is here demythologizing the Valentinian depiction of Christ as the firstfruits of the pleroma. On the diversity of causes for the descent of souls, see Alcinous, *Didascalicus* 28; Iamblichus, *On the Soul* 28–29.

34. Harl, "La préexistence des âmes"; Laporte, *Théologie liturgique chez Philon d'Alexandrie at Origène*, 99.

to logos in his dialogues, and that Gnostic imitations of his writing in this vein are easily recognized, whereas Origen's exegesis has the same goals and observes the same principles whatever its subject matter. We have no reason to doubt that he understands the descent of souls as literally as the fall of angels, a topic on which he is more loquacious than any previous writer, and often (as we have noted) with the aim of supplying the literal sense of a passage in the scriptures that he takes to be allegorical. Anyone who imagines human souls to be the rational beings whom God created to govern the world at *First Principles* 2.9.1–2 must explain how Origen came to use almost the same vocabulary of the angels at 1.8.1; if the same dethronement of the intellect, in a greater or lesser degree, produces angels, souls, and demons, why should Ezekiel's mockery of the Prince of Tyre be construed as a veiled account of the fall of Satan when it was equally true, in its literal sense, of the Prince of Tyre himself? Nor has any reader of his answer to Celsus accused him of speaking in riddles when he insists that daemons are not the sublunar viceroys of the gods but a rebel horde who live in perpetual defiance of their Maker, inadvertently furthering his purposes by freeing the souls of those whose flesh they torture and destroy.

Acquainted as he is with the Book of Enoch, and we presume with the writings of the Greek apologists, Origen holds that demons work on human souls primarily by deception, and above all by the terrors and blandishments of false religion. Not being gods, they feed on blood and incense,[35] but the hidden price for the worshipper is that the soul "is estranged from God and bound to the body of humiliation" (*Against Celsus* 8.54). The healings ascribed to Asclepius are examples of the quackery that humans can sustain with the aid of demons; even pagan sorcerers, however, have discovered a peculiar potency in the name of Jesus and in scriptural appellatives for God (5.45). Celsus imagines that the very name daemon connotes a being who belongs to God and is therefore worthy of the sacrifices prescribed by law (8.25). Origen replies that these are laws of human origin, and that Christians are bound to refrain from the worship of such beings (8.26), since they know them for fallen angels (1.31). They do not believe, with Plato, that every soul is assigned at birth to a daemon who determines its future lot (8.34); nor will fear of retribution compel them to offer sacrifice, since they have a God who will not permit them to suffer (8.27). It is a measure of his credulity that Celsus applauds a superstitious testimony to the deeds of Apollo while slighting the prayers that Christians address to the one God worthy of our devotion (3.28). He does not perceive that he is handing the reins of power to rebels when, in order to justify his own charge

---

35. *First Principles*, Book 1, proem 10; 2.3.3.

that Christians are bad citizens, he asserts that they owe the same respect to demons as is paid to the viceroys of an earthly monarch (8.35). If "it is not without the help of demons that kings have won their thrones," that is only to say that God allows tyrants to flourish in their season (8.66). Christians accept their earthly rulers by divine ordinance, but will pray to no being and swear by no being other than God himself (8.65).

Deception brings its own penalty—as when Adam forfeited the image of God for that of Satan[36]—but it may also be the cause of more tangible evils. In Origen's world, it was by debauching the conscience of the many that the demons afflicted the bodies of the few who remained unfallen. In AD 235, when he witnessed a brief persecution under Maximinus Thrax, he ascribed it to demons, and exhorted Christians not to fatten them with timorous offerings of blood and incense (*Exhortation to Martyrdom* 41). In fact, it is the demons who are daunted by the courage of martyrs (*Against Celsus* 8.44) and give way for a time before the souls of the righteous dead (8.34). After a time, they gather and return in force, but as a rule they have no power to wound the church except by stirring up the enmity of pagans. Only at 8.31 is it conceded that they may be capable also of sending famine, blighting viticulture, and sowing plague among beasts and humans; even these atrocities are permitted to them, however, only so long as God elects to use them as instruments of his wrath. In the words of the psalmist, God entrusts judgment to the evil angels (8.32); these temporary ministers, however, are not to be mistaken for those whom have been appointed as permanent guardians of the cosmos (8.36), and if they are sometimes allowed to exceed their remit—a matter concerning which we possess no certain knowledge (8.32)—that is not a reason for offering them the firstfruits that in the law of Moses are set aside for God. Still less should the fear of disease tempt us to dedicate a part of the body to each of thirty-six demons, as the doctors of Egypt do (8.59), or to meddle in the putative arts of cajolery and coercion, the only fruit of which will be to deliver the practitioner into the power of those same demons in the place that God assigns for punishment (8.61). When Origen contrasts the Christian Eucharist with the bloody sacrifices of the pagans (8.54), he will not have forgotten Paul's admonition that even those who eat and drink unworthily at the Lord's Table may "fall sick."

---

36. *Homilies on Genesis* 1.13, in *Homilien zum Hexateuch*, ed., W. Baehrens, 17.26–28.

Demonic Action and Human Responsibility

Why does God permit the tribulation of his saints? One answer, as I have hinted in the last paragraph, is that no one in this world belongs entirely to the party of the righteous, because the Adam in each of us colludes with Satan. The expulsion from Eden and Satan's fall from heaven are two historic events that are signified in Ezekiel by the translation of the Israelites from Jerusalem to Babylon;[37] the saying at Genesis 3:22 that "Adam has become like one of us" is glossed by the prophecy at Psalm 82:6 that "you shall die as humans and fall like one of the princes"—that is to say, you shall fall like Satan.[38] The judgment on Adam, "earth thou art and to earth thou shalt return" (Genesis 3:19) suggests to Origen that "earth" in Ezekiel 14:13 is a cipher for all who sin.[39] In his *Commentary on Romans*, Origen does not question the historicity of the Adam in whose loins we are all contained.[40] Assuming, on the contrary, that there is a distinct time of Adam (*Commentary on Romans* 5.1.38), and a measurable epoch from Adam to Moses (5.2.7), he infers (almost two hundred years before Augustine) that we inherit the likeness of Adam's sin not only by imitation but by physical descent (5.1.34–35). His argument for the baptism of infants at *Homilies on Leviticus* 8.3.1 is that each of us enters the world in a state of defilement (*sordes*), with the exception of Christ, who had no human father. Our personal culpability, however, is in no way lessened either by this congenital frailty or by the assiduity of Satan. Only by God's special dispensation can he wound us either by illness or by natural disaster; as we have seen, his usual ploy is deception, which prevails because we are willingly deceived.

Hence, it will never be just to shift the blame for our sin to Satan. Even when he is said to have entered into Judas Iscariot, he was not more than a catalyst to the sinful disposition of his host. Christ said on the eve of his own betrayal that it was "written" (Mark 14:21), and the psalm in which it is written—"let his days be short and his bishopric pass to another" (Psalm 109:8)—was cited by Peter as evidence that even the crucifixion was ordained (Acts 1:20). Furthermore, he appears not to be a free agent, for when Satan enters into a man, it is only the power of Christ that can deliver him; yet Christ is the one who opens the heart of Judas to Satan by foretelling his

---

37. *Homilies on Ezekiel* 1.3, in *Kommentar zu Samuel, zum Hohelied*, ed. W. Baehrens, 326.1–13.

38. *Homilies on Ezekiel* 1.9, in *Kommentar zu Samuel, zum Hohelied*, ed. W. Baehrens, 333.14–16.

39. *Homilies on Ezekiel* 4.1, in *Kommentar zu Samuel, zum Hohelied*, ed. W. Baehrens, 359.25–26.

40. Bammel, "Adam in Origen," 72–73.

treason, and once he is resolved to sin says to him only "What thou doest do quickly" (John 13:26–27). Origen is thus at pains, in his *Commentary on John*, to refute the inference that Judas was already fated to be a sinner by his own nature or by divine ordinance. His perfidy flowed from his character (*Commentary on John* 32.6.68), but this is the meaning, not the negation of freedom; the fact that, when Christ predicted his betrayal, every disciple began to suspect himself is proof of the mutability of *proairesis*, the faculty of choice (32.19.255). Judas retained this faculty up to the point where the sop was handed to him, and Christ refrained from unmasking him in order to give free play to his own conscience. Recognizing at this point his own unworthiness (32.22.283), he succumbed to the tempter and went out into the night, which symbolized the fall of darkness upon his soul (32.24.313). Once Satan has gained his way, it is impossible to say whether he or Judas is the addressee of Christ's injunction "What thou doest do quickly" (32.23.297); at first, however, Judas was as capable as any other saint of repelling the darts that Satan looses at all of us many times a day (32.2.19).

Origen contends that we are all capable of showing the same resolution when we are moved by the spirit of anger, and that any woman can offer the same resistance to an assault upon her chastity, so long as it is Christ who rules the soul (*First Principles* 3.1.4). In the Latin of Rufinus we encounter the Latin equivalent to the Stoic term *propatheia*, which signifies the instinctive movement caused by an impression of an object of fear or desire. According to the Stoics, it will not assume the definite character of fear or desire in the wise man, although there is difference of opinion among modern, if not among ancient, commentators as to how far his soul is susceptible to the first motion. Hence, there is also difference of opinion as to how well Origen renders the Stoic position; he is not to be judged, however, by his accuracy as a scholar, for his text is not Chrysippus but the Bible, his subject is not the wise man but the God-man, and his chief aim once again is to avoid sacrilege, not to settle a philosophical dispute.

Stars as Signs, Not Causes

Chrysippus, of course, has no conception of an evil spirit who goads humans into sin. On the other hand, Origen accepts the common view of the Stoics as fatalists, and either they or the Gnostics who appealed to them must be his silent interlocutors in the digression against astrology, which is prompted by the creation of celestial signs at Genesis 1:4. What do the sun and moon signify, said his adversaries, except the things to come? And if they signify truly, so that that which they signify cannot fail to occur, how are we free (*Philokalia* 23.1)? Origen's first reply is that, by robbing us of "that which lies with us" (*to eph' hêmin*), this doctrine renders exhortation useless, and leaves us no rationale for punishment and reward. The adversaries to whom he directs this argument are heretics whose mentors in the pagan world are astrologers and skeptics; in such company it is lawful to borrow even from Epicurus (*Gnomologicon Vaticanum* 40), who had urged against the determinists of his day (that is, the Stoics) that if their reasoning were true they could not know this, since the same reasoning entails that they believe only what they are fated to believe (*Philokalia* 23.2). Origen also holds with the Epicureans that no true oracles can be obtained from the shrines of the gods; whereas they argued, however, that it would compromise the serenity of such lofty beings to meddle in our affairs, he avers that, being no gods but demonic impostors, they possess no faculty of precognition (23.21). At the same time, it is they who have spread the falsehood that the stars are causes and not merely signs (23.6). Yet signs they are, because God cannot be ignorant of the future, as reflection on the concept of divinity teaches us even in the absence of the scriptures (23.4). For those who require empirical proof, the anticipations of Christ's coming in Daniel, Isaiah, and the First Book of Kings will suffice;[41] the treachery of Judas was foreseen not only by Christ on earth but by the psalmist, writing under inspiration centuries before. Both Stoics and astrologers reasoned that if what is foretold is necessarily true, the event itself is necessary: a Peripatetic can deny the premiss, but a Christian, while denying the validity of the inference, takes the premiss as an article of faith.

The symmetry of past and future furnishes Origen with the strongest part of his case against the astrologers. They admit that a person's destiny is, in part at least, the product of antecedents that are woven into the causes of the astral configurations that predict these antecedents; these configurations therefore bear infallible witness to the past, but it would be absurd to argue that they cause it (*Philokalia* 23.5). They do in fact signify both past and future: the only written evidence for this is an extracanonical text, the Prayer of Joseph (23.19), but it is reasonable to assume that the God who sets the way of life before us in scripture should communicate his ordinances to the angels through this medium (23.21). The words of Genesis 1:4 on which Origen is commenting imply that God makes use of the heavenly bodies as a cipher, just as on another occasion he made Pharaoh a sign to the nations—though again it must be understood that he hardened the heart of Pharaoh only insofar as he attempted to persuade him by miracles, knowing

---

41. *Philokalia* 23.4–5, adducing 1 Kings 12:32 and 13:1–5; Isaiah 45:1–4; Daniel 2:37–40 and 8:5–9.

in advance that they would fail of their effect (23.20). To ordinary denizens of this world the heavenly alphabet is illegible, since knowledge of the future would induce lassitude or despair (23.10); the pretensions of the astrologers are false because they presuppose an accuracy that no human can attain (23.17). That which God foresees in his omniscience, by contrast, cannot fail to occur (23.8), but that is a consequence of the logical relation between all knowledge and truth, not an index of any necessity in things themselves.

If Satan and the stars are not to blame, still less is God. So much would be obvious were it not for the admonition in Romans 9 that God spares only those on whom he wills to have mercy, creating us to be vessels of honor or vessels of dishonor as he pleases, and with no more right to gainsay him than the pot has to cry out against the potter. When he addresses these texts in his *First Principles* (3.1.16–21) and his *Commentary on Romans*, Origen takes what we now call the Arminian view that God creates us knowing but not determining the choice on our own part that will shape us as vessels of honor or dishonor. If the apostle seems to have forestalled this interpretation by adducing the case of Jacob, who was preferred to Esau even in the womb, we must understand him in a manner that does not belie the justice of God in apportioning his gifts to human merits. That is to say, we must presume that Jacob was reaping the merits of his previous life (*First Principles* 2.9.7). Since Origen did not believe that a "man of the church" could entertain any argument for the transmigration of souls from one human body to another (*Commentary on John* 6.11.66), it has generally been assumed that he alludes here to a fall into the corporeal realm from the intellectual cosmos. Since, on the other hand, he certainly held that the child in the womb is already a person, it is possible that Origen was alluding to the rabbinic traditions that charged the foetus of Esau with impiety, emulation, and attempted homicide. This is another case in which he is more concerned to proclaim the truth than to vindicate it by philosophy.

God's power to elicit good from evil is illustrated again in Origen's *Homily on Numbers*, where he hints at an analogy between Judas and Balaam, the pagan diviner who blessed the people of Israel against his will (Numbers 22).[42] Judas by meditating evil brought about the salvation of the world (*Homilies* 14.2.4); Balaam, because he was bent on disobeying God's express command, was permitted to carry out the commands of his enemy, and thus became a harbinger not only of Israel's victory but of the birth of Christ (13.7.4). Since the star whose rising he proclaimed was the one that led the Magi to Bethlehem, we can answer those who ask why God permitted this friend of demons to go on practising astrology with

---

42. On the divine use of Balaam's free will, see Hall, *Origen and Prophecy*, 125–36.

success and thereby drawing others into this superstition. God, who ordains no evil, may permit it so long as it serves his providential design: unwilling, therefore, to leave the gentiles without some presage of Christ, he confided their instruction to fallen angels, who, in creating this false science from the remnants of their own knowledge, would inadvertently teach them more than the lawful prophets were able to teach the Jews.[43]

Divine Justice and Divine Victory

A theory of the origin of evil is incomplete without some theory of a cure. It can be argued that Plato begins by defining the problem—or rather two problems, ignorance and injustice—and excogitates his theory of transmigration as a solution, whereas Paul and the Gospels thrust the resurrection upon the world as the solution to a problem that had yet to be defined. If the resurrection was to be understood as the firstfruits of the new life purchased for us by Christ's death for our sins, it followed (since he was also said to have died under the law) that the term "sin" now included much that had hitherto been taken for righteousness. This was sufficient evidence that we could not know what sin is without revelation; it was not so clear what Christ had done, in addition to exposing the inadequacy of the law of Moses, to make the restoration of innocence possible. To Origen it was self-evidently heretical to deny that Christ was the Savior of all humanity, and equally heretical to imagine that salvation could be independent of our own exertions. Attributing both errors to the Gnostics, he maintained for his part that just as every human shared in the fall of Adam so every human inherited Adam's freedom to cooperate with God: the notion of the fall of souls, in whatever form he held it, was the philosophic combination of these two truths, both of which he held to be clearly written in the New Testament. The consequence is that, while he does not suppose that the divine image, lost in Adam, can be restored without divine grace,[44] he does not see the cross as a more efficacious instrument than the example and teaching of Jesus or the nourishment of the soul through his continuing incarnation in the scriptures, which for that reason are rightly called the word of God.[45]

He is credited indeed with an early defence of the theory that Christ died as a ransom to the devil. Commenting with his characteristic pedantry on the saying "you were bought with a price," he argues that it would be

43. For further questions about divine foreknowledge, see Edwards, "Providence, Freewill and Predestination."

44. Alviar, *Klesis*, 81–87.

45. See, e.g., Martens, *Origen and Scripture*, 239–41.

absurd for God to pay the price to himself, and hence that it must Satan who received that precious blood which outweighed all other souls in value. This passage from his *Commentary on Romans*, however, refers not to the cross but to the circumcision of Christ, and may be inspired by the apotropaic circumcision of Moses's child when he is attacked by the Lord (Exodus 4:24–26). Like most theologians before Nicaea, Origen appears to regard the death of Christ as the climax of his obedience, the fulfillment of a prophecy, and the necessary condition of our own dying to sin; this dying on our part, however, and the spiritual regeneration that follows upon it are not the results of an automatic process. They are not bestowed upon us by imputation; they are not imparted to us by the performance of any sacramental act, and they will not even come to us through the perusal of scripture if our thoughts cannot rise above the literal sense. The Christian virtues are acquired like the Aristotelian virtues, through constant practice and exercise, in which every soul will exhibit some proficiency, while almost none will be perfect (*First Principles* 3.1.1). For this reason Christian ethics requires what is lacking to Aristotle—an eschatology, which will afford sufficient time and more powerful means for the purification of both body and soul than has been vouchsafed to them in the present life.

This posthumous itinerary leads the soul first to the earthly paradise, guarded since the fall of Adam by a flaming sword through which we can pass only with great suffering, unless we have already been made holy in the present world by God-sent chastisements and tribulations. The majority of humans are not so fortunate, and belong to that type of whom Paul says that they build with hay and stubble, not with stone and precious metals, and must therefore endure the destruction of their works so that they themselves may be saved as by fire. Once they have entered paradise, they will undergo further obstruction until they are fit to ascend through the heavenly spheres, learning much in the course of this journey that was previously hidden, so that they come to a better understanding of the scheme of providence and of their own place within it.[46] Access of knowledge brings with it a further refinement of moral vision as the whole record of its merits and demerits is spread before the soul in the twinkling of an eye. Once the harmony of soul and spirit, which was broken by the soul's "cooling," has been restored, we shall know at last that consummation of the image and likeness of God that enables us to dwell in his unmediated presence, distinguished only by our subtle bodies from the three persons of the Trinity,

---

46. See further, Blosser, *Become Like the Angels*. On the texture of the resurrected body, see Schibli, "Hierocles of Alexandria."

who have now become (as in truth, of course, they have always been) the creature's "all in all."[47]

Origen in Chalcidius

Origen is therefore at one with the Platonists, and indeed with most philosophers, in regarding the soul's enslavement to lower appetites as the principal cause of evil. He agrees that the soul is riveted more firmly to these appetites by the body that it inherits from the fall, but he does not hold that embodiment in itself is an evil or an inescapable cause of sin. Matter, if there is such a thing at all,[48] is a product of God, not a recalcitrant coefficient of creation; even the lower cosmos, which serves as a theatre for the probation of virtue and vice, does not compel us to sin and is not produced by our transgressions, let alone, as the Gnostics asseverate, by those of a divine agent. Nevertheless, there is one ancient reader of some intelligence and discernment, an author of Christian sympathies though by no means a rigid churchman,[49] who makes Origen a party to his own dispute with the Platonists who blame the faults of creation on its substrate (*Chalcidius* 276–78). We may nonetheless hesitate to speak of creation, for Moses's view that God is the author of matter is rejected (cf. 277),[50] and Chalcidius accepts without hesitation the equation of Plato's receptacle or nurse with the Great and Small of the *Philebus* (286), and with Aristotle's prime matter, expatiating at some length in the difference between the four elements, each of which depends on matter as the permanent milieu of change and generation that receives all predicates but possesses none. Echoing Aristotle (*Physics* 192a) he nonetheless declines to identify matter with the mere privation of predicates: as the permanent substrate of the impermanent, it has a nature that embraces all ten of Aristotle's categories, not excepting substance (336).[51] No category is evil in itself, and if we take

47. On *apokatastasis* in Origen, see Ramelli, *Christian Doctrine of Apokatastasis*, 137–221.

48. See *Philokalia* 24 and *First Principles* 4.4.7.

49. Reydams-Schils, "Calcidius Christianus?," argues that he is a Platonist who sometimes makes a politic concession to Christian readers. In *Calcidius on Plato's Timaeus*, 191–215, where her principal interlocutor is Waszink, *Plato Latinus*, she contrasts Calcidius with other Christians who were undoubtedly more circumspect in their adoption of pagan tenets.

50. See further Reydams-Scils, "Calcidius on Matter," with the response of Bakhouche, "Le dualime en question."

51. On Calcidius's interpretation of Aristotle (which is eccentric but not always indefensible), see Van Widnen, *Calcidius on Matter*, 75–92.

evil to mean the absence of good it is in the privation, not in the matter itself, that evil resides.[52]

Since Moses and Plato are independent sources of authority for Chalcidius, he accepts the theory that souls expiate their sins by transmigration into new bodies (297–98).[53] He also makes a distinction, not anticipated in Plato but familiar to the student of Plotinus, between the substrate of the perceptible cosmos and the truly primordial matter, which he styles noetic or intelligible.[54] If the fourth-century date that most scholars assign to him is correct, Chalcidius is unlikely to have been ignorant of Neoplatonism.[55] It is not to Plotinus, however, but to the opening verse of Genesis that he turns for a proof that God created this eternal substrate for the ideal realm before he initiated the temporal order at Genesis 1:2, where the earth "without form and void" is taken to signify prime matter (276). This is not the exegesis of Hermogenes, for whom the earth of Genesis 1:1 is ontologically superior, though temporally posterior, to that of Genesis 1:2. The priority that is accorded to the intelligible here would suggest the influence of Origen, even if Chalcidius had not imitated the Alexandrian's practice of collating the Septuagint with the translations of Aquila and Symmachus. In fact, we see more than influence, for Chalcidius quotes, as Origen's own exposition of these verses, a passage that does not survive in the Greek remains of either his commentary or his homilies on Genesis.[56]

Didymus and Evagrius on the Fall of Souls

We should be wary of spurious precision in dating the birth and death of Didymus, since all that is known for certain is that he was in his eighties in the last decade of the fourth century. Even before his works were condemned at the Council of Constantinople in 553, he was stigmatized by Jerome as an ardent defender of Origen (Letter 73). No doubt it would have been almost an obligation for him to defend his predecessor if it is true, as some ancient reports suggest, that he and Origen both presided over the

52. See above all ch. 354 on the providential use of the receptivity of matter.

53. Though denying that Plato teaches transmigration from humans to beasts. On his antecedents, see Waszink, "Le rapport de Calcidius."

54. See 276 and Van Winden, *Calcidius on Matter*, 52–66.

55. On the juxtaposition of Platonic and biblical teachings, with arguments for a date in the reign of Constantine, see Edwards, *Religions of the Constantinian Empire*, 54–58.

56. 276–78. Reydams-Schils, *Calcidius on Plato's Timaeus*, 199–203 issues a salutary warning against postulating Origen as a source where he is not named.

Catechetical School in their native Alexandria.[57] The very existence of this school in either man's day, however, is open to doubt. Little credence need be given to the story of his meeting with St. Anthony, but his association in legend with this pillar of orthodoxy is an index of his high repute in his own time, both as theologian and as exegete.[58] Jerome did not question his orthodoxy when translating his treatise *On the Holy Spirit*, and the three books *On the Trinity*, which are extant under his name in Greek, are neglected today because they are dull and unlikely be authentic. Although other works are ascribed to him on Migne's *Patrologia Latina*, I shall follow the practice of specialists in building this discussion chiefly on the remains of his commentaries on Genesis, Job, the Psalms, and Zechariah, discovered at Tura in 1941.[59]

Born around 345 in Pontus, Evagrius was in early life an intimate of the Cappadocian fathers, and is said to have been ordained as a deacon by Basil of Caesarea (Palladius, *Historia Lausiaca* 38.2). In 379 he joined Gregory of Nazianzus in Constantinople, but in 382 (a year after Gregory's resignation of the episcopal office) he departed for Jerusalem, with the purpose of taking up the monastic life (Palladius, *HL* 38.3). Despite his friendship with Bishop John of Jerusalem, he elected to pursue his vocation in Lower Egypt, first in Nitria and then in Kellis (Socrates, *Church History* 4.23). His death in 400 coincided with the eruption of a controversy regarding the orthodoxy of Origen, in which both John of Jerusalem and the monks of Nitria took the side of the Origen against Jerome, Epiphanius, and Theophilus.[60] Only in 415 was the charge of Origenism laid against Evagrius himself, but in 553 he was condemned as a heretic at the Second Council of Constantinople.[61] Scholars have observed that his ascetic works (the *Practicus, Antirrheticus*, and *On Evil Thoughts*) offer little evidence to support this judgment; more warrant for it can be found, however, in his dogmatic compositions, the *Letter to Melania*, and the *Kephalaia Gnostika*—particularly in the Syriac version of the latter, which Guillaumont has shown to be more faithful to the author's text than the Greek that we now possess.[62]

Didymus, while he was bound as a Christian to reject the doctrine of metempsychosis, concurs with the Platonists (and as we have seen, perhaps with Origen) in conceiving the initial fall as a shift from a more tenuous

57. Bayliss, *Vision of Didymus*, 13–14.

58. See further Layton, *Didymus the Blind*, 20–21.

59. Puech, "Les Nouveaux écrits."

60. See further Katos, *Palladius of Helenopolis*.

61. Guillaumont, "Évagre et les anathémathismes."

62. Guillaumont, *Kephalaia Gnostica*.

form of embodiment to a grosser condition, which he believes to be figu-
ratively described in God's creation of coats of skin for Adam and Eve at
Genesis 3:21 (*Commentary on Genesis* 1.107.5–7). Where Gregory of Nyssa
assumes the creation of the androgynous inner man to be simultaneous
with that of the outer man who is endowed with sexual organs, Didymus
(once again perhaps following Origen) sees the demarcation of sexes as one
of the physical corollaries of the fall.

Since Didymus, like Origen, seldom reveals more of his system than
is required by his purposes as a commentator, doubt remains as to whether
he believed that even the tenuous state of embodiment is the consequence
of a fall. Certainly our souls existed before they inhabited our present bodies (*Commentary on Job* 1.57.14–11.58.1), as we deduce from Jeremiah 1:5,
Romans 9:13 (on Esau and Jacob) and Luke 1:44 (on the leaping of John
the Baptist in the womb); while, however, Didymus speaks with apparent
approbation of the tenet that souls have entered bodies both on account
of their own wrongdoing and for the sake of others, he does not allude to
a previous state of embodiment, either for individual souls or for the human race collectively in Adam. While there are hints that matter is always
necessary for individuation, we also read that before they were implanted
in bodies souls were *homoousioi* (consubstantial) with the Creator.[63] Bayliss
observes nonetheless that the ontological gulf between God and his creatures is reaffirmed in many other passages, and that where an unencum-
bered pre-existence is attributed to the soul, the motive is to exempt it from
all suspicion of being naturally subject to corruption and thus to ensure the
priority of virtue to vice.[64] He certainly holds that the soul is immortal and
that after death it will continue to undergo reformative punishment until it
has been made fit for the presence of God.[65] While immortality implies simplicity, this is consistent with a Platonic division into rational, irascible, and
concupiscible elements, which after the manner of Porphyry are styled both
parts and powers. Didymus also seems to accept the Stoic enumeration of
psychic faculties. In short, his statements regarding the nature of soul are
so eclectic that we cannot derive from him a consistent theory of the soul's
relation to its luminous vehicle, either before or after the present life.

Evagrius too subscribes to the threefold division of soul, and his
frequent exhortations to liberate *nous*, as the highest element, from the
gross sources of temptation could be taken to signify that he envisages a

63. For this comment on Romans 7, see Bayliss, *Vision of Didymus*, 110.

64. Bayliss, *Vision of Didymus*, 116–17, citing *Commentary on Psalms* 4.259.16–31.

65. Bayliss, *Vision of Didymus*, 101, citing *Commentary on Genesis* 2.158.20–21 and
Commentary on Ecclesiastes 6.349.9–14.

permanent survival after death without a body (e.g., *Kephalaia Gnostica* 2.77). His most considered formulation is that body, soul, and mind will be one—a position resembling that of Origen, except that he seems to regard the body itself as a fallen mind.[66] At *Kephalaia Gnostica* 1.65 he writes that the saints will be naked intellects free from satiety: this may be a clue to his understanding of Origen, or it may be that later generations read Origen through Evagrius. He might seem to annihilate the distance between the Creator and his creatures when he says that all will be gods (4.51); on the other hand, he and his readers knew that Christ had said as much at John 10:35. His language is often ambiguous, in conscious acknowledgement of the ambiguity of the scriptures, and he certainly does not presume, any more than Plotinus or Origen, that it is always the corporeal that corrupts the incorporeal. On the contrary, the sins of the rational soul are more pernicious than those if its lower parts—and also more native to us, inasmuch as they are less likely to be instigated by demons. Pride is the vice of the intellect, while freedom is both the most characteristic and the most perfidious of its virtues. Naturally mobile, it finds its stability only in the contemplation of God; the misuse of its freedom (the likelihood of which is, of course, inherent in the very notion of freedom) disturbs the simplicity that was grounded in God's immutability, and the ensuing descent immerses the intellect in the denser medium of soul, which ties it to a body. We are left in doubt once again as to whether Evagrius is speaking of a literal descent from an incorporeal state; his idiom being at all times hortatory rather than scientific, the passages that appear to distinguish a sensible from an intelligible body remain obscure.[67] His comments on transmigration are also tentative,[68] and the heresy more often imputed to him by ancient critics is a doctrine of universal restoration (*apoktastasis*) which implies a cessation of the pains of hell.[69]

Conclusion

Origen's reputation as a heretic is ancient; his modern reputation as the arch-Platonist has been fostered by those who treat him as a synecdoche for all that is wrong with traditional Christianity. In contrast to our own

66. See *Letter to Melania* 6 with Cartwright, "Soul and Body in Early Christianity," 186.

67. Corrigan, *Evagrius and Gregory*, 114–19.

68 Corrigan, *Evagrius and Gregory*, 127–28.

69. For a concise account of Evagrius's doctrine of apokatastasis and its sources, see Konstantinovksy, *Evagrius of Pontus*, 170–77.

movers of opinion, he believes in a transcendent God, a fall from a state of relative innocence and a world to come that is inaccessible to our carnal senses. If we label these tenets Platonic—inaccurately enough, and doubly so if we add that they were derived by allegory—we can pretend that they are not Christian, and that when the same tenets are echoed by church fathers of better standing, such as Gregory of Nyssa, it was only to baptize them and thereby exorcise the residual Platonism of the ante-Nicene church. The capital evidence of his debt to Plato in this caricature is his doctrine of pre-existence, if the term "doctrine" is applicable to a handful of extemporary remarks that are designed either to elucidate the obscurity of a scriptural text or to reconcile that text with the church's axiom that we cannot be punished for sins that we cannot avoid. Plato's doctrine of the soul's pre-existence is, by contrast, an axial premise of his myths, and is grounded in reasonings that Origen could not endorse—for instance, that soul is naturally immortal, that every soul undergoes an endless series of embodiments, and that the knowledge that it acquires in one embodiment is inherited in the next.

When Origen denies the transmigration of souls and conjectures that there are some souls that come into this world from God and some that do not, he is consciously speaking the language of the church and is as far from Plato as anyone can be who holds his theodicy. His speculations are never motivated by a desire to account for the origin of motion or the presence of latent knowledge, but only by his conviction that it would be unjust for God to be as indifferent to our merits as the Stoics and the Gnostics imagine. In contrast to both these movements and to Plato, he combines his *a priori* vindication of God with a qualified faith in the historicity of the fall of Adam. In later Christian thought it became more customary to treat the fall of Adam as the sole pre-existent factor in personal sin; but as we shall discover, they did not all draw the consequence that we are born in a state of perfect moral liberty, uncircumscribed by the errors of the past.

8

Providence and Order in the Platonic Tradition

WE SPEAK OF MIDDLE Platonism, of Neoplatonism, of Christianity, and the varieties of Gnosticism: and certainly we cannot efface these distinctions in the third century,[1] though we might venture to multiply them. Origen tenaciously differentiates the teaching of the church from its Platonic echo, Porphyry refutes the charge that his master borrowed everything from Numenius,[2] Hippolytus insinuates that heresies are as numerous as the Greek schools that nurture them. In the second century, however, we see less evidence of a parting of traditions than a coalescence or mutual fermentation. Much of the literature that we call Gnostic draws on Plato, but it carries his notion of a Good beyond being to an extreme that the pagan Platonists had not yet reached, denying to the ineffable Father any but negative predicates, or even the right to use those as signifiers.[3] The analysis of the noetic realm into being, life, and mind is a Neoplatonic commonplace only after Plotinus, yet is partially anticipated in texts written by his "Christian, yet heretical" adversaries.[4] Comparisons can be drawn with the *Chaldaean*

1. *Pace* Digeser, *A Threat to Public Piety.*
2. Origen, *Against Celsus* 4.3–5, 4.40; 6.43; 7.38–42. Porphyry, *Life of Plotinus* 17.
3. Dillon, "Monotheism in the Gnostic Tradition."
4. Porphyry, *Life of Plotinus* 16. On the noetic triad in the anonymous commentary on the *Parmenides*, see Rasimus, "Porphyry and the Gnostics." On the *Chaldaean Oracles*, see Majercik, "Existence-Life-Intellect Triad."

Oracles and an anonymous commentary on the *Parmenides*, but the date of the latter is doubtful while the former has been thought to show more affinity with the system of Valentinus than with that of any pagan contemporary. Christian apologists, as they don the philosopher's cloak, are less inclined to contradict Plato than to accuse him of plagiarism from Moses;[5] conversely Numenius is thought by some to have been indebted to Philo,[6] and even those who demur cannot deny that he shares with a work ascribed to Longinus a high estimation of the "lawgiver of the Jews."[7]

Numenius is conventionally regarded as a Middle Platonist or Pythagorean who was not ashamed to learn from Jews and Gnostics. There are elements in his work that seem more redolent of Christian apologetic than of any of these traditions—for instance, his extension of immortality to the *empsykhon* or ensouled body,[8] his allegoretic reading of a story concerning Jesus, and his belief in the active malevolence of daemons.[9] There is no doubt that Plato was an authority to him—so far as we know, his chief if not sole authority[10]—and that the First and Second Minds in his cosmogony are the Good of the *Republic* and the Demiurge of the *Timaeus*, the other forms being engendered by the Second Mind's contemplation of the First.[11] The demiurgic activity of the Second Mind, however, is not, as in Plato, a spontaneous diffusion of its goodness, but the result of an aberration that bears less resemblance to anything in Plato than to the fall of Sophia (Fr. 11.11–16).

In the extant remains of Numenius, which are admittedly sparse and tendentiously unrepresentative, we hear nothing of the evil soul in matter that Plutarch supposed to be attested in Plato's *Laws*. While the most natural reading of the passage quoted above implies that the cosmos has an origin in time, we do not know whether the world-soul was created at this time or whether it was produced by the marriage of form with a hitherto inchoate principle of motion, as Alcinous seems to opine.[12] We know that his First God is not entirely idle, for he is called the sower of souls, if not the

5. Justin Martyr, *First Apology* 59–60, etc.

6. Whittaker, "Moses Atticizing." On the possibility of Gnostic mediation of biblical concepts, see Edwards, "Atticizing Moses?"

7. Numenius, Fr. 30. 4–6 Des Places, quoting Genesis 1:2; Longinus, *On the Sublime* 9, quoting Genesis 1:3.

8. Fr 46a Des Places, with Edwards, "Numenius," 65.

9. Frs 1c and Fr 37 Des Places.

10. For his appeals to Pythagoras, see Frs. 1.5 and 36.9.

11. Frs 11 and 16 Des Places, with O'Brien, *Demiurge in Ancient Thought*, 144–58.

12. Alcinous, *Didascalicus* 10.4, p. 165.14 Hermann; cf. Dillon, *Alcinous*, 18.

seed.[13] One passage even suggests that every being in this cosmos is subject to providence, a position that Plotinus found absurd when he encountered it in the Gnostics:

> As God looks upon and turns to each of us, the consequence is that bodies live and are animated by being joined to[14] the rays of God. (Fr. 12.17–18, from Eusebius, *Preparation for the Gospel* 11.18)

The flaw in this world is not to be sought in its substrate or in one of two warring forces within it, but in the demiurgic intellect to which it owes its form and its very existence.[15] How this assumption is to be reconciled with his belief that the cosmos is beautiful by participation in this Second Intellect, which is good by participation in the Good itself or First Intellect, is a question that cannot be answered from our fragmentary testimonia. Numenius is the alleged mentor of Plotinus, the acknowledged precursor of Porphyry;[16] he is also, as we shall see in the present chapter, the precursor of the Gnostics whom Plotinus opposed, and also of the new men who sat uneasily between Platonists and Gnostics. We shall see, in short, that the Gnostic repudiation of the cosmos and the qualified affirmation of it in Neoplatonism are two distinct yet not entirely independent precipitates of the intellectual ferment that also gave rise to Christianity. We shall also see how easily a Platonist could find himself aping the tenets of a Christian, or a Christian those of a Gnostic, when one was defending the justice of the gods or the other denying the pre-existence of the soul.

The System of Plotinus

The element in Neoplatonism that distinguishes it from all second-century systems that claimed Plato as an ancestor is the postulation of a transcendent principle superior to being.[17] For this, and for the equation of it with

---

13. Fr. 13.5. See Edwards, "Numenius Fr.13," where the criticisms of O'Brien, *Demiurge in Ancient Thought*, 149 are already anticipated.

14. Or "fostered by the rays" if we accept the emendation of Dillon, *Middle Platonists*, 370–71.

15. See above on the schism in the Second Mind. For Dillon, *Middle Platonists*, 371–72, the Third Mind is the fallen aspect of the Second; for Proclus, *On the Timaeus* 1.303.27f. Diehl (= Fr. 21.3 Des Places), it is the world, while at *ibid*. III.101.32 (FR. 22.4) it appears to be the world-soul.

16. See the comment of Proclus at Numenius, Fr. 37.24–26 Des Places; Frs. 30–33 and 36 are all taken from the works of Porphyry.

17. Halfwassen, *Der Aufstieg zum Einen*.

the One of the *Parmenides* and the Good of the *Republic*, there may have been precedents in Pythagorean literature;[18] the reasoning by which Plotinus mounts to the One, however, commences with his solution to a problem that had long divided Platonists: the relation between the Demiurge of the *Timaeus* and the forms. Those for whom the Demiurge was himself the highest principle were apt to regard the forms as the contents, and perhaps creations, of his own intellect; for those who set the Good above the Demiurge, the forms were in some sense independent of him, which was not to say that his mind was incapable of compassing them. The most literal exegesis of the *Timaeus*, upheld in the time of Plotinus by his critic Longinus of Athens, implied that the forms are external to the demiurgic intellect:[19] this is the position that Plotinus finds untenable, not so much because it lacks philological cogency as because it would be unbecoming in Plato, as the prince among philosophers, to ascribe to the Demiurge anything less than perfect comprehension of the essences that he brings into existence. Plotinus follows Aristotle, rather than Numenius and the Gnostics, in deducing the eternity of the cosmos from the rationality of its final cause, which of course he takes to be the Good. Since the forms are the progeny of the Good, the Demiurge has that knowledge of them that, as Plato hints and Aristotle says, can be achieved only by an unqualified union between the perceive and the thing perceived. Since such a union is possible only for a perfect agent, and the perfect will never choose to be less than perfect, the forms will be the sole and eternal contents of the Demiurgic intellect; since neither they nor the Demiurge have any material substrate, they will not only be contained in but coterminous with him. In short, they and the Demiurge will be one.[20]

They will indeed be as absolutely one as anything in the realm of being. Yet just as any object in the sensible world is a compound of form and matter, so even in the intelligible cosmos there is an insuperable duality between knowing and being known. The principle of unity, therefore, cannot reside in intellect itself, which is at once and two, a One-Many; being must owe its unity to that which is higher than being, that of which Parmenides says, in Plato's dialogue of that name (*Parmenides* 137c–142d), that the being of the One would exclude the being of anything else, as a second predicate would make the One more than one. Where Plato had maintained that the One is superior to being, Plotinus adds (with an echo

18. See Dodds, "The *Parmenides* of Plato"; but also Hubler, "Moderatus."

19. See Porphyry, *Life of Plotinus* 20.92–104, with *Enneads* 5.5 and Armstrong, "The Background of the Doctrine."

20. On *Enneads* 5.5 as an interpretation of Aristotle, *Metaphysics Lambda* see Gerson, *Plotinus*, 48–56.

of Origen, whether conscious or unconscious) that it is superior to thought, which is to say that we can form no conception of it.[21] It follows that it has no thoughts of its own, since any thought can be an object of intellection. In one experimental treatise Plotinus expresses the absolute independence of the One by ascribing to it the capacity to will, to live, and to energise itself.[22] Even such terms, however, are accommodations to our linguistic poverty, and the One is not said, even metaphorically, to exercise either love or will in relation to the world. Hence, Plotinus arrives, by a different route, at the position of Valentinus, that the Demiurge is inferior to a first principle, which surpasses all thought and speech, but he does not follow Valentinus in making him inferior also to the realm of being. Still less does he concur with Philo in setting a creative and providential will above the eternal forms. The One does not love and was not, for Plotinus or his successors, the object of any cult. Even to speak of a philosophic communion with One does not seem true to his usage, for *nous* is the highest object with which the Plotinian self can undergo a union or *henosis*.[23] The One is not a possible object of union, and Plotinus cannot even use the makeshift adverb *ekei*, "there," as he does of the intellectual realm, to hint at some undiscovered place where this union might occur. Just as "the equal" in Plato is a synonym for equality, and "the just" for justice, so Plotinus is often better understood if we follow Mackenna in styling his first principle not "the One" but "Unity."[24]

Unity must be the unity of something, and the reason for the existence of anything lies in the nature of the Good to superabound. While this is said by Plato of the Demiurge, Plotinus transfers it to the higher principle without denying that it also holds true of all that participates in goodness. It seems that this superabundance results not only in the procession of *nous*, as the first objectification of the One, but also in the presence within *nous* of a kind of matter, which accounts at once for the mutual coinherence and the plurality of the forms.[25] The unity of intellect is sustained by the con-

21. Whittaker, "*Epekeina nou kai ousias*," citing Origen, *Against Celsus* 7.38 and Plotinus, *Enneads* 5.1.8.6.

22. On *Enneads* 6.8, see Leroux, *Plotin: Traité sur l'unité*.

23. See Meier, *Plotinus on the Good*, 307, citing *Enneads* 4.4.2.26.

24. Mackenna, *The Enneads of Plotinus*. Cf. Meier, *Plotinus on the Good*, 94–95. Bréhier, *Philosophy of Plotinus*, 157n6 suggests that Plotinus was forced to describe the first principle as the One because the Greeks had no term for zero. Westra, "Freedom and Providence," 127, retorts that "a cursory glance at *Enneads* VI.8" would refute this—as no doubt a cursory glance at the equally mythological language of the *Timaeus* would refute all that Plotinus says on the impassibility of the demiurgic intellect.

25. See especially *Enneads* 5.2.1.7–13, with Rist, "The Indefinite Dyad"; Emilsson, "Relation between the One and Intellect."

templation of its origin; its very possession of unity, however, implies that it is something other than unity, and hence that the largesse of the One has produced a new thing that is other than, hence inferior to, the Good. Thus, this *aporroia*, or flowing away from the One to intellect, is at the same time a necessity and, in language that Valentinus had made infamous, a *tolma*, or act of temerity.[26] It would not be in the nature of the Good to stint its self-communication, and Plato's *Sophist* (248–52) declares it unthinkable that there should be no life in the realm to which all life in our lower sphere is subject. While *nous* itself, the paradigm of the *Timaeus*, remains immutable, its ectype is impressed by Soul on the lower extreme of being, which Plato calls space and Aristotle matter.[27] The demiurgic function is therefore shared by *nous* and soul, the first constituting the formal and the second the efficient cause of that which, although it is good that it should exist, is less good than either of its causes. As all that lives is ensouled, the physical cosmos itself has a soul, whose creation is mythologically depicted in the *Timaeus* as a temporal event. The relation of the world-soul, and indeed of all particular souls, to Soul itself is open to some debate,[28] but it is clear that both the world-soul and Soul itself remain unfallen. The cosmos fashioned by Soul through the instrumentality of souls is nevertheless the seat of that which we know as evil, and it is in his attempts to explain this that Plotinus shows himself at once the most trenchant and the most seminal reader of Plato since Aristotle.

In *Enneads* 4.8 Plotinus undertakes to resolve apparent inconsistencies in Plato's teaching on the fall of souls. On the one hand, we read that the body is a tomb for the soul, that the cause of its confinement is its own sin or a wilful shedding of wings; on the other hand, we are told that the function of souls is to animate bodies, that the first act of the Demiurge was to fashion a soul for the world and that individual souls descend at times appointed by the gods. Is the soul then the captain or a captive of its material domain? The answer requires Plotinus to draw a number of distinctions, all of which are repeatedly affirmed or presupposed in his other writings. The most fundamental is that between the actuality (*energeia*) of the Intellect and its capacity (*dunamis*) for action in lower realms of being, which is exercised by soul. Every soul has the ability to contemplate both the unchanging realm of forms and the perpetual flux of matter, without forgetting either its subjection to the one or its obligation to master the other. Aristotelian terms will

---

26. *Enneads* 5.1.1.4; see further Rist, "Monism," 340–42.

27. Noble, "Plotinus' Unaffectable Matter," suggests that Aristotle, *Physics* I9 is one source of the doctrine that matter cannot be affected because it lacks the properties to which it acts as a substrate.

28. Discussed at length by Helleman-Elgersma, *Soul-Sisters*.

not so readily capture the distinction that Plotinus goes on to draw between the animation of bodies from a higher plane and a *neusis* or descent that involves the soul in the privation, pain, and travail of the body. (We must guard ourselves from a spatial understanding of this descent, remembering that for a Platonist it is less true to say that the soul is in the body than that the body is in the soul.)[29] The soul of the world, says Plotinus in tacit rebuttal of Numenius, has undergone no *neusis*, and maintains the just rhythms of growth and decay without any experience of vicissitude. Lest we imagine this to be possible only of a body that has nothing external to it, Plotinus accords the same impassibility to the sun and other stars (*Enneads* 4.8.2). The bodies of human beings, on the other hand, are governed by souls that have undergone two descents, the first for the purpose of governing the body (4.8.4.1–2), the second without any purpose, as it arises from a surrender to corporeal passions and their concomitant vices.[30] Even the first descent may be styled a *tolma*, or act of temerity (4.8.5), for which attachment to the body is its own punishment; for the second, the most benign antidote is swift death and transmigration to a new body, and the worst a period of retributive chastisement, administered by daemons.[31]

From this it appears to follow that most incarnations are not wilful acts of defection on the part of the soul but therapeutic expedients; it is only by the experience of wrongdoing and its consequences that such souls learn what is good. If some descents are ordained by the gods themselves, the reason is that it is better for souls to err than to remain for ever in a state of unrealized potentiality: the order of the cosmos requires that each denizen should perform its appointed task. At the same time, no soul is permitted to suffer complete degradation, for unless there were some part that remained unfallen it would be impossible for the soul to recover its knowledge of the forms and achieve the deliverance that Plato promises to the philosopher.[32] This treatise was written some time after Origen had conjectured that the sun and moon have willingly exposed themselves to vanity without falling into sin, and that if certain souls are expressly said to be sent into the present world by God there must be others whose descent has a different cause. Even more time had elapsed since Irenaeus, using almost the same vocabulary as Plotinus, had argued that the *experimentum mali*, or empirical knowledge of evil, is a qualified good although it is a

---

29. Because it is soul that unifies body, being unified in turn by God or intellect, as this is unified by the One: Porphyry, *Sententiae* 28 and 31.

30. See further Rist, "Plotinus on Matter and Evil."

31. Stamatellos, "Plotinus on Transmigration."

32. On *Enneads* 4.8.8.1–3 see Caluori, "The Embodied Soul," 220–21.

consequence of transgression, since it is only by making trial of both that we learn to discriminate between good and evil (*Against Heresies* 1.9.1). Since no one will suggest that Plotinus was influenced by Irenaeus, affinities between Origen and Plotinus cannot be taken to prove that one had read the other, or even that they are rehearsing the doctrines of a common master: it is enough that they belonged to the same intellectual milieu.

Plotinus on Fate and Providence

Porphyry gave the title *On Fate* to *Enneads* 3.1, the third of his master's treatises in chronological order. It opens with the stipulation that nothing in the realm of change and movement can occur without cause—least of all when the subject is the soul, which is always moved by the desire to attain some end (*Enneads* 3.1.13–24). To see that one man steals when another refrains, and that one grows rich in the same fields where another fails to prosper (3.2.4–7), gives the lie to every species of physical automatism, whether it be the Epicurean reduction of all phenomena to a fortuitous dance of atoms, the Stoic belief in the universal hegemony of fate, or the stargazer's confusion of foreknowledge with predestination (3.2.4.9–15). The Epicurean are manifestly wrong because the aimless careers and collisions of invisible particles cannot account for the regular succession of like events to like events that is a fact of daily experience (3.23.6–13); nor would such anarchy permit either mental deliberation on our part or the inspired prediction of future events (3.2.3.15–29). The Stoic position frees us from chance at the cost of annihilating all causality, since it banishes all active powers from nature (3.2.4.9–20); it also defies experience by robbing us of all that we know to lie within our own power of choice and action (3.2.4.20–28). The astrologers, whose mouthpiece appears to be Ptolemy, maintain that all persons born under the same skies share the same character, yet observation teaches us that members of the same nation differ as much from one another as from members of other nations (3.2.5.1–15). Like Origen, Plotinus grants that the future may be predicted from astral phenomena, but not that this heavenly script is the *cause* of that which it foretells.[33]

Plotinus's most extensive discussion of providence was divided by his pupil into two treatises, now numbered as *Enneads* 3.2 and 3.3. In the opening chapter of 3.2 Plotinus appears to disclaim the intention of proving the operation of providence in detail, undertaking only to demonstrate the justice of the cosmic order in which every being does and suffers only such things as are proper to its station. At the same time he admits that, if we are

33. See Adamson, "Plotinus on Astrology."

to vindicate this order, we must explain why the wicked thrive at the expense of the just; true though it is, it will not be enough to say that ill fortune cannot detract from the happiness of the just and that good fortune brings no advantage to the wicked (*Enneads* 6.3.2.6.1–5). Before he proceeds to show that we each receive our due reward, however, he lays down certain principles that have been ignored by those who assign the blemishes of the world to matter, to chance, to fate, or to an evil demiurge (3.2.1.1–10). Above all, one must remember that the part exists for the whole, not the whole for the part (3.2.39–18);[34] order is good in itself and does not exist for the purpose of controlling that which is disordered (3.2.4.26–28). Furthermore, we are apt to see disorder where there is none because we demand from the lower planes of being that which can be true only of the highest, where there is neither chance nor change and hence no cause. We cannot blame animals for their lack of reason, which has at least the advantage that they never act against nature (3.2.9.31–37). We cannot blame the gods because they do not permit our crimes to mar their felicity, or even require of good men, who are living the life of the gods, that they should step down from this height to restrain our follies (3.2.9.12–15). The finger does not perform the office of an eye (3.2.4.40–41) nor the mind that of the foot (3.3.5.13–15). Where there is order there are degrees, and since evil is nothing but a lesser degree of goodness (3.2.5.26) we cannot dissent from the judgment of Plato that evils will never be banished from the world.[35]

The power of choice, and therefore of error, sets us apart from both beasts and gods (*Enneads* 3.2.8.9–11). All things that befall us externally are natural, but the test of our probity is our receiving them either in accordance with or in opposition to nature. Actions of the latter kind do not proceed from providence (3.3.5.25 and 47), but neither do they frustrate it, for it lies with us to use whatever place has been allotted to us according to reason and nature (3.2.17.23–25). We have, moreover, some liberty to decide not only how but what we suffer: if a group of youths who put their trust in prayer and neglect to exercise lose their clothes to a gang of robbers, they have no right to blame their own indolence on the gods (3.2.8.16–21; 40–46). If there were no such failures to be provided for, we should have no cause to speak of providence: if its vigilance sometimes disappoints us, we may sure that due reparation will be made when the soul undergoes a new embodiment, in which the criminal will become the victim of the same crime (3.2.13.1–13). Plotinus seems to assume that this principle can

34. On the cosmos as a living intellectual unity, see *Enneads* 3.2.1.30–33, with Boot, "Plotinus, On Providence."

35. *Theaetetus* 176a5, quoted at *Enneads* 3.2.5.29. At 3.2.15.9–10 the same words explain the persistence of matter.

be strictly applied, though he also repeats the dictum of the *Republic*—"the blame lies with the chooser; God is blameless"[36]—which implies that we are free to learn from our sins and choose a better life than the one that we misused. At the same time he points out that it is merely a type of life that falls within our power of election, the course of the actual life being partly determined by our own choices, as though we were actors in a play who imparted something of our own to the role prescribed for us by the poet (3.2.17.28–32).

It has not escaped some readers of Plotinus that his satire on those who expect to be saved by prayer alone would fall with some force on Christians. Paul's use, long before Plotinus, of the argument that not every limb in the body can be the head is not, of course, any proof of borrowing on the part of the Greek philosopher, any more than Paul is likely to have borrowed the analogy from Menenius Agrippa; on the other hand, the position disowned by Plotinus, that order exists for the sake of the disordered, finds no closer parallel in antiquity than Paul's dictum that the law was introduced for the sake of transgressions. Whether Plotinus knowingly encountered any mouthpiece of the church we cannot say, unless we set aside the ancient testimonies that forbid us to identify the Origen who was a colleague of Plotinus with the Christian theologian. Porphyry tells us, however, that it was a certain group of "Christians, albeit heretics," whose criticisms of Plato inspired the acerbic vindication of the natural order that we now know as *Enneads* 2.9, "Against the Gnostics or against those who say that the Author of the cosmos is malign."

The boast of these men, says Porphyry, was to have penetrated being to a depth that was hidden from Plato; their sources were books attributed to Zoroaster, Zostrianus, Allogenes, Nicotheus, and Messos, the last four names being otherwise unknown to the Greek tradition, although Nicotheus is invoked by the alchemist Zosimus, while the other three, together with some fragments of a book of Zoroaster, have been rediscovered in the Nag Hammadi Codices.[37] Many would now assign both the *Zostrianus* and the *Allogenes* to the Sethian tradition (that is, the one that was strictly called Gnostic in antiquity), while our references to the Book of Zoroaster are embedded in one version of the text that seems to have fathered this tradition, the Apocryphon of John.[38] To Plotinus himself, his adversaries are erstwhile

---

36. *Republic* 617e4, quoted at *Enneads* 3.2.7.19–20.

37. See Porphyry, *Life of Plotinus* 16; Edwards, "Neglected Texts"; Jackson, "The Seer Nikotheus."

38. See chapter 4.

friends—that is, students from the school of Ammonius Saccas[39]—who, instead of deducing the principles of being from the book of nature under Plato's guidance, have interpolated hypostasis after hypostasis between the realm of essence and the activity of the Demiurge (2.9.1.12–16 and 41), as though it were not the same intellect that contemplates the transcendent and informs the material order. They teach that matter is evil, though coeternal with the divine,[40] and that the cosmos came into being only because Sophia, the lowest of the hypostases, was ensnared by her own reflection in the nether realm, to which she descended, not only begetting the Demiurge but bringing in her train the other souls and the "members of wisdom" who appear to be the only beings capable of escaping the prison fashioned by her son.[41]

This is the torso of a myth whose limbs are scattered in Gnostic and the works of Catholic heresiologists. Plotinus, unlike the latter, cannot deny the fall of souls, and has his own use for the term "members." In common with Irenaeus and Hippolytus, he repudiates the notion that creation arose from a rupture or transgression in the divine realm; on the other hand, he was widely regarded as the heir to Numenius and hence to a cosmogony that assumed the coeternity of intellect and matter and traced the origin of the material world to a lapse of vision in the intellect, comparable to the lapse of vision that Plotinus himself imputes to the erring soul.[42] It could have been said on Numenius's behalf that he did not multiply hypostases, did not graft the biblical figure of Wisdom on to Platonism, and did not exclude the first principle from the governance of the cosmos; nevertheless, Plotinus finds it expedient to take his appeal against the Gnostics directly to Plato, whose parable of the cave admits that our present state is one of bondage and ignorance, but only for so long as we go on choosing that it should be so.[43] Where the Gnostics create their own tragedy of terrors (2.9.13.7),[44] the true doctrine holds each soul accountable for its fall and thus endows it with means of its

39. Edwards, "*Aidôs* in Plotinus." On Sethianism before Plotinus, see Turner, "The Platonizing Sethian Treatises."

40. See further Narbonne, *Plotinus in Dialogue*, 12–53; Spanu, *Plotinus, Ennead II.9 [33]*, 70–73.

41. The myth of *Enneads* 2.9.10 appears to originate with the primitive Gnostics, often called Sethians in modern scholarship. See Rasimus, "The Sethians and the Gnostics of Plotinus"; Burns, *Apocalypse of the Alien God*, 32–47 and 161–66.

42. See Porphyry, *Life of Plotinus* 17.1–2. On the relation of Numenius to both the Gnostics and Plotinus, see Athanassiadi, "Numenius: Portrait of a Platonicus."

43. *Enneads* 2.9.6.8–10; Plato, *Republic* 514aff.

44. Cf. Proclus on Numenius, Fr. 21.6 Des Places; Hippolytus on Valentinus, *Refutation* 6.42.2.

own salvation. No soul is doomed by its nature to eternal reprobation, and conversely none is saved, as the Gnostics imagine, by suddenly perceiving itself to be a son of God.[45]

This could be a jibe against any Christian, as could the complaint that the Gnostics imagine that providence has some special concern for each of them that does not require that they attune themselves to the harmony of the cosmos. Where Christians had hitherto been coupled as atheists with the Epicureans, Plotinus compares the Gnostics to them as fellow-deniers of providence;[46] at the same time, he takes up Celsus's quip (itself purloined from Epicurus) that those who genuinely hate the world can leave it in an instant.[47] The Gnostic in Plotinus, like the Christian in Celsus, is an *idiotês* or private individual who cannot act out his role in the scheme of things. On the other hand, the fear of the stars that the Gnostics exhibit is not a vice that earlier polemicists had detected in the Catholic form of Christianity; nor, of course, would any adherent of this tradition have quarrelled with Plotinus when he challenges his antagonists to imagine a more beautiful adumbration of the noetic realm than our own material cosmos. A Christian might have smiled when he heard the Gnostic compared to a tortoise who is trampled because the music to which the rest of the world is dancing is not adapted to his own gait.

For all that, our physical cosmos is not the best of all possible worlds; indeed, it is the worst of all actual worlds. The *Treatise Against the Gnostics*, thirty-third in chronological order, is often (though not invariably) regarded as the last quarter of an integral text, entitled by Robert Harder the *Grossschrift*, the remainder of which is now represented in Porphyry's arrangement by treatises 30–32, that is *Enneads* 3.8, 5.8, and 5.5. A writing of the length of Harder's *Grossschrift* would be unparalleled in the Plotinian corpus, as would the postulated redistribution, although Porphyry did not shrink from dividing a single text into two or three consecutive treatises.[48] Be that as it may, the Gnostic myth of Sophia's fall is preempted in *Enneads* 3.8,[49] the first of the four extant treatises, by a personification of nature that is perhaps less characteristic of the Platonic tradition than of the Stoics and

45. *Enneads* 2.9.9.56–57; cf. Acts 5:27, where "servant of God" is also a possible meaning. Cilento, *Paideia Antignostica*, 248 compares Clement of Alexandria, *Stromateis* 7.16.103.1.

46. *Enneads* 2.9.15.8; cf. Lucian, *Alexander* 25.

47. *Enneads* 2.9.9.17; cf. Diogenes Laertius, *Lives of the Philosophers* 10.126.

48. Harder, "Ein neue Schrift Plotins"; Cilento, *Paideia Antignostica*.

49. At 3.8.4.3 she says of herself that she works in silence (*siôpê*); compare the personification of silence (*sigê*) in Valentinian myth at Irenaeus, *Against Heresies* 1.1, etc. For commentary on this treatise, see Deck, *Nature, Contemplation and the One*.

their Peripatetic opponents. Nature, in this conceit, is not so much a distinct hypostasis as a power or operation of soul, excelling all human artisans not only in working without either tools or limbs but in having no substrate but prime matter (*Enneads* 3.8.2.23–25), whereas the human craftsman derives his colors from that which already has color, and polishes a surface that is already stone or wood. As a *logos* or principle of soul, which acts as a logos or principle of *nous*, she is not so far from her source as to fall on one side or the other of the divorce between subject and object, between the contemplative intelligence and that which it contemplates. Like intellect, she is herself a mode of *zoê* or life and a mode of *theôria* or contemplation.[50] Nevertheless there are gradations of life, of Logos, of the contemplative faculty, and nature, because her workshop is the lower domain of being, is capable only of the physical, not the noetic exercise of the contemplative faculty, which weakens it by translating it into a *praxis* or activity. The Logos that nature imparts to material entities is indeed the reflection of a Logos superior to nature herself because it originates in *nous*; nevertheless, as Plotinus says at the opening of treatise 31, the sculptor who translates his noetic vision into a tangible form deprives it of actuality, for the matter in which it takes shape has the potential to be transformed into something else.

Theôria or contemplation is in fact the true end of all *praxis* (*Enneads* 3.8.6.1–2). The more closely we approach this end, the more perfect the coalescence of subject and object. Yet even on the plane of *nous*, coalescence is not identity: if the objects of pure intellection are never external to the intellect, as Plotinus maintains at length in *Enneads* 5.5 (the third portion of Harder's *Grossschrift*), thought and its objects will be coextensive; yet even here, at the farthest point that thought can reach, there remains the duality of that which thinks and that which is thought. At the end of 3.8 the endeavor to grasp the principle of unity beyond intellect throws both thought and speech into *thambos* or bewilderment (3.8.11.32)—a hint that Plotinus had understood the cause of Sophia's fall in the Valentinian allegory. In *Enneads* 3.5, his treatise *On Love*, Plotinus departs from Plato by characterizing the proper object of the mind's striving as the infinite or indefinite, the *apeiron*; distinguishing two forms of love—the Uranian, which seeks knowledge of the whole, and the pandemic, which attaches itself to a part—he concludes that the latter is always seeking more than it comprehends, and this is the reason, as Plato says, for its rashness and incontinence in the pursuit of earthly beauty. The greater the *aoristia* or indefiniteness that comes between the soul and its object, the more the soul takes on the condition of matter, which shares with the One the predicates (if predicates they are) of *aoristia*

---

50. *Enneads* 3.8.3.14–18, 3.8.7.2, 3.8.5.25–30, 3.8.8.26–29.

and *apeiria*. Although in *Enneads* 3.5 this is said only of the love that has the part, not the whole, for its object, the final treatise in Porphyry's arrangement of the corpus reveals that the soul comes even closer to dissolution when it outsoars finitude, only to recoil from the sublimity of the One.

Fate and Freedom

As we have said, Plotinus thinks it inevitable that the One should superabound, since that which is good, in Plato's dictum, has no particle of envy. In explicating the myth of Poros and Penia in the *Symposium*, Plotinus declares that a soul that is drunk with *logoi* from above will descend as Poros descended to the Garden of Zeus, and share the fruits of its contemplation with the needy inhabitants of the lower realm. It is in this way that the good populates the lower realm, yet at the cost of bringing into being that which is other than the One, and thus inferior, and of causing even the secondary and tertiary vessels of this superabundance to fall below their proper station in the cosmos. The emergence of *nous*, as we saw above, is a *tolma*; in contrast, however to that of the Valentinian Sophia, this primordial transgression is also the primordial good, existence as something other than the One. His objection to the Gnostics seems to be that, in making Sophia fall because she is seduced by the matter below her, they fail to perceive that the impetus to descend is in that which descends. Consequently they also fail to perceive that the descent is not wholly evil and that in some measure that which descends remains unfallen. Of the hypostases *nous* and soul, indeed, we can say that they have never fallen; at the other extreme, Plotinus can evoke the myth of Narcissus or speak of souls who drown in the mirror of Dionysus; as we have seen, however, there is a part of these also that remains above.

There is thus no question of blaming all evil on matter; if Plotinus describes it in one treatise as the prime evil, this is not because the soul plays no part in its own delinquency but because it is only in the presence of matter that it can turn away from the good. If Denis O'Brien is right, however, the soul not only commits the fault but creates the conditions for it, since she herself is the one who generates matter before she "covers" it in an attempt to endow it with form that too often results in her losing her own.[51] There is a striking analogy here to the Valentinian conceit that matter is formed by the tears of the penitent Sophia, who then sets about the redemption of the cosmos. The question is too intricate to be determined

---

51. O'Brien, *Plotinus on the Origin of Matter*. On the subsequent history of discussion of *Enneads* 1.8.14.51–54 and other texts in Plotinus, see Narbonne, *Plotinus in Dialogue*, 44–46.

in a book of the present scope, and it will suffice for our purpose to say that whatever the origin of matter in Plotinus, the ineradicability of evil is not a corollary of the existence of matter but of very nature of being itself. Indeed, we can hardly ascribe existence to matter, for as a possible receptacle of predicates it has no existence of its own, and ought not even to be described as the *ametron* or "unmeasured," but rather as *ametria*, "measurelessness."[52] It is not the cause of individuation, nor is individuation an evil in itself, for intellects completely emancipated from matter do not lose their identity, though they do not retain any anecdotal memories, and are totally penetrable to one another because they are all engaged in the contemplation of the same timeless objects. To say that matter is infinite or indefinite is not so much to accord it a property as to deny it all properties: that is a state into which a soul cannot enter with impunity, but the tragedy of all souls is that they are not the One and that if they aspire, as they must, to the condition of the One, they may forfeit their unity even as souls.

As matter cannot cause evil without the complicity of soul, so we cannot infer that because we sin *in* the body we sin *on account of* the body. *Enneads* 3.4, *On Our Tutelary Daemon* is a commentary on a passage near the end of the *Timaeus* where, having admitted that a bodily indisposition may be the cause of a vicious character, Plato declares that nevertheless the gods have placed in each of us a daemon to be the ruling principle of thought and action. Since the term daemon may be applied in Greek to any accident that we suspect to be supernatural, it may also connote one's fate. Plotinus argues, therefore, that the choice made by the soul on the threshold of each new incarnation determines a paradigm or pattern of life, which will be realized if it remains true to its hegemonic principle and forfeited if it yields itself to the ebb and flow of matter. The tutelary daemon that is assigned to every soul at *Timaeus* 90a–d is equated in this treatise with the star that is said at 41c–42b to be its proper home.[53]

Plotinus himself concedes in *Enneads* 4.4.40, that the magician achieves his ends when he is able to exploit the natural sympathy between

---

52. See *Enneads* 2.4.15. At 1.8.15 the necessity of evil, as a corollary of the necessity of matter, is asserted, although its reality consists only in its counteraction of unity, and hence of our aspiration to the Good. Scholars have often perceived a hesitation in Plotinus between a theory of matter as mere privation and a theory in which it is actively inimical to the Good. See Long, "What Is the Matter with Matter?," on the conflict in his thought between the Aristotelian notion of matter as substrate and the Platonic conception of a timeless receptacle for the forms.

53. For criticism of Porphyry, *Life of Plotinus* 10, where he states that Plotinus composed this treatise after his daemon was found to be a god, see Edwards, "Two Episodes."

elements.[54] Earlier in the same treatise (*Enneads* 4.4.32) he concludes that the operation of this sympathy enables the stars to act at times as causes and not merely as signifiers. The question is agitated at greater length in *Enneads* 2.3, to which Porphyry attached the title *On Whether the Stars Are Causes*. Plotinus's answer is not a simple negative, though he is certainly not on the side of the astrologers. While such eternal configurations cannot be wholly fortuitous it is possible for stars can signify without being causes (2.3.1.1–5), and quite impossible that glory or disgrace can be products of sidereal influence (2.3.1.6–10). It is true that we owe our souls to the stars (2.3.9.10–16; cf. *Timaeus* 41, etc.) and not absurd to suppose that they have imbued the soul with certain dispositions (2.3.11, 2.3.15; 4.4.31); each of us, however, possess not only a soul but an intellect, and, since this remains unfallen, it is only when we belie our twofold nature and abandon the higher soul that we become enslaved to fate (2.3.9.27–31).

Divinity and Demonology in Porphyry of Tyre

For Plotinus, therefore, the conviction that nothing in nature is evil does not entail that matter is good, but rather that the evil that we impute to it consists only in a deficit of being. Its place is at the extremity of being, or at both extremities if we apply the term "noetic matter" to that which underlies the forms as a precondition of multiplicity and of the intellect's being other than the One.[55] On the other hand, it has no place among the contents or the immediate products of intellect, though it may be an emanation of the soul. This etiolation of matter is often assumed to be characteristic of all Neoplatonists, but Plotinus may be the last to speak of it with such disdain. He was also a much less religious man than his student and eulogist Porphyry of Tyre, who, whether or not he was raised as a Christian, sets up his master's system as a rival to that of the church by adopting Origen's formulae "God above all" and "three principal hypostases" as designations for the transcendent principles to which Plotinus himself gave no such names.[56] Proclus alleges that he conflated the One with the Father of the Chaldaean triad, that is with the first existence rather than with the ineffable source of existence.[57] If this is true, his first principle has more in common with the personal deity of Philo and the New Testament than with the One of the

---

54. I have been greatly helped by the discussion of Adamson, "Plotinus on Astrology."

55. See *Enneads* 2.4.2–5, with Nikulin, *Neoplatonism in Late Antiquity*, 90–116.

56. Porphyry, *Life of Plotinus* 23; Plotinus, *Enneads* 5.1 title.

57. See Edwards, "Porphyrius," 1338.

Enneads, who neither thinks nor is. The Christian heirs to Philo and the New Testament, as we know, maintained that nothing, not even matter, exists independently of his will, and Porphyry also appears to have held in his *Commentary on the Timaeus* that matter owes its origin to the Demiurge.[58]

The descent of souls to bodies (which, in Porphyry's exegesis of the myth of Er, takes place through the gates of Capricorn) is not in itself an evil, for it not only gives life to the animate but enables the soul to cultivate virtues for which there is no occasion in a world without death or adversity.[59] Nevertheless the association of soul and body is deadly to the former when it ceases to exercise its natural mastery and permits appetite to get the better of virtue. In the *Sentences*, which distil the teaching of Plotinus, the practical virtues mark the first stage in a process of deification that leads us through the political virtues to those of the true philosopher and finally to the paradigmatic virtues which confer upon us the status of "father of gods" (*Sentences* 32). No other means to this goal are prescribed or proposed than the assiduous subjection of the passions to the disciplined intellect. In other works, however, he maintains that the irrational soul cannot be set free without rites and incantations, disdained by Plotinus but inculcated under the name of theurgy by the *Chaldaean Oracles*.[60] This loss of faith in the sovereignty of reason can be blamed, if we will, on Porphyry's youth, on his age, or on the senescence of Greek culture; its metaphysical premise, with which Christians concurred more readily than his fellow-Greeks, is that impiety springs not only from human ignorance but from minds and wills superior to ours.

For Porphyry, as for his master Plotinus, the superabundance of the divine is symbolized in myth as a stupor of intoxication, causing the intellect to sink down to earth. In the *Cave of the Nymphs* the sweetness that overwhelms Cronus is the same influence that draws the soul from heaven; perhaps it is the same influence, or its converse, that in the *Phaedrus* and the myth of Sophia tempts the lower intelligence to reach for a height from which it cannot but fall. Porphyry's narrative culminates, however, in the emasculation of Cronus, which denotes the impassibility of the intellect to the matter that it informs.[61] The surrogates of the gods, who rule the lower world from within, are daemons who excel us in longevity and sagacity

58. Proclus, *In Timaeum*, vol. 1, 300 Diehl = Sodano, *Porphyrii in Platonis Timeeum*, Fr. 50. See further Smith, "The Significance of 'Physics.'"

59. Augustine, *City of God* 10.30,20–53 = Smith, ed., *Porphyrii Fragmenta*, Fr. 298 (p. 341). Augustine notes that his views are at variance with those of other Platonists.

60. See Smith, *Fragmenta* 283–303 (pp. 319–50); Hadot, "La métaphysique de Porphyre."

61. *Cave of the Nymphs* 16, in Porphyry, *Opuscula Selecta*, ed. A. Nauck, 68.6.

but are subject to passions of which the gods know nothing. In his treatise *On Abstinence*, Porphyry argues that animal sacrifice is a custom imposed on the world by rebellious members of this race who, instead of acting as deputies and ambassadors, have usurped their names and the worship due to high powers, battening on our misplaced oblations and threatening us with pestilence, famine, and earthquake if we decline to shed the blood of our fellow-creatures, and even that of our fellow-humans, in compliance with their demands.[62] No Christian had attributed such power over natural forces to fallen angels, but Porphyry is entirely at one with Justin, Athenagoras, Clement, and Origen in explaining false religion as an artifice by which beings indebted to us for their corporal sustenance become tyrants of our souls.

Porphyry is no Christian, since he maintains at all times that the gods exist and are worthy of our reverence. His treatise *On Statues* is written for the edification of those who see nothing in images but wood and stone, as others see nothing on books but ink and paper.[63] Another work *On the Philosophy of Oracles*, known now only from disapproving excerpts in Eusebius, admits that the shrines are inhabited by daemons rather than gods, who speak by constraint and not without some measure when they prescribe the modes of sacrifice due to each of three classes of deity.[64] Even those who require the killing of animals are not said in our remains of this work to be evil or inimical to the true order of the cosmos. Nor will Porphyry ever admit that a god can be the cause of our wrongdoing, even if our own choices, as he warns his wife Marcella, may open a place in our souls to an evil daemon.[65] His marriage to Marcella is a propitiation of his natal daemon, which seems to be the equivalent of the tutelary daemon of Plotinus and the *Timaeus*.[66] This now represents, however, not the higher state of life that acts as a beacon to the soul, but the conditions that are imposed upon its freedom in the present world by the choice that it made before birth. In the *Cave of the Nymphs*, the appeasement of these marine and material deities is a work of perpetual sacrifice, by which we are surely

---

62. *On Abstinence* 2.36–43, in Porphyry, *Opuscula Selecta*, ed. A. Nauck, 165.3–173.8.

63. Smith, *Fragmenta*, Fr. 351 (p. 408). On the Christian reception of this work, see Viltanioti, "Cult Statues in Porphyry."

64. Smith, *Fragmenta*, frs. 303–50 (pp. 351–406). On its scope and the questionable veracity of Eusebius, see Addey, *Divination and Theurgy*, 83–126.

65. *Letter to Marcella* 11, in Porphyry, *Opuscula Selecta*, ed. A. Nauck, 281.24–282.1.

66. *Letter to Marcella* 2, in Porphyry, *Opuscula Selecta*, ed. A. Nauck, 274.5–15, citing *Phaedo* 61a.

to understand not only cultic oblations but the moral and intellectual probation of the soul.[67]

The blinding of Polyphemus in this episode is construed in the *Cave of the Nymphs* as a metaphor for the attempt to escape the body by suicide.[68] Plato inveighs against suicide as a desertion of the post that has been assigned to us by providence. Plotinus held that this act will be committed only by those who are still in thrall to the passions from which they seek deliverance, and Porphyry was informed by a certain Egyptian that the soul of a suicide lingers in the vicinity of the corpse.[69] He records with gratitude that Plotinus dissuaded him from a sudden resolution to kill himself, which he attributes to a fit of melancholy (*Life of Plotinus* 11.14). If, therefore, the adversity that we experience as evil in this world is better perceived as a test of our progress in the virtues, does it follow that the soul retains its reason whatever body it occupies? Porphyry does indeed maintain in his third book *On Abstinence* that beasts are rational;[70] nevertheless, in his fragmentary work *On That Which Depends on Us*, he seems to have drawn a clear contrast between the choice of life as a beast, which deprives the soul of its autonomy, and the choice of a human life, which circumscribes but does not extinguish freedom of will.[71] Elsewhere, however, if credit is to be given to competent witnesses, he maintains that the transmigration of rational souls into beasts is a myth.[72] It may be that no philosophical ingenuity, and no demonstrable theory of development, will rid Porphyry's thought of all its contradictions, but we may be sure at least that he never admitted the presence of evil in the divine realm, and never ascribed to daemons, fate, or matter an influence powerful enough to absolve the soul of responsibility for its sins.

---

67. *Cave of the Nymphs* 35, in Porphyry, *Opuscula Selecta*, ed. A. Nauck, 80.8–22.

68. Lamberton, *Homer the Theologian*, 131, suggests that Porphyry is tacitly alluding to his own thoughts of suicide.

69. *On Abstinence* 2.47. The conjecture of Edwards, "Porphyry's Egyptian" that the "Egyptian" is Origen the Platonists is partly corroborated by Marx-Wolf, *Spiritual Taxonomies and Ritual Authority*, 17–23, where she proposes the treatise *On Daemons* by this Origen as the model for Porphyry's denigration of daemons in *De Abstinentia*. She also takes this Origen to be the Christian of the same name.

70. Cf. Plutarch, *On the Cleverness of Animals*.

71. Smith, *Fragmenta*, Frs. 268–71 (pp. 295–307). See further Coope, *Freedom and Responsibility*, 172–73.

72. See now Helmig, "Porphyry and Plutarch." The evidence from Augustine, *City of God* 10.30 and other sources is cited at n. 9.

Iamblichus and Theurgy

Among the more inscrutable of the lost works that are attributed to Porphyry is the letter to Anebo, which must now be reconstructed from quotations in Iamblichus, and Eusebius of Caesarea, together with an exultant paraphrase in Augustine.[73] While these sources do not coincide exactly, all agree that this letter impugns the efficacy of the rites by which the Egyptians undertake to coerce or cajole the daemons whom they profess to worship. In the course of his diatribe, he insinuates that practices that dishonor the gods will also corrupt their votaries, and challenges the coherence of the underlying theology with objections to which Porphyry himself supplies an answer in other writings. We are free to doubt his authorship, as Iamblichus never names him in his rebuttal of the letter; we may read it, with Bidez,[74] as a recantation of his youthful credulity in the *Philosophy from Oracles*; or, waiving any pretence of being able to date his works without circular reasoning, we may surmise that he wrote it with the intention of calling forth just such a reply as the work *On the Mysteries*, which is plausibly ascribed to his pupil Iamblichus.[75] To vindicate the utility of external forms, Iamblichus cites the doctrine of the Egyptian Hermes that materiality is not the polar opposite of being, but a purposeful abstraction by the Demiurge from the "substantiality" (*ontotês*) that constitutes the intelligible realm.[76] At the same time, there is evil because the soul that descends to the body leaves no part of itself above, as Plotinus imagined, and is therefore all the more apt to forget its duty of mastering the body that it informs.

We escape from the dominion of matter by exploiting both the natural properties and the symbolism of the material. Of the appointed rituals, some are applied cathartically to the soul, others coercively to daemons, who are all too ready to make a show of their power and therefore easily persuaded to employ it in our service. The objects of those who summon them, however, are not those of the philosopher, for whom theurgy is not the use of divine things for our own objects but the surrender of every object to that of becoming like the gods. Inferior as they are to the ineffable One that precedes existence, and even to the monad that it generates as the overture to existence, the gods who superintend the material order from their seat in the intelligible are good without qualification. Although, in

73. Sodano, ed., *Porfirio, Lettera ad Anebo*.

74. Biidez, *Vie de Porphyre*.

75. Addey, *Divination and Theurgy*, 127–44.

76. Iamblichus, *On the Mysteries* 8.3. Cf. 3.28, but also 6.4, 5.12, and 5.18 on the seduction of souls by matter, with the article on Iamblichus by R. Chiaradonna in the *Stanford Encyclopedia of Philosophy* (online).

contrast to daemons, they are not cowed by incantations, flattered by sacrifice, or touched by the forces of sympathy that bind one part of the cosmos to another, they reward us in accordance with the purity of our devotions, and the sage who enters into communion with them has no further need of material instruments. But for their condescension, which can hardly be reduced to some impersonal principle of superabundance, the human soul would remain irretrievably fallen; on the other hand, this soul is not, as Porphyry had alleged, the slave and dupe of maleficent daemons. On the contrary, daemons are masters only of those who fail to make servants of them, while those who no longer need them as servants are masters in the present world and gods in the world to come.

The *Hermetica*

Our path in the present world is not entirely of our own choosing, says Iamblichus, for astrologers assign to us two tutelary powers, the *oikodespotês*, who determines our external circumstances, and the paradigm, which represents the highest mode of life that the soul can attain in its present cycle.[77] In the first we may recognize the natal daemon of Porphyry, in the second the allotted daemon of *Enneads* 3.4. In the treatise *On the Mysteries*, however, the authority is neither Homer nor Plato, but a foreign science to which Iamblichus never appeals elsewhere. In his other works, he is either an expositor of Plato or an advocate for Pythagorean austerity; this is not so much an argument against his authorship of *On the Mysteries* as an illustration of the increasing readiness of Platonists to acknowledge that wisdom has not been imparted only to the Greeks. Christian apologists had revived every pagan testimony to the cultural and intellectual primacy of the barbarians, but even without such a stimulus Iamblichus will have been as conscious as Porphyry that his ancestors had not always spoken Greek. Both were provincial citizens of an empire that, in promoting certain tongues, had levelled all nations; if one turned to the Chaldaeans for supplementary revelation and the other to Egyptians, the latter had at least the sanction of Plato, who had said in the *Timaeus* that the Greeks were but children compared to the builders of the pyramids.

Debate goes on as to how much native Egyptian matter is present in the *Hermetica*, a collection of nineteen metaphysical and hortatory tracts, eighteen in Greek and one in Latin, which have been somewhat artificially

---

77. See *On the Mysteries*, Book 9, with Shaw, *Theurgy and the Soul*, 217–19; Iamblichus, *On the Mysteries*, trans. Clarke, Dillon, and Hershbell, 326–44.

extracted from a larger and more diverse miscellany.[78] Verifiable references to these writings are not to be found before the first quarter of the fourth century, and Iamblichus is perhaps the one pagan author who can be plausibly credited with some knowledge of them.[79] They are plainly not free of Jewish and Christian influence, and the third book in the corpus is little more than a polytheistic embellishment of the first chapter of Genesis.[80] In the nineteenth the ministers of the Demiurge (who, as ever, is both good and free) are neither the lesser gods of the *Timaeus* nor biblical angels, but daemons who act as intermediaries between their creator and humankind.[81] Here, as in many other *Hermetic* treatises, is the turbulence of matter that tempts the soul from its proper object: the pervasive assumption of the *Hermetica* is that, notwithstanding the divine provenance of the soul, we cannot escape from our captivity without help from above. The sudden transformation that the initiate undergoes in tract 13 supervenes on a diligent preparation of the soul, yet does not come wholly from within. The proof is that it not only purges the inner man but renders the body luminous; in *Hermeticum* 4 the rebirth or *palingennesia* is effected by the immersion of souls in a chalice, which appears to unite the baptismal font and the mixing-bowl of Plato;[82] if an allusion to the Eucharist is also discernible, it reinforces the lesson that deliverance is as much a work of grace as of moral endeavor

It is in the first tract of the corpus, often though not invariably believed to be the earliest, that the causes of the soul's exile and the means of return are most vividly expounded. It commences with a meeting between the unnamed seer and Poimandres, the Mind of the Sovereignty, whose name may be derived from that of Ra, the Egyptian creator, despite intimations elsewhere in the *Hermetica* that it signifies Shepherd of Men.[83] Even to see him is to be enveloped in a light that not only exhilarates the visionary but reveals to him the mystery of creation. This commences with the emergence from the primordial *nous* of a demiurgic *nous*, the former being apparently the first of all things and not, as in Iamblichus, the offspring of a

78. See Fowden, *The Egyptian Hermes*, 22–23.

79. Scott, *Hermetica*, vol. 4, 28–103, quoting freely from *On the Mysteries*, but also from the *Commentary on the Timaeus*.

80. Dodd, *The Bible and the Greeks*, 210–34. On the coalescence of native Egyptian and biblical elements in the cosmogony of *Poimandres* and other texts, and on the internalization of these by the reader, see Mahé, "La création dans les Hermetica."

81. *Hermetica* 19.5 This dialogue, entitled *Asclepius*, is preserved entire only in Latin, and attributed to Apuleius. See Hirsfall Scptti, "The *Asclepius*."

82. See *Timaeus* 41d; but baptismal imagery is also present: see Cophenhaver, *Hermetica*, 131–39.

83. See Kingsley, "Poimandres"; but also *Hermetica* 1.2, 1.6–9; 13.15.

cause for which we lack words. Its procession is accompanied by a descent of the elements into the lower realm, but from this cascade there leaps up a Logos, or Word, that populates the demiurgic mind with incorporeal ideas of material bodies (1.10). It is into this upper realm that Anthropos, the primal human being, is born, and as he looks down he sheds the radiance of the Divine on the lower world (*Hermetica* 1.12–13). And yet his largesse is his ruin, for catching sight of his reflection, he becomes enamored and falls like the Gnostic Sophia, or (as Plotinus would say) like a soul into the mirror of Dionysus (*Enneads* 4.3.12.1). As primal man is our archetype, his descent is ours, and the soul remains a prisoner of this voluntary yet intractable darkness until, by a combination of grace and merit, she recovers her portion of light.

Arnobius and the New Men

Hermes is one of the teachers invoked by the *novi viri*, or new men, who are denounced by the Christian apologist Arnobius in the second book of his treatise *Against the Nations*. According to Jerome, this work was composed around 326 when this aged teacher of rhetoric elected to join the church, which hitherto "he had always impugned," and was required to submit this proof of the sincerity of his conversion. Many scholars feel that parts of *Against the Nations*, especially the second book, have a tone that suggests experience of active persecution, and some internal evidence suggests a date as early as 297. As there are other elements, however, that do not sit well with this chronology, it may that we should regard Book 2 as the nucleus of a work that was completed many years later, at a time when the church had been freed from persecution but was still labouring to refute the charge of weakening the prosperity of the Roman Empire by her innovations.[84] The strategy of Arnobius is to demonstrate that the religion on which Rome prides herself is the product of serial innovation, egregiously represented in his own day by the new men (*novi viri*), who have fused the Platonic belief in the transmigration of souls with a medley of cults, both new and old. This is no philosophy but the most recent of the superstitions imposed on the Romans by their own conquests, and it is not the Greeks but the Christians who possess the only medicine by which purity of worship and native virtue can be restored.

The doctrines of the new men are adumbrated in chapters 13 and 14, not directly but by assimilation to the Christian beliefs on which they vent

---

84. See Edwards, "Some Theories," replying to Simmons, *Arnobus of Sicca*, 47–93, and *Universal Salvation*, 56–63. See now also Gassman, "Arnobius' Scythians."

their satire. You (he exclaims) who follow Mercury, Plato, and Pythagoras, why do you mock our decision to venerate only the Father and Lord of all when the *Theaetetus* exhorts you to seek the greatest possible likeness to God in thought and disposition? Can you deride us for teaching the resurrection of the body and yet embrace the prophecy in the *Statesman* of a time when the world will turn back in its course and men born old will end life as children in their cradles? Why do you cavil when we provide more carefully for our souls than for our bodies, when you too admit that the soul is our proper self and that the body is its prison? And why is it more ridiculous for us to speak of the suffering of the reprobate in Gehenna than for Plato to lace his dialogues with mages of Cocytus, Phlegethon, Acheron, and the Styx?[85] The capital mistake of the *novi viri* (designated as such for the first time in chapter 15) is to credit the soul with a natural immortality, when in fact it is of an intermediate character, and God alone determines its longevity in accordance with its merits.[86] In morality we fall below the beasts, none of which ever acts against its own nature;[87] even in intellect, we are debtors to society, and if a child were reared alone from infancy, with only silent nurses to feed and tend him,[88] we can be sure that he would never display the knowledge that is elicited from the slave-boy in the *Meno* with the sophistical pretence that he could not have acquired it in this life because he has never been to school.[89]

Pierre Courcelle conjectures that the new men are disciples of Porphyry,[90] yet the taunts attributed to them do not recur in the handful of passages that can be securely assigned to that author's work against the Christians. As Chiara Tommasi observes, the first Platonist to rank Hermes Trismegistus with Pythagoras and Plato was not Porphyry but his pupil Iamblichus;[91] the latter, we know, was not ignorant of Numenius,[92] and allusions in Arnobius to secret rituals and the coercion of daemons sit more easily with his treatise *On the Mysteries* than with his master's *Letter to*

85. *Against the Nations* 2.14.2, alluding to Plato, *Phaedo* 113d. Cf. Tertullian, *Apology* 23.13.

86. *Against the Nations* 2.14.6. Arnobius leaves open the possibility of transmigration at 2.16.13, although at 2.14.4 he asserts that souls that are not saved return to nothing.

87. *Against the Nations* 2.17.1–2. For antecedents, see Seneca, *Letter* 90.

88. *Against the Nations* 2.20–23, a parody of Herodotus, *Histories* 2.2.

89. *Against the Nations* 2.24.1, ridiculing Plato, *Meno* 82b–86a.

90. Courcelle, "Les sages de Porphyre"; Festugière, "La doctrine des *viri novi*," had argued for a more eclectic pedigree.

91. Tommasi, ed., *Arnobio contro i pagani*, 184–85n108.

92. *On the Mysteries* 1.5.

Anebo.[93] Moreover, it is Iamblichus, not Porphyry who is known to have written commentaries on the majority of the dialogues that are cited in confutation of the new men.[94] Even the surviving works of Iamblichus, however, cannot throw light on the reference to the mysteries of Etruria near the end of the disquisition (*Against the Nations* 2.62); the name of Cornelius Labeo has also entered scholarly discussions,[95] although even the date of this author is in dispute.

The rebuttal of the new men is a tissue of borrowings from the Platonic tradition. The first Greek to maintain that individuals owe their virtues to society was Protagoras, as a speaker in Plato's dialogue of that name. The interpretation of the rivers of Hades as conceits for the anguish of the delinquent soul can be traced to Pythagorean literature. The contention of the new men that souls are sent into the world for their edification is attested both in Porphyry and in Iamblichus; the vehement retort of Arnobius is that no benign deity would condemn us to bondage in a realm where we find no antidote for evil and can hope for nothing better than a quick death as a reprieve from tribulation (*Against the Nations* 2.39–43). We may call this Gnostic reasoning, but it is redolent also of the more pessimistic strain in Plato, which derives the noun *soma* ("body") from *sêma*, or "tomb." It raises a problem for orthodox Christianity that appears to be soluble only by returning to the notorious doctrine of Plato himself that the soul is by nature a denizen of the heavens, which descends to the lower world only as a result of its own temerity. Arnobius does not reach for this solution (which had already been castigated as Origen's heresy), but neither is he ashamed to cite the *Timaeus* in corroboration of the biblical doctrine that the world has a beginning and endures only by the will of its Creator (2.36.2). In keeping with his regular professions of agnosticism regarding the existence of pagan deities, he does not quarrel with the delegation of sovereignty to the lesser gods in this dialogue; in this book he prefers the term *dii* to *daemones* or *angeli* (both of which he attributes only to the Platonists) and admits their existence so long as it is granted that they do not demand sacrifices, being creatures of the one God and immortal only by his will (2.35).

---

93. See *Against the Nations* 2.13.8; also 4.12.2, with Tommasi, *Arnobio contro i pagani*, 360n55, citing *On the Mysteries* 3.31.

94. See Dillon, ed., *Iamblichi Chalcidensis Commentaria*. Arnobius cites *Theaetetus* 158b at 2.7.7; *Phaedo* 113b at 2.13.2; *Statesman* 270b at 2.13.6; the main subject of the *Phaedrus* at 2.34.2; *Timaeus* 41d at 2.52.2.

95. Mastandrea, *Cornelio Labeone*, 127–29; Smith, "Porphyrian Studies since 1913," 66–768.

Conclusion

The influence of Plotinus on Christian thought is apt to be overestimated when we do not take sufficient notice of chronology. If he and Origen both affirm the first principle to be higher than thought and being and not merely (as Plato had it) higher than being, it is almost certain that precedence must be accorded to Origen. If Porphyry, his pupil, smuggled the formula "three hypostases" into the title of one of his treatises, and styled the One "God over all" with none of his master's reservations, that is evidence of his desire to present the system to the world as a rival to Christianity, not of a Christian debt to Platonism. Since the originality of Plotinus was uncontested (though in his own time not uncensured) we cannot assume that thoughts that are first attested in his writings had any precedent, even in Numenius of Apamea. Neither he nor Porphyry is the source of the Christian doctrine of the Trinity, though the latter may have refined some technical terms that acquired a new salience in the vocabulary of the church. His argument for the harmony, or rather for the complementarity, of Plato and Aristotle may also have promoted the first-hand study of both authors; yet Gregory of Nyssa can sow his *Commentary on the Song of Songs* with echoes of the *Phaedrus* without embracing Plato's doctrine of pre-existence, while Aristotle could be deployed on every side of the Christological debates without arriving at any position that Aristotle would have owned.

Theodicy, as a speculative rather than a dogmatic science, is perhaps the only branch of thought in which Christians were as heavily indebted to the conceptual as to the lexical armory of Platonism. The arguments that evil is, properly speaking, nothing and that the principle of order implies the subordination of lesser to greater goods were to prove invaluable to Augustine and Dionysius, and we shall see in the following chapter that Augustine was not the first to see the utility of these Platonic commonplaces against the Manichaeans. We shall also observe that Christians of the fourth century concurred with the Platonists against Irenaeus and his contemporaries in maintaining that the fall has robbed us not only of immortality but of the higher cognitive powers that humans exercised in the immediate presence of God. At the same time, those who were not Origenists rejected the doctrine of the soul's pre-existence without a body or even in a more tenuous body; the doctrine of special providence, which Origen himself had not surrendered, continued to be a desideratum of Christian theodicy, but may not have been wholly unpalatable to Platonists of the fourth century who espoused the Iamblichean defence of sacrifice and prayer.

9

Dualism and Its Opponents in the Fourth Century

SCHOLARS CONTINUE TO WONDER how the Gnostics and their kindred passed as Christians, and it must be admitted that the heresiologists (who confess this to be the case) do nothing to dispel the riddle. As we have seen, however, the theology of the ancient critics of Gnosticism had more in common with that of their opponents than with the orthodoxy of modern times, in which the term "Gnosticism" is pejoratively applied to all that savors of otherworldliness, dualism, and divine transcendence. If Gnostics proclaimed that the highest God is unknowable, so do not a few of the recognized church fathers. If they divided Christians into the psychic and the pneumatic; so does Paul, and so does the vociferous Tertullian, who is no more willing than any modern liberal to grant the existence of anything that is not in some sense a body. The high valuation of *gnosis* or knowledge, which may be all that the epithet *gnostikos* signifies, is not foreign to Paul or to later ecclesiastical writers, even when they did not concur with Clement and Evagrius in styling themselves by this epithet. The heretics held this world to be damned and they rejected the works of the body: the Johannine Christ, though he dies for the world, proclaims that he has defeated it, while Paul expresses a yearning, which may be his own, to be released from this body of death. Gnosticism has never been the religion of the whole church, but it can scarcely be profitable to seek its origins in Platonism or Orphism, in Egypt or Iran, when, as Simone Pétrement says, the Christianity of the

New Testament is more dualistic than any of these;[1] for even Sassanian Zoroastrianism did not assert, with John and Paul, that an evil power is the prince or the god of this world.[2]

The school that still looks to Iran as the cradle of Christian dualism can point to at least one hybrid of Zoroastrian and Christian thought whose origins can be dated, and which proved itself the most tenacious of ancient heresies. Manichaeism is not the prototypical form of Gnostic thought, and the Christian sect into which its founder was born does not merit the appellation "Gnostic," but the readiness of Mani's opponents to trace not only his teaching but that of his Gnostic predecessors to Zoroaster is matched by the rising frequency of appeals to the Persian seer in Gnostic literature after Mani's teaching began to penetrate the Roman Empire. On the other hand, Manichaeism begins as a religion and ends as a heresy: in the interim, although it may have been partly accountable both for the recrudescence of earlier heresies and for the vigor of catholic writing against them, it was not yet the principal object of polemic. As we shall see in this chapter, there was still a need, or at least an audience, for the deployment of familiar arguments against familiar names.

A New Religion

Mani, the form and origin of whose name is still contested,[3] appears on the evidence of the encyclopaedia known as the *Fihrist* to have spent his early years in Mesopotamia.[4] The Greek text purporting to be his autobiography, discovered in 1969, relates that he grew up among the Elchasaites, a sect famous for its frequent performance of baptism.[5] This and a number of other witnesses credit him with a strong belief from infancy in the guidance of a heavenly twin, together with a capacity to perform miracles, or at least the appearance of miracles, which excited at once the reverence and the hostility of his elders.[6] All sources again concur in dating his rise to prominence from his migration to Persia, where he enjoyed, at least for a time, the patronage of Shapur I, the second monarch of the Sassanian dynasty. Superseding the Parthians, the Sassanians proclaimed their native origins by espousing Zoroastrianism, not in its early monotheistic form

1. Pétrement, *A Separate God*.
2. See Shared, *Dualism in Transformation*, 13–26.
3. Gardner, *The Founder of Manichaeism*, 31–36.
4. Gardner, *Founder of Manichaeism*, 26.
5. Gnoli, *Il Manicheismo*, vol. I, 26–29.
6. See Sundermann, "Mani's Revelations," 83–93.

but in the dualistic variant that sets Ormuzd the Creator against his twin, Angra Mainyu or Ahriman, who mars all the works that come perfect from his hand. We hear on dubious testimony that Shapur enlisted Mani into his army,[7] but also that he became his persecutor.[8] Since Mani retained the favor of Shapur's son and successor Ormuzd I, it may be that his suffering under Shapur was a retrospective invention of the Magian or Zoroastrian priesthood, who liked his teaching none the better because it bore some resemblance to their own. The Emperor who played the tyrant to Mani was in fact Ormuzd's successor Bahram or Wahram, whose hostility to his doctrines was compounded by his bungled attempt to cure a royal patient whose sickness had already defied the most eminent physicians.[9] The unprotected Mani now fell an easy prey to Kartir, the leader of the Magian priesthood, although there are many traditions concerning both the cause and the date of his death.[10]

Mani appears to have styled himself the Paraclete,[11] or at least to have professed to be the mouthpiece of that Spirit whom Jesus promised to his apostles. The cosmogony that underlay his rejection of alcohol, meat, and sexual congress was as dualistic as that of the Zoroastrians, but made the evil power the principal agent of creation, the powers of light being first his enemies, then his unwilling captives. The purpose of the regimen, which he and his disciples observed, was to keep the body free of all complicity in the cycle of killing and reproduction, even at the cost of having one's food prepared by acolytes lest one fall into the sin of inflicting death upon a plant.[12] Vegetarianism was mandatory, since the duty of the elect was to ingest, and thereby liberate, the particles of light that were trapped into the world, and that were supposed to be more abundant in vegetables than in beasts.[13] Whatever they owed to the Jains,[14] the Manichaean communities spread more widely in Asia and Africa, and may have exerted an influence

---

7. See Alexander of Lycopolis, *Against the Manichaeans* 3, with Van der Lof, "Mani as the Danger from Persia."

8. Gardner, *Founder of Manichaeism*, 65–67.

9. See Sundermann, "Mani."

10. Gardner, *Founder of Manichaeism*, 73–82; BeDuhn and Mirecki, "Placing the Acts of Archelaus," 3.

11. Gardner, *Founder of Manichaeism*, 35, observes that he appears only under this title in Coptic documents from Kellis. Cf. however, Gnoli, *Il Manicheismo*, 74 and 78, where the "Paraclete of Truth" is spoken of in the third person.

12. Augustine, *Against Faustus* 30.4; Beduhn, *Manichaean Body*, 32–33.

13. Beduhn, *Manichaean Body* 93, 167–70, etc.

14. Woschitz, "Der Mythos des Lichts," 105–8.

on both Buddhist and Christian monasticism.[15] So hardy and intrepid were his disciples that there is scarcely an Asian tongue that cannot boast at least one specimen of Manichaean literature;[16] since Mani numbered the Buddha,[17] Zoroaster, and Jesus Christ among his harbingers, they did not think it dishonest to present themselves as Buddhists in one territory and Christians in another, posing always as enlightened practitioners of the dominant creed. Driven from Persia as heterodox Zoroastrians, they were bitterly persecuted as Persian renegades by the Emperor Diocletian, whose edict of 302 that they should be burnt with their books was more severe than any of the four that he was to issue against the church in the following year.[18] At much the same time, a bishop of Alexandria published a letter to his flock that denounced the Manichaean meal of bread as a parody of the Eucharist:[19] to him, as to every Christian who writes against them, they were not so much pagans as heretics, and it is under that description that they appear in the literature from the Roman era, both Greek and Latin, which will be examined in the present chapter.

The Cologne Mani-Codex

Before 1969 only excerpts survived of Manichaean literature in Greek. No doubt this dearth led scholars to exaggerate the importance of the mutilated codex, purporting to be Mani's autobiography, which was discovered in that year;[20] but even those who think it a later work than it purports to be have acknowledged that its chronology of Mani's career in Persia is verified by other witnesses. We therefore have no reason to doubt its report that Mani was reared by a sect related to the Elchasaites,[21] on whom our principal source of information is the *Elenchus*, or *Refutation of All Heresies* attributed to Hippolytus of Rome. According to this author, Elchasai claimed to have received a vision from two gigantic angels in the third year of Trajan (that is, AD 100), which promised relief by a second baptism to those who

15. See Lieu, *Manichaeism in Central Asia.*

16. See, e.g., Franzmann, *Jesus in the Manichaean Writings.*

17. See Scott, "Manichaean Views of Buddhism." Shem and Enoch were also reckoned among his precursors: see Gnoli, *Il Manicheismo*, 68–70.

18. *Collatio Legum Romanarum et Mosaicarum* 15.3, cited by P. Corcoran, *Empire of the Tetrarchs*, 135–36.

19. Beduhn, *Manichean Body*, 131–32.

20. First edition by Henrichs and Koenen, "Kölner Mani-Kodex"; critical edition by Koenen and Römer, *Kölner Mani-Kodex.*

21. I adopt this tentative formulation in deference to de Jong, "*A quodam Persa exsisterunt.*"

had committed the hitherto unforgivable sins of fornication and adultery.[22] His evidence is selective, since his aim is to show that Bishop Callistus of Rome had favoured this teaching as a charter for his own indulgence to murderers, adulterers, and apostates, but he adds that this rote of pardon was administered in the name of seven witnesses—heaven, water, the holy spirits, the angels, oil, salt, and earth—and that repeated immersion were also prescribed for those who were bitten by dogs, possessed by demons, or troubled by other bodily distempers. It is possible that the dog symbolizes the influence of Sirius the dog-star, which was sometimes thought to stimulate powerful eruptions of lust, for it seems to be one of Elchasai's cardinal tenets that there are days on which no holy works can be performed because of the baleful influence of the stars.[23] The *Refutation* also says that this heresy originated in Parthia, that it recognized the inspiration of Christ but not his divinity, and that its errors included the mandatory circumcision of its adherents;[24] there is no allusion to Mani (who may not yet have commenced his mission), and no intimation that Elchasai traced the origin of the world to two antagonistic powers.

Indeed, there is only one fleeting attestation of the doctrine in the treatise *On His Body*, as Mani begins to promulgate his doctrine to the Persians in the reign of Sapor I.[25] In the prefatory chapters, which corroborate many details of the independent account in the *Refutation of All Heresies*, the followers of Alchasai are depicted as vegetarians, who are astonished to discover that Mani is able understand the speech of plants.[26] They are more incensed than astonished when Mani challenges their belief that they can sustain their moral purity by baptizing the foods to which they restrict their diet: it is all too apparent, he scoffs, that our malice, selfishness, and frailty survive these corporal ministrations.[27] Yet Mani seems to be far from despising matter, for his argument against baptism is an anecdote relating that when Alchasai tried to immerse himself first in a river and then in the sea, he was admonished on both occasions that he should not pollute his body with the filth that had stained this element every time it encircled the body of a sinner.[28] These disclosures he seems to owe to his sysygos, or heavenly double, perhaps the same being whom

22. *Refutation of All Heresies* 9.13.3.
23. *Refutation of All Heresies* 9.15.4 and 16.2–3.
24. *Refutation of All Heresies* 9.13.1, 9.14.1.
25. Gnoli, *Il Manicheismo*, 48 (Codex 21–23).
26. Gnoli, *Il Manicheismo*, 40–44 (Codex 8–12).
27. Gnoli, *Il Manicheismo*, 86 (Codex 81–82).
28. Gnoli, *Il Manicheismo*, 94–96 (Codex 94–97).

he sees beckoning to him when he looks into a stream.[29] This seems to be a reversal of the Gnostic motif according to which a being of higher station is seduced by its image in matter. In this text Mani appears to be separated from his twin, yet he is not only guided by constant revelation from above, but is able to rehearse visions imparted to his predecessors Adam, Shem, and Enoch.[30] There is no hint in the surviving text that his lineage includes the Buddha, Zoroaster, or any sage whose name is not preserved in the Hebrew or Christian scriptures.

Alexander of Lycopolis

By the common consent of scholars, the earliest extant refutation of Mani in Greek is a treatise bearing the name of Alexander of Lycopolis, a bishop, according to Photius of Byzantium, who flourished around AD 300, and hence at a date consistent with the author's claim to have ascertained the doctrines of the sect from living *gnôrimoi* or associates of its founder.[31] There is less consensus, however, as to whether the author has been correctly identified as a Christian, or even as a bishop, when there is much in the text that seems to the editors of the one English commentary to stamp him as an "Alexandrian Platonist" who contemplates Christianity as a sympathetic outsider.[32] In his synopsis of Mani's cosmogonic myth[33] the two principles (as he styles them in the manner of Greek doxographers) are God and matter under the sobriquet of light and darkness;[34] the turbulent motion of matter resembles that of the receptacle in the *Timaeus*, and its designs on the higher realm are so redolent of the aspiration of matter to form in the physical theory of Aristotle that, as the author quips, they ought to have been welcomed rather than spurned.[35] The first instrument by which God attempts to curb the disorder of matter is Soul, as a reader of the *Timaeus* would foresee, and all

---

29. Gnoli, *Il Manicheismo*, 46 (Codex 17).

30. Gnoli, *Il Manicheismo*, 62–70. The Sethel who comes between Adam and Shem would appear to be Seth, the surviving son of Adam (Genesis 4:25).

31. For text with introduction, see Alexander of Lycopolis, *Contra Manichaei opiniones disputatio*, ed. Brinkmann.

32. See Van der Horst and Mansfeld, *Alexandrian Platonist*, 46–47.

33. *Contra Manichaei opiniones disputatio*, ed. Brinkmann, chapter 2, p. 3.

34. *Contra Manichaei opiniones disputatio*, ed. Brinkmann, chapter 6, p. 9 is compared with Diogenes Laertius, *Lives of the Philosophers* 3.69 by Van der Horst and Mansfeld, *Alexandrian Platonist*, 59n319.

35. *Contra Manichaei opiniones disputatio*, ed. Brinkmann, chapter 9, p. 15.

the more so if he had read it with Plutarch's commentary.[36] When Soul itself becomes captive, the power that God creates to extract the imprisoned light and drive matter into nothingness is "that which we call the Demiurge."[37]

In his rejoinder, the author often turns to Greek philosophy for his touchstones, as when he likens the dismemberment of Soul to that of Dionysus in Orphic myth and contrasts the baseless fabrications of Mani with the more coherent dualism of the Pythagoreans.[38] His argument that matter cannot subsist without form, which he here equates with God, was a platitude for more than one school, and he marries Plato with Aristotle when he urges that, if God and matter are two productive yet independent principles, each would be required to produce its own matter, and we should be bound to posit four principles rather than two.[39] He adds, with no more than a nod to the *Categories*, that motion has effects that are measured by quantity whereas "good" and "evil" are qualitative predicates.[40] No more than Aristotle can he understand how matter, which Mani equates with baser elements, could have any inclination to rise to a higher plane; we may hear an echo of the same philosopher's animadversions on Speusippus when he observes that random motion has no more tendency to generate good from evil than evil from good.[41] Against the tenet that God and matter are mingled in the cosmos, he draws on both Platonic and Aristotelian discussions to show that no such mixture is conceivable, whether God be incorporeal (as the true philosophy holds) or corporeal, as the Manichaeans imagine in agreement with the Stoics.[42] A mingling of incorporeals would be nonsensical, as incorporeals occupy no place, and therefore neither can be in the other,

36. *Contra Manichaei opiniones disputatio*, ed. A. Brinkmann, chapter 3, pp. 5–6, with the commentary of Van der Horst and Mansfeld, *Alexandrian Platonist*, 54. The author speaks of that which "we call soul," but the adoption of Greek philosophical terms need not exclude his being a Christian.

37. *Contra Manichaei opiniones disputatio*, ed. A. Brinkmann, chapter 3, p. 6. Van der Horst and Mansfeld, *Alexandrian Platonist*, 55n194, seem to infer from the pronoun "we" that the author is a Greek and not a Christian. Certainly a Christian would either eschew the term Demiurge or reserve it for the true God (see e.g., *Adamantius*, ed., Bakhuysen, p. 4.11), but Alexander may be imposing Gnostic terminology on a myth that initially styled the second principle "Living Spirit."

38. *Contra Manichaei opiniones disputatio*, ed. A. Brinkmann, chapter 5, p. 8; chapter 6, p. 10.

39. *Contra Manichaei opiniones disputatio*, ed. A. Brinkmann, chapter 6, p. 10.

40. *Contra Manichaei opiniones disputatio*, ed. A. Brinkmann, chapter 6, p. 10. Cf. Aristotle, *Metaphysics* 986a22ff. on the Pythagorean opposites, with Van der Horst and Mansfeld, *Alexandrian Platonist*, 61n227.

41. *Contra Manichaei opiniones disputatio*, ed. A. Brinkmann, chapter 8, p. 13.1–3.

42. *Contra Manichaei opiniones disputatio*, ed. A. Brinkmann, chapter 8, pp. 13–14.

unless some valid analogy could be drawn between the presence of God in matter and that of grammar in the mind. The occupation of the same space by two bodies at the same time is known by every student of Peripatetic writings against the Stoics to be impossible; the mingling of the corporeal with the incorporeal is patently unimaginable except in the special case of body and soul.[43]

This conclusion might be thought to contradict John's dictum, "the Word became flesh" (John 1:14), were it not that Christians at the beginning of the third century were divided as to whether the incarnation ought to be characterized as a mixture of the human and divine.[44] Nemesius of Emesa was later to find a paradigm for Christology in the unconfused commingling of soul and body as this was taught by Ammonius, the tutor of Plotinus, who may for some part of his life have been a Christian.[45] The author of this tract against the Manichaeans is certainly not a Platonist in a sense that precludes his being an adherent, and not merely an observer, of Christianity. He assumes throughout that God, the first principle, is a personal being wholly distinct from matter; his argument that if God can create an immaterial power he must be able to create whatever he wills without a substrate presupposes the Christian doctrine of creation out of nothing.[46] It is as a Christian, rather than as a Platonist, that he takes exception to Manichaean doctrines that imply that the Father suffered on the cross and that the purpose of the cross was to release the imprisoned intellect from matter.[47] The gulf between the image of God and the rest of creation is such that no capacity for intellection can be allowed to animals, while daemons are so gross in body and intellect that they depend for their nourishment on the smoke of sacrifice. Both of these tenets are foreign to pagan Platonism, though both are found in Origen. The author also shares Origen's belief

43. On the author's ignorance of, or indifference to, the Neoplatonic tenets that the body is contained in the soul and the soul in the intellect, see Van der Horst and Mansfeld, *Alexandrian Platonist*, 31 and 67.

44. Origen, *Against Celsus* 3.41 speaks of an *anakrasis* of the divine and the human in Christ.

45. Dorrie, *Porphyrius' Symmikta Zetemeta*, 45–46, citing Nemesius, *Nature of Man* 39.16–20.

46. *Contra Manichaei opiniones disputatio*, ed. Brinkmann, chapter 24, p. 35. See also Van der Horst and Mansfeld, *Alexandrian Platonist*, 13; the assertion in chapter 12, p. 18 that it would be more worthy of God to annihilate matter than to subject it to form does not imply that matter is in itself "non-existent" in any sense of that term; it does, however, assume that God has an absolute power of determining what will exist, and no such power is accorded to the highest principle in Platonism.

47. *Contra Manichaei opiniones disputatio*, ed. A. Brinkmann, chapter 24, pp. 24–35.

in the veracity of the scriptures, asserting as a fact that a brother's killing of his brother was the first murder.[48] He extols the wisdom of Jesus, and if he commends the simplicity of Jesus's followers with more sympathetic detachment than apologetic zeal, it may be because he anticipates some cultivated readers who are not Christians, and who may need to be persuaded that it is better to be simple than sophistically obscure.[49]

With the same intent he commences with an account of Christianity as a simple creed that has suffered fissiparation through the rise of sects that no longer perceive that Jesus came to teach a way of life rather than a system of metaphysics. We may read this as an apology for the ordinary believer who cannot match the Manichaeans in a battle of wits, but it is also an application to Christianity of a story that it had told of the decadence of the pagan schools and the consequent pullulation of heresy. Plotinus does not inveigh against the Gnostics in this fashion because he is either unaware of or indifferent to their profession of Christianity; in this exordium the author known as Alexander of Lycopolis tempers his faith with philosophical detachment, which enables him to present his opponents as enemies not only to truths revealed but to truths that were never gainsaid by reason. It is good to have the world on one's side, when arguing, against a certain exegesis of Paul, that virtue and vice proceed not from an excess of matter or spirit in our natures but, on the contrary, from our freedom to act or not to act according to natural law.

The *Acts of Archelaus*

In contrast to Alexander's formal refutation, the *Acts of Archelaus* is a dialogue,[50] in which Manes himself is not only the defeated interlocutor but a fugitive, who in the epilogue is recaptured by his Persian countrymen and justly imprisoned for his offences.[51] He masquerades at all times as a Christian, and, although the debate is set in the reign of Probus,[52] during which the real Mani died at the hands of Zoroastrian priests, it is not implied that

48. *Contra Manichaei opiniones disputatio*, ed. A. Brinkmann, chapter 10, p. 19, where the author expects his readers to recognize Cain from an anonymous allusion. Cf. chapter 24, p. 36 on Abraham and Isaac (Genesis 22) and chapter 25, p. 37 on the descent of angels at Genesis 6.

49. See *Contra Manichaei opiniones disputatio*, ed. A. Brinkmann, chapter 1, p. 3 on the simplicity of Christians; chapter 2, p. 4 on the sophistry of Mani.

50. Most probably composed in Greek, though the full text now survives only in Latin: BeDuhn and Mirecki, "Placing the Acts of Archelaus," 8–9.

51. *Acts* 55–56, in *Acta Archelai*, ed., C. Beeson, pp. 94–95.

52. *Acts* 31–32, in *Acta Archelai*, ed., C. Beeson, pp. 44.24 and 45.4.

his heresy was either derived from or purposely opposed to the dualism that was ascribed to the ancient prophet of Iran. He is denounced at one point as a priest of Mithras,[53] a more familiar bugbear to Christians than Ahriman, the dark twin of the Creator in Sassanid cosmogony. The true father of his doctrines, however, is said to have been a certain Scythianus, whose disciple Terebinthus took the name Budda—a name invoked by Mani indeed, but without projecting onto the Indian sage his own myth of creation by the reluctant synergy of light and darkness.[54] In the *Acts of Archelaus* he admits to no predecessors but styles himself the Paraclete, or Holy Spirit, whom Christ had promised to send in the Gospel of John.[55] Archelaus, retorting that Christ would not have waited three centuries to fulfil a promise made to his own disciples, argues that the prophesied instrument of revelation was St. Paul, who, in contrast to Mani, not only worked miracles but exhibited that foreknowledge of his own destiny, which is the least that we ask of a prophet.[56]

The dialogue ends with a passage commending the study of certain barbarians who have traced the good and the evil in the cosmos to two distinct principles. We are told that the author was Basilides,[57] a Christian of the second century known from other sources. While he does not appear to have been a dualist, there may be a trace of his teaching in the narrative that is put into the mouth of Mani's emissary Turbo while Archelaus awaits his coming. Turbo relates the encroachments of the Lord of darkness upon the realm of light, the expedition of primal man in his panoply of five elements, and his defeat by the powers of darkness.[58] They devour his armor, which Turbo equates with his soul, or perhaps with all soul, but the subsequent liberation of primal man by the Holy Spirit is the stroke that reminds us of the restoration of the third sonship to the Father in Basilides.[59] The soul

---

53. *Acts* 40, in *Acta Archelai*, ed., C. Beeson, p. 59.28; epilogue, p. 9829–30.

54. *Acts* 52, in *Acta Archelai*, ed., C. Beeson, pp. 90.16 (Scythianus), 91.7 (Terebinthus); and *Acts* 53, p. 91.12 (Budda). Similarities between Hegemonius's life of Mani and earlier accounts of a proto-heretic are noted by Spat, "The 'Teachers' of Mani."

55. *Acts* 11, in *Acta Archelai*, ed., C. Beeson, p. 19.4; *Acts* 25, p. 37.2; *Acts* 37, p. 52.32.

56. *Acts* 38, in *Acta Archelai*, ed., C. Beeson, p. 58.1–2; cf. *Acts* 41, p. 60.5–25. At *Acts* 31, p. 44, he asks with an allusion to John 14:18 why Christ would have left his disciples without their promised teacher for two hundred years.

57. *Acts* 57, in *Acta Archelai*, ed., C. Beeson, p. 96.10ff., expressly making Basilides a disciple of Scythianus. Cf. *Acts* 42, p. 61.33. or the longest account of the doctrine of Basilides, see [Hippolytus], *Refutation* 7, with Löhr, *Basilides und seine Schüle*.

58. *Acts* 7, in *Acta Archelai*, ed., C. Beeson, pp. 9–11, preserved in both Greek and Latin.

59. *Acts* 8, in *Acta Archelai*, ed., Beeson, p. 11.4–6. Cf. *Refutation of all Heresies* 7.5.1 and 7. In this passage the living spirit crucifies the archons.

remains trapped in the cycle of transmigration, every crime being expiated by an exact retaliation of the same act upon the criminal in the next life.[60] Plutarch agreed that the gods sometimes exact such compensations in the present life, and was willing to imagine that, as Turbo avers, the moon and the sun act as havens for those elements in us that quit the body at death.[61] Since he did not, however, regard the soul as a massy particle of light, he could not entertain the Manichaean doctrine that the waxing of the moon is caused by an influx of souls, or its waning by their exodus to the sun. It is not easy to read this as allegory; on the other hand, it is hard to take Turbo literally when he says that earthquakes occur when the giant Omophorus, who suppers the cosmos, shifts it from one shoulder to another.[62] When we read that plagues are caused by the erotic dalliance of a certain virgin with the archons of the material realm, the Gnostic model is easily discernible, but the conceit is not therefore any less opaque.[63]

The myth makes little reference to scripture, except to say that the body of Adam was shaped by the rulers of the present cosmos in the image of primal man. Turbo's statement that all humanity forms one mass with Adam prefigures similar expressions in the Cappadocian fathers and Augustine;[64] whereas they, however, represent Christ as a second Adam leavening the flesh of his descendants, the Christ of the Manichaeans puts on only the semblance of flesh, the true object of his mission to this realm of shadows being the redemption of the soul.[65] The benighted adherents of the Demiurge cling to the law of Moses, which both they and their Manichaeans detractors take in its literal sense.[66] We could make our own sense of the narrative by construing the light as a symbol of the gospel and the darkness as the foreshadowing of the gospel in the Old Testament; the sole hint of such an allegory, however—and another anticipation of Augustine— is a passing equation of paradise with *concupiscentiae*, or carnal passions.[67] Even when light itself—the substance of God and the souls that emanate from him—is said to be a constituent of the foods that are prescribed for the

---

60. *Acts* 10, in *Acta Archelai*, ed., C. Beeson, pp. 15–16.

61. *Acts* 8, in *Acta Archelai*, ed., C. Beeson, pp. 12–12–13.3.

62. *Acts* 8, in *Acta Archelai*, ed., C. Beeson, p. 11.9–11.

63. *Acts* 9, in *Acta Archelai*, ed., C. Beeson, pp. 14.6–15.5. Cf. *Hypostasis of the Archons.*

64. *Acts* 11, in *Acta Archelai*, ed., C. Beeson, p. 19.3.

65. *Acts* 55, in *Acta Archelai*, ed., C. Beeson, pp. 80.7–81.5.

66. *Acts* 15, in *Acta Archelai*, ed., C. Beeson, pp. 24–26.

67. *Acts* 10, in *Acta Archelai*, ed., C. Beeson, p. 18.16 (*epithymiai* in the Greek of 18.2).

elect, we can hardly doubt that Turbo means to be understood literally: why else would the Manichaeans require that their meals be prepared by others, and commence the breaking of bread with a prayer disclaiming any part in the death of the crop from which it is made?[68]

Laughable as they found such petitions, opponents of the Manichaeans reproached them all the more when they concealed their peculiar doctrines and adopted a position close to the heterodox Christianity of Marcion. Mani himself in this dialogue, on the few occasions when he is permitted to speak, rests his case on the more dualistic affirmations of the New Testament, or else on the contradictions between the Old Testament and the New, which seem to him to bespeak two different sources of inspiration. Had not Jesus denounced the Jews as children of the devil,[69] and was it not these same Jews who had been taught to make war and to punish murder with murder, whereas the God of Jesus Christ had taught us not only to abstain from harm but to love our enemies?[70] This was now stale criticism, and Archelaus shows little desire for novelty in his responses. Mani, he alleges, has no grasp of Paul's distinction between the outer and the inner man, and therefore fails to perceive that soul and body are of different natures only because the one is a lamp to the other, expelling the darkness that is a product of its moral corruption rather than its material creation.[71] Since body and soul (as Irenaeus averred) were created together when God decided to form a creature in his own image,[72] we cannot say that the law was intended only for the body. Paul, in describing the law as a type, a shadow, and a chaperone, teaches us not to despise but to value it for the sake of that to which it leads.[73] As mercy is superior to justice, so the gospel is superior to the law, but we ought not to follow Marcion in treating as evil that which is in fact a provisional good.

The one philosophical argument of any weight in this dialogue is that nothing can be judged to be good or evil in disposition unless this disposition is manifest in action.[74] If matter or the power that shapes it is evil, how was it known to be such before it was created, and what use would it be

---

68. See *Acts* 10.7, in *Acta Archelai*, ed., C. Beeson, p. 17.4–9.

69. John 8:44, quoted at *Acts* 38, in *Acta Archelai*, ed., C. Beeson, p. 46.19–21.

70. *Acts* 65.19–24, as quoted by the indignant Diodorus.

71. *Acts* 21, in *Acta Archelai*, ed., C. Beeson, p. 33.14–17; *Acts* 24, pp. 25–27.

72. Acts 22, in *Acta Archelai*, ed., C. Beeson, p. 34.2–16. Cf. *Acts* 16, p. 27.6–9.

73. *Acts* 46, in *Acta Archelai*, ed., C. Beeson, p. 67.25–28, alluding to Galatians 3:24.

74. *Acts* 20, in *Acta Archelai*, ed., C. Beeson, p. 31.11–18, in the mouth of the judges but addressed to Archelaus.

to create a body unless its rival had seen fit to create the soul?[75] How can humans be said to have been evil before the first sin was committed?[76] If the sin was voluntary, that is proof of the mutability of our nature, and hence that we are not evil by necessity but by choice;[77] if we are evil by nature, and hence by necessity, why did the creator give us a law that could not be obeyed? Why indeed, being evil himself, would he even envisage our acting in a manner that proved us to be his moral superiors?[78] And how could he be a jealous god, when jealousy always accompanies desire and desire will always be directed to that which is better?[79] Here Archelaus anticipates the reasoning of Augustine, that if that which is evil yearns for anything higher than itself it must already be in some measure good.

Maximus and Methodius

Mani's doctrine was at once traditional and innovative because it unites the notion of evil as a product of will with that of evil as an inert condition or corollary of existence. Plotinus, in maintaining the second view, had all but banished malice from the cosmos, leaving his successors to reintroduce it through the caprice or vanity of daemons. In Gnostic thought, the divine seduces itself when it falls in love with its own reflection, and the evil that is engendered by this lapse is a myopic, and for that reason all the more resolute, substitution of the image for the substance of divinity. For Mani also the presence of evil betokens an evil will, which he is no more willing than Plato or the church to trace upward to the first principle: he relegates it, therefore, to the lower domain, assimilating it even more closely to matter than the malign world soul of Plutarch.[80] This Platonic antecedent had barely inspired either opposition or imitation in Christian apologetic: where the devil is said to be the Lord of matter, as in Athenagoras, he is not its natural king but a usurper, being a fallen creature rather than the instigator or architect of creation. If it was in the fourth century that Christians united to oppose the doctrine that evil originates in matter, it may be because the rise of Manichaeism had imparted new vigor to heresies that were no longer so formidable in their second-century garb. We shall see, when we come to examine the dialogue of Adamantius, that

---

75. *Acts* 23.5–8, said on behalf of Archelaus by the judges.

76. *Acts* 19.10, in *Acta Archelai*, ed., C. Beeson, p. 31.4–6.

77. *Acts* 18.8, in *Acta Archelai*, ed., C. Beeson, p. 29.7–9.

78. *Acts* 20 in *Acta Archelai*, ed., C. Beeson, p. 32.1–9.

79. *Acts* 20.5, in *Acta Archelai*, ed., C. Beeson, p. 31.29–30.

80. For a comparison of Mani with earlier dualists, see Gardner, "Dualism in Mani."

Mani may have left his stamp on the latter's picture of Marcion. In censuring only the second-century heresies by name, he may be intimating that Mani said nothing new, and therefore nothing that had not been refuted before him; and it may be to make the same point that he and his predecessor Methodius (who, if he composed the dialogue *On Free Will*, was one of his sources), avail themselves of arguments against the existence of matter that were not only ancient but had their origin outside the church.

One of the longest texts in the compilation of choice passages from Origen that is known as the *Philokalia* is a disputation between an orthodox Christian and a heretic, who contends that, if God is not the author of evil, it must be already inherent in the uncreated matter of the cosmos.[81] The same exchange forms part of a longer dialogue on the origin of evil that is attributed to Methodius of Olympia, one of Origen's first detractors;[82] Eusebius, however, reproduces much of it as the work of a certain Maximus,[83] whose very obscurity indicates that this is the true attribution. It is the first sustained defence in European literature of the thesis that philosophy can dispense with the notion of matter by treating bodies as bundles of qualities brought into existence by the mere will of God. Origen is familiar with this position, but hesitates to make it his own: the presence of the text in the *Philokalia* is best explained by supposing that it was discovered in his Caesarean library, and mistaken for his own work by disciples less erudite than Eusebius. Maximus will therefore by a philosopher of the second century, possibly the same one who was remembered as a colleague of Numenius, who was willing to entertain doctrines of special providence and bodily resurrection that we are apt to think more Christian than Platonic.[84] His acquaintance with Gnostic thought is hardly disputable,[85] and it would therefore be no surprise that a Valentinian should act as the interlocutor in a writing by one of his friends.

The Valentinian begins by reflecting on the turbulent motions of the sea and goes on to complain, in a style notoriously typical of his sect, of

81. Origen, *Philokalia* 23.

82. Methodius, *Werke*, ed., N. Bonwetsch, 143. For the Slavonic version of this work see Vaillant, "Le De Autexousio de Methode." On the possibility that it is "covertly critical" of Origen, see Patterson, *Methodius of Olympus*, 35–37. On the relation between Methodius and Adamantius (*Acta Archelai*, ed., C. Beeson, 146.15–162.3), see the interesting, though not decisive, article by Barnes, "Methodius, Maximus and Valentinus."

83. Eusebius, *Preparation for the Gospel* 7.22.

84. See Porphyry, *Life of Plotinus* 17; Edwards, "Numenius," 64–65 on Fr. 46a Des Places.

85. See Fr. 16 Des Places, with Edwards, "Numenius," 61, and Edwards, "Atticizing Moses," 69–72.

the tragic vicissitudes and miscarriages of justice that impair the moral harmony of the cosmos.[86] Either, therefore, the Creator himself is evil or it is not true that he created all things from nothing.[87] The former view might be characterized as Marcionite, the latter as Platonic; the Valentinian doctrine partakes of both, imputing ignorance rather than malevolence to the Demiurge and tracing the instability of matter not to the sin but to the repentance of Sophia. The orthodox speaker retorts that if matter and God are both uncreated they share the same essential attribute, and will therefore be identical unless they are separated by a third substance, which, being equally uncreated, will entail an infinite regress.[88] If God is assumed, with the Stoics, to be not identical with but immanent in matter, he must either undergo some contraction in order to dissociate himself from matter, or else, if he remains extensive with matter, we must grant that God himself is the seat of evil and disorder.[89] If neither of these positions is tolerable, we must conclude that God is eternally distinct from the matter out of which, as the heretic concedes, he fashioned the cosmos. To make him the artificer of the world is to say, however, that he is responsible for the properties that give his work its character as an artefact, just as his human counterpart is responsible for imposing the form of a temple or an image upon his substrate.[90] But are we not then compelled to say, if matter in its initial state is devoid of all form and property, that the cause of evil resides not in the substrate but in the artificer himself?

It is useless to answer that God modifies the qualities of matter but is powerless to modify its *ousia* or substance. If substance is form, and the substrate is by definition formless, the substance originates with the artificer (163.17–19). We may reply that, according to common usage, evil resides not in substance but in agency: the murderer becomes evil only when he commits his crime.[91] We cannot maintain, however, that evil is present in matter only as agency, for every act requires an agent, and who, if we assume matter to be passive, can that agent be but God? Hence, a new interlocutor suggests that we should assume matter to be already endowed with form.[92] He admits on interrogation that this thesis attributes properties to matter,

---

86. *On Free Will* 2–3, in Methodius, *Werke*, ed. N. Bonwetsch, pp. 147.21–155.2. Cf. [Hippolytus], *Refutation* 6.42.4.

87. *On Free Will* 3.6–8, in Methodius, *Werke*, ed. N. Bonwetsch, pp. 152.5–153.13.

88. *On Free Will* 5.3.3–4, in Methodius, *Werke*, ed. N. Bonwetsch, pp. 158.4–159.1.

89. *On Free Will* 6.3–5, in Methodius, *Werke*, ed. N. Bonwetsch, pp. 160.5–161.6.

90. *On Free Will* 7.4–9, in Methodius, *Werke*, ed. N. Bonwetsch, pp. 163.7–164.13.

91. *On Free Will* 8.9–10, in Methodius, *Werke*, ed. N. Bonwetsch, p. 166.171. 5.

92. *On Free Will* 9.1–3, in Methodius, *Werke*, ed. N. Bonwetsch, p. 169.1–13.

and that therefore we must assume that God is either powerless to change them—in which case he is far from omnipotent[93]—or else that he displays his power in changing them. If, however, the change is from good to evil, he will belie his character as God; if the change is from evil to good, the presence of evil in the cosmos is inexplicable.[94] Since, then evil does not originate either in God or in the fictitious resistance of matter, it must originate in our own free will, and the tragedies that are denounced by scoffers and heretics are the consequences of our own misuse of this faculty.[95]

The orthodox speaker turns to Aristotle, without acknowledgement, for a supplementary argument that suggests, not only that evil is not attributable to matter but that the very concept of matter is otiose. The properties that we regard as elemental are those of water or fire, of air or earth: we define these elements by the permutation of four contraries, the dry and the moist, the hot and the cold, which are mutually destructive. Since, however, nothing is destructive of itself, it is impossible for all four to be the properties of one thing, namely matter.[96] This apologetic supplement is lacking in the *Philokalia* of Origen and the parallel citation in Eusebius's *Preparation for the Gospel*. A coda to the excerpt from the *Philokalia* informs us that, although it is attributed to Maximus by Eusebius, the excerpt appears in Origen's refutation of the Marcionites. It would seem in any case that we must give credit to Methodius or Adamantius for this marriage of cosmology to theodicy, with its recognition that once we release the Creator from all conditions we lay the whole responsibility for that which falls short of perfection in the creature. At the same time, it was Origen who perceived that the evil will is itself a phenomenon to be explained, and it is in his *First Principles* that we met not merely an intimation but a bold statement of the thesis that philosophy can dispense with the concept of matter. The fact that he advances this as a thought entertained by others, whom he does not name, must lend weight to the suspicion that the discourse on matter in his *Philokalia* is neither his own work nor an interpolation from some later source but, as Eusebius says, the flotsam of an otherwise unremembered Maximus.

Methodius is a fierce opponent of Origen on the resurrection, so far as he understands him:[97] to reserve immortality for the soul, he argues, is to judge that God created the material world in vain.[98] But God creates for

93 *On Free Will* 11, in Methodius, *Werke*, ed. BN. onwetsch, p. 175.1–2.

94. *On Free Will* 10–11, in Methodius, *Werke*, ed. N. Bonwetsch, pp. 170.11–175.10.

95. *On Free Will* 13, in Methodius, *Werke*, ed. N. Bonwetsch, pp. 178.13–180.10.

96. *On Free Will* 12, in Methodius, *Werke*, ed. N. Bonwetsch, pp. 175.11–178.12.

97. Perhaps not solely Origen: see Patterson, "Who Are the Opponents?," 221–29.

98. Methodius, *On the Resurrection* 1.19, in Methodius, *Werke*, ed. Bonwetsch,

ever, and when the fashion of this world—that is, its fallenness—passes away, the abiding beauty of his handiwork will be all the more evident. Taking up Paul's description of the body as the temple of the Spirit at 1 Corinthians 6:19, he likens sin to a fig tree supported by the wall of the temple and throwing out roots that begin to dislodge its stones: the stones will nonetheless outlive the tree, and can be restored to their pristine design when it has withered, just as the body, which was never intended to die, can be remolded into a new and enduring shape when the sin that slew it is overthrown.[99] When God created humanity in his image, he was no less careful than a human sculptor to preserve it from destruction;[100] the author of sin is the devil, who fell away from God of his own volition and set up his kingdom in matter, as Athenagoras records.[101] The surrender of the soul to his enticement is recounted in the *Symposium*, where God is said to have furnished the means of life to us by his commandments first to Adam, then through Noah, then through Moses, and in the last days through the apostles: with the last he vouchsafed to us also Christ himself as an enduring image of purity, which the devil cannot counterfeit, and through whose example not the soul alone but the entire cosmos will be saved.[102]

The Dialogue *Adamantius*

The customary dating of the *Acts of Archelaus* to the first half of the fourth century rests primarily on the liberal use that Epiphanius makes of it in his *Panarion*, or *Medicine-Chest*, where Mani is the sixty-sixth of the eighty heretics whose poisons he undertakes to neutralize.[103] He appears not to have heard of the Elchasaites,[104] and takes advantage of this supposed dependence on the Greeks to show that Mani must have been ignorant of the

---

p. 241; 1.24, p. 250. At 1.20, pp. 260–61 he argues that there is even less reason to punish the body by annihilation if embodiment is the penalty of sin on the part of the pre-existent soul. See further Patterson, *Methodius of Olympus*, 141–83.

99. *On the Resurrection* 1.41, in Methodius, *Werke*, ed. N. Bonwetsch, pp. 285.12–286.11.

100. *On the Resurrection* 1.35, in Methodius, *Werke*, ed. N. Bonwetsch, p. 274.5–9, citing Genesis 1:26–28, but alluding also to the famous image in Plato, *Phaedrus* 252d–e. For Methodius's knowledge of Plato, see *On the Resurrection* 1.62, p. 327.10.

101. *On the Resurrection* 1.37.1, in Methodius, *Werke*, ed. N. Bonwetsch, p. 278.

102. *Symposium* 10.2.262–65, in Methodius, *Werke*, ed. N. Bonwetsch, pp. 123–24.

103. On his occasional preservation of the Greek, see Lieu, "The Self-Identity of the Manichaeans," 208.

104. Though there is evidence of his having read Hippolytus: Pourkier, *L'hérésiologie chez Epiphane*, 26 and 477.

opening verses of Genesis, in which God creates darkness by creating light, thereby acknowledging the necessity of both in the economy of nature. Conscious that Mani, in styling himself the Paraclete, might be claiming an inspiration superior to that of Moses, he asks how Christ's undertaking to give the Spirit to his disciples could have remained unfulfilled for two centuries (66.59.1; *Acts of Archelaus* 22.78.1). In accounting for evil, he follows his predecessors in reducing it to sin, though he also pauses to sneer at the explanation of natural disasters that is offered by Mani's spokesman in the *Acts* (66.22). It follows, of course, that evil is not a substance (66.16.5–17.7) but the consequence of an aberrant use of freedom by those creatures of God to whom he vouchsafed this gift so that they might crown his work by ruling the lower creatures in his image (66.18.6–13). The recognition that evil is the property of actions rather than substances entails that before the creation we cannot judge either of the two equipollent deities to be more evil than the other; taking up well-honed arguments against Marcion, Epiphanius adds that if neither deity contains or produces the other, a third must be postulated to keep them apart (66.14).

Since victory rather than originality is his object, he is happy to number Origen, Eusebius, and Titus of Bostra as his precursors in the refutation of Mani (*Panarion* 66.21.3); since, however, Origen died in 252, we may surmise that Epiphanius has been, for once, unduly generous to the man whom he had come to regard as the coryphaeus of heresy in his own time.[105] The writing that he attributes to his dead adversary is most probably the dialogue *Adamantius*, a work that bears Origen's name and upholds some tenets of his that had never been deemed unorthodox, while rejecting at least one heresy that was commonly laid at his door.

This dialogue is the most extensive work before Augustine devoted solely to the refutation of false beliefs on the origin of evil. Its eponym, Adamantius, is the principal speaker and perpetual victor in successive controversies with two species of Marcionite, a Valentinian, a disciple of Bardesanes, and a heretic who adheres to no named sect.[106] Because Adamantius endorses the term *homoousios*, and even seems to quote it as part of a creed,[107] and because he informs the Marcionite that under the present Emperor the true Church has regained her liberty and her buildings

---

105. See Dechow, *Dogma and Mysticism*.

106. For text, see Bakhuysen, *Der Dialog des Adamantius*.

107. *Adamantius*, 4.11–15, ed. S. Bakhuysen: "I believe in the one creator and demiurge of all and in his consubstantial (*homoousion*) word, who exists for ever and in the last times has assumed man from Mary, and in this one crucified and resurrected from the dead. I believe also in the Holy Spirit who exists for ever."

have been restored,[108] it is widely assumed that its date of composition falls between the Nicene Council of 325 and the death of Constantine in 337. If this were so, it would possibly be the only work of this period to cite a creed other than that of Nicaea in which *homoousios* is a watchword of orthodoxy. The translation into Latin by Rufinus, which avoids this anachronism and differs in other particulars from the extant Greek, appears to be based upon a more primitive text:[109] the counter-argument that it was he who modified the original to purge it of elements inconsistent with the thought of Origen would be plausible only if he had ever attributed it to Origen, and only if he had taken more pains to align the position of Adamantius on the resurrection with Origen's doctrine of the spiritual body. The unparalleled use of *phalsa* (Latin *falsa*) in the Greek where *pseudê* would be the native term suggests, if anything, that the current redaction was undertaken with knowledge of the Latin.[110] The original Greek, however, must have been written early enough to be available to the compilers of the *Philokalia* of Origen, who appear to have surmised (unlike Rufinus) that he was the Adamantius of the dialogue, and hence the true author of the disquisition on the insubstantiality of matter that now occupies a large part of section 4. Thus, even if it was not composed, as it seems to hint, before the death of Constantine, this dialogue was certainly current before AD 370.

Whatever its date, the dialogue was written some years after the first promulgation of Mani's teachings in the west. Nevertheless, the only indication that the author was acquainted with this heresy is his attribution to the second Marcionite of the tenet that there are two gods, one of whom is good and the other *poneros* or wicked (*Adamantius* 2.1 [Bakhuysen, p. 61.16]). The first Marcionite, by contrast, agrees with those described by Epiphanius in setting a just creator between the good God and the wicked devil (2.6 [p. 69.15–16]). The Marcion of Tertullian and Irenaeus, as we have seen, opposes the good God to the just creator, imputing to the latter not only the chastisement of wrongdoers but every eruption of jealousy of vindictiveness that the Old Testament relates as an act of God. In replying to both, Adamantius deploys many of the arguments that were being urged at much the same time against the Manichaeans in the *Acts of Archelaus*. This need not surprise us, since the *Acts of Archelaus* represents Mani as little more than an exotic Marcionite; whereas, however, Archelaus (having no living Marcionite to refute) can simply assume the compatibility

---

108. At least in the Latin at 40.20, ed. S. Bakhuysen. See Barnes, "Methodius, Maximus and Valentinus," 49–50.

109. See further Ramelli, "The Dialogue of Adamantius."

110. *Adamantius*, 8.25, ed. S. Bakhuysen, corresponding to the Latin at 9.27.

of goodness and justice, Adamantius demonstrates this by quoting texts in which Christ foretells the everlasting punishment of sinners (1.10 [pp. 22.30–25.21]). Conversely, he can cite passages from the Old Testament enjoining kindness to enemies, and can therefore prove, against both his interlocutors, that compassion is not the prerogative of the good god, and therefore not a sufficient pretext for his incursion into a world that was not of his making (1.12 [pp. 26.22–29.11]). Granting that the scope of mercy is wider in the New Testament than in the Old, Adamantius advances a novel theory of progressive revelation, according to which it was not merely in his liturgical prescriptions but in his moral legislation that Moses accommodated himself to the barbarity of the Israelites (1.9 [pp. 18.22–21.12]); the Savior's wider extension of the Mosaic law, which requires us to love our neighbor, is foreshadowed in the precept to return our enemy's ox to him when we find it going astray.

Now that justice is shown to be part of goodness, says Adamantius, we must inquire which of the three gods inflicted punishment on Judas (*Adamantius* 1.16 [Bakhuysen, pp. 32.38–35.23]). If it was the good god, his act was presumptuous, while at the same time it belies the Marcionite's identification of goodness with mercy. If it was the Demiurge, he dealt justly with his own, and if it was Satan he does not deserve in this instance to be labelled wicked. The Marcionites assume that the natures of their two or three principles are eternally fixed, yet the nature of an agent can be judged only by his actions (2.2 [pp. 62.29–63.35]). Before the creation of humans, there was no oppression by one God, no deliverance by another; hence it makes no sense before the creation to declare one deity better than the other, any more than it makes sense after creation to draw an antithesis between goodness and justice. Against the second Marcionite, Adamantius also presses Tertullian's argument that two gods would entail two infinities, unless one were capable of containing the other, in which case the latter would not be a god (2.1 [pp. 60.12–63.18]). Thus we are prepared for the confirmation of the disciple of Bardesanes, who argues in the third section of the dialogue that while there is only one God he is not the sole principle, since the matter from which he creates the world is coeternal and not in all respects tractable to his will.

The argument that ensues is complicated by the intervention of both the Valentinian and the heretic who speaks for himself, and Adamantius is therefore obliged to contend with different views as to whether matter is created or uncreated, and whether spirit or soul is the emanation of God that must be released from the physical cosmos. Nevertheless, since all three affirm that evil springs from matter,[111] all three succumb to most of the objections that are urged by Adamantius. Anyone who holds that matter is uncreated must say whether God contains matter or is contained by it, and how, if he contains it, he can avoid responsibility for evil; he has no response, or is not given time to advance one, when his catholic opponent asks him what third principle keeps God and matter apart (*Adamantius* 94.3–5 [Bakhuysen, pp. 144.27–149.23]) or how, if the two are coextensive, there be any space for creation without some contraction of the divine infinity. The reasoning that he purloins from Methodius, on the other hand, is equally potent against all three, for if matter has no substance of its own, the conclusion that any evil that it harbours resides in its *poiotêtes* or qualities is as inevitable as our previous conclusion that an agent is only as evil as his actions (4.6 [pp. 142.1–143.6, etc.]). On the other hand, if God formed the cosmos from a substrate that was endowed with evil properties, he must have transformed these properties, leaving intact the substance that was not evil (2.8 [pp. 154.10–155.16]). Even if we prefer, with one Valentinian, to speak of a conversion of evil properties, it is no longer intelligible that matter, after this transformation, should be the cause of evil (2.8 [pp. 156.10–157.13]). But if there is no substance to resist him, there is nothing that sets a limit to this transformation, and therefore God himself would be to blame if the world that he shaped from matter were less than perfectly good.

To these borrowings from Methodius, Adamantius adds that if God was prepared to assume a body of flesh he cannot have regarded matter as an evil so long as it remained uncorrupted by sin. To those who assert, with Marcion and his supposed disciple Apelles, that the body of Christ was spiritual (*Adamantius* 4.16 [Bakhuysen, pp. 172.30–173.36]), he replies that this is the postulate of those who maintain that God did not assume a body but underwent a change from one mode of spiritual being to another. But that is to forget that a change entails the destruction of that which existed before the change, which in this instance means nothing less than the destruction of God himself (4.16 [pp. 174.4–175.20]). Once we acknowledge that God was not ashamed to become incarnate, we shall not be ashamed to believe that the body of the resurrection will be the same body that housed the soul in the present world (5.3 [pp. 178.1–179.10]). The only celestial bodies of which Paul knows are the sun and the moon (4.2 [pp. 176.20 and 177.16]); scripture and observation alike will teach us that the body is not the prisoner of the soul but its coadjutor (5.21 [pp. 218.9–11; 219.6–8]). Scripture itself employs the word "soul" to denote the whole person, unless we suppose that Jacob was accompanied to Egypt by seventy disembodied

111. *Adamantius* 4.2 [Bakhuysen, pp. 140.30–143.7].

souls at Genesis 46:15 (5.20 [pp. 214.22 and 215.21]). The argument that the flesh may be good but the body evil is proved to be nonsense by Paul's equation of these terms at 1 Corinthians 6:16 (5.22 [pp. 22.30–25.4]). Those who assert that the body causes the soul to sin refute themselves when they argue that the soul descends to the body from a higher realm, for this voluntary abandonment of perfection for imperfection would itself be the root of all the ensuing sin (5.21 [pp. 216.10–219.5]).

Conclusion

Methodius and Adamantius are perhaps the first Christian writers for whom the unreality of matter is a cardinal premiss in the refutation of dualism. So long as the principal object of theodicy was to prove against the Gnostics that evil cannot originate in the divine realm, it was hardly necessary to say more than that matter, being God's creation, must be as free of intrinsic evil as all other products of his will. This reasoning was of equal force against Plutarch's understanding of the *Timaeus*, in which matter exists independently of the Demiurge and resists the imposition of form because it is curdled by an evil soul. In denying to matter not merely an origin outside God but any substance of its own before God forms it, Methodius and Adamantius echo the Platonism of the third century, which denied the existence of a second principle. If matter can be said to be pre-existence, either on the noetic or on the cosmos plane, it is only as a potentiality for the existence of something that is other than, hence inferior to, the unity and goodness of the first principle. If it proceeds from soul, as some texts in Plotinus are thought to imply, it does not constitute a new object until it is covered and informed by soul itself. Even to call it privation is misleading, because, considered merely as matter, it has no properties to lose. It is rather the indefiniteness, the measurelessness, that, when conjoined with form, ensures that that which receives the form will always fall short of its permanence, its perfection, its unchanging self-identity. It is for this reason that matter in Plotinus is the prime evil, and it may therefore seem imprudent of Adamantius to say, in the course of his reply to the Bardesanian, that evil is mere deficiency of good. Is he not here conceding that evil and matter are synonymous—the very thesis that he purports to deny?

We may answer for Archelaus, as well as for Adamantius and Methodius, that when they deny that either evil or matter is a substance, they do not reduce them to the mere negativity of formlessness, indeterminacy, or disorder. The consequence of reducing the phenomena of the natural world to their properties is to deprive them of any source of permanence other than the will of their Creator: since there can be no want of either good-ness or the power to confer existence in his willing, there is nothing in the cosmos, not even a substrate devoid of properties, that can be characterized as evil. Since it is moral, not natural, evil that taxes the faith of Christian theologians, they look for the cause of it not so much in the presence or absence of properties as in the pious or impious exercise of volition: if they say that evil is nothing, they mean that a volition is not a substance but an *energeia* or function of a substance—that is, of an agent, endowed with free-dom by the same God to whom that agent owes the good of existence. This identification of evil with agency is common ground between catholics and Manichaeans: they differ in that the latter maintain that evil agency must be the consequence of an evil nature, whereas, according to the former, it is the will that gives a perceptible force, and hence the appearance of sub-stantiality, to that which in itself is nothing more than the corruption and debilitation of nature. How the will that shares in this corruption becomes not merely weak but malignant was a question for a greater mind than those of Methodius, Adamantius, and Archelaus; before we turn to Augustine, however, we must consider some further examples of theodicy in the fourth century, which were undertaken in answer either to pagans or to heretics less audacious than the Mesopotamian prophet.

10

Christian Theodicies in the Later Roman Period

THE DYNASTY OF CONSTANTINE presided over the first, and the most inventive, age of Christian humanism. Those who now joined the church in great numbers were not prepared forgo the pleasures and consolations of literature, and the wealthy among them did not wish to see it removed from a curriculum that was designed to ensure that those born to the few positions of privilege were equipped for them by the rarity of their attainments. Even had it been possible to substitute a Christian for a pagan syllabus, who would have dared to put into the hands of children the very texts that were being quoted to justify heresy, faction, and political contumacy. There was after all little danger that Christian souls would be debauched by poets who had always been mocked as liars or by orators and historians who had failed to sway their own contemporaries. Since their moral blemishes could be palliated by allegory, or used as the basis of Christian admonition, the only quarrels that they were likely to spawn were philological, which was no bad thing for a young man's training in rhetoric.[1] For now it was no longer sufficient, even when composing a theological treatise or a biblical commentary, to write plain and grammatical Greek without grace or ornament; we may rejoice that it was still less pardonable to heap clause upon clause into

---

1. On the common literary culture of pagans and Christians, see Kennedy, *Greek Rhetoric under Christian Emperors*. On Christian appropriation of pagan rhetoric, see now Ludlow, *Art, Craft and Theology*.

monstrous coacervations, as Eusebius and Clement had done in the hope that pomp would pass for eloquence. Christians now dominated the republic of letters, enjoying close friendships with pagans of equal refinement, and, for Greeks at least, thus was the first era in which they produced apologetic works that a pagan might have thought worth reading for the style.

Of course it did not follow, even when the matter of pagan literature had been absorbed with the manner, that Christian texts would suffer any loss either in cogency of argument or in purity of doctrine. Just as the application of pagan tools to scripture elucidated the grammar, revealed the *skopos* or intention of the whole passage, and deterred the commentator from wilful reverie, so a closer acquaintance with the tenets and terminology of the pagan schools enabled a polemical or dogmatic writer to give more precise expression to his own teachings and to bring the errors of his adversaries into sharper relief. Lactantius, for example, has nothing to say of the fall or the atonement and does not even quote the Sermon on the Mount when he contends that perfect justice is perfect love, yet by this thesis he deprives all property of its moral sanction, together with the artificial codes of war and law that are invoked in its defence. Both the limpid prose of Athanasius and the more ornate diction of Gregory of Nyssa present more persuasive accounts of the fall than had yet been advanced in Christian apologetic. At the same time, Gregory takes Ecclesiastes as the text for a series of sermons on the vanity of human wishes that might not have been out of place in a pagan seminar. Theodoret's treatise on the goodness of God is classical not only in the lucidity of its style but in asking the reader to accept no other theological premiss than the goodness and power of the deity. This is a theological economy, but not a falsification of Christian teaching; we shall see at the end of this chapter, however, that in the hands of a poet even a vivid account of Satan's seduction of humanity may be so beholden to its pagan models that it becomes a redaction rather than a paraphrase of the biblical narrative.

Lactantius on the Origin of Injustice

The previous chapter ended with Arnobius, a maverick among Christian apologists, who does not insist that his is the only God, rejects the pre-existence of the soul with the Gnostic argument that no soul could be tempted to enter a world so full of evil and tribulation, and denounces the inhumanity of sacrifice in terms reminiscent of Porphyry, though without arraigning the daemons as its authors or beneficiaries. In its present form the treatise *Against the Nations* runs to seven books, the second of which may be the remnant of an earlier draft.[2] Most scholars agree that traces of redaction and amplification are also evident in the seven books that make up the *Divine Institutes* of his pupil Lactantius, whose vivid narrative of the persecution in Bithynia follows the dedication of his fifth book to Constantine at a time when the latter was exercising authority in the west but had not yet repealed the edicts of Diocletian (*Divine Institutes* 5.1). It is in this book, which may have formed the nucleus of an enterprise spanning fifteen years, that he states his intention of combining eloquence with instruction, thus excelling not only the propaedeutic tract of Minucius Felix and the rugged declamations of Tertullian but even the polished compositions that Cyprian had addressed to his flock in Carthage (5.4). If he hoped to make Constantine not only his protector but his pupil, we see evidence of his success in the latter's *Oration to the Saints*, composed some time between 312 and 328:[3] it is also likely, however, that Lactantius wrote with the aim of giving heart to his fellow-Christians, for the fifth book of the *Institutes* sets out to reveal not only the origins of false religion, the secret causes of persecution, and the superiority of Christian piety to all pagan notions of virtue, but also to explain the purpose of God in permitting the good to die and the wicked to boast their triumphs as he postpones the day of wrath.[4]

Lactantius bases his argument in the first half of the book on the common sentiment of the pagans and their philosophical principles, as revealed in the literature of the classical era. Only in the second half does he expose the machinations of the demons and invoke prophetic warnings of divine wrath. He pursues the same strategy in the first two books of the *Divine Institutes*, for it is only in Book 2 that the gods who haunt the pagan shrines are unmasked as angels in revolt (*Divine Institutes* 2.2, etc.), whereas in Book 1 false cults are represented, on the authority of Ennius in his translation of Euhemerus, as rituals commemorating mortals who were particularly distinguished for their crimes (1.11, 1.13–14, 1.22). As in the Greek apologists, it is not so much by demonstrations of supernatural power as by collusion with our foolish propensity to revere the dead that the demons propagate false religion (1.11); all the more blame is therefore to be attached to the timid philosophers who have failed to unmask this subterfuge and the folly of those who succumb to it.[5] Yet how can we expect better of them, as Lactantius says in one of his more original disquisitions, when all the pagan

2. Digeser, "Lactantius and Constantine's Letter," argues for completion in 313, against the widespread opinion that redaction continued up to 324.

3. For text and review of scholarly opinions, see Girardet, *Konstantins Rede*.

4. On the interweaving of Christian and pagan sources in Lactantius's eschatology, see Coleman, *Lactantius the Theologian*, 61–92.

5. See above all 5.12–13 on the allegories of the Stoics.

philosophers—even Plato, Cicero, and the Stoics—have been ignorant of the true nature of justice? The maxim of rendering to each his own[6] presupposes a system in which there are some who have and some who have not, some who are lawful masters and others whose duty is to serve them. The true elements of justice are piety and equity, the first of which is the knowledge of the true God, while the second is an acknowledgment of the equality of all humans under his laws (5.15). The story that justice fled the earth in the reign of Saturn[7]—that Saturn to whom his devotees now sacrifice their own children (5.10)—is a pagan testimony to the necessity of right worship as a condition of righteous conduct (1.5). Humans in their primitive state knew no division of property or rank (5.5–5.6).[8] If all acknowledged the one Lord, there would be no wars for the subjugation of other nations, no theft or adultery, no prison and no bloody conflicts for temporal goods (5.8). He exclaims in Book 6 that empires created by conquest and coercion, for all the glory that they ascribe to themselves, subvert true virtue by making virtues of tyranny, discord, cruelty, and spoliation (6.6.23). It is therefore no surprise that the church, in which this ideal pattern has been restored, should be an object of envy and enmity (5.12, 5.20); if it appears surprising that God should permit the oppression and slaughter of the righteous, Lactantius can reply, with a quotation from Seneca and a distant echo of Irenaeus, that if they were unmolested they would not feel any temptation to injustice, and would therefore exhibit no virtue in being just.[9]

Lactantius knew that philosophers did not regard the mere willingness to die as a proof of virtue, and would therefore think it absurd for God to demand this unless it conduced to some rational end. In the second half of Book 5, Lactantius argues that the fortitude of the Christians is grounded in their conviction that the soul is immortal and designed by its Maker to live for ever in his presence (*Divine Institutes* 5.18; cf. 1.8–9). Their willingness to be stripped of all that this world deems good, to the point of renouncing life itself, is therefore grounded, no less securely than the best philosophies of the schools, in their awareness that the sensible world can offer us neither secure nor abiding happiness (5.19). The church is the one society of which it can be said, as Cicero claimed of the legislation of Romulus,[10] that it unites the practical and the theoretical; the reason is that its hopes rest not on

6. *Divine Institutes* 5.17–18; cf. Plato, *Republic* 433a; Cicero, *Nature of the Gods* 3.38.

7. See further Zanker, "The Golden Age."

8. On the antcedents of the "primitivism" of Lactantius, see Boas, *Primitivism and Related Ideas*, 15–41;. Colot, *Lactance*, 107–74.

9. *Divine Institutes* 5.23, substituting God for the gods in Seneca, *On Providence* 1.6. Cf. Irenaeus, *Against Heresies* 4.39.

10. Cicero, *On the Commonwealth* 1.21.

demonic imposture but on the sure authority of scripture, coupled with the perfect life of Christ, which, as he shows at length in Book 4, was foretold infallibly by the prophets of Israel.[11] And while the philosophers scoff, the deaths of his followers have had robbed the demons of their empire over the masses (5.22), who are not persuaded by logomachy but by the force of example (5.23). As Christ had already been made to say in Book 4:

> Should anyone say, "Your precepts are impossible," he can an-
> swer, "I do them myself, yet I am clothed in flesh, whose nature
> is to sin. . . . It is hard for me to despise wealth, since one cannot
> live otherwise than in this body. Yet I too have a body, but I fight
> against every appetite." (*Divine Institutes* 4.24)

This might be a Stoic commendation of moral autarky, or of the ancestral virtues that were so often extolled by Stoicizing Romans, were it not that the Stoics held up the wise man only as an ideal (cf. *Divine Institutes* 5.17), while Lactantius himself did not regard courage in furtherance of conquest as a virtue. It is not without design that his last quotation from the pagan classics in Book 5 is a passage in which Seneca writes that because the just are children of God, he perfects them by adversity and will not permit their strength to be impaired by ease and pleasure (5.23). Christian teaching not only refutes the errors of philosophy, but vindicates the truths that the best philosophers have extolled while betraying them by their unworthy conduct (5.14). Cicero would have been a true sage had he lived as he wrote (3.16; 6.18), and even Lucretius shows an occasional consciousness of a soul that will not be resolved into indistinguishable atoms at his death.[12] At the same time, it is a leitmotif of the *Divine Institutes* that poets have done more harm to the soul by falsehood than philosophers by error. At *Institutes* 5.5 the hardships that Jupiter puts in the way of agriculture are attributed to the devil and represented, against the clear intent of Virgil, as a tyrannical artifice to weaken his subjects rather than as a fatherly provision to foster resilience and invention.[13] Lactantius gives no account of the biblical fall, and this transference to a false deity of the curse on the soil, which scripture ascribes to God, is as close as he comes to explaining natural evil.

11. *Divine Institutes* 4.5–21; see further Edwards, "Scripture in the North African Apologists."

12. See the quotation *of On the Nature of Things* 2.999–1001 at *Divine Institutes* 3.16. Cf. *On the Workmanship of God* 17–19, where he also appeals to Lucretius against the Epicurean doctrine. On the sources of his anthropology (which in this treatise also involves no fall), see Roots, "The *De Opificio Dei.*"

13. Cf. *Georgics* 1.126; *Georgics* 4.361 is evoked at *Divine Institutes* 5.10, this time as a veridical prophecy of Pharaoh's death. Lactantius is not wholly wrong: see Tarn, "Alexander Helios," on Virgil's indebtedness to the *Third Sibylline Oracle.*

It is not the whole truth, however, to say that God permits the affliction of the righteous as an exercise in virtue. Where the philosophers frequently ascribe no more to the Author of the cosmos than the framing of benign laws that reward prudence and virtue, together perhaps with measures for the rectification after death of particular injustices, the Christian must believe in a special providence that reveals itself in this world as the visitation of God's wrath on the wicked (*Divine Institutes* 3.11.19–20). Lactantius devotes a whole treatise to the proof that wrath is no less a proper trait in the divinity than love,[14] since we express by the one term a steadfast disposition to bestow goods in proportion to merit and by the other an equally steadfast disposition to punish those who inflict harm or deprive others of their due.[15] The pagans have witnessed the vengeance of God on every persecutor of his saints. Decius died in battle, Valerian was conquered, humbled and flayed after death, Aurelian was killed by his troops before he could execute his purpose (*Deaths of the Persecutors* 4–6). Maximian was executed by Constantine (30), his son Maxentius was driven with his army unto the Tiber (44), the instigator Galerius expired of a wasting illness (48), Diocletian was reduced to ignominy (42), and Maximinus Daia was defeated by an army less than half the size of his own (49). Christians are not Stoics, who look for no reward but that of dying as nobly as they have lived.

From Philosophy to Theology

Lactantius claims philosophers as his allies, yet repeatedly declares that, in their ignorance of Christ's teaching and example, they have failed to grasp the root of justice or to display its fruits. Even those who have understood that piety is the prerequisite of justice have connived at the propagation of false religion and of myths that corrupt the soul. For them the wise man is an ideal, not to be realized in the present life, just as they held that there is no earthly polity that embodies even their own definition of equity as giving to each his due. Christians have a superior philosophy because their founder proved that one can live and die without sin, and because, in imitation of his humility, the church has done away with the unnatural disparities of wealth and power that shelter under the maxim to each his own. Indeed in Book 5,

---

14. On Lactantius and his pagan predecessors, see Girgenti, "Dell' ira de Achille."

15. Pohlenz, *Vom Zorne Gottes*, 50, observes that this is our sole surviving treatise on the anger of God from the ancient world, but finds no evidence on p. 53 that it was inspired by Marcion's strictures on the Old Testament. At p. 52 he observes that Lactantius grants to (the unnamed) Seneca that anger may be forbidden to the human agents of God (cf. *On the Anger of God* 18 with Seneca, *On Anger* 1.14–21).

which may be the earliest portion of the *Divine Institutes*, Christ is above all else the consummate sage, the wise man of whom the Stoics despaired: it is only in other books—the fourth in particular, which is barely represented in the *Epitome*—that we read of his existence with the Father before creation (*Divine Institutes* 4.8.14–16), his second birth from a virgin (4.12.4), and the inspired foretelling of this in the ancient scriptures. Even the reader of this book would not easily divine that Jesus had died to erase the penalty of sin, or enabled his followers to escape its power through sacramental communion and the insufflation of the Holy Spirit. The one respect in which, throughout the *Divine Institutes*, Christ does more than he can require of us is his judgment of the dead.

The most obvious shortcoming in Lactantius's anthropology is one that he shares not only with his pagan but with his Christian precursors: he assumes that, notwithstanding the universal fall from innocence, we have only to will with sufficient strength to overcome both the natural weakness of the body and the vices induced by nurture and education. The fatalists and astrologers of his time drew a strict dichotomy, which even they must have known to be chimerical, between fate without and freedom within, between the subjection of bodies to natural forces and the supremacy of reason in the soul.[16] To those who were more conscious of their infirmities, the ubiquity of sin appeared to betoken some profound vitiation of the Creator's handiwork—a sentiment that leads Origen to speculate on the pre-existence of souls and to say that with the loss of paradise we became chattels of the devil.[17] Since, however, neither off these hypotheses curtail his belief in the sovereignty of the will, at least when it chooses to be assisted by the Spirit, he is scarcely any more capable than Lactantius of explaining why we not only need a model of perfection but need God to be that model, and how the death that he foreordained for himself was not only a testament to his own righteousness but an antidote to sin.

Athanasius, bishop of Alexandria from 328 to 373, is remembered as the champion of the Nicene Creed against all pretended substitutes—or, as some would say, of his own interpretation of it, which decried all others as Arian but fell short of the later canon of orthodoxy.[18] He was also the author of the first apology that plainly sets the church's doctrine of sin and redemption before the eyes of pagans. In the first half, under the title *Against the Nations*, he informed his idolatrous readers that the one true image of God

---

16. See Edwards, "Astrology and Freedom."

17. *Homilies on Genesis* 1.13, in Origen, *Homilien zum Hexateuch*, ed. Baehrens, p. 17.26–28.

18. See Gwynn, *The Eusebians*, 169–244.

in the crested realm is the incorporeal soul. This honor accrues to it, however, because it is modelled on the Word or Logos, in whom the likeness to the Father is so perfect as to admit no distinction in nature. The object of the second half, *On the Incarnation of the Word of God*, is to explain how the clothing of this invisible image in visible flesh delivered the human race not only from the penalty of sin but from its natural liability to death.

Evil and the Fall in Athanasius

The treatises *Against the Nations* and *On the Incarnation of the Word* were both composed at the behest of Athanasius's friend Macarius,[19] but the former is addressed chiefly to philosophers while the latter disarms first the Jew and then the Greek of their objections to the paradox at the heart of Christian preaching. The origin of evil is the first question to be discussed, and the solution takes the form that had already become perfunctory for many Greeks—that evil cannot be part of the creation, since it is nothing but a failure to participate in that which is eternal and divine (*Against the Nations* 2.2). To fall short of the good is possible only for a being that has both knowledge and the freedom to abuse it: human beings, to borrow another commonplace from the Neoplatonists, have the choice between fixing the gaze of the intellect on the invisible realm, which God himself inhabits, or on the world that plays home to our bodies, whose shifting phenomena darken the very senses by which we perceive them (2.2–4). To imagine that evil resides in the nature of things would be to make the Creator himself the cause of evil (6.1–2), or to posit a second deity, equal or even superior to him in the material order (6.5); as though this tenet did not sufficiently jeopardise our salvation, there are some who reduce the true God to idleness by imputing the whole creation to his adversary (7.1). The origin of evil lies not in God nor in the creation but in the apostasy of the soul, which, once it forgets its affinity to God and becomes enamored of that which is bodily and sensible, begins not only to covet but to worship the products of matter, and all the more readily when they are fashioned by our own hands. The objects of idolatry may be the heavenly bodies, the elements, our carnal desires, or fabulous entities of our own devising (9.1–3); among the Greeks veneration is most frequently accorded to the dead, whose crimes and

---

19. Not the bishop of Jerusalem, but a neophyte. Meijering, *Orthodoxy and Platonism*, 108–13, upholds the dating of this treatise to the years before the Arian controversy against the later dates proposed by Gentz, "A Reconsideration," and Kannengiesser, "Le témoignage des Lettres Festales." For further consideration, see Anatolios, *Athanasius*, 26–30.

frailties Athanasius proceeds to catalogue with more relish than originality (10–14). Reason and scripture concur in exposing the folly of this homage to human artifice (14–15); if it be urged that the sculptors follow the poets, while the poets represent the gods as they are, we may grant that they do indeed tell the truth, but not about the gods (16–18).

Thus it would appear to be a misreading of history, rather than the chicanery of demons,[20] that has tempted humans into false religion. Philosophers have made their own contribution to this triumph of the senses, notwithstanding Plato's strictures on the deceitfulness of the plastic arts. Athanasius seems to be acquainted with two defences advanced by Porphyry: that the attributes of the gods may be symbolically represented in iconography (Against the Nations 19.3), and that the images, though powerless in themselves, may act as vessels of the dynameis or powers that the gods communicate to lesser agencies (19.4).[21] To the first of these arguments Athanasius retorts that it would be unworthy of God to wait for humans to fashion a medium in which he could manifest his power (20.4) and that no corruptible artefact can be a true image of that which is invisible and imperishable (22). As to the theory that statues act as conduits of divine power, it would be more fitting to worship the beings whose power they transmit (21.1), or even the men who have created these useful organs (21.3) In fact, the very diversity of cults is sufficient evidence that they are false (23); the animals who are adored in Egypt are immolated in Greece (24), while the frequency of human sacrifice among barbarians shows how quickly the soul is hurried to its moral destruction when it parts from God (25). The veneration of the stars and elements, which are works of God himself, has some color of piety; nevertheless, it belies the manifest harmony of the cosmos, handing it over to a multitude of suzerains, each of whom will be jealously bent on aggrandizing his own domain (26–29).

The harmony of the world, the regularity of its cycles and its perfect adaptation to the needs of its denizens proves that it cannot be under the sway of more than one God, any more than it can be the product of accident or of blind determinism.[22] The delicate interdependence of its mobile elements and its living creatures must be sustained by a single animating principle, which the gospel teaches us to call the Son and the Word of God (Against the Nations 40–43). The one proper image of him in this world is the human soul, which he created in his own likeness (34.3): invisible as it

20. See, however, On the Incarnation 12.6; 13.1; 15.1.

21. Perhaps an allusion to the opening of Porphyry's treatise On Statues. On which, see Viltanioti, "Cult Statues in Porphyry."

22. On the Nations 35–39; see also On the Incarnation 2.1–2 against automatism.

is, the Word is known by its effects, which appear not only in the motions of the body (32.2–3) but in the acts of imagination and intellection which carry it beyond its visible envelope, revealing the body to be its vehicle rather than its prison (33.3–4). As the soul in its essence is the loftiest manifestation of the good in the world of common experience, so the soul that betray its essence by sinning is the only source of evil (34.1). Nothing is said in the treatise *Against the Nations* of disease or disorder in the physical realm; and as we have seen, there is barely an allusion to fallen angels, let alone to any disturbance of the soul or the cosmos by their machinations. It does not, however, follow that because we are responsible for our own sin we are able to effect our own deliverance from moral turpitude or its consequences. On the contrary, it is the intransigence of sin, the impossibility of recovering our lost virtue by our own efforts, that furnishes Athanasius with the theme of his treatise *On the Incarnation of the Word*.

He begins by recapitulating his proof in the first treatise that the world is governed by a single immanent principle, the Logos, which orders all things for good (*On the Incarnation* 3). This much being granted, however, it is all the less credible to the unbeliever that this same Word of God, who is no less incorporeal, no less impassible, no less invisible than his Father, should assume a fragile body and undergo the meanest of deaths (1.3). The task before the apologist is now not only to lay bare the evil for which this scandal was the remedy but to show how it could be possible or fitting to conquer evil by inflicting a greater evil. For this, as Athanasius says with a simultaneous echo of a promise by Jesus and a recurrent chorus in Euripides,[23] one requires the assistance of God through whom the impossible becomes possible (1.2). With revelation and reason as our guides, we must go back to the creation, which, if God is to be truly God, can no more be a product of mere artifice upon pre-existent matter (2.3) than it can be the result of chance (2.2). Plato is as blind as Epicurus if he imagines God to be a mere demiurge, limited by his materials, and not the omnipotent Creator of all things out of nothing (2.4). The absolute contingency of all that is not God (3.1–2) entails a natural tendency in created things to fall back into nothing.[24] For all that he says of the grandeur of the soul in *Against the Nations*, Athanasius says in this text that even human beings, the crown of God's handiwork, are by nature mortal (3.4). We enjoy the hope of immortality only because the Word endowed the human race with his image and likeness, placing it in a paradise where it was capable, by obedience to

---

23. Matthew 19:26; Euripides, *Bacchae* 1389–90, etc.

24. On the complementarity between creation from nothing and redemption, see Anatolios, "*Creatio ex nihilo*."

his commands, of attaining the perfection of Godlikeness.[25] Of this destiny humans were robbed by turning from God and failing prey to the fickle pleasures of the flesh.[26]

Quotations from scripture fall more thickly into this account of human apostasy than in the corresponding chapters of *Against the Nations*. On the other hand, as it makes no reference to a historical Adam and Eve, it could be taken as a parable of Everyman's fall from innocence into ignorance. When the remedy is supplied by the "pity" of God we catch an echo of a serio-comic passage in the *Symposium*, which is avowedly myth.[27] Nevertheless, the dilemma that is set before God is not one that would have troubled Plato's Zeus, for it proceeds from his obligation to be true to his own admonition, "In the day that you eat thereof, you shall die."[28] Thus he was bound to visit a capital penalty on those whom, since they bore his own image and likeness, he did not wish to annihilate (*On the Incarnation* 6.3; 7.1).[29] Moreover, the concomitant of mortality was corruption, and no contrition by the fallen creature could have stemmed the tide of lawlessness (5.3–5). And even if we had listened to the prophets, or had discerned the invisible hand of the Creator rather than worshipping his creation, repentance would at most have curbed transgression; it would not have restored the presence of the Word, and nothing less than this presence would have erased our natural liability to death (5.2). There was only one expedient that would enable God to exact the threatened penalty without extinguishing his own image and likeness, and this was the assumption of flesh by the archetype of that image and likeness, the Word himself, who in contrast to his creatures was by nature a stranger to mortality (13.7).

But why, says the unbeliever, must the death be so ignominious? Christians before Constantine had seldom made a symbol of the cross and when they spoke of the death of Christ as theologians or apologists, the manner of it was frequently ignored or allegorized. No one before Athanasius had offered such a battery of arguments to prove that *crucifixion* was the only mode of death that served every purpose of the Savior. Having manifested his providential love and power in so many acts of healing, he could not succumb to any of the bodily disorders that he had vanquished (*On the*

25. *Incarnation* 3.3 and 5.2, with a reference to Wisdom 2:24 on the envy of the devil.

26. *Incarnation* 5.3ff, quoting Romans 1:26.

27. *Incarnation* 3.3; 8.2; 11.1.

28. *Incarnation* 3.5, citing Genesis 2:17.

29. Kannengiesser, "Athanasius of Alexandria," 108–10 finds her an ideal Adam whose interior being consists of mind but not soul, of whom he discerns no trace in the other works of Athanasius.

Incarnation 22.4–5); he could not die in private or in a desert place (23.1), lest it be suspected that he had not died at all and therefore had not risen; his elevation symbolized his victorious struggle with Satan, the lord of wickedness in high places (25.5); his hands are outstretched to beckon Jew and gentile (25.3); the shameful mode of execution not only fulfilled a prophecy but bespoke his solidarity with the fallen race whose likeness he had assumed in all but sin (20.4–5). As God he was immortal and his resurrection was therefore inevitable (20.6); but just as the abundance and variety of his miracles revealed his superiority to the prophets (38.5), so his superiority to death was the more evident because it was contrived in the manner chosen by his enemies (24.2). These enemies, if they are Jews, are now confounded by the fulfillment of their own prophecies and the destruction of the temple (40.4); if they are Greeks they have witnessed the desertion of their oracles, the waning of idolatry, the acceptance by the common people of teachings that they had not been willing to learn from any philosopher (46.1–2; 50.4). Barbarians have embraced not only the faith of the evangelists but the ways of peace, which Rome had labored in vain to impose by arms (51.4; 52.2).

All this he had achieved by the incongruous feat of taking on a body as a means of communicating supernal truths to those who possessed only carnal senses (54.2): to doubt that he who exercises providence throughout the world could exercise it at the same time in a finite shape is as foolish as to doubt that the soul that animates the whole body could be active at the same time in one of its members (41.5; 42.3) or that the tongue should be an expression of the mind (42.7). Even if there were no testimonies to his resurrection, the intrepidity of a host of martyrs proclaims that death has lost its terrors (28.4, etc.); and those who imputed his miracles to Beelzebub,[30] if they were not already confounded by the gospel, would be bound to recant in our own day, says Athanasius, when they see the demons everywhere put to shame (32.4, 32.6; 37.5). Since their power lay wholly in deception (47.2), Athanasius does not pretend that their flight has been followed by any cessation of natural calamities: but at least it is clear, when the oracles are mute and sorcery impotent (48), that sin has no other cause than the truant will. Even if an analogy can be drawn between the work of Christ and that of the Demiurge in Plato's *Statesman*,[31] it is only the Demiurge who turns back the course of history to redeem the world from chaos. Christ's revolution takes effect in the soul, the most precious part of us, expelling the sin that hitherto stood between whole nations and the unseen God.

---

30. *Incarnation* 48.7, alluding to Matthew 12:24, etc.
31. *Incarnation* 43.7, alluding to *Statesman*.

After Athanasius

Athanasius has been commended for his simplicity, yet in this short treatise he at once subsumes and supersedes all previous narratives of sin and redemption in Christian literature. With Origen, and in contrast to Irenaeus, he maintains that humanity sinned in a state of knowledge rather than from lack of knowledge; he does not imply that an incarnation might have taken place as a prophylactic had it not required as a remedy for transgression. At the same time, just as in Irenaeus, the final state is to be more perfect than the initial one, and just as in Origen humans are called to win for themselves the likeness that is wanting to the image, so in Athanasius salvation is not merely a return to innocence but the acquisition of immortality, and with it the impeccability that was not imparted to souls in their first creation. Because the soul is not by nature immortal, as Lactantius imagined—not by nature even capable of immortality, as we might infer from Theophilus—we cannot make ourselves worthy of this renewal by an exertion of the will. What lies in the will is simply to put our sinful disposition to death in Christ, so that we may rise to life as the image of him who resembled us in everything but sin. Because he is our universal archetype, the death that each must undergo is already accomplished for all by his crucifixion, which now becomes, for the first time since Paul's letter to the Colossians, the instrument of his victory over Satan. Both our enthralment to sin and our release from it are objective conditions, not produced but ratified by our own choices: the condition of those who have made such a choice is not the autonomy of the Stoic wise man but, to use a modern term, the theonomy of a mind that is attuned to the indwelling Word. As Athanasius says, not only here but in his *Oration against the Arians*, God became human that we might be made divine.

As we have seen, Athanasius is no Origenist, notwithstanding his conception of the fall as a surrender of reason to sense and of salvation as the attainment of divinity by partaking of the Word in body and soul. Where Origen speaks of a fall in Adam and a descent of individual souls, Athanasius mentions neither but invites us to read our own history, both collective and individual, in his narrative of a primaeval loss of wisdom. In Origen the soul grows cooler, forfeiting the divine image and assuming that of the devil, perhaps before and certainly after it joins itself to flesh and blood through the filthy medium of sexual congress. By contrast, Athanasius represents demons as the enemies of the soul but not its captors, and since he does not trace the origin of sin to one individual, he is not obliged to propose any mechanism for its transmission. In these respects he fails not only to follow Origen, but to anticipate his persecutors in the late fourth

century, who asserted the historicity of Adam and Eve as a truth irreconcilable with the doctrine of pre-existence. While the foremost doctors of the
church confessed that some particulars in the description of paradise were
not to be taken literally, Epiphanius spoke for most or all when he maintained that the entire history of God's providential dealings with humanity,
from creation to the cross, would be imperilled if the fall itself were merely
an allegory. How could Christ be the second Adam if there had been no
first? Why would there be a bodily resurrection if the body were only the
prison of the soul in its exile from heaven? Was not the precondition of the
corporate salvation of humanity in the last man its genetic solidarity in the
first?

Athanasius, as we have noted, did not arrive at what is now the orthodox confession of three persons in one divine nature, without any greater
or less. We owe this tenet not so much to Nicaea as to the three men who
are commonly known as the Cappadocian fathers—Basil of Caesarea, his
brother Gregory of Nyssa, and their yokefellow Gregory of Nazianzus,
whom the Orthodox world regards as the best theologian of the three. The
western church, however, has Nazianzen more oracular than instructive,
while consenting to forgive the logical failings in Nyssen's efforts to decipher the ineffable. He insists that the nature of God cannot be known, yet
is unwilling to resign the perfidious analogy between the three persons and
three human people; he tends to reserve the term "image" for the incarnate
Christ while affirming that in us the image is not the outer but the inner
man. As we shall see, his account of the fall suggests that the animality of
the outer man is the cause of the fall, although our sexual differentiation is
a proleptic result of it. In his *Commentary on Ecclesiastes* a similar distaste
for the present state of the world is apparent, and salvation lies not so much
in discerning the hand of providence in apparent evils as in turning away
from its delusive goods.

Gregory of Nyssa on the Fall

Gregory's *Hexaemeron*, a completion of the treatise on the six days of creation that was left unfinished by his brother Basil (GNO IV.1, 6.1), rejects
at the outset any suspicion of deficit or imperfection in the works of God.
Tacitly refuting the Valentinian myth in which Wisdom (Sophia) tries to
create independently of her consort Will (Thelema), he asseverates that
the true Artificer lacked neither will nor wisdom to give perfection to his
handiwork, and that the power of execution is implicit in his will (15.15–
21). He also has a caution for the Platonists who, while they agreed that

neither power nor wisdom were wanting in the noetic cosmos, regarded the material world as a product of superabundance rather than voluntary benevolence, and its blemishes as inevitable consequences of the imposition of form on a labile substrate. There is nothing, says Gregory, in the constitution of the world that can impair the design of God, since he created it from nothing;[32] the "earth without form and void" of Genesis 1:2 is not an unregulated chaos but the cosmos as it exists "spermatically" in the mind of God, where it lacks nothing but conversion from the potential to the actual (27.10–17). Nor did this conversion require a substrate, which God had the good luck—and as Sethians thought, the bad judgment—to find at hand for his purpose: matter is merely a name for the totality of the elements, and neither the existence nor the combination of elements has any cause but the divine will (16.1–11). There is no presentiment here, as is sometimes alleged, of Berkeley's denial of the very existence of matter:[33] on the contrary, this theory of supervenience accords more solidity to it than the Aristotelian theory, which makes it prior to all the elements. Nevertheless, this redefinition of matter serves the same end in Gregory that the denial of it serves in Origen, or in the Maximus whose thoughts have crept into Origen's *Philokalia*: it takes from matter the status of a necessary substrate which it retains in Greek cosmogony even when it is stripped of every attribute that would enable it to exist alone.

What and whence is evil, then, if all things come from nothing? The Greek word *kakos* occurs over eighty times in the *Great Catechism*, yet it always signifies either that which is alien to the nature of God or that which, though equally alien to the nature of the world, is brought into it by an exercise of the freedom that belongs naturally to the souls that God created in his own image. No reference is made to natural evil, and if Gregory can speak of an evil deity, it is only because he must quote the heretical oxymoron in order to confute it.[34] Because it is by the doing of good or evil that a good or evil disposition is formed, the power of the soul to do good is vitiated by evil actions. Deliverance from sin and its consequences therefore depends on the working of God through inward and outward mortifications to which Gregory, following Origen, often applies the imagery of fire. Nothing that proceeds from God's will rather than ours can be evil; it was

32. See Gregory's extraordinary analysis of the word *ouden* (nothing) at 28.12–29.17, for which he finds authority in the translations of Genesis 1:2 by Aquila and Symmachus.

33. See Edwards, "Christians against Matter." On Related passages in Basil, see Zachhuber, "Stoic Substance, Non-Existent Matter?"

34. *Great Catechism*, prologue 7, GNO III.4, 7.21–23.

he who became the victim of our iniquity when he became the one human being whose flesh remained untouched by sin.

The universal fallenness of humanity is repeatedly affirmed in Gregory's writings,[35] yet he never infers that since we are all come of wicked stock we cannot refrain from sin. In words reminiscent of Origen, he says that the corporeal state defiles the soul;[36] at the same time, however, he is so far from regarding birth as a fall or descent of the soul from a higher sphere that in his treatise *On the Making of Man* he will not admit even its temporal priority to the body. He does ascribe a moral and ontological precedence to the rational soul, which he takes to be both the inner man of Paul and the common element in us that, according to Genesis 1:26, was fashioned by God in his image and likeness.[37] The image of God, with whom each individual human is properly to be identified, is not denumerable:[38] plurality is a consequence of embodiment, which, while it differentiates one human from another, is also that which unites all humans to the animal creation. Gregory holds, with Origen, that the creation of this vehicle is recounted in Genesis 2, although he takes the narrative form to be an accommodation to mortal understanding. The soul is placed in the body to rule it and thereby to exercise mastery over the whole of the natural order:[39] that is its role in Plotinus also, and as in Plotinus, its fall consists not so much in its embodiment as in its enthralment to sensory perceptions. Sin in Adam is the prototype of sin in us, the surrender of reason to the carnal appetites: a champion, if not a lifelong exponent of virginity,[40] Gregory contends that God endowed our first parents with genital organs only because he foresaw that the fall would render them incapable of spiritual propagation.[41]

Gregory does not quite concur with Philo in equating Adam with reason and Eve with pleasure, nor does he represent the virgin's dedication to God as a Christian analogue to Plato's begetting in the beautiful. As we

---

35. See, e.g., *Homilies on the Lord's Prayer* 5; *On the Making of Humanity* 16; Zachhuber, *Human Nature in Greory of Nyssa*, 145–62.

36. See, e.g., *On Virginity*, GNO VIII.1, 301.11 and often in this treatise.

37. *On the Making of Man* 6.2 and 6.4, in Gregory of Nyssa, *De Hominis Opificio*, ed. L. Sels, pp. 136 and 137.

38. *On the Making of Man* 16.10, in Gregory of Nyssa, *De Hominis Opificio*, ed. L. Sels, p. 138.

39. *On the Making of Man* 4, pin Gregory of Nyssa, *De Hominis Opificio*, ed. L. Sels, 130; 8.8., p. 148.

40. While it is not known whether he was married, he famously exclaims in *On Virginity* that he wishes that he were a virgin.

41. *On the Making of Man* 22, in Gregory of Nyssa, *De Hominis Opificio*, ed. L. Sels, pp. 227–28.

have seen, he differs from both these predecessors in making human nature itself the subject of the fall.[42] It is evident from such works as the *tunc et ipse filius* that our nature includes the flesh (GNO III.2, 8–9)—indeed, that "flesh" is its scriptural name—and that its integrity could not be restored until we were united to God by the incarnation and thereby reunited to one another. Our unity as a race depends not only on our common possession of the image of God but on our common descent from Adam. Although it is sometimes said that Gregory speaks of a depravation of human nature in the abstract without explaining its transmission to individuals, he seems to echo Origen and anticipate Augustine in making lust in the parents the cause of moral incontinence in the offspring (*Great Catechism* 16.3).

As in Adam, so in our parents, pleasure gets the better of reason, and each new generation comes into being through an iteration of the original fall. Gregory may not entertain a doctrine of total depravity but he takes the psalmist literally when he says that the wicked are sinners from the womb (Psalm 51:5).

Gregory of Nyssa on the Fallen World

The revelation of God's ineffable majesty and goodness through the visible cosmos is a recurrent theme in Gregory's writings, whether they be pastoral, exegetic, or dogmatic. Should polytheists or atheists ask the neophyte why he believes in a Creator, he says in the *Great Catechism*, proof can be found in the ceaseless regularity of the natural order and in the adaptation of all its changes and cycles to the needs of life.[43] The origin of the elements, the path of the winds, and even the operations of the intellect that admires and observes them are mysteries to the wisest and the most learned of us: how then, he demands of Eunomius, can a mere human profess to know the essence of the Father who made these things and pronounce it distinct from the Son through whom they were created?[44] While Gregory is apt to assume that such arguments are unanswerable, he discovers the most formidable challenge to them in a book that is not only recognized as scripture by the church but bears the name Ecclesiastes, thereby signifying that, as the church is the *ecclesia* or gathering of the elect,[45] so Solomon, the wisest of

---

42. Thus at *On the Making of Man* 4, in Gregory of Nyssa, *De Hominis Opificio*, ed. L. Sels, p. 130, it is human nature that is an image of the divine nature.

43. *Great Catechism*, prologue 4, GNO III.4, 6.16 and 10.19.

44. *Against Eunomius*, GNO I(II), 247.9–15, etc.

45. Cf. Gregory's observations at GNO V, 279.5.

men, had resolved to gather in these few sentences all that was necessary to release the soul from error and set it on the way of life.

Why then does this lesson to the faithful commence with the exclamation, "Vanity of vanities, all is vanity"? Origen had maintained that since the realm of vicissitude is the realm of sin, every creatures that inhabits it, whether voluntarily or involuntarily, is subject to vanity; Gregory offers two different interpretations, both of which, like that of Origen, have their roots in Plato.[46] On the one hand, it is vanity to combine our own concepts to produce a new concept that exists in the mind alone without any counterpart in the world;[47] on the other hand, it is also vanity to covet those things outside the mind that vanish as we enjoy them, and are therefore no more capable of imparting a lasting good to the soul than a children's sand castle can withstand the tide (GNO V, 281.11–18) or all the rivers of the world can enlarge the sea (286.20–23). The second meaning is evidently the one intended by Solomon, who would not have committed the heresy of denying the reality of the material creation or the benevolence of its Author: the axiom, at once Platonic and biblical, that since God is good his creation must be good supplies both introduction and peroration to Gregory's *Homilies on Ecclesiastes*.[48] Although he addresses only the first three chapters, he finds in these abundant evidence that the Israelite sage believes in two creations, one of the intelligible realm and one of the sensible, and that the latter is good insofar as it conveys some notion of, and thus awakes a desire for, the former.[49] Ecclesiastes 1.9 echoes Plato in reminding us that matter is the realm of "was" and "will be," not of the things that endure for ever (294.17–295.13). Solomon himself, though a natural denizen of the intelligible realm, elected to taste for himself every gratification that the senses could offer so that when he proclaimed their futility he could not be accused of teaching without experience (305.19–306.11).[50] While Gregory draws no comparisons, Christians would perceive that the future bridegroom of the Song of Songs is here anticipating Christ in another way, by being voluntarily tempted as

46. At 289.20 the two objects of vanity are distinguished as the *anoêton rhema* (word without concept) and *anonêton pragma* (work without profit).

47. GNO V, 281.6–10. Cf. Origen on the meaning of *eidolon* at *Homilies on Exodus*.

48. GNO V, 283.18–285.12, alluding to Romans 1:18–20 and Wisdom 13:3–5 on the error of worshipping the creation instead of its Creator; GNO V, 440.2–3, commenting on Ecclesiastes 3:11.

49. See, e.g., GNO V, 293.2–11; 311.15–19; 373.17–374.3. At 293.6, the fatigue of the mind is reminiscent of Origen, *First Principles* 1.3.8–1.4.1 and also Plotinus, *Enneads* 2.9.3. At 324.20–325.3 the soul's pursuit of supernal beauty in the *Symposium* is fused with the quest of faith for things unseen at 2 Corinthians 4:18 and Hebrews 11:1.

50. At 317.19–20, however, Gregory raises the possibility that his career of worldly pleasures was invented for our instruction.

we are; Platonists would perceive in him the historical type of a figure who in Plato remains hypothetical, the philosopher who returns from the sunlit world to liberate the remaining prisoners from the cave.

Gregory follows Plato in contending that mundane pleasures prove themselves to be illusory by their failure to impart lasting satisfaction. At the same time, he agrees with Aristotle and the Stoics that sin cannot be reduced to mere miscalculation, and that the wrongfulness of an act is often revealed by its conflict with the natural order. Fusing Platonic with biblical imagery, he identifies the straying of the lost sheep with the defection of our nature from its "celestial way of life" (GNO V, 305.3–5). Thus he builds an entire catena of satirical metaphors on Aristotle's remark at *Politics* 1258b that money is sterile and therefore cannot beget interest (*tokos*) merely by being lent (344.11–345.11). And when he derides the notion that a human may purchase another human being as one purchases an inanimate object or a senseless beast,[51] he is denouncing an institution that Zeno had banished from his ideal republic and that other Stoics declared (against Aristotle) to have no foundation in nature. But of course he is also acquainted with scriptural condemnations of usury which are more forcible than any in pagan literature, and if slavery is not proscribed in either the Old Testament or the New, his principal ground for denying that one man may buy another is the teaching of both testaments that human beings are made in the image of God.[52]

To realize in itself the image and likeness of God is the duty of every rational soul (GNO V, 295.15–16); and since God never changes, the virtues by which we resemble him should be equally immutable. When, therefore, the preacher tells us that there is a time to love and a time to hate, a time to embrace or a time to refrain from embracing, the word "time" must be taken as a generic term for "measure" (374.15–376.11). The Greek maxims "follow the mean" and "nothing too much" may be derived from a literal reading of the preacher's precepts (375.13–14), but a closer study will reveal that this literal reading is no more consonant with the true intent of the text than with the gospel. There is not, in the life of a Christian, one time for love and another for hatred, one time to embrace and another time to refrain from embracing: at all times we are required to love what is good and to hate what is evil; at all times we are bound to embrace the needs of our fellow-humans but to shun their unrighteous ways (417.10–418.10). Those who live by the law alone will assume that Solomon's "time for the casting

---

51. GNO V, 335.338.22, commenting on Ecclesiastes 2:7.

52. On the vehemence of Gregory's opposition both to slavery and to neglect of the poor, see Ramelli, *Social Justice and the Legitimacy of Slavery*, 197–203.

of stones" occurs when a man is found gathering sticks on the sabbath;[53] yet the text speaks too of a time for gathering stones, and no such time is allotted by any ordinance of Moses (391.11–14). Solomon in fact was saying obliquely to his own age what the apostolic writings teach us now in the plainest terms, that *every* time is a proper occasion for building up an armory of virtues in the soul so that we will never lack stones to cast against our sins (396.14–20).

The natural order is perfect in its kind, and while injustice is a ubiquitous symptom of the fall, it is neither a cause of nor an excuse for sinning. If then we are told by Solomon to make the world our study, but only in order that through this study we may rise to the contemplation of higher truths, why is it that so many souls remain bound to the things below? Gregory replies, in terms once again reminiscent of Plato, that God is blameless for the evils that arise from the abuse of our autonomy and from that liberty to choose good, which implies the liberty not to choose it (GNO V, 427.15–428.1). Echoing *Enneads* 3.9.3, he observes that the soul is free to ascend or descend by fixing its love on either the higher or the lower (409.9–420.18); he does not suggest that our power of choice is compromised by the fall of the race in Adam or by the intrigues of the devil. When he writes that the object of the soul's progress in virtue is its *apokatastasis* or restoration to its initial perfection (296.17), the soul's fall from the supercelestial place in the myth of the *Phaedrus* comes to mind; nevertheless, it is evident from the other works of Gregory that he never posits a fall of individual souls from heaven, and that he means by *apoktastasis* the restoration in us of that which was lost in Adam. He borrows the term *apokatastasis* from Origen, and he uses it, as Origen did, to signify a consummation of all things in which not only sin but the physical word that we know will be superseded by the immediate presence of God to all his creatures.[54] Platonists, by contrast, have no eschatology for the world, and no concept of a divine predestination that can guarantee the spontaneous conversion of every soul.

We must look beyond the *Homilies on Ecclesiastes* for Gregory's attempts to reconcile the ineluctable purpose of God with our licence to sin. He makes no reference here, for example, to the death of Christ as a means of deliverance independent of our own wills. It is in the *Greater Catechism* that he propounds his theory that Christ was offered to the devil as a bait, in swallowing which the devil found himself captive and stripped of the

---

53. GNO V, 390.13–391.5, commenting on Numbers 15:32–36.

54. See further, Ludlow, *Universal Salvation*, 38–44 and 77–111; Ramelli, *Christian Doctrine of Apokatastasis*, 373–440.

souls whom he himself had reduced to bondage.[55] Another of Gregory's presuppositions, affirmed in the *Homilies* but without the consequences that he develops elsewhere, is that God is infinite not only in power but in his communication of love and felicity to his creatures: although he evokes the language of the *Symposium* when describing the intelligible objects of desire, he conceives of God as a higher object, who fulfils our love by arousing a greater capacity to love. Thus there can be no question of repletion once the thirst of the soul is quenched, no falling away from the vision of God through *koros* or satiety: as Gregory asserts in the *Homilies on Ecclesiastes*, the seeking is its own reward. Gregory differs from Plato in embracing the doctrine of bodily resurrection, with its corollary that no more than one body is ever assigned as a tenement to the soul: indeed, he holds that the soul retains its attachment to the atoms of this body even after their dispersion, and will be able to reintegrate them on the final day.[56] In the meantime, it would seem that the soul undergoes purgations and illuminations similar to those posited by Origen, with the same result that at last there will be no soul that refuses to turn of its own free will to its Creator. The ministry of grace is indeed more catholic in Gregory than in his predecessor, for he says what Origen expressly denies, that even the devil will be saved.

Theodoret and Theodicy

As in pagan so in Christian philosophy one could meet the problem of evil by denying it or by arming the soul with the means to overcome it. Against Nyssen's adoption of the second method one could set a number of texts maintaining the goodness of the world, including the 38th Oration of Gregory Nazianzen and a meandering fable by the poet Synesius of Cyrene,[57] who may never have been less than half a pagan. It will be sufficient here, however, to notice only the most comprehensive essay in this vein by a prolific and versatile author of the fifth century, Theodoret of Cyrus. He was so admired that even the condemnation of his fusillades against Cyril of Alexandria could not prevent the survival of his histories, theological tracts, and biblical commentaries; if his orthodoxy was doubted, his caustic *Cure for All Greek Maladies* left no doubt of his apologetic zeal.[58]

55. *Great Catechism* 24.4, GNO III.4, 62.9. Cf. *On the Three Days' Space*, GNO IX,281.13.

56. *On the Soul* 44–48. See Ramelli, ed., *Gregorio di Nissa sull'anima*, 380–86.

57. For Synesius's *Egyptian Tale* (also known as *On Providence*), see Long, "The Wolf and the Lion."

58. On his deployment against the pagans of their own medical metaphors, see Papadogiannakis, *Christianity and Hellenism*, 30–39.

It is therefore all the more remarkable that he should make so little use of peculiarly Christian dogmas in his treatise *On Providence*.[59]

On Providence

The first book opens with a resonant assertion of a claim that we might think most in need of proof. God is the everlasting and eternal Creator, more worthy of love and gratitude than any other being and hence to be vindicated with more zeal than we would bring even to the defence of our parents (*On Providence* 1.3). Above all we must defend him against the pagans who imagine that there are many warring gods who either neglect the world or enter it only to sow misfortune and corruption. The ranks of our adversaries include the philosophers whenever they disguise the immorality of these gods by reducing myth to allegory (1.7). Many of them, moreover, entertain doctrines as false and pernicious as those of the poets. Some deny providence, some abandon works to chance and others to fate; some trust only the senses and some imagine a plurality of worlds (1.8). Having thus reproached in turn the Aristotelians, the Epicureans, the Stoics, and any latter-day dupes of Democritus (among whom one might number Plutarch), he proceeds to denounce the heretics who have severed the power of God from his grace by denying the common nature of the three persons. Some proclaim Marcion's three gods and others the two principles of Mani (1.9). Arians make the Son a creature, Apollinarians rob his body of a soul, Macedonians deny divinity of the Spirit (1.10). All are confounded, declares the peroration to the first book, by the spectacle of the imperishable heavens and their eternal rotation, together with all the benefits that accrue from the change of seasons and the alternation of night and day (1.14).

Purloining an image from Aristotle's exoteric treatise *On Philosophy*, he argues at the beginning of Book 2 that to imagine such regularity in the world without a designer would be as irrational as to imagine that a ship could hold a straight course without a pilot (*On Providence* 2.1–2). Once the dependence of the natural order on God is established, we can hardly doubt that he who raises water to the mountains for our sake (2.12) might be as jealous or niggardly as the Gnostics suppose in his other dealings with us (2.13). It is no less absurd to maintain that he lacks not the will but the power to preserve his creatures (2.14). Tacitly following Plato and his Christian imitators, Theodoret reminds his interlocutors that God is infinite and in need

---

59. Halton, trans., *Theodoret of Cyrus*, 3–6, concludes that the precise date of this work cannot be determined, and that, while it is highly derivative, not all of its pagan sources can be traced.

of nothing (2.16); the equally trite corollary that he was under no obligation to create would be acceptable only to Platonists who read the *Timaeus* as literally as Christians read the opening chapter of Genesis (2.15). The diversity of phenomena and the juxtaposition of contrasting elements are not signs of deficiency in him but of his solicitude for us, as we shall see by meditation on the advantages of travelling by sea rather than by land (20).

At 3.1, echoing other works on providence and his own *Cure for Greek Afflictions*, Theodoret recommends the study of human anatomy as a third cure for the malady of doubt. Who cannot be amazed by the delicate fashioning of our instruments of speech (*On Providence* 3.10), the versatility of the alimentary system (3.12–13), the uninterrupted functioning of the respiratory organs (3.17), and the artful design of the ear (3.36)? We are all the more to blame if we do not exercise the reasoning faculty, which has speech as its handmaid (3.23), and do not listen to the voice of God in scripture and Christian sermons (3.38).

Against those who argue, with Seneca (Letter 90), that the plastic and mechanical arts have been fatal to human innocence, Theodoret urges in Book 4 that it is good for us to imitate the creativity of the divine Artificer (*On Providence* 4.3–5). No organ is given in vain, and Theodoret agrees with Augustine that only the fall has taught us to be ashamed of our genital organs (4.10). The uselessness of the hand as a means of defence is compensated by its agility in digging, climbing, building, or steering a ship (4.16–20). Nevertheless it is not from ourselves but from God that we have received these skills, together with those of mining, cooking, and weaving (4.23–24); if, as Pliny says, the worms surpass us in weaving, God has permitted us to gather the produce of the worms (4.26–27). Pliny and many Christians had already noted that grammar sets us apart from the brute creation (4.31); Theodoret, a copious writer of letters, adds that we alone are able to speak with those who are far away because of the fitness of the hand to hold a pen (4.31–33).

The fifth book refutes the objection that a God who cared for humans would not have forced us to learn our crafts by long apprenticeships yet given bees the power of making honey and constructing hives by instinct (*On Providence* 5.4–5). We must remember that bees make honey for us (5.6), and that they provide us with a natural of modesty and harmonious intercourse (5.7–13). Our shortcomings in strength and speed are supplied by the horse, the ox, and the ass, whom we dominate by reason (5.20–30). The wild beasts whom we cannot tame are a chastisement to our evil disposition, and are no more a proof of the weakness or malevolence of God (as the Manichaeans opined) than surgical cautery or a flogging at school are evidence of a moral defect in the doctor or the teacher (5.40–41).

The exordium to book 6, deploring the obstinacy of the wicked, takes up the objection that wealth and poverty are unequally distributed and not in accordance with virtue. So much the better for the poor, says Theodoret, for that virtue which is the true end of life (*On Providence* 6.5) often flourishes in poverty, as experience testifies (6.11–12), and as the Stoics, Socratics, and Cynics confess by their exhortations to live in accordance with nature (6.13–14). Wealth is not of itself an evil (15), and every class of society has its function, like the members of a body (6.17–21): the poor, without whom no one would be rich, enjoy better health and are more inured to adversity (6.35–41). If the wicked are often rich, it is not God's policy to anticipate in this world the judgment that awaits us all (6.29, 36–37).

Theodoret turns wearily in book 7 to the argument that a benign creator might tolerate poverty but not slavery. Equality, he avers, was indeed the original dispensation (*On Providence* 7.8–9): slavery is a consequence of the fall, which has made it impossible for humans to survive except in societies where the majority submits to the few who rule (7.9–19). The fall has doomed us all to labor (25–26), and scripture gives many examples—Noah, Abraham, Rebecca, Jacob, and Moses—of masters who worked harder than their servants (7.28–33). A slave is free from many of the anxieties of his master (7.22), and the wise ruler performs the duties of teacher and guardian to his subjects. Hence, God requires the angel to submit to the archangel, the wife to the husband, the laity to its priests (7.36). God in his justice cannot curb the freedom of rulers and masters who abuse their charge (7.37–38), but the remedy is to pray with confidence in his boundless mercy (7.39–41).

The presence of slaves in a church that made no distinction between the bond and the free (Galatians 3:28) had troubled Christian prelates before Theodoret, who is not so ready as Gregory of Nyssa or John Chrysostom to denounce the institution.[60] In Book 8 he compiles a list of biblical figures who had profited by a season of unmerited servitude or humiliation, concluding that those who allege that the good fare worse than the wicked do not know the inscrutable ways of God (*On Providence* 8.57). In Book 9 he argues that even those who belittle providence exhort us to practice virtue (9.13) and that even wrongdoers pay homage to it by their dissimulation (9.18). Anticipating Joseph Butler's arguments from analogy, he argues that just as prudence and thrift are visibly rewarded in the present world (9.15), so there must be a reward for virtue, in a future life if not in this (9.19–20). Many of the poets and philosophers say as much (9.24), though we cannot follow them in supposing that only the soul is immortal, for the body would

---

60. See Ramelli, *Social justice and the Legitimacy of Slavery.*

then protest that it has been the soul's partner in fortitude, just as the soul has often been its confederate in sin (9.27–33).

Book 10 at last addresses a topic peculiar to Christian theology, the general resurrection of the dead. Its reasoning, however, is entirely on the manifestation in Jesus Christ of the Word who judges all. This revelation exposes the limits of philosophical reasoning, extinguishes vain curiosity, and teaches us to revere the inscrutability of God (10.1–4). Yet we know that Christ came to make us by adoption what he is by nature (10.13), that his divinity was attested by his incomparable works (10.19–32), that on the cross he paid our debt to the devil and made the devil in turn his captive (10.33–37), and that his conquest of death was the earnest of a general resurrection (10.38–43). Cavillers who ask why he did not come sooner must learn that the incarnation was eternally ordained (10.44) and prepared by many acts of providence in Old Testament times (10.45–57). Even the apostasy of the Jews was employed by God to create opportunities of witness for the saints (10.58–62). The doctrine of the incarnation propounded here is generally agreed to betoken Theodoret's acceptance of the Council of Ephesus (431–33), and since his own statement to Pope Leo I in 449 implies that he wrote the treatise twelve years before, the likeliest date for its composition would seem to be 437.[61]

Back to the Fall

We find, then, that Greek theologians of this epoch either ignore the biblical story of the fall or strip it of elements that would now be deemed fantastic. No doubt, Athanasius, Theodoret, and Gregory of Nyssa were all aware of the philosophical traditions that posit a history of social and moral decadence without laying the blame at the door of one transgressor. On the other hand, we have seen in chapter 2 that Latin literature in the era of civil war is haunted by a dim consciousness of ancestral sin. Catullis and Ovid trace it to Romulus, Horace to Laomedon, Virgil to the uncharted past. Lactantius would have scoffed that these putative culprits merely personify the fratricide and perfidy that are implicit in the creation of an empire; other Latin Christians, less inimical to the culture in which they were reared, could see no need to make a mystery of a truth for which the pagans had already been prepared by their own conceits.

The fall of Adam and Eve at the prompting of Satan is retold, with little innovation on the biblical narrative, by Firmicus Maternus in his treatise *On the Error of Pagan Religions*, which exhorts the Emperors Constans and

61. Bardy, "Théodoret," 299–301.

Constantius to put into force the Deuteronomic laws against the worship of false gods. Firmicus, whose manual of astrology had been dedicated to Constantine when he was ruling as a Christian, does not expressly say that he has renounced this science or his belief that each planet has a ruler who may be worshipped as a god subordinate to the Creator. Whatever his former allegiance, he claims an intimate acquaintance with the cults of both Rome and her subjects, and can testify that, where they are not diabolical parodies of the Christian sacraments, they honor the fiend himself in the serpentine guise under which he appeared to our forebears in Eden. All pagan worship, therefore, is not merely a result but an iteration of the fall.

No heterodoxy can be laid at the door of Avitus of Vienne, who recounts the fall in the second book of his versified paraphrase of the books of Genesis and Exodus.[62] Like all Christians, he takes the serpent in paradise to be Satan, who after his expulsion from heaven marries the powers of an angel with infinite malice, an unctuous tongue, and an ability to adopt whatever form is most serviceable to his design. He conquers Eve first by flattery and then with the Gnostic insinuation that only a jealous god reserves to himself the capacity for judging good and evil, which ought to be the prerogative of any rational mind (2.145–97). Even then she hesitates repeatedly before she plucks the fruit, but once she has done so she cannot resist its aroma. With a boldness that she has never displayed before, she seeks out Adam and immediately persuades him to eat with the promise, suggested but not expressly given by the serpent, that he will thus become the equal of his maker (2.201–3). Thus woman succumbs to vanity, man to pride, and man more quickly to woman than she to temptation from without. The punishment of the erring pair is postponed to the third book (3.45–209), but even in the second the pullulation of sin is so rapid, as it overtakes cities, loosens the reins of crime, and establishes lust as the only law, that we can hardly believe them to have been once the sole denizens of the world (2.260–410). It therefore seems that, as in many Christian texts of this era, we are permitted to take them as paradigmatic figures. There is certainly no propagation of an irresistible tendency to sin, for Avitus at once contrasts Adam with Lot, who elected to lose his wife rather than join her in flouting God's command.

The master in the inversion of poetic tropes in this era is Prudentius,[63] who retains a high reputation as a hymnodist and inspired a long vein of mediaeval exercises in the personification of vice and virtue. The serpent is

---

62. For commentary see Shea, *Poems of Alcimus Ecdicius Avitus*.

63. Dykes, *Reading Sin in the World*, maintains that the aim of the poem is to awaken a sense of accountability in the reader.

a recurrent image in his poetry, as in that of Virgil, but as in Firmicus he is no longer a natural predator.[64] The *Hamartigenia* begins with a salvo against the polytheists who imagine that a world so fair and ordered as ours could be the creation of more than one divinity, and goes on to denounce the reveries of Marcion, whose Demiurge is competent only in evil, while the unknown Father above him takes no part in the creation. With a brusque transition to the manner of Ovid, Prudentius shows us an allegorical picture of Envy as a gigantic beast whose lips overflow with gall and whose forehead never sheds its crown of hissing serpents. It is not clear whether this monster personifies Marcion or his imaginary creator; if this were the *Psychomachia*, Prudentius's celebrated depiction of the warfare between the passions, we should assume that the human passion of envy is being indicted here as the primordial cause of sin. But in fact, just as *phthonos* at Wisdom 2:24 is not only the passion from which God is exempt but the vice that defines and constitutes his adversary the devil, so in the *Hamartigenia* Envy takes possession of Satan, already a fallen angel, and transforms him into her own sibilant image as soon as he learns that God has planted his own image in another creature and told all other beings pay him homage. There is no account, however, of the temptation of Adam and Eve, and it seems to be a spontaneous consequence of this corruption of Satan that the natural realm begins to teem with malice. The lion attacks the goat, the wolf is a sudden foe to the shepherd, the fruits that we wrest from the soil are often poisonous, and the very winds conspire against our efforts to preserve our livestock and protect our bodies. Scarcity begets greed, which is quickly followed by a retinue of sins that set one human against another. Women turn to cosmetics, men to gold, war becomes a perpetual recreation, and beasts are trained not only to the plough but to the torture of those whom their fellow-sinners have branded as criminals.

This plague of self-inflicted injuries comes to an end with the birth of Christ, which in the *Apotheosis* of Prudentius is the signal for the other fallen angels to quit the shrines in which they have masqueraded as deities and deceived generations of suppliants with their ambiguous replies. In the *Hamartigenia* the result of Christ's teaching is the emancipation of souls from error and the reopening of a path to the stars, from the first soul descended to Adam's body. This heterodox parenthesis is the only mention of Adam, its purpose being not so much to inculcate a new doctrine as to assimilate the afterlife promised by Christ to the catasterism that pagans were wont to imagine as the destiny of their great men. Just as the fall is almost

---

64. Serpents in Virgil: *Eclogues* 3.93; *Georgics* 1.53; *Aeneid* 2,205–21, 471–75; 5.80–84, 273–75; 7.346; 8.432. Serpents in the *Kathemerinon* of Prudentius: 3.101–2, 126–27; 6.140–45; 9.88–90; 10.163–64; 11.91–92.

reduced to an allegory and the pullulation of sin is described in terms that mirror pagan accounts of human decadence, so the Christian doctrine of the last things is clothed in imagery more palatable, and therefore more alluring, to philosophers; it may be that writing in verse, or writing in Latin, shielded Prudentius from the charge of Origenism, which would have been inescapable had he set down such an inaccurate theodicy in Greek prose.

Conclusion: Looking Forward

Prudentius is famous also for his eulogies of martyrs and his retort to the learned polytheists who opposed the removal of the Altar of Victory from the Forum.[65] Yet even he, in a poem on the genesis of sin, adapts biblical narrative to his epic models. Christians of the fourth century were at one in maintaining that human nature had been debased by a fall—how else explain the presence of sin in the handiwork of a sinless Creator?—and if they were pressed to say whether they believed in the biblical paradise, they could hardly fail to reply in the affirmative. Yet even those of unquestioned orthodoxy opined that particulars of this ancient tale might be fabulous, and it was seldom considered politic to dwell on them for the purpose of theodicy. The consistent application of the whole narrative to this end by Augustine will be the subject of the next chapter, in which we shall see why the most consistent biblicist of the early church, who was also its most consistent philosopher, found himself unable to account for the ubiquity of sin or its expiation on the cross without subscribing literally to the claim that all men and women who have ever lived were contained in Adam's loins.

---

65. See now Kraus, *Prudentius' Contra Symmachum.*

11

Augustinian Variations

AUGUSTINE IS ONE OF the fathers of Roman Catholic and Protestant orthodoxy, yet even in these circles he now has an evil reputation. He is accused of a Neoplatonic contempt for the body (although he goes to great lengths to explain how our bodies can be preserved without blemish in the life to come); he is accused of a pathological distaste for sexual intercourse (though, in contrast to many others of his time, he condemns no intercourse that is not illicit); he is accused of an inhumane indifference to suffering (though he sends fewer people to hell than his Pelagian or Donatist adversaries); and he is accused of denying the freedom of the will (although he avers at all times that only an act that is freely performed can be rewarded in heaven or punished in hell). In his own time he was accused of wedding two incompatible theories of the origin of evil, one Manichaean and the other Catholic, one openly denying while the other purported to vindicate the freedom of the will.[1] He is certainly unusual among Catholics in his preoccupation with the question of evil, and it was no doubt this preoccupation that led him, before the event that he calls his conversion, into the company first of Manichaeans and then of Platonists. He does not admit, however, to any substantial alteration in his opinions between the works in which he upholds the goodness of the natural order and the freedom of the will against the Manichaeans and those in which he asserts against the Pelagians that all humanity has been enslaved to sin by the fall of Adam.[2]

1. See further Lamberigts, "Was Augustine a Manichaean?"
2. For a review of modern controversies regarding the intellectual development of

The present chapter cannot hope to render his mature doctrine palatable to every reader, but it can at least hope to show that he spoke the truth when he denied that he ever traduced the material creation or denied to Adam's posterity the one freedom that can be rationally ascribed to it—the freedom to commit sin at the behest of a sinful will.

How Augustine Saw the Problem

In Augustine we see every shade of Christian culture as it appeared to us in the last chapter. He is a humanist who disowns the humanities with consummate eloquence, a dogmatist who quotes scripture against the philosophy of his youth, yet also an exegete who philosophizes even as he explains his text. In a book that fathered the European tradition of autobiography, he recalls his futile tears for the death of Dido, his apprenticeships as a Manichaean and a Platonist, and his miraculous conversion to the Christianity of the New Testament. Yet perhaps the most famous episode is one in which, as a child, he refuted Plato without having heard of him, by committing a sin not for any good that would come of it, but because it was a sin:[3]

> It was my will to commit a theft, and I committed it, driven by no need but by a poverty and disdain for what was right, indeed by a surfeit of wickedness. For I stole that which I had in copious and much better supply, and the thing that I wished to enjoy was not the thing that I wished to acquire by theft: that thing was the theft itself and the sin. (*Confessions* 2.4.9)

In this celebrated passage, Augustine proclaims what Plato and Aristotle denied—that it is possible to do evil in the full knowledge that it is evil, without disguising it under any semblance of the good. Together with his observation of infant twins denying each other the breasts that had milk for both, the remembrance of this trespass was for him an abiding proof that Paul was right to speak of a law in our members that compels us to do the contrary of that which our mind or *nous* would have us do in the service of God (Romans 7:23; *Confessions* 7.21.27). Although the apostle may have thought this the peculiar dilemma of believers, Augustine was freed by Cicero and Plato from the Manichaean doctrine that a sinner sins

---

Augustine, see BeDuhn, *Augustine's Manichaean Dilemma*, 12–14. He is no doubt right to maintain that it is often better to speak of the amplification of belief by understanding than of a change in Augustine's opinions.

3. Text from O' Donnell, ed., *The Confessions of Augustine*. Although it is obvious that the first sin cannot be repeated, I do not think it wholly true to say, with O'Donnell, vol. 2, 136–37, that "the sin of the tree of Genesis is not here."

by nature,[4] and Plato might have accused him of mistaking the soul for a character in tragedy who "sees and applauds the good yet does the worse" (Euripides, *Hippolytus* 389). In his later years, the theological innovation for which he became notorious was his teaching that the unregenerate will, for want of charity, is *bound* to do evil even when it shows all the colors of virtue.[5] For this loosing of human agency from the sovereignty of reason he has won a name in some quarters as the founder of the modern sensibility, the godfather of the Faustian soul, the discoverer of the will. In others it has been argued that he is not without precursors, and that, in recognizing will as a faculty distinct from reason, he was applying to theology what he had learned as a philosopher from the Stoics.

The truth appears to lie not so much between the extremes of scholarly opinion as in both of them. On the one hand, there are few thoughts of Augustine that were not anticipated by the philosophers; on the other hand, he mixes all the elements of reason in the alembic of revelation, adopting nothing that he does not transform. We shall see that while he never renounced the position that good may accrue to the whole from the existence of particular but subordinated evils, he could say with the Platonists that good without evil is inconceivable. While he could endorse the Stoic definition of freedom as acting in accordance with one's nature, he could neither accept that our weaknesses are simply given to us without any fault on our part nor accord to our wills the power to overcome these weaknesses without divine succor. In his explanation of the enthralment of the will to the flesh in this world, it can be said that the part of the pre-existent soul is played by Adam;[6] his doctrine of creation, however, rules out any analogue of the necessary descent of the soul to matter or of its all but inevitable subjection to matter; if there is any necessity in the fall, it resides in the soul, not in God or in matter, and even this account is not complete without some argument that the more perfect a creature is the more it will be disposed to fall.

---

4. For the *Hortensius*, see *Confessions* 3.4.7 and 8.7.17; for the *libri Platonicorum* 7.9.13ff.

5. See *On the Spirit and the Letter* 4.6, etc.

6. There is no doubt that in early works he entertained the concept of a pre-existent soul as one of four possible hypostases (*On Free Will* 3.18.52–53.25.76). For criticism of O'Connell, *St. Augustine' Early Theory of Man*, see P. di Leo, "Plotinus and the Young Augustine," 286–87, comparing the pride of the Augustinian sinner with the temerity of the Plotinian soul. *Pace* BeDuhn, *Augustine's Manichaean Dilemma*, 462n47, I cannot see a narrative of the descent of souls from one order to another at *On Free Will* 3.5.14–15 or 3.11.33–33.12.35.

Evil as Disorder

In the *Confessions* Augustine presents the development of his thought as an epiphenomenon of a life in which love of self, love of the flesh, and love of the world were secretly but inexorably consumed by the love of God.[7] Born in 354 in the small North African town of Thagaste, he could find no Catholic teacher, even in Carthage, who was equal to the Manichaeans in scriptural disputation, and spent nine years as a member of the sect. Rescued from their "fantasies" by the study of certain Platonic books (*Confessions* 8.2),[8] he exchanged the view that sin is the product of an evil nature for Plato's doctrine that evil is a deficiency of goodness that can never be banished from the material realm. This is the tenet to which he gives a Christian dress in his dialogue *On Order*, composed in 386 at Cassiciacum shortly before his decision to accept baptism as a Catholic and to embrace the church's canon of scripture as his sole rule of faith. In contrast to most of his subsequent reflections, it has more to say of the place of evil in the external world than of its origin in the soul. Nevertheless, it establishes in the clearest terms the difficulty that never ceased to trouble him—that he cannot hold as a Christian either that evil is God's creation or that it enters the world in defiance of his will.

According to its proem, the treatise *On Order* was written at the behest of Augustine's eminent friend Zenobius (*On Order* 1.1.1). Throughout the work, attention is drawn to the evolution and recording of the argument, since one of his aims is to demonstrate that the presence of divine order in the cosmos is visible only to those who have taken pains with the ordering of their own thoughts. In the opening scene, he is startled by a sudden ebullition of water from the neighboring baths while he is working late at night (1.3.6). His young friend Trygetius explains that the usual channels of egress for the water have been choked by autumn leaves (1.3.7), but Augustine affects to be puzzled that God would countenance such a breach of order (1.3.7; 14.11). Trygetius's friend Licentius replies vehemently that order means conformity to the principles of causation, and that since there is no event without a cause there is no event that breaches the order of the cosmos. Adapting the Epicurean manoeuvre that Origen had borrowed in his discussion of astrology, he avers that if his thesis is refuted, he will regard his defeat as a further exemplification of the ubiquity of order (1.3.9). We cannot doubt that all things have causes even where they elude us: if

---

7. See *Confessions* 10.30.41, echoing 1 John 2:16.

8. Chiefly if not exclusively those of Porphyry, according to Beatrice, "Quosdam Platonicorum Libros."

a Chaldaean book had foretold this accident, its author would be a true prophet even if he could not explain the coagulation of the leaves (1.5.14).

Augustine, who will later have much to say against astrology, is most concerned at this point to ascertain the moral consequences of his friend's position. He inquires of Licentius whether he thinks the order of his own argument good or bad; Licentius replies that no doubt it mingles truth and error, but even the errors result from a certain order of reasoning; he adds that order in itself is neither good nor bad (*On Order* 1.6.15). If that is so, says Augustine, must we attribute all the ills of the world to the God whom we believe to be the sole architect of its order (1.7.18)? Licentius responds that God hates evil as he loves the good, and that both dispositions express his love of order (1.7.18). When, however, Licentius defines order as that by which all things in God's creation are directed (1.10.28), Augustine wonders whether God does not direct himself (1.10.29).

On the next Augustine day elicits from Licentius a new statement of his position, according to which divine order is necessary only because the world contains evil as well as good (*On Order* 2.1.2). The corollary is that order is not imposed upon that which is good, since it is not susceptible of change or motion. He may therefore have withdrawn his claim that order is neither good nor bad, but not his claim that both the good and the bad are implicit in the concept of order. At the same time, he admits that it is only the good that is properly said to exist. To be good is indeed to be with God, whereas all things below the heavens (and even much that we see in the heavens) exhibit a mobility that shows that they cannot be with God, even if, inasmuch as they obey his will, they cannot be said to be without him (2.2.4). On further interrogation, Licentius comes to the view that, since it is only the ordered soul that apprehends the true order of the cosmos, the wise man's goal is to be with God by practising the perpetual contemplation of the intelligible and eternal (2.2.5). Augustine reminds him, however, that the wise man also has a soul and body (2.2.6), and that he will have need of memory, if only to exercise his duty of teaching others (2.2.7). Neoplatonists had distinguished between the anecdotal memory that is proper to brutes and the anamnesis or recollection of eternal verities that is proper to the rational soul; Plotinus had gone so far as to deny that an emancipated intellect has any memory of its past.[9] The writing of the *Confessions* is a testimony to Augustine's high valuation of the anecdotal memory, the loss of which would render the saints insensible of God's mercies and hence of

---

9. See *Enneads* 3.6.5; 4.4.5, etc., with Clark, "Plotinus: Remembering and Forgetting."

the causes of their own salvation.[10] He could also appeal, however, to Plato's argument that the philosopher will return to the cave in order to liberate his fellow-prisoners, and we may guess, from an allusion to the Pythagoreans near the end of the dialogue, that he was also familiar with their custom of reflecting on the transactions of the day before going to sleep.[11]

It is highly characteristic of Augustine to raise the question whether the wise man knows stupidity (*On Order* 2.3.8), just as he was to wonder in the *Confessions* whether the contents of our memory include forgetfulness. Without such knowledge, no one could teach the ignorant, yet how can wisdom be conscious of that which it has banished from the intellect? The conclusion to which Augustine draws his companions is that stupidity is not a thing in itself but the absence of wisdom, just as darkness is not a thing in itself but the absence of light (2.3.10). It is thus not properly an object of knowledge, although we cannot be aware of what we know without an awareness of it, just as without some awareness of shadow we cannot appreciate that which is illumined. Now we see the purpose of the admission that that which properly exists is the good, for if evil is only the absence of good we cannot hold God responsible for its creation. We can, however, see that he has a purpose in permitting it, for a shadow can add to the beauty of what is perceived, just as a well-chosen solecism can add to the beauty of a poem (2.4.13). This discovery enables Augustine to point out the inadequacy of Licentius's thesis that order is merely that which subdues by the proper allocation of reward and punishment, in accordance with Plato's definition of justice as "allotting to each his own." If that were so, all evils would be in origin *praeter ordinem*, extrinsic to divine order (2.7.23). We grasp the divine plan only when we perceive that we have a choice between goods and evils insofar as we have a choice between pursuing that which is and that which is not. If we were unable to err, there would be no divine justice, as there would be no injustices to punish (2.7.22), and the intellectual disciplines by which we free ourselves from error would be otiose (2.7.24).

Precedents for this theodicy can be found, as we have seen, in Plutarch and Seneca; it is possible that Augustine had already encountered Porphyry's hypothesis (which he repeats in the *City of God*) that souls are sent down into bodies to acquire virtues that cannot be manifested in heaven. Having thus established both the providential purpose of tribulation and the necessity of intellectual discipline for the understanding of the ways of providence, Augustine undertakes a long excursus on the cultivation of

10. See, e.g., Breyfogle, "Memory and Imagination." Kotzé, *Augustine's Confessions* contends that its principal aim to convert the Manichaeans.

11. *On Order* 2.20.33–34.

wisdom. We begin by accepting both religious truths and moral precepts on authority.[12] As we grow in understanding, we find that reason is exhibited above all in the exercise of sight and hearing, which in contrast to the other senses are capable of grasping not only pleasure but harmony (*On Order* 2.11.33–34). Without pretending to have fathomed those mysteries that will always exceed comprehension, we come to perceive through the study of mathematics (which supervenes on that of music) that unity is the presupposition of both beauty and harmony (2.18.48). This is a shaft against the Manichaeans—and a proof that it is inconsistent with the nature of God that evil should have existed but not been subject to his power. Without commenting explicitly either on Plato's notion of pre-existent matter or the heresies that it has generated, Augustine concludes that the secrets of nature cannot be fathomed by our own exertions (2.16.44). The aim of pedagogy is not to foster curiosity but to imbue the soul with virtue. The test of our education will not be our mastery of science but our progress in courage and temperance, which cannot be acquired without the tribulations that we all too readily lay to the charge of God (2.17–45).

Evidently the author of this treatise has not outgrown his Platonism. In becoming a biblical theist, however, he has permitted two new axioms to transform the familiar principle of plenitude into something less Platonic, which we may call the principle of compensation. The first axiom is the identity of the first principle with the Creator, the second the contingency of all things that are not the first principle. The Good, or One, of Plotinus does not know, does not love, and does not will its progeny, but since it cannot fail to superabound it communicates its goodness to every plane of being, first as essence to *nous*, then as essence to soul, and at last through soul in its most tenebrous form to matter. While it is impossible for the poverty of matter to grasp the plenitude of form, it would be an even greater diminution of plenitude to restrict being to the plane of essence. Hence, it can be said that evil is ineradicable, and at the same time while it remains subordinate to the good it is no true evil. Once we replace the One by the Creator, however, we cannot affirm the existence of anything other than God to be inevitable. Hence, the existence of anything imperfect can no longer be excused as an ineluctable consequence of the imperfection of its medium: evil is no longer a lesser good but a positive blemish, which cannot be excused on the grounds that it could not have been otherwise. Its very contingency indicates that it cannot have been willed or even condoned by the Creator; in the absence of any second principle, its presence in the

---

12. *On Order* 2.9.26. On the necessity of juvenile faith in authority as the basis of future reasoning, see Augustine's tract against the Manichaeans *On the Utility of Belief*.

world is barely explicable, and it finds its place in the natural order only when it is judged—that is to say, only when it is authoritatively deemed to be antithetical to the good.

Against Dualism

As a bishop, Augustine wrote voluminously against the Manichaeans, and the transition from authority to reason that he inculcates in his treatise *On Order* provides a frame for his diatribe *Against the Epistle of Mani called Fundamental*, which condenses into one argument his reasons for abandoning the religion of his youth. He is our principal witness to the epistle, which was written (he says) with the supposititious authority of an apostle but without the accreditation that the true apostles received both from the apostles and from the church. Their reverence for this document thus exposes the Manichaeans to the same charge of credulity that they urge against simple adherents of the church which has the apostolic succession; and since, in contrast to Catholics, they profess to despise the material creation, they also court the charge of self-contradiction by embracing a myth in which God is portrayed as an infinite domain of light, flanked on one side by a realm of darkness whose denizens are the offspring of shadow, vapor, smoke, and fire. Like Plato and Origen, he confines the use of allegoresis to those who are of his own party, convicting his opponents of three errors, two of which we might call philosophical, while the third is a profound misapprehension of the power and purpose revealed in God's creation of this world.

The first error, as any Platonist can inform them, is to attribute to God a body of any kind, for it is in the nature of body to occupy space and admit of division: it follows that no body, however subtle, can be present as a whole in every place.[13] Yet only a little reflection on the operation of thought and memory, even in brutes, will teach us that the soul has this capacity: how then can we deny it to the Author of the soul (*Against the Epistle of Mani* 15.20–16.20)? The second error, obvious once again to all students of Plato, is to attribute substance to evil, for there is no substance without some measure of form, of harmony and of activity, all of which are in themselves good (35.39–36.41). If shadow were really a body and not merely the absence of light, if fire and smoke were able to produce offspring, if the five progenitive agents of the realm of darkness were able to maintain an eternal concord, each performing its work without encroachment on the others—all this would be evidence of their participation in the Good, which, as the church and Plato agree, can flow only from God

---

13. In *Acts against Fortunates* 12, Fortunatus denies that the soul resembles God.

(31.34–34.37). Augustine seems, however, to be correcting not only Mani but Plato himself when he diagnoses the third of the heretic's trespasses against reason as a failure to grasp that omnipotence is a necessary attribute of God.[14] Once this is granted, we cannot suppose that God would create a domain of evil or that, if such a domain existed already, he would delay his conquest of it or allow his conquest to remain incomplete (27.30). Any notion of a recalcitrant substrate that frustrates his design is impious, and the only position consistent with his dignity is that he brings all things but himself into existence out of nothing (25.27). When we hold together the two assertions that God is our Creator and that we are created from nothing, we have the solution to the problem of sin, which is the root of the problem of evil. On the one hand, we are good because God created us without any admixture of evil; on the other hand, because we have wills of our own, we are free to fall back into the nothingness from which only his power can preserve us (40.46–41.47). The way to redemption, therefore, is not through the study of arbitrary myths but through the cultivation of our noblest faculties, which will furnish our incorporeal souls with objects of contemplation more enduring than a heretic's sensuous dreams.[15]

Few Manichaeans would have been troubled by these animadversions. It was open to them to construe their founder's writings allegorically, so that even the assault of darkness on light (related in other versions of this myth) could be taken to represent the aspiration of matter to form;[16] it was equally open to them, as we learn from Augustine's debate with Felix, to disclaim any knowledge of works ascribed to Mani which had now been confiscated by their opponents (*Against Felix* 1.1). They had no reason to endorse the Platonic equation of evil with non-existence, for them, as for many pagans, the *a priori* argument that the world must be good because its Creator is good was belied every day by our encounters with the natural causes of sickness, pain, and death. If it were urged, with the Stoics, that the only evil is to set one's will against nature—that is, as Christians say, against God—how often in the Old Testament does the Author of nature permit or require the performance of acts that would now be sins on the eyes of the church. And if the church responds that it is only the *will* to disobey the Creator himself that is sinful, the rational interlocutor will ask why, if he

14. Cf. *Acts against Fortunates* 13–14.

15. *Against the Epistle called Fundamental* 2.2; cf. *Confessions* 3.6.10; 4.4.9; 5.9.16, etc.

16. Cf. Plutarch, *On Isis and Osiris* 374c, where Poverty and Plenty at *Symposium* 203b come to represent matter and form. On the other hand, BeDuhn, *Manichaean Body* argues that such a "hermeneutic of charity" may be only an outsider's excuse for refusing to take the insider at his word.

has given us such a will, it is we and not he who are held accountable for the crimes that we cannot avoid.

Augustine was a tenacious controversialist who did not leave objections unanswered. The argument from the manifest universality of evil is rebutted in *On the Ways of the Manichaeans*, where he contends that nothing is evil in the absolute sense unless it is so on all occasions and to every agent. The venom of the scorpion, for example, is toxic to us but is so far from being toxic to the scorpion that it cannot survive without it (*On the Ways* 8.11). The rays of the sun are painful to the eyes of the Manichaeans who revere it, but not to those of the eagle; if we can inure ourselves to poisons by the consumption of small doses, it is evident that the evil is in our use of a thing and not in the thing itself (8.13). The claim that the God of the law is the author of sin was advanced by the Manichaean Faustus, who asked how the bloody slaughter of beasts or the taking of a concubine was consonant with the teaching of the New Testament. Augustine rejoins that sacrifice must be understood typologically, as a prefiguration of that death which put an end to all killing in the name of holiness (*Against Faustus* 18.6; 19.10; 20.18, etc.); Abraham's infidelity to Sarah was both natural and permissible because he had not yet been promised the miracle that would satisfy his desire (which was also his duty) to people the earth with worshippers of the true God (*Against Faustus* 23.32–38). The proof that our capacity to sin does not relieve us of blame demanded a longer and subtler chain of reasoning, which Augustine pursues in his three books *On Free Will* (*De Libero Arbitrio*), the first of which was composed around 388, the second and third between 391 and 395.

What Is Freedom?

The dialogue commences with a question, put abruptly to Augustine by his pupil Evodius: is not God the author of evil (*On Free Will* 1.1.1)? Although he adds that by evil he means both that which we do and that which we suffer, the first book is concerned primarily with the causes of human maleficence. Evodius doubts whether anyone sins unless they have been taught to do so, but quickly admits, when pressed by Augustine, that no intellectual discipline can have evil for its subject matter if evil is not a true object of understanding (1.1.2). As in other works of Augustine against the Manichaeans, understanding is held to be answerable to faith, which teaches us that God cannot be the author of any evil (1.2.4–5). Yet sin exists, so our first task, says Augustine, is to ascertain why such an act as adultery is sinful. Not, as Evodius first proposes, merely because it is painful to the husband, for if it were to take place with the husband's connivance it would be for that reason all the more culpable (1.3.6). Not because it contravenes the law, for if what is unlawful were already sinful, the early Christians would have committed sin in defying the Roman government (1.3.7). As Plato's Euthyphro answered that the gods do not confer holiness on that which they love but love it because it is holy,[17] so Evodius and Augustine hold that it is the evil in an act that makes it unlawful, not the unlawfulness that makes it evil. Augustine suggests that the evil consists in surrendering the governance of the soul to *libido* or unrestrained desire (1.3.8). This is the root of all sin, so that even homicide, if committed involuntarily or on account of others, would not be sinful. The slave who kills his master because he fears death is not to be blamed for his fear of death but for the indulgences that have inspired his master's displeasure (1.4.10). To yield to lust is wrong because it flouts not merely the laws of society but the immutable ordinance of God (1.5.12–130).

The bishop of Hippo shares with the recluse of Cassiciacum the conviction that the best is the *ordinatissimum*, the most ordered (*On Free Will* 1.7.15; 1.8.16). At the pinnacle of the earthly creation, order means the subjection of the passions to the intellect, which guides us by its knowledge of things immutable and eternal to that wisdom whose fruits are happiness and virtue (1.7.17–11.9.19). Why then, do we allow our passions to throw us out of the path to life that is set so clearly before us? The answer lies, as Paul and our own experience remind us, in the capacity of the will to act against reason (1.11.21–22). Silently applauding the Stoics, Augustine concludes that the sole good for humanity is the good will (1.12.25). In language that is as free from scriptural echoes and as redolent of Plato as any speech at Cassiciacum, he declares that we mean by evil the soul's defection from the eternal and immutable and by good its restoration (1.16.34–35). Thus we are led to the question that supplies the theme of the second book: why, if it can be employed as readily for evil as for good, did God give us this freedom of the will (2.1.1)?

Augustine's first reply is that the evil is an inevitable concomitant of the good. No act can be properly ascribed to its agent unless it is voluntary, and for an act to be voluntary it must be possible to do otherwise. Consequently, that good which consists in obeying God implies the capacity to disobey (*On Free Will* 2.1.2–3). Evodius wonders whether this possibility of disobedience might be too high a price for the good of obedience (2.2.5).

17. On the evolution of the view that evil is nothing (*Confessions* 7.1.1; 7.12.18) from Plotinus, *Enneads* 1.8.3–6, etc., see Evans, *Augustine on Evil*, 34–35, although, as she also notes, Plotinus seems inclined to predicate of matter both a certain kind of being and a certain kind of evil (*Enneads* 2.4.16).

Augustine replies that if we put our faith in the goodness of God, as Christians, we shall quickly find an argument to justify that faith (2.2.5–6). It is universally granted (as Plato had argued in the *Philebus*) that merely to live is less of a good than to be conscious of living (2.5.11–12); Evodius is easily persuaded, on the principle, to subordinate sensation to consciousness, consciousness to reason, and reason itself to its noblest object, which is once again defined as the immutable and eternal (2.6.13–14). The phenomena of sensation are multitudinous, yet it is possible for two humans to share a single experience of this multiplicity—to see the same object, hear the same noise, or taste the same food (2.7.15–19). In this common enjoyment of externals we have a common awareness of number, which is so fundamental to order in the cosmos that the wisdom by which we grasp this order is held by some to be nothing other than number (2.8.20–21). Arithmetic is possible because, while 3 or 7 are more than 1, there is only one number 3 or one number 7: anterior to both is the number 1 without which no multiplicity is conceivable (2.8.21–24). This reasoning shows that wisdom itself is number and hence that the truth[18] that constitutes nature is number (11.30–32). Since therefore wisdom is one for all human beings (2.12.33–34), and our highest good is to live in accordance with truth (2.13.36), it follows that God, who is ultimate truth, is also our sovereign goal (2.15.39). The use of our free volition to attain this ultimate good delivers us from sin (2.13.37), but the price of that freedom is the possibility that instead we shall cleave to our sin.

This argument ignores a number of difficulties that had exercised Augustine's predecessors, both in the schools and in the church. Despite the exertions of Origen, it had yet to be shown that the freedom of the will was consistent with divine foreknowledge, which, according to the Aristotelians, logically necessitates the truth of the thing foreknown. Again, it had yet to be shown that human freedom precluded the moral infallibility that all Christians ascribed to God himself, the unfallen angels, and the saints. On the other hand, if it was Adam's fall that robbed us of our aboriginal goodness, what reason can be given for this transgression against his own nature, what blame can be attached to those who inherit the evil consequences of his sin, and what answer can we give to the Manichaeans who hold that the wicked sin by nature and not from choice? The reconciliation of divine prescience with human liberty is accomplished quickly enough, in the manner of the Stoics,[19] by including the exercise of the power to choose

18. In 3.16.46 *veritas* is God, or more accurately Christ, as at John 14:6. Elsewhere Augustine is fond of quoting Wisdom 11:20: "thou hast made all things in measure, number and weight."

19. See Diogenes Laertius, *Lives of the Philosophers* 7.1.23, where Zeno declares

among the things that God foresees (*On Free Will* 3.3.6). In the third book Evodius accepts that God's foreknowledge of contingencies is analogous to ours without asking either how he achieves the certitude that is denied to us or how he can escape responsibility for a crime that he foresees but does not forestall (3.2.4–4.11). He accepts again that evil has its place in the order of the created world so long as God foresees both the sin and his punishment of it (3.5.12–15.15). The argument that humans might be free and yet infallible is countered by a further appeal to the principle of order: as the natural economy of creation is richer because it accommodates lights that are weaker than the sun (3.9.24–25), so its moral economy is enriched by an order of beings who enjoy at present neither the blessedness of the unfallen angels (3.12.35) nor the unreasoning innocence of beasts (3.9.28). For all that, it is the fault of Adam rather than his Creator that his descendants are born with the power, and indeed the propensity, to sin (3.24.71). If the first humans were not, as Irenaeus thought, infants in reason, they had yet to acquire the wisdom that comes of acting habitually in accordance with reason (3.24.72). Had they followed this Aristotelian precept, they would at last have become impeccable.

What then is to made of the claim that Adam's sin, elective yet inexplicable, has deprived his posterity of the power to choose either good or evil? Augustine's observations on the relation of choice to volition in this treatise made an important, though often unnoticed, contribution to the history of ideas. An act that is free and hence liable to punishment or reward, he contends, must originate in the will. What then are the conditions for pronouncing the act of will itself to be free? If we stipulate that it too must originate in the will, we must apply the same condition to this antecedent act of will, and in turn to an infinite series of precursors; if we avoid the regress by denying that the act of will must be willed, we admit that willing is not an act that can be explained (*On Free Will* 3.17.48–49). As later students of the same question have argued, our freedom consists in the rational choice to do as we will, but the freedom to decide what we shall will is a chimera. That which we decide to will can only be that which we already will.[20] That Adam sinned is clear, though we cannot say why, and it is equally clear that sin has corrupted the whole human race, with a consequent enervation of both the reason and the will. Since, however, we still have the freedom to act as we will, and since it was never logical to demand that we have the

---

that the agent who punishes is acting in accordance with fate no less than the one who does wrong.

20. See, e.g. Russell, "Hume's Lengthy Digression." Chappell, *Aristotle and Augustine on Freedom*, 179–80, argues that Augustine sometimes lapses into expressions that imply liberty of indifference, i.e., freedom to will what we shall will.

freedom to will what we will, we cannot escape culpability by denouncing the misfortune of our birth (3.2.5).

Augustine hesitates here, as throughout his life, between two theories of the origin of the soul's origin, but neither, in his view, relieves us of culpability. If we embrace the traducian theory of Tertullian, that the soul is transmitted in the father's seed,[21] it will follow that we were already present in Adam and therefore partake of his guilt. If instead we accept the creationist theory that a new soul is infused into new body, we must grant to this soul the power to resist the moral debilitation of the flesh. We may note here that the dilemma for Augustine, at 3.21.59 as in later writings, is that traducianism implies the corporeality of the soul, and yet comes nearer to accounting for that which Plato explains by his theory of pre-existence.[22] In either case, our nature, as created, is good, while sin is merely one of its affections and not even, as the Manichaeans argue, an inevitable one. Augustine adds that where an apparent evil cannot be traced to sin, as in the innocent suffering of animals, it will be found to be no evil:[23] the order of the present world permits nothing to be immortal, while the struggle of all living creatures against dissolution testifies to the unity of the cosmos and hence to the undivided sovereignty of God (*On Free Will* 3.11.34).

Memories and Origins

It is in this third book *On Free Will* that Augustine's arguments take on a distinctly Christian color. The soul that falls in Adam, metaphorically or historically, does not sin alone and cannot redeem itself by its own exertions. Here, as in his dialogue of the same period called *The Teacher*, Augustine maintains that Christ is present to every soul as a standard of truth,[24] but this internal monitor would inform us, at best, of our plight, not the means of escaping it, if the same Christ were not revealed to us in the gospel as the one who accepted the penalty of sin for our salvation. "The one whom we forsook within in pride we have found outside us in humility" (*On Free Will* 3.10.30). The treatise *On Free Will* was completed shortly before the writing

21. *On the Soul* 25.2; 27.6; 36.1 against the Valentinian notion of a spiritual seed.

22. See *On the Soul and Its Origin* 2.7.11ff.; On Genesis according to the Letter 10.17.31–24.40; *Unfinished Work against Julian* 1.1, etc. For differing modern opinions, see Clark, "Vitiated Seeds"; Keech, *The Anti-Pelagian Christology of Augustine of Hippo*, 144–47.

23. At *On Free Will* 3.23.69 their pains reveal the vitality of their souls and their appetite for unity, while at 3.14.40 physical decay is not an evil because it is not the penalty of vice.

24. See Fuhrer, "Ille intus magister."

of the *Confessions*, in which Augustine recounts his slow deliverance from the conceits of the Manichaeans and the arrogance of philosophy. Although from his youth he was conscious of the pleasure that we derive from sin, even where we enjoy no profit, he allowed the Manichaeans to persuade him that the soul could remain untouched by the defilement of the body. Fornication and worldly ambition consumed him even while he imagined himself to be a Christian (*Confessions* 3.1.1; 8.7.17, etc.), and although the study of Platonism guided him to a better understanding of the nature of God, it taught him nothing of the law in his members that competes with the law of Christ (7.21.27). Still less did it enable him to comprehend how the Word of God through whom all things were made could have taken flesh for the sake of a fallen creature (7.9.13–14).[25] For all his erudition and conversation with learned friends—whom, as he came to see, he had loved without knowing what love is (3.1.1; 4.6.11)—it was only the chance over-hearing of a child's song that induced him to "take up and read" God's direct command to him in Paul's letter to the Romans.[26] From this he learned that what was required of him was not the cultivation of a higher self but humble submission to the God whose gratuitous mercy offered the sole atonement for his imperfections.

Augustine's autobiography is not only an account of this quest for God but a continuing iteration. As we have noted, anecdotal memory has a value for him that was never accorded to it by the Platonists. No doubt the detractors of the new bishop of Hippo had reminded him of his sins, and his answer is not to deny or extenuate them but to aggravate the recital of his misdeeds with a disclosure of inward motives that he might have hidden from all but God, his ostensible addressee. "Not because I love them, but that I may love thee," he exclaims at *Confessions* 2.1.1—and also to demonstrate that for Christians the test of integrity is not forensic innocence but purity of heart, by which standard no one can merit salvation. The nine books of personal history are succeeded by a meditation on memory, which concludes that God is not to be found there by some process analogous to Platonic *anamnesis*. The works of creation proclaim him, but to hear them crying not "I am God" but "he made us" (10.6.9) do we not need also the testimony of scripture? The Platonists blamed the evil in the world on its turbulent substrate, Marcion on its purblind demiurge, Mani on a combination of both. The act of recollection by which Augustine refutes them all in the last three books of the *Confessions* is a sustained perusal of the Mosaic narrative of creation, which is also his key to the origin of matter

25. See further Smith, "What Augustine Did Not Find."
26. *Confessions* 8.29, quoting Romans 13:13–14.

and time, and hence to an understanding of the soul's place in the scheme of providence.

In Book 11 he quotes an old conundrum that is obliquely yet inescapably related to the origin of evil: what was God doing before he made the world (*Confessions* 11.13.15)? As we have seen, the common (though by no means uniform) view of Platonists since Aristotle was that, since it could no be less good to create at one time rather than another, the temporal activity of the Demiurge in the *Timaeus* must be construed as an allegorical representation of eternal superabundance. Augustine prepares us for his own defence of the biblical narrative by surmising that the word of creation is not a discrete command but the expression of God's eternal will through the second person of the Trinity (11.7.9). Only the product of creation is temporal, which is to say that it is coterminous with time. It is therefore absurd to ask what God was doing before creation, for that which is anterior to creation—ontologically, not chronologically—is eternity, in which all is simultaneously present to the mind of God (11.12.14). This does not mean that time is to be identified with the motion of celestial bodies, for we can easily imagine, both of these and of other bodies, that their motion might be retarded or expedited, and thus performed in a longer or shorter time (11.23.29–30). The measurement of time presents a great mystery, for in contrast to God we inhabit a "now" to which nothing is present, for no duration can be ascribed to the instant of present experience, in which even as we try to grasp it the hitherto unknown future is slipping into the irrecoverable past (11.15.19–16.21).[27] It is through our own mental faculties, through memory and foresight, that we are able to reclaim and measure any stretch of time (27.34–28.37). Just as Seneca draws a moral precept from every inquiry into a natural phenomenon, so Augustine ends by extolling the proper use of memory in bringing to mind God's ceaseless acts of love.

Temporal creation, then, is not imputed either to accident or to divine caprice. Pursuing his exposition of the opening verses of Genesis in Book 12, Augustine does not attempt to determine whether creation in the beginning denotes creation in the Logos, or Wisdom of God, or merely the initiation of divine activity. If we take the second view, we must understand the heaven of Genesis 1:1 as the eternal yet contingent heaven of heavens, which precedes the creation of the visible firmament of Genesis 1:6 (*Confessions* 12.8.8–9.9).[28] The antitype to its perfection is the earth without form and void, the chaotic abyss, of Genesis 1:2. This too is not a temporal

27. Carter, "Augustine on Time," maintains that time in Augustine represents an *ordo* of change for the fallen creation and an *ordo* of endurance for the redeemed.

28. On this adaptation of the Neoplatonic notion of intelligible matter, see Tornau, "Intelligible Matter."

creation (12.12.15), but the imagery of chaos represents absence rather than substance, just as the darkness (*tenebrae*) from which the light shines forth in the following verse is not a thing in itself but the absence of illumination (12.17.25). In contrast to this darkness (which only Augustine's silent interlocutors, the Manichaeans, mistake for a second kingdom),[29] the earth of Genesis 1:2 is close to nothingness without being nothing (12.3.3; 11.6.6, etc.), and numerous accounts of this inchoate state can be offered which may all fall within the intention of the Holy Spirit, if not within that of the author who wrote at his prompting (12.17.25). Augustine inclines to the view that this darkness is matter that (as the Platonists say) is anterior to concrete being, not in order of time or in order of ends, but in order of logical precedence: a sound is logically prior to a note because sound is the genus of which the note is a species, and hence we cannot sing a note with also emitting a sound (12.29.40). Just as our making the sound is not an overture to singing but its necessary concomitant, so matter is not a preliminary creation but a concomitant of the act—a strictly instantaneous rather than sequential one—that brings the world into existence. Time and matter are both created media, not prerequisites for the exercise of God's will; that which is not from his substance, like the persons of the Trinity, is summoned by omnipotence from nothing (12.22.31, etc.).

It is only in the thirteenth and final book, as he ponders the works of God on each of the first six days, that Augustine breaks into open invective against the detractors of the natural world, who cannot admit that if all creation is good in the eyes of its Author, the faults that they see in it testify only to their own want of vision. God's purposes are concealed from us by his secret predestination (*Confessions* 13.34.49), but that is no argument for the Manichaean fatalism that entails that we are saved or damned by nature (13.30.45). Neither sexual difference nor sexual intercourse can be evil, since humanity was created male and female (13.23.33). At the same time, our being created in the image of God, in which there is no distinction of sex, implies that the carnal nature was given to us in the service of the spirit (13.32.47). Each new enrichment of the natural order has both a corporeal and a spiritual sense (13.25.38): the lights that divide the day and night are the visible sun and moon, but we also see that the denizens of the spiritual world receive different measures of illumination (13.18.23–19.25). The earth that brings forth fruit is a parable of the godly soul (13.26.39–41), while the creatures of the sea that we lawfully use for our sustenance are also emblems of wisdom and subtlety in the midst of spiritual trials (13.20.27).

---

29. On the evenings and mornings of Genesis 1 as indices of the *modus naturae* rather than of time, see *On Genesis according to the Letter* 2.14.28.

It is God's part to give and ours to reap the fruit of what is given; when that which is good in his eyes is good in ours, we learn to repay his bounty with love, not for his sake but for our own (13.7.8–9.10).

Ignorance and Volition

Much of Augustine's teaching on evil and sin in the final decade of the fourth century can be reduced to two philosophical commonplaces: the Platonic equation of evil with mere lack of being or deficit of goodness, and the Stoic principle that no evil befalls us to which we do not consent. At the same time, he was not enough of a Platonist to reduce all sin to ignorance and the infirmity of reason, or enough of a Stoic to hold that we can render ourselves immune to both vices by our own resolve.[30] Even before he assumed episcopal office, the quarrels of children at the breast and his own gratuitous theft from a pear tree had convinced him that our propensity to evil is more active than many philosophers imagined; the homiletic and controversial activities in which he engaged as a bishop seldom failed to afford new evidence that the root of human sin was neither ignorance nor infirmity, but pride (*On Genesis according to the Letter* 11.14.8–15.19, etc.).

Even in Platonism ignorance is a supervenient rather than a primordial cause of sin. The fall of the soul from the supercelestial heaven in the *Phaedrus* is the consequence of striving too recklessly for the vision of truth; the gravity of the soul's trespass (together perhaps with some mysterious fatality) determines the character of the first embodiment, while subsequent lives are chosen by the soul itself, with as much self-knowledge as it can redeem from its tribulations. In Alcinous, Plotinus, and Porphyry, descent is not so much a sin as an exercise of the soul's proper function, albeit one marred in almost every case by the surrender of mind to the blandishments of matter. Since Adam takes the place of the pre-existent soul in Augustine, there is no possibility of his sinning through ignorance—he has the fullness of reason, if not of wisdom[31]—and although he has a body, it is a direct product of the will of God that has not yet succumbed to corruption. Adam's apostasy therefore must originate in the pride of reason, whose subsequent captivity to the appetites is its punishment rather than its apology. As a Christian who holds that nothing occurs without God's will, Augustine cannot be content to say "the blame lies with the chooser; God is blameless" (Plato, *Republic* 620); in his *Commentary on Genesis*, however, he can still

---

30. See e.g., *City of God* 14,2.1, 14.8.1, and 14.9.4.

31. On this important distinction, which allows for some imperfection in the original state of Adam, see *On Free Will* 3.5.17, 3.22.64–65, 3.24.72–73.

argue that divine foreknowledge is not the cause of that which it foreknows (11.9.12). God foresaw not only sin but the chastisement of sin (11.11.14), foreseeing that both would be useful to a race of creatures endowed with free will but not with the wisdom to apprehend the good without knowledge of evil (11.11.14). We may wonder how the inference that Adam was bound to sin can be avoided, just as we may wonder how the tendency of that which came from nothing to fall into nothing can fail to be realized; Augustine nonetheless stops short, throughout his works, of maintaining that Adam's sin was preordained.

He did not have to look back to Eden, or even to his own pilfering of a fruit, to witness the malign consequences of pride, for the church in Africa in his own day was divided almost equally between his own coreligionists, whom he styled Catholic, and the schismatics who traced their orders to Donatus. They repudiated both the ordinations and the baptisms of the Catholics because they believed that the latter had incurred the taint of collaboration during the last persecution under pagan Emperors.[32] Augustine's retort was not so much to dispute their historical claims as to urge them to recognize their own sins, which they confessed every day in reciting the Lord's Prayer (Letter 185). Their pride has beguiled them into a breach of charity, and severed them from the saving love that Christ imparts to the members of his own body, but to no other. While the implication that they thought themselves free of every sin, and not only that of apostasy, may be tendentious, the same reasoning could be deployed with more justice after 412 against the British monk Pelagius, who protested that a doctrine of universal peccability encouraged the lax to hope that they could saved without that victory over sin that is both promised to and demanded of all believers.[33] By this point in his life, however, Augustine had not only ocular but scriptural proof of the inevitability of sin in the present world.

Three passages in Paul's letter to the Romans had come to bear for him a meaning that had not been found in them by his predecessors, or even by his younger self.[34] At 5:12, where the Latin translates the anacoluthic Greek by the equally cryptic *in quo omnes peccaverunt*, he took this to mean that all have sinned in Adam, and hence as a vindication of his own conjecture in *On Free Will* that all humans are guilty, in God's sight, of the primordial

32. See further Edwards, "The Donatist Schism and Theology."

33. On "Pelagianism," see now Bonner, *The Myth of Pelagianism*, with the caveat that the fifteen charges enumerated in chapter 1 were not created, or even pressed, by Augustine, but answered by Pelagius with some success, as Augustine admits, at the Synod of Diospolis.

34. On the contrast between the *Exposition of Certain Passages in Romans* and the anti-Pelagian writings, see Edwards, "Augustine and Pelagius."

transgression.[35] This reading, he says, he derived from Ambrosiaster,[36] while careful reflection had taught him a better understanding of the passage in Romans 7 where a sinner complains of a law in his members that mocks his endeavors to serve the law of God (*Retractations* 7.23). Origen and Chrysostom had opined that the apostle is speaking not in his own person but in that of a gentile who has put on the yoke of the Jewish law. Augustine, who initially agreed with them, came to think it more natural to apply the words that Paul speaks in the first person to Paul himself. It followed, of course, that if Paul was not blameless, no one is free from sin.[37] And it seemed to Augustine that Paul himself confesses as much in Romans 9, where, far from saying that each of us will be rewarded in proportion to our endeavors, he declares that God makes some to be vessels of wrath and others vessels of destruction (Romans 9:21), showing mercy where he will without regard to our notions of merit (9:15; cf. Exodus 33:19). Previous commentators had surmised that, when Jacob is said to have been saved without works, Paul meant that he was saved on account of the faith that God foresaw: yet this, as Augustine protests, would be to make his election dependent on his merit, and none of us has any merit that we may plead against God (*To Simplicianus* 1.2.6). The guilt and depravity that we inherit from Adam are manifested in the struggle between the spirit and the flesh, which even Paul could not put to rest; the logical converse of our inability to save ourselves by works is predestination, the creation of good works from nothing in those whom God has saved.[38]

The Legacy of Eden

Augustine's masterpiece of apologetic, *On the City of God*, was prompted by a calamity that, as a Christian, he believed to be no calamity—the sack of Rome by the Goths in 409 or 410. To pagans this was proof that Rome's ancestral gods had forsaken her now that her emperors were Christian, the Altar of Victory had been removed from the forum,[39] and the senate had

35. *On the Deserts and Forgiveness of Sinners* 1.9.9–15.19. The verse is not discussed in his early *Exposition of certain passages in Romans*.

36. *Against two Letters of Pelagius* 4.4.7, apparently citing Ambrosiaster at *Patrologia Latona* 17.97. See Leeming, "Augustine, Ambrosiaster and the *Massa Perditionis*."

37. See further Squires, "Augustine's Changing Thought."

38. For doubts regarding the original content of the tract to Simplicianus, dated to 397 by Augustine at *Retractations* 2.1.1, see Wilson, *Augustine's Conversion*. Its strangely proleptic character is recognised by Wetzel, "Pelagius Anticipated."

39. See Croke and Harries, *Religious Conflict*.

put its trust in mercenaries who, being Christians themselves, were not ashamed to destroy the city that they had been hired to preserve. Augustine responds with his celebrated contrast between two cities, one of which, in the pomp of worldly dominion, is permitted to despoil and enslave the nations (*City of God*, Book 1, preface), while the other is known to God alone as he chooses those who have humbly turned to him in each generation to be the subjects of his everlasting kingdom (1.35). Rome has fallen already, into the service of idols, the folly of war, the worship of pride and cruelty as virtues: even her best philosophers have scorned Christ and invoked the fallen angels as mediators of salvation (3.3.5; 10.16). In the second half of the work, Augustine undertakes a review of history as narrated in the scriptures from creation to the advent of the Savior, digesting into one argument the numerous replies that he had already made to pagan and heretical detractors of revelation. Having unmasked the veneration of daemons as the source of pagan religion and the scandal of philosophy, he dwells at some length on the origin of angels, concluding that, since they must have been created in time, they are represented at Genesis 1:3 by the light that antedates the sun (11.9). In reply to the Manichaeans, who contend that scripture acknowledges a principle of darkness when it pronounces Satan a liar from the beginning (*principium*), he maintains, as ever, that darkness and sin are not beings but deficiencies of being, and takes the noun principium to denote the instantaneous defection of an agent whose true *principium*, in the sense of origin, is the Wisdom in which all things are made (11.15–17 and 22–23). It is in his role as a liar, wielding power by seduction rather than coercion, that Satan returns in Book 14 to test the strength of Eve.

Augustine will accept no account of the fall that suggests that Adam and Eve were disarmed by any natural imperfection. Had they been infants in reason as well as in malice, as Irenaeus supposes, they could not be held guilty of sin.[40] Nor could he say, with Philo or Gregory of Nyssa, that Adam's reason was overcome by passion, for in an unfallen agent passion will always be subject to reason. Those who think such constancy inconsistent with the freedom of the will are impugning the freedom of the saints and of God himself.[41] We libel the Creator again if we hold, with the Stoics, that any of our natural passions has no right use except to be suppressed and replaced by a better disposition (*City of God* 14.9.1–6). Augustine goes on to argue that since marriage is a good ordained by God it would have been possible for Adam and Eve to have sexual congress in paradise without sin

---

40. See *City of God* 13.4 and 14.12.

41. On the impeccability of the saints, see *Enchiridion* 28.105; on the liberty of God, see *Unfinished Work against Julian* 1.81.

and to bring forth children who would be proof against temptation (14.22–23). His ostensible opponents are the Manichaeans, but many ascetics also rejected marriage and Pelagius reserved the kingdom of heaven for virgins, even if he did not assert, with Gregory of Nyssa, that some other way of propagation would have been found if Adam had not sinned.

Augustine repeats what he had said so often to the Manichaeans, that Adam and Eve were created from nothing and therefore free of original imperfection in soul or body. For the same reason, however, neither was yet exempt from mutability, and Eve, as Adam's inferior in reason, was more easily seduced (*City of God* 14.11.2). Augustine refrains from echoing his remark in On *Genesis according to the Letter*, that had God given Eve to Adam for fellowship rather than procreation, he would have made her a man.[42] He does maintain, on the other hand, that Adam was not deceived but elected to join Eve in her sin because his love for her outweighed his love for God (14.11.2). We are not to infer that love between human beings is transgressive in itself but that it becomes so when it assumes a place in our reasoning disproportionate to its place in the natural order: as Augustine says elsewhere, the good of our neighbor is always instrumental to our enjoyment of the one true good that is God.[43] Both Eve and her husband acted in pride (14.14), and it is by the pride of one and the humility of the other that the two cities are distinguished in this world (14.13.1)

By the same token the tree of knowledge is not in itself maleficent (since God creates nothing evil), but becomes so when the eating of its fruit violates a positive command. The evil will is the will to disobey, the pride of a creature whose own perfection tempts it to forget that it is created out of nothing. Since paradise was not only a corporeal but a spiritual locality, it is allegorically true to say that the evil will is itself the fruit of knowledge (*City of God* 14.11.1). Understanding the knowledge of good and evil to be the experience of wrongdoing, Augustine never concedes to Irenaeus that it might be a prerequisite of maturity: the knowledge of their own nakedness that disquieted Adam and Eve in the wake of the fall was the earliest symptom of the corruption of the sexual appetite (14.17). It was one of Augustine's most original theories to derive both a proof and an explanation of our endemic sinfulness from the disobedience of our genital organs. The protoplasts, had they remained in paradise, would have exercised these members as they exercised all others, under the tutelage of reason; even the wisest of their descendants, however, finds the organ recalcitrant to the

---

42. *Genesis according to the Letter* 9.5.9; cf. 9.17.31 and 18.34. On the innocence of the sexual act in Eden, see 9.9.14–10.18.

43. See O'Donovan, "'Usus' and 'Fruitio.'"

will and is unable to consummate intercourse without an irrational—and often unsummonable even when summoned—awakening of lust (14.23.3). Even Christian parents cannot procreate without this carnal motion, which communicates itself to the soul of the infant in the form of concupiscence, or inordinate desire. Marriage is not sinful, as too many ascetics imagined (14.21), but its principal office cannot be performed without sin, and hence cannot fail to bring new sinners into the world.[44]

Is Original Sin Defensible?

In the light of our common descent from Adam Augustine argued also that we inherit not only a tendency to sin but the guilt of a crime committed long before we were born. Hence the necessity of infant baptism, a sacrament that Pelagius may endorse but cannot explain.[45] In modern times the forensic transmission of guilt is inconceivable, whatever views we may hold on the heritability of vicious inclinations. Those who would trace the notion to Augustine's Berber or Carthaginian ancestry[46] are confessing their own genetic fatalism, and also forgetting that both the transmission of sin and the transmission of guilt receive ample countenance in the Roman literature that he studied in his youth. More than one Latin poet warned his contemporaries that the crimes of their fathers called for expiation;[47] even if they do not say that the soul of the offspring may be vitiated by the evil thoughts of the parents, some were prepared to believe that even its color could be influenced by a strong impression upon the mind of the mother at the moment of conception.[48] Porphyry, who did not discount such evidence, maintained that the perturbations of the mother's soul may impinge upon the imaginative soul of the child in the womb.[49]

It was not against the philosophers but against Pelagius and his supposed disciples that Augustine had to vindicate his doctrine of original sin.

44. Cf. *On Marriage and Concupiscence* 1.24.27.

45. *Against two Letters of Pelagius* 4.29–31. Yet Augustine has little authority for this argument, other than the cryptic statement of Cyprian, Letter 64, that infant baptism washes away the sins of another: see Beatrice, *Transmission of Sin*, 131–57. The difficulty of reconciling transmission of sin and guilt with an incorporeal soul is acknowledged in Letter 166, on which, see Teske, "St Augustine on the Incorporeality of the Soul."

46. On the "fiery African monk," see Williams, *The Ideas of the Fall.*

47. Horace, *Odes* 3.6.1; Virgil, *Eclogue* 4.31. For a more expansive treatment of these points, see Edwards, "Willed Causes and Causal Willing."

48. Heliodorus, *Aethiopica* 4.8.5; Augustine, *Retractations.*

49. Porphyry, *To Gaurus on the Ensoulment of the Embryo* 5, ed. L. Brisson, pp. 160–62.

It is possible that he misrepresents his opponent when he accuses him of believing that the moral law can be kept in its entirety so long as our wills collaborate with the power that God vouch safes to us at birth. On the other hand, much the same teaching was attributed to Pelagius by Jerome, who never embraced Augustine's views on human depravity or predestination; nor was it Augustine who brought Pelagius before the synod of Diospolis on a list of fourteen charges.[50] Far from malignantly pressing these charges after his acquittal, Augustine is willing to waive the majority of them on the word of the defendant, but protests that he clings to a notion of human freedom that both scripture and experience forbid us to entertain. Even after conversion, the will to good is the will of God in us, as we learn from Paul's admonition to "work out our own salvation in fear and trembling, for it is God who is at work in you, both to will and to do of his purpose" (Philippians 2:13–14).[51] If even the fall of Adam is explicable only because he failed to rely on the auxilium, or supernatural aid, of the God who created him from nothing, how much more need must Adam's posterity have of an auxilium that not merely preserves them from evil but enables them to do good (*On Punishment and Grace* 12.34–35). And if it was urged, on apostolic authority, that God wills all to be saved, this was not a text to be set against the more perspicuous teaching of Romans 9 (14.44; 15.47; 16.49). Thus it must signify either that God wills us to desire the salvation of all, or else that he himself wills the salvation of people from every class, or simply that whoever is saved is saved by the will of God.

Augustine's most tenacious and eloquent critic in his later years was not the ascetic Briton but an Italian bishop, Julian of Eclanum, who cannot have been in the strict sense a Pelagian, since he accused Augustine of stigmatizing marriage (*Unfinished Work against Julian* 1.61–62). He also accused him of traducianism[52]—a position that, as we have seen, could hardly be held by one who denied the corporeality of the soul—and of reverting to the Manichaean principles of his youth (*Unfinished Work* 1.73, 1.75; 2.129, etc.). In his *Retractations*, Augustine pleads that he was not obliged to say more to the Manichaeans than would suffice to refute their belief in two opposing principles of good and evil. To Julian's objection that sin entered the world through one man according to Paul, and not (as Augustine implies) through the sexual union of the first man and the first woman, Augustine can reply that the deposition of the man's seed is the cause of birth, and that where this is lacking, as in the case of Christ alone, there will be no transmission of

---

50. *Pace* Bonner, *Myth of Pelagianism*, 2.
51. See *On the Spirit and the Letter* 2.2, etc.
52. *Unfinished Work against Julian* 1.1, 1.6, etc.

sin.[53] But the strongest argument of all against the libertarian view of Julian is that, far from upholding the justice of God, it implies that he has no regard for justice. If all sin came through the imitation of Adam and redemption through the imitation of Christ, it is hard to account for the sins of those who never heard of Adam and impossible for those who have never heard of Christ to be saved (2.146, 2.176). Even if it were not a sin against love to demand perfection of the imperfect, it would be perverse to argue that the nations that have never known Christ are free to emulate him.

Conclusion

Has Augustine solved the problem of evil, or at least his problem of evil? Or has he regressed from adolescent Platonism to juvenile Manichaeism, as Julian of Eclanum insinuated? Certainly he no longer believes, with the speakers on his dialogue *On Order*, that God's tolerance of that which resists his will can be palliated by defining evil as a lesser good and assigning it to its natural place. At the same time, his espousal of predestination threatens to make nonsense of all resistance to the divine will. So long as Augustine takes the Stoic position that only that to which we consent by will or judgment can be evil, he must assume that such resistance can proceed only from the will of a rational creature; yet if we cannot will the good because we cannot waken the love of the Spirit in our hearts, it would seem that we cannot be held accountable for sinning. Augustine's own reflections on the opacity of the will have brought him close to the Stoic definition of a free action as one that proceeds from the agent's nature, however the agent acquired that nature; the Stoics, however, had no doctrine of creation out of nothing. The Christian God is accountable for the existence of every nature and of every creature that instantiates it. Even if we accept the claim—for which have only the testimony of scripture, not of reason—that the will and the rational faculty of every human being since Adam have been impaired by his voluntary transgression, it is arguable that God abetted his sin by foreseeing and failing to prevent it. Furthermore, neither the principle that a sinner's descendants share his guilt nor the principle that corruption in the inner man can be passed on like a bodily distemper is a truism: Pelagius denied both, and so do our modern courts of law.

To accept Augustine's theory we must accept—what is easy enough to believe—that no one can be saved by good acts alone if the criterion of a good act is that it be performed with perfect charity. Yet this would be a

---

53. *Unfinished Work* 2.56. See 2.49 for the argument that if imitation were the cause of sin, the apostle would have blamed the devil as the first exemplar.

tyrannical condition for God to impose if he had not created Adam with the capacity to perform such works of love and to go on performing them for ever. Many ancient thinkers held that a tendency to err, both epistemically and morally, is a natural concomitant of the mobility of the soul and the fragility of the body; even Augustine argues that without God we must slip back into the nothingness from which we were created. He does not wish to infer that Adam's sin was unavoidable, but can he explain how, if it was avoidable, a perfect creature could have been guilty of it? To say that he failed to rely on divine assistance is to make his fall analogous to the soul's turning from its source in Platonism; for the Platonists, however, this is the consequence of the soul's inferiority to intellect, whereas Augustine holds that Adam lacked nothing in rationality, even if he had not yet attained to wisdom. But if God had created him thus, is it not unjust of God to require him not to sin?

The argument that evil is outweighed by the good of punishment becomes threadbare if the punishment is not only everlasting but arbitrary. Because he held salvation to be contingent on an explicit profession of faith, Augustine believed that most of Adam's descendants were destined for hell. We who are not disposed to admit that anyone can be punished for another's fault, or that even divine retribution could outweigh the evil of perpetual suffering, denounce this as a theodicy that defends God's justice at the expense of his love. It is salutary to remember that Pelagius too believed that the vast majority of humans will be damned. Indeed, it seemed to Augustine that the terms in which Pelagius offered salvation—perfect obedience to the law through strength of will—would close the doors of heaven to everyone but Christ. Far from being an antidote to sin, the aspiration to be perfect leads us into the sin of pride, for we are striving to be better than the apostle Paul, who has taught us that whatsoever is not of faith is sin.

Pelagius, by contrast, holds that sin was no more paradoxical in Adam than it is necessary in us. Adam failed to use all the strength with which God had endowed him, and his posterity has been all too apt to imitate him. Nevertheless, by the grace of God, our strength is as great as his and we are capable of succeeding where he failed. To Augustine this is pride because it implies that we have the means of holding ourselves above the voids: if he can give any reason for Adam's fall, it is that pride (as Evagrius saw) is the one temptation that is fostered rather than quenched by the extinction of base desires. The godly are more apt than the ungodly to forget their need of God. The more the Pelagian boasts of his innocence, the more he sins, because where there is pride there can be no love and hence no work of God. Augustine hesitates at times as to whether we have any power to accept or spurn the offer of grace, but he is in no doubt that the offer itself is always gratuitous, as is the gift of perseverance once we have believed. The elect, therefore, are not only the foreknown, as the young Augustine and Origen held, but the predestined. This too we are apt to style a loveless doctrine, though we never say this of Origen's thesis that every rational being is predestined to consent in the fullness of time to its own salvation. Augustine himself spoke only of predestination to life, not to death, and whatever corollaries he may have drawn from it, there is nothing in his doctrine of divine sovereignty that obliges God to send one soul to hell, just as there is nothing in the libertarianism of Pelagius that increases one soul's chance of entering heaven.

12

On Christianizing Plato

AUGUSTINE, AS WE HAVE noted, has for the centuries been the lodestar of
Christian thinking in the west. When the subject of discussion is the problem of evil, however, he shares his primacy with a Greek who might be regarded as his superior, since he professed to be Dionysius the Areopagite, an
early convert and follower of Paul.[1] The modern scholar wonders how intelligent and learned readers were duped for a millennium by the pretensions
of an author who is not quoted before the fifth century, and whose Greek
is a thesaurus of abstractions and technicalities that would have seemed re-
condite to a trained philosopher, let alone a Christian neophyte, in the reign
of Nero.[2] Scholars of the Renaissance were more perceptive, and Luther,
who disliked his ecclesiology even more than his metaphysics, declared that
this feigned companion of the apostle was no Christian but a Platonist.[3]
In the last decade of the nineteenth century, this charge became more

1. The Christian hinterland of Dionysius is explored by Golitzin, *Mystagogy*. Platonic parallels and antecedents are marshalled by Wear and Dillon, *Dionysius the Areopagite and the Neoplatonist Tradition*. Since Dionysius was a reputed convert of Paul,
we should not forget that Paul's speech on the Areopagus was a proclamation of the
unknown God and that his own conversion followed an encounter with Jesus in which
he was temporarily robbed of his vision. The first point is not lost on Norden, *Agnostoc
Theos*, while both are developed at length by Stang, *Apophasis and Pseudonymity*.

2. For the argument that Dionysius is a pagan see Mazzuchi, "Damascio, autore
del Corpus Dionysiacum"; Lankila, "The Corpus Areopagiticum as a Crypto=Pagan
Project." For criticism see Perczel, "Dionysius the Areopagite," 222–23.

3. Zachhuber, "Luther on Dionysius," 517.

invidious—even for those who had no quarrel with philosophy—when it was discovered that the author to whom Dionysius is most indebted is not Plato, or even the reputable Plotinus, but Proclus, the scholastic pedant and coryphaeus of intellectual decadence,[4] whose chief contribution to the study of Plato in the late Athenian school over which he presided had been a rubbish-heap of commentaries and the insertion of an incomprehensible entity called the henad between the One and the intelligible realm. Proclus had tried, in the manner of Iamblichus, to marry the austere reasoning of Plotinus to the superstitions of popular religion; he had taken up theurgy as a technique for the manipulation of fictitious deities, and Dionysius had proved himself his satellite when he applied the same term to Christian liturgy.[5] At times he was not content to merely imitate Proclus but reproduced his words verbatim, the most notorious instance being his disquisition on the problem of evil, of which more will be said below.

Scholarship has ceased to belabor Proclus for his failure to be Plato or Plotinus, and no longer assumes that a Christian cannot learn from the Greeks without unlearning the gospel. It is no more true to say that Dionysius scorns the Bible than that Proclus spun his system from his own head without any warrant in the imagery and vocabulary of Plato. It is as perverse to ignore the liturgical element in the church of Dionysius as to ignore the fact that theurgy in Proclus is the prerogative of a small guild, if not of a lone practitioner.[6] It is prejudicial to say that love means *eros* rather than *agape* in both Dionysius and Proclus without observing that *eros* in Proclus is almost always the attraction of the lower to the higher, whereas in Dionysius it is always predicated of God.[7] It remains true that no other Christian of antiquity ever wrote like Dionysius, and that careful study has proved him to be not only an imitator but a plagiarist of Proclus. How much they have in common we shall learn in this chapter from the mere juxtaposition of their theories; every theory, however, has a base, and, as we shall see in the following section, the differences at the base between Dionysius and Proclus are such as neither the Christian nor the Platonist would have wished to see played down.

---

4. Schäfer, "Hugo Koch and Josef Stiglmayr."

5. For defence of theurgy in both Proclus and Dionysius, see Shaw, "Neoplatonic Theurgy and Dionysius the Areopagite"; also Louth, "Individual and Liturgical Piety."

6. See especially Louth, *Denys the Areopagite*.

7. See the end of this chapter and M. Schiavone, *Neoplatonesimo e cristianesimo*, 86–87. As to whether this is the divine *agape* that inspired the incarnation, see Osborne, *Eros Unveiled*, 190–200; Ivanovic, "Eros as a Divine Name."

Preliminary Observations

Theology in classical Greek means sometimes prophetic discourse about the gods (often phrased with mythological obscurity), sometimes the elucidation of myth as allegory, and sometimes, thanks to Aristotle, the philosophical quest for the ultimate principles of being, which (again thanks to Aristotle) we are accustomed to call metaphysics. In the *Elements of Theology* by Proclus, the last sense is paramount, although provision is made to accommodate both the others by (1) the initial postulate of an ineffable source of goodness and unity; (2) the identification of being with the noetic or intelligible; (3) the devolution of being through the triad of existence, life, and intellect; and (4) the postulation of a participable unity below the transcendent One, which corresponds to the realm of the gods in popular worship and poetic myth:

1. For every Neoplatonist the first principle has two appellations, the "One" as in the *Parmenides* and *Philebus*, and the "Good" as in the *Republic*;[8] but only for Christian readers, or for those who forget to put off the spectacles of Christianity, does this principle take the form of a God who is both one and good. The first antinomy of the *Parmenides* argues that "if the One is, it can have neither parts nor predicates, since to speak of either creates plurality." Plotinus and his followers extend this reasoning to the exclusion of being itself from the One, and interpret its goodness and unity as the power to confer these predicates on all things to which existence can be ascribed. The first principle is thus a progenitive cause, inasmuch as unity produces multiplicity and goodness is predisposed to superabound,[9] and a final cause inasmuch as every being strives for identity with its own essence and the fulfillment of the end that is proper to it. When we conceive the first principle in itself and not as cause, however, we can say of it only what it is not.[10]

2. True being, as all Platonists agreed, is to be found in the realm of forms or ideas, each of which is always and necessarily identical with its essence. In the *Timaeus* intellect or *nous* is a designation for the artificer or demiurge who fashions the world in the image of the paradigm, or realm of forms, which contains the archetypes of all natural

---

8. See *Philebus* 15a, etc.; *Republic* 509b; Halfwassen, *Der Aufstieg zum Einen*.

9. The source of this notion is the asseveration at *Timaeus* 29e–30a that the good will always strive to communicate itself.

10. See Proclus, *Platonic Theology* 2.10, etc.

kinds.[11] In Neoplatonism *nous* or intellect itself is the seat of forms, and hence of being or essence.[12] Since the forms are coterminous with the demiurgic mind that contemplates them, the subject and object of knowledge are in substance one; for all that, the polarity of knowing and being known remains, so that *nous* is at once a unity and a dyad. Its principle of unity must therefore lie beyond it, and Platonic epistemology confirms the metaphysical necessity of postulating the unconditioned One.

3. The paradigm is the formal cause, or pattern, of creation in *Timaeus*, while the efficient cause of the Demiurge; in the less mythological diction of the *Sophist*, "life" is the term that signifies the dynamic propensity of intellect to communicate form to matter. In the *Philebus* Socrates defines being as a mixture of two contraries, limit and the unlimited, both proceeding from the One. It is probable that all these texts coalesce in the formulation of two triads that furnish the scaffolding of the intellectual word in the successors of Plotinus.[13] In the *Chaldaean Oracles* the three terms are *hyparxis*, *dynamis*, and *nous*—existence, power, and intellect—while in the Gnostics, Iamblichus, and Proclus they are *hyparxis* or *ousia*, *zoê* and *nous*, existence/being, life, and intellect, the order being codified by Proclus with the argument that *nous* pertains to all rational entities, *zoê* to all that are sentient (including, of course, the rational), and *ousia* to everything that exists, whether sentient or non-sentient.[14] He also correlates being or existence with the noetic or intelligible (i.e., the object of intellection), *nous* with the noeric or intellectual (i.e., the subject of intellection), and life with an intermediate category, the noetic-and-noeric.[15]

4. From Iamblichus onward, the Neoplatonic tradition maintained that, since there is no participation in that which has no parts, a participable unity must be intercalated between the primordial One and the contents of *nous*. It is not clear whether Proclus was the first to characterize this mediation of absolute unity by adopting the rare term

11. *Timaeus* 48a; 28b–29b.

12. See Porphyry, *Life of Plotinus* 20, with A. H. Armstrong, "The Background of the Doctrine."

13. See further Hadot, "Être, vie, pensée"; Majercik, "The Existence-Life-Mind Triad."

14. See *Elements of Theology* 101. See further Dillon, "The Early History of the Noetic Triad"; Ramelli, "Some Overlooked Sources."

15. See R. Majercik, "Chaldean Triads."

henad from the *Philebus*,[16] but he is certainly the first author whose extant works define the peculiar manner in which the henad is both one and the One. Since the One to which every individual and all things as a totality owe their unity is not one, the first subject of this predicate is the henad. The henad is participable where the One is imparticipable, but the realm that it inhabits does not yet admit of the difference that appears, in contradistinction to sameness, at the level of *nous*.[17] Consequently its relation to the One, and to other henads, is closer to identity than to any other relation that we can express. Every henad is in a sense the One and is distinct from other henads but without difference. To participate in the henad is thus the highest possible appropriation of unity; at the same time, in order that participation may not destroy the unity of that which is participated, there must be one henad of *nous* (for example) and another of soul.

Point (4) not only adds another plane to the ontology of Plotinus but introduces a strain of demotic religiosity, which Plotinus disavows in his allegorical readings of the ancient poets and his audacious dictum "The gods should come to me, not I to them" (Porphyry, *Life of Plotinus* 10.45). For Dionysius there can be no divorce between theological and philosophic approaches to the knowledge of God, for the substrate of philosophical reflection is God's revelation of himself in scripture. For him, as for any Christian, it is God who is (1) the One and the Good; (2) the lone occupant of the plane of Being; (3) the first exemplar and primordial source of existence, life, and wisdom; and (4) the henadic Trinity who is known to the theologian, as to the laity, by no other means than his own accommodation to our capacity and condition:

1. While they made free use of privative epithets for God, augmenting the pagan lexicon with Philo's neologisms, Christians also favored the appellative *pantokrator* (omnipotent, almighty), which savored less of the first than of the second antinomy of the *Parmenides*: "if the One is then everything can be predicated of it." Moreover, they had inherited a biblical vocabulary that implied that God is capable of love, of hatred, of anger, and of willing into existence that which he might have willed to be otherwise. This they could not discount or explain away by allegory; Lactantius affirms that his wrath is as real as his love, and

---

16. *Elements of Theology* 6 and 113–65; cf. Plotinus, *Enneads* 6.9.9.33 and Plato, *Philebus* 15a–16b.

17. On the indivisibility of the henad, see Proclus, *Commentary on the Parmenides* 1220.

that neither is inconsistent with his incorporeality, his ineffability, or his impassibility. Dionysius gives lucidity to a hitherto turbid tradition in his *Mystical Theology*, maintaining that the negative or apophatic epithets must be balanced against the positive or kataphatic epithets, and that while the latter contain more untruth than the former, their very falsehood is a corrective to any temptation to take the negative epithets for propositions.

2. For Christians there is no question of denying existence to the God who revealed himself as I AM[18] (or as Philo has it, he who is), just as there is no question of denying unity to him of whom both Moses and Christ proclaimed, "Hear, O Israel, the Lord our God, the Lord is one."[19] Origen may be the author of the variation on Plato that sets God above both intellect and being, yet for the most part he represents God as the supreme existent. In Dionysius too the dictum that God is superior to existence and non-existence is peculiar to the mystical theology,[20] while the *Divine Names* casts no doubt upon the accuracy of the formula "He who is."

3. The triad of being, life, and intellect was taken over, either from Porphyry or from the Gnostics, by the belated convert Marius Victorinus, whose refutation of Arius correlates being with the Father, life with the Son, and intellect with the Spirit. The one Latin author after him who shows knowledge of this triad is Augustine, who does not distribute its members among the persons, but asserts at *On the Trinity* 10.10.13 that existence, life, and intellection are activities of the Godhead as a whole.[21] When Dionysius alludes to the triad, the biblical substantive wisdom replaces intellect, and all three functions are once again exercised not severally but in unison by the three persons of the Trinity.[22] The three triads into which he divided the angels do not correspond to being, life, and intellect, let alone to the noetic, the noetic-and-noeric, and the noeric, but to Origen's three stages of scriptural pedagogy—ethics, physics, epoptics[23]—which Evagrius had interpreted for

18. Exodus 3:14, at least in the Septuagint. On the reluctance of Dionysius to sever the One from the first existent, see Vlad, "L'Être premier," 101–4.

19. Deuteronomy 6:4, quoted at Mark 2:29, etc.

20. *Mystical Theology* 5, in Dionysius, *Corpus Dionysiacum* II, eds. Heil and Ritter, p. 149.6.

21. See further Manchester, "The Noetic Triad."

22. *Divine Names*, in Dionysius, *Corpus Dionysiacum* I, ed. Suchla, 2.5, p. 129.1; 2.7, p. 131.10; 5.1, p. 181.1–6.

23. *Commentary on the Song of Songs*, in Origen, *Comilien zum Hexateuch*, ed.

monks as the purgation of soul, the illumination of intellect, and the perfection of the image and likeness of God through contemplation.

4. The teaching of Proclus, according to which each henad is identical in some sense with the One and yet distinct from other henads,[24] offers the nearest pagan analogue to the Christian understanding of the Godhead as a triad of discrete hypostases sharing one essence and constituting one God. For Christians, however, henad is a noun that has no plural. Origen, preempting both Iamblichus and Proclus in his retrieval of the noun from Plato, differs from all three of them in applying it directly to his first principle, God the Father, whom he also calls the monad.[25] Dionysius, for his part, styles the whole Godhead a "tri-hypostatic henad"[26]—a coinage that could only have been a fruitless paradox in the school of Athens. "Three in one" is not an impossible conceit for Proclus, but neither is it a possible denomination for the first principle.

Proclus: To Theodore on Fate[27]

Proclus is the author of three treatises vindicating the goodness of the cosmic order and defending the gods against accusations of ignorance or neglect. They survive entire in the Latin renderings of William of Moerbeke, which are unfortunately poor specimens of the translator's art, as he not only coins a new term to represent the definite article but sometimes fails to capture the idiomatic sense of a verb and frequently produces incomprehensible constructions by his servile imitations of Greek syntax. The reader's difficulties have been partly alleviated by Helmut Boerse's discovery of large portions of the original in the writings of Isaac Sebastocrator; Isaac has not, however, been wholly faithful in transcription, omitting many passages that offended his orthodoxy, suppressing the names of pagan deities, and occasionally adding a commentary of his own. It is he who asserts, for example, that Proclus's treatise *On the Existence of Evils* is a paraphrase of the excursus on the same

Baehrens, p. 75. On Evagrius, see Edwards, "Didymus and Evagrius."

24. See further Butler, "Polytheism and Individuality."

25. *First Principles* 1.1.1, reproducing the locution of the *Philebus*; cf. *Divine Names* in Dionysius, *Corpus Dionysiacum* I, ed. Suchla, 1.4, p. 112.11. This is not to deny that Plotinian *aporroia* ("emanation," or rather flowing away) is also in a sense from nothing: see Gerson, "Plotinus' Metaphysics."

26. *Celestial Hierarchy* 7.4, in Dionysius, *Corpus Dionysiacum* II, eds. Heil and Ritter, p. 32.9.

27. For commentary, see Steel, *Proclus: On Providence.*

question by Dionysius, thus revealing that the likeness between the two authors was already so obvious in the first millennium as to leave no doubt that one had appropriated the thought of the other.[28] At the same time, a comparison of the two texts will expose some striking differences, not least in their asymmetric understanding of the role of love.

The dissertation on fate addressed to the engineer Theodore lacks an introduction in the Greek, perhaps because the Christian editor did not wish to perpetuate his impious belief that the world is governed by an implacable mechanism that not only preempts any exercise of freedom on our part but makes the gods prisoners to necessity. In his use of the term *mêchanêma* (unaltered in Moerbeke's Latin at *Theodore* 2.22), Proclus not only smiles at Theodore's profession but hints that he has fallen into the tragic mode, which Plato had taught his followers to contrast with the more reverent—or as Proclus would say, theological—practice of understanding the worst in the light of the best. He announces that there will be three heads to his reply, none of which proved palatable to the editor of his Greek. The first is that providence—"seeing before" in Latin but *pronoia*, or prior cognition, in Greek—is administered by the gods who cannot fail to serve the Good from which all things proceed, both those that are fated and those that are free; accordingly, it is providence that encompasses fate, not fate that determines providence (3.9–11). The second is that souls are of two kinds, one of which is immutable by nature and thus exempt from all the frailties of embodiment, while its labile sister roams the tides of ignorance and passion (3.14–19). The third (which appears to follow from the second) is that the knowledge that the soul possesses in the higher realm is blotted out by its descent into the body, so that the truth that we are now seeking cannot be grasped in its fullness until the mind is once again disencumbered from the senses (3.19–24).

In explaining the subordination of fate to providence, Proclus begins from the axiom that the Good extends to all things, from the highest to the lowest, so that providence must have for its sphere not only the supercelestial realm where everything is eternally identical with its essence, but also its dusky ectype where the hour of generation is the beginning of decay. The intelligible substances that populate the higher realm are primordial exemplars of the Good. They are therefore subject to providence but not to fate, if we mean by the former term perfect conformity to one's natural end without compulsion from without (*Theodore* 7). Where providence reigns alone there is no motion, although all the causes of motion are to be found

28. See Paparella, ed., *Proclo: Tria Opuscula*, 46. For the Greek text I shall use page numbers from this edition; for the Latin, which can be found in other editions, I shall use standard chapter headings.

here; the simulacra of being in the lower realm are constantly in motion, the causes of which are always extraneous to them (10). If on one side we have an eternity whose inhabitants know only the eternal, and on the other a realm of time in which all knowledge is conditioned by temporality, there can be no commerce between them unless we posit some mediator that is native to eternity, yet capable of experiencing the linear flow of time. This is the soul, which is neither unmoved like the intelligibles nor moved from without like bodies but the source of motion, both for itself and for all that resides below (9.12–23).

When Proclus speaks of two souls, he does not mean (like the Gnostics or the rogue Platonists whom both Porphyry and Arnobius had ridiculed) that each of us contains two rival centres of volition, one from heaven and one from earth. He means rather that, as Socrates says repeatedly in the dialogues of Plato, every soul is divided into a rational and an irrational element, one monadic and fitted to rule, one multiform and created for subjection. The natural occupation of the higher or rational soul, as we learn from the *Phaedrus*, is to contemplate the forms that people the supercelestial heaven (*Theodore* 19); at the same time, every soul has the task of regulating a portion of the corporeal realm, which at the same time is subject to an inescapable nexus of causation (20). Yet, bound though it is to the wheel of transmigration, it is not a slave to necessity, since each of its successive lives is the consequence of its own choice. Proclus admits, with Plotinus at *Enneads* 4.8.1, that Plato also speaks of divine tribunals and of periods appointed for the fall of souls (34); it is our exercise of choice over that which lies within our power that weaves us into the fatal concatenation of causes (36). It is by its wilful surrender to passion and ignorance, its refusal to master the stages of ascent from shadows to their supernal archetypes and thence to the contemplation of divinity (25–31), that the soul exchanges providence for fate.

Proclus now takes up a number of arguments that Theodore urges against the efficacy of the human will. Echoing Alexander of Aphrodisias, he observes that, while we are universally confident of our own power to shape the future, we are apt to blame fate for all that goes awry while taking the credit to ourselves when God or fortune or fate conspires with our endeavors (*Theodore* 38). While the infallible prescience of the gods is attested by numerous oracles, two kinds of divination can be distinguished, one of which leaves no appeal against the future, while the other apprises us of an impending danger that can be averted by prayer and sacrifice (39). As providence subsumes fate, so the gods know intelligibly that which is not intelligible, and timelessly that which unfolds for us in time (65.1–15). Knowing us more profoundly than we know ourselves (65.15), they do not need to predetermine our willing to have determinate foresight of the outcome. If Theodore maintains that we cannot reason to any purpose because there is no universal view as to what is good, he has forgotten that we are creatures of intellect as well as of sense: the tastes and pleasures of one nation differ from those of another (45.16–26), but the sovereignty of reason imparts to all a common faculty of discerning that which is good (46.12–20). It is fatuous to object that even Socrates knew nothing, for by his confession of ignorance he apprised us that the true objects of knowledge lie in a realm inaccessible to the senses (48–49). He commends the sciences in numerous dialogues, and when he appears to belittle them, it is only by comparison with that direct contemplation of the ideal that is the prerogative of philosophy (51–52). He is not denying that it lies with us to initiate the soul's return to the supercelestial "Plain of Truth."

Proclus: Ten Doubts Regarding Providence

But if providence means foresight, how can it be exercised by one who knows nothing of before or after? And if it is a condition of our freedom, as Alexander of Aphrodisias says, that the future should be the domain of the *mê on* (the non-existent), how can it be an object of foreknowledge? The second question is briefly canvassed in the *Commentary on the Parmenides*, where Proclus explains that for every order of being there is a different order of knowledge, the higher being always more holistic than that of the lower but communicable to the lower by participation.[29] The longest discussion of this topic, however, is found in another of the *Opuscula*, the *Ten Doubts Concerning Providence*, which is once again extant only in the anfractuous Latin of Moerbeke, while excerpts from the original Greek were stealthily baptized by John Philoponus, omitting most allusions to pagan teachers and their multiple objects of worship, in his diligent work *Against Proclus on the Eternity of the World*.

The first inquiry is whether all things, the definite and the indefinite, can be governed by the same providence. Proclus replies that while our own minds cannot grasp the contingent in its wholeness because we do not grasp the intelligible, and even a mind that apprehends the intelligible might be ignorant of the contingent, there is a form of cognition, possessed by the gods, whom he elsewhere calls the henads, that encompasses every order of being *holikôs*, or as we would say holistically (*Doubts* 4.23), from the highest to the lowest. The second question is whether the contingent—that

29. As Trouillard, *Mystagogie*, 203–4, shows—quoting Proclus *Elements of Theology* 120—the gods have pre-noetic noesis through their relation to the One.

is, whatever remains indefinite until it is realized in the course of time—can be an object of providence if the proper objects of definite knowledge, and therefore of divine knowledge, are necessary and atemporal. The premiss is that that which is not definitely known is also indefinite in nature, but all Platonists believed, on the authority of the *Philebus*, that the definite and the indefinite flow equally from the One. Hence, Proclus argues, the gods possess a definite comprehension of the indefinite (8.12–14), because even contingent events have causes, and all causation originates in the realm of the gods (8.24–26). The third question is whether providence can be in the same sense the cause of both the definite and the indefinite. Once again the answer is that it can because the knowledge of the gods, from whom providence flows, is always definite (10 and 15), and it is only because the energies that descend to us from this plane are dissipated by our own weakness that we receive knowledge in an indefinite form (14 and 19). Even the daemons have in an anecdotal form the knowledge that the gods enjoy by virtue of their perfect discernment of causes (16). Thus Proclus can maintain, against many Christians, that daemons have some cognizance of the future, while denying, with Augustine, that the gods employ them as intermediate sources of information (15). This answer gives rise to a fourth doubt: can there be entities that do not participate in the activity of the gods? The principle that every agent receives from the gods according to its capacity assures us, on the contrary, that each will receive such goods or incur such evils as are proper to its nature and commensurate with its merits (22–23): in other words, providence meets the Platonic definition of justice by allotting to each its own.

We have already half a solution to the next and most formidable question: how, if there is providence, can there be evil? The response distinguishes two kinds of evil, one in bodies that is counter to nature and one in souls that is counter to reason (*Doubts* 27.15–22). Decay of the body is counter to nature for the particular entity that it reduces to non-existence, but since decay is the inescapable counterpart to generation, the loss of one member sustains the antiphonal unity of the whole (28–29). The ills of the soul require a more searching diagnosis, for soul is by nature prone to both ascent and descent, and while neither motion is counter to its nature, its very mobility creates the possibility of error. As intellect aspires to the condition of the divine, so the rational soul aspires to that of intellect and body to that of soul (30.40–45); on the other hand, it is good that such a soul should descend to animate a body that would otherwise remain irrational, even at the cost of succumbing to the corporeal appetites and suffering all the miseries that afflict the souls of beasts (31.7–22). As in bodies, so in souls the motion that is contrary to nature is the corollary of that which effects the work of providence (31.45–56). If we raise, as a sixth objection, the failure of providence to dispense its blessings according to our deserts, the philosopher knows that the soul may be all the healthier for being denied the specious goods that providence grants to others (34), and that when such gifts are bestowed upon the wicked we may infer that the gods have given them up to their sins (37).

If a seventh doubt is raised by the uneven fortunes of animals, we must either suppose that they too are moral agents, in which they too may earn their lot (*Doubts* 44), or else that they are automata, in which case they invite neither praise nor pity (45 and 47). The eighth problem, which arises from the tardiness of divine punishment, can be laid to rest once again with Plutarch's arguments[30] that the gods know when to administer their nostrums and that the world would have been impoverished if certain sinners have been cut off in youth (51–56). Against a ninth group of skeptics, who deny the legitimacy of vicarious penalties, Proclus follows Plutarch again in arguing for the organic unity of human societies, and a particular community of nature between progenitors and descendants (59–60).[31] The colophon is not so much the solution of a tenth doubt as a delineation of the cosmic hierarchy, each tier of which has shed a little more of the integrity and refulgence of the gods, but without abandoning its tutelary role in the sphere assigned to it (63–64). Only the soul can be guilty of dereliction, by the exercise of that liberty that defines its special character, and thus perfects the graduated unity of the whole (65.32–34).

Proclus: *On the Existence of Evils*

The question implied by the title of the treatise *On the Existence of Evils* is whether we use the term "evil" of a substance, and it is clear at once that the answer must be in the negative (*Existence of Evil* 2).[32] To say that whatever exists must partake of being is a tautology, and it is a Platonic axiom that being receives both unity and goodness from the first principle. If, therefore, evil were to partake of being it must also partake of the Good; since, however, evil is the antonym of good, there can be no participation of one in the other. Only if we postulate some other principle than the Good could we admit the subsistence of evil; such a conjecture, however, is inconsistent

---

30. Parallels with Plutarch are noted by Opsomer and Steel, trans., *Proclus: Ten Problems*, 66–67.

31. We may compare Augustine's doctrine of the unity of the human race in Adam, but also Porphyry, *Isagoge* 20.1–14, on the meaning of genus.

32 *On the Existence of Evil* is found in Proclus, *Tria Opuscula*, ed. H. Boese.

with the unity of the cosmos, unless we set the One above the Good as a principle of both good and evil (3). If evil is a ubiquitous phenomenon of the world, it must be, as Plato intimates, a consequence of superabundance rather than deficiency in the first principle (7.10). The goodness of the Demiurge overflows to all possible levels of existence, the lowest of which inevitably participate less in being than the highest. Non-being is present in them, not as an absolute, for the existence of absolute non-being would be absurd (7.39), but as the qualified non-being, the disparity between existence and essence that makes it possible for a particular both not-to-be another particular and to change into something other than itself (8). This mutual implication of being and not-being introduces evil insofar as the particular fails to realize its own essence, which is its good (5). The good of the whole, however, is not impaired, for it is part of that good that there should be an ordered scale from existence to non-existence. That which is closer to non-existence exhibits less order, and thus suffers evil, but the subjection of the disordered to the ordered is what we understand by the ordering of the whole (9).

Thus evil, which has no being of its own, may nonetheless be present to that which has being—yet not to every occupant of the scale of being, as Proclus proceeds to demonstrate. The gods, since they exemplify henadically the goodness of the One,[33] do not fall short in any way of perfection (*Existence of Evil* 11–13). The angels too are perfect in their own kind (14), and it now emerges as a maxim for Proclus that nothing that is perfect in its kind can be reckoned evil (15). Thus he will not concede to Plutarch[34] that even daemons can be evil, for those appointed to punish wrongdoers are contributing to the order of the whole, and hence are not evil in themselves, or even for those who are punished once the evil has been expelled from their souls (16–17). Subordinate to the daemons are the heroes who display an irascibility that would be alien to a god, but is native to a being of this rank (18). By the same principle, fierceness in a lion is no evil, and neither is the impact of one body on another: that humans should be devoured by beasts or struck by weapons is not to deplored when the death of the body conduces to the edification of the soul (18–19).

The irrational soul—the *eidolon*, to use an expression from Plotinus— is naturally mobile and subject to passion, but is capable of accepting the *metron* or regulation of the higher soul (*Existence of Evil* 25). Alluding in a later chapter to Plutarch's reading of *Laws* 988, Proclus declares that the

---

33. *Existence of Evil* 13.14, p. 502 Paparella: *ex primaque unitate procedunt primae unitates.* Cf. *Ten Doubts Concerning Providence* 10.

34. Whom he nonetheless quarries repeatedly when accounting for apparent delays in the operation of providence at *Ten Doubts Concerning Providence* 8–9.

evil in the soul of the world is not maleficence but instability (45–46); and this is not so much a defect as the precondition of the soul's capacity to move between the higher and lower realms (22–24). Without such motion there could be no communication of goodness from the immutable to the mutable. Now even in the immutable realm there must be some loss of unity, for inasmuch as all things that exist have being in common but differ in essence, all existence is the result of the joint procession of the definite and the indefinite—or, in the language of Plato's *Philebus*, of limit and the unlimited—from the One (34). In the mutable or phenomenal realm, which is further from the One, the unlimited is more apt to prevail, but it does not follow that the ruin of the soul is an inevitable consequence of its proximity to matter. If that were so, Proclus argues, we should have to conclude that soul is not free but subject to an external determination (*to automaton*), which belies its character as the source of motion (33). As the lowest extreme of the scale of being, matter disturbs the order of the cosmos whenever it gains the ascendancy over soul; in this specific sense it is, as Plotinus said,[35] the prime evil (30.23–31), but to assert that it is evil in itself is to give a substance to evil and hence to find ourselves saying either that evil proceeds from the Good or that there is more than one principle of being (31). Matter is the necessary condition of a cosmos in which the good is potentially evil and the evil potentially good; where these possibilities coexist, says Proclus the necessary is neither good nor evil but the contrary to both (36–37).

Ought we say that evil in the body is worse than evil in the soul? Yes, inasmuch as the evil in the body corrupts its substance, where evil may pervert the operations of the soul but cannot deprive it of its immortality. On the other hand, while it is true that *dynamis* or power is a function of substance and hence inferior to it, the *dynamis* of the soul stands higher in the scale of being than the substance of the body. Hence, we may argue that evil in the soul, as the corruption of something greater, is a greater corruption than evil in the body (*Existence of Evil* 39). Neither in the soul nor in the body is evil itself a substance: it derives the appearance of substantiality from that which it inhabits, being weakest when it destroys the very substance of its host and strongest when it eats away the virtue but leaves the substance unimpaired (51).

The Peregrinations of the Soul

The discussion of transmigration in this treatise is wholly omitted by the Christian redactor of the Greek. Souls, according to Proclus, are capable both

35. See further Opsomer, "Proclus vs Plotinus on Matter."

of ascent and of descent (*Existence of Evil* 23.1–15), and it is by their descent that they violate the order of nature and thus succumb to evil. The expiation of the sin of one life by migration into another is preceded by the draught of forgetfulness, which deprives them sometimes of their proper disposition (Latin *habitus*)[36] and sometimes of their proper operation, although it never annihilates their immortal substance (21.20–29). The evil that they suffer is the corollary of their being out of joint with the world, and is not suffered by the whole. On the contrary, it is better that souls should animate the lower order of being than that they should limit themselves to the contemplation of the transcendent (23.15–25); their trespass is to concede to the lower nature the mastery that they were appointed to exercise over it (23.26–36). This reasoning suggests that the good for soul is not so much to be free from body as to be exempt from the weaknesses and passions that it regulates—a doctrine entirely consonant with Proclus's teaching elsewhere that even the rational soul will never subsist without the chariot that the myth of the *Phaedrus* allots to it in the supercelestial realm.[37]

We should note, before passing on to Dionysius, that the reconciliation of the soul's choice before embodiment with its liberty when embodied was a recognized difficulty for Platonism, analogous to the difficulty in Christian thought of reconciling the freedom of individuals with the inherited corruption of humanity. In his *Commentary on the Republic*, Proclus maintains that once the soul has chosen its lot, the gods impose a cluster of accidental circumstances—time, location, bodily and mental capabilities—that they know to be commensurate with its character and deserts.[38] When Origen, two centuries before, asserts that God has allotted stations in this world to rational beings who have fallen from perfection, we cannot be sure whether human souls undergo the same fall or one analogous and sequential to it; certainly Origen would not have granted that incarceration in an animal's body could be a penalty for human sin.[39] Nor is Tertullian's argument, that the soul will derive no profit from its afflictions if it cannot remember the cause of them, entirely rebutted by the Neoplatonist's

---

36. Evil is defined at 27.23–24 as the privation of the *habitus* which is in virtue.

37. See Van den Berg, "Proclus, *in Platonis Timaeum*"; Griffin, "Proclus on Place," 178–81.

38. See *Commentary on the Republic*, II, ed. Kroll, 264 and other passages discussed by Coope, *Freedom and Responsibility*, 175–81, where she observes that the reincarnated soul does not cease to be human.

39. See Origen, *First Principles* 2.9.1–2. Proclus's comments on custom and habit at *Existence of Evil* 26.25–37 bear comparison with Origen's remarks on the vitiation of the embodied soul at *First Principles* 3.4.3.

conjecture that the rational soul retain a shadowy image of the supernal realm when it passes into a beast (25.10–21).[40]

Dionysius on Evil

We have seen above that in Christian thought a single plane of being, which is nothing less than Being itself, encompasses all the properties and functions that are assigned to at least two levels in the cascade that begins for Platonists with the One. The One may be conceived with religious awe, but is not an object of cultic worship, not a datum of childhood faith awaiting the adult seal of ratiocination, not an agent who wills and loves into being that which might have been otherwise; and neither, although we can credit it both with existence and with demiurgic action, is *nous*, the supernal intellect. For Christians the first principle is God not adjectivally but by name, while being and unity are the attributes concomitant with his supremacy: he attracts to himself the predicates that are conferred by philosophers on the highest principle, but his title to them would not be secure if they were not attested in the same scriptures that also affirm the temporality and contingency of the world, thus bearing witness to the primacy of will in his operations and preparing us (as Christians urged) for unconditioned acts of love that belie any philosophical definition of his essence. The God who creates a universe from nothing by simple fiat, only to make himself a being of no account within that universe, is neither the first nor the second One of the *Parmenides*.[41]

For all his reticence on the creation of matter, the cosmology of Dionysius is never expressly at odds with Christian orthodoxy; neither on the other hand, does it favor the sharp antitheses between pagan and biblical teaching that are drawn by other fathers of the church. Nowhere are the fruits of Dionysius's study of Proclus more conspicuous than in the chapters of the *Divine Names* on the origin of evil. He begins with the axiom that the defining attribute of God is his goodness (*Divine Names* 4.1 [Suchla, 143.11])—a biblical truth no doubt, but one that Plato too had invoked to account for creation and thus banish evil from the realm of being (*Timaeus* 29d–e). Dionysius borrows from *Republic* 509b a preposition and a simile when he likens the sun in our world to the God who is *epekeina*, superior to all of which we can know or speak (4.4 [147.2–15]). As the sun is known by the light that renders all other objects visible, so we know God, without

---

40. For *ydolon* at 25.20 cf. Plotinus, *Enneads* 4.3.27.

41. A Neoplatonist might see the Dionysian God as a conflation of the first and the second One: Corsini, *Il trattato* De Divinis Nominibus.

being able to look on him directly, by the goodness that he disseminates to every order of being, from the most glorious of the angels to the most corrupt of demons and the most ignorant of beasts.[42] This is Plato's doctrine of the natural superabundance of the Good—or, as Dionysius says in an echo of Plotinus, of the power of God to communicate goodness, and therefore being, by his mere existence (4.1[144.2–5]). From God no evil can emanate, for that would imply that the good is not of his essence (4.21[169.13–16]); once we confess that everything is a product of his bounty, we must infer that even that which is evil partakes of the good insofar as it comes from his hand (4.7 [152.10–12]; 4.20 [167.11–168.6]). This is certainly a position held by Christians before Dionysius—by Augustine, for one, in his tract *On the Nature of Evil*—but it sits a little uneasily with biblical texts that imply that God is the author of evil no less than of good (Amos 3:6; Isaiah 45:7). On the other hand, it is perfectly consonant with the teaching of Proclus and Plotinus that, although every being has fallen away from unity in some degree, it owes whatever existence it has to the presence of the One.

Dionysius therefore reasons that even a depraved soul or a demon, so long as it has the power to do evil, participates in the good of being alive and of having the power to exercise its essential functions (*Divine Names* 4.23 [Suchla, 171.16–21]). Insofar as a body is necessary for the sustenance of life and its operations, the possession of a body is not an evil (4.27 [173.17–174.3]). The same may be said of matter inasmuch as it is constitutive of bodies; if it be objected that evil is the privation of good and that matter in itself is nothing but privation, it will not follow that matter is the cause of evil, for privation in itself cannot be a cause of any kind (4.28 [174.4–7]; 4.29 [175.5–9]). Privation is always parasitic on being, as a consequence of some weakness in the agent; while the misuse of his agency must be blamed on his weakness, the agency itself is the proper and natural corollary of his place in the order of being, and in that respect is good. If Dionysius here contradicts the teaching of Plotinus in some passages of the *Enneads*, he is all the closer to Platonists of his own day, who no longer regarded matter as the prime evil. Again he concurs for the most part with Augustine, except that the latter explains our falling away as a consequence of our being created from nothing, whereas Dionysius never clearly enunciated this doctrine.[43] His argument that the attraction of the soul to matter cannot be the cause of evil, as some resist the attraction (4.28 [174.21]), would perhaps

42. As Perl remarks in *Theophany*, 59, the acknowledgement of evil in the angelic realm (entailed, of course, by the teaching of the church on the fall of Satan) is one of the salient differences between Dionysius and Proclus,

43. Knepper, *Negating Negation*, 26, denies that he held it. Pavlos, "Theurgy in Dionysius," 165, appears to infer from his silence that he did.

have seemed to Augustine to exaggerate our capacity to remain innocent after the fall. Greek Christians would be more apt to take the Dionysian view, and all the more readily because it struck at a universal tenet of Platonism that, whether or not the soul sins in descending to the body, embodiment will invariably beget the temptation to sin. For Dionysius sin is a corollary of freedom, and he seems once again to differ from Augustine, in common with all Greek Christians and Platonists, when he denies that providence ever converts an agent to the good against his will.

On the other hand, he does not embrace the Platonic doctrine of transmigration, and he attributes to his God a greater propensity to intervene in the world than any Platonist since Numenius would accord to providence (*Divine Names* 4.33 [Suchla, 178.3–17]). Throughout his discussion of evil he reminds us that it is not because God neglects the world that the world has neglected God (4.35 [179.5–13]). To such a privileged saint as Moses he shows himself as the light that transcends all form and hence can impart all forms to his creatures; the nations have been permitted to infer his invisible sovereignty from the inexhaustible glory of his visible creation. They fail to discern him because of their weakness, not through any parsimony on his part, just as they fail to apprehend his love because the everyday syllables that spell the word *erôs* suggest to them only carnal gratification (4.12 [157.18–158.6]). The scriptures substitute *agapê* for *erôs* (4.7 [150.16]), although the Platonists will recognize their own vocabulary when they read of the synagogic and teleiotic operations by which he retires the unity of the cosmos (4.6 [150.10]). Sometimes the inspired commentators on scriptures call God love, sometimes the object of love—the first insofar as he draws all things towards him, the second insofar as he is the good and the beautiful, and therefore worthy of their desire (4.14 [160.1–11]).

Of evil Dionysius says, in Aristotelian terms, that it is an accident to the being of the agent who performs it (*Divine Names* 4.37 [Suchla, 177.3]). Of God, by contrast, he says in the words of Plato (*Symposium* 211a), that his beauty is not perishable, nor subject to growth or decay, nor present in one respect but wanting in another (4.7 [151.10–17]). Yet neither is God to be credited with the indifference or inactivity of a mere object: on the contrary, divine love is "ecstatic" in that it seeks no good of its own but only the good of its inferiors (4.13 [158.19–159.2]). That *erôs* should be a property of the divine, and hence a mark of plenitude rather than of deficiency, is nonetheless inconceivable to all Platonists but Proclus, and even he says nothing of this downward-tending *erôs* except in his *Commentary on the First Alcibiades*, where he has to explain why Socrates approaches Alcibiades instead of allowing the pupil to come to him in accordance with the more usual practice.[44] No Platonist could have made sense of the saying "my *erôs* is crucified," quoted from Ignatius (*to the Romans* 7.2) at *Divine Names* 4.12 [157.11] and applied by Dionysius to Christ himself; and when he construes the jealousy of God at Exodus 20:5 as the outpouring of his love upon those who seek him (4.13 [159.14–18]), he cannot have forgotten that jealousy is a trait that Plato jealously denies to the Creator (*Timaeus* 29e). And while Dionysius makes no explicit reference to the Trinity, the Pauline motto "from whom, through whom, and in whom" (Romans 11:36) is an intermittent refrain to his panegyric on the ubiquity of divine love (4.4 [148.12–15]; 4.10 [154.11 and 155.5–7]; 4.14 [160.12]).

Conclusion

In his treatise against the Gnostics Plotinus likens the critic of providence to a tortoise who cannot keep up with a dance, but when he is trampled lays the blame on the other dancers. Evans-Pritchard writes that the Azande see witchcraft everywhere as they cannot believe in accidents: they are not content to ask why houses fall (which would lead them, as we would say to science) but demand why this house fell on this passer-by, which leads them, in the absence of an Aristotelian theory of chance, to magic. It cannot be denied that the Christian theory of providence throughout the Middle Ages and the early modern period has amounted to little more than a substitution of divine miracle for human magic. All things, on this theory, work for the good of the elect and the confutation of the ungodly; although it might be admitted that the good often comes in strange guise, the suggestion that the object of divine concern is the part and not the whole was deemed to be pagan or deistic. If all that remained of the Areopagite were the *Divine Names* and the *Mystical Theology*, his Protestant critics might not have been wholly wrong to assign him to the former category; but once we grant equal status, as mediaeval authors did, to the *Celestial Hierarchies*, we must grant at least that his paganism is not that of the Platonists, since no one in the tradition would have held that every soul in the present life has been provided with the means of eternal salvation. Strict Augustinians may protest that Dionysius allows too much to rest on our own volition, but in this respect his doctrine is that of the Greek church from antiquity to the present. Nor does it seem reasonable to accuse him of lacking a doctrine of grace when he is the one Neoplatonist who frees the term *eros* from any hint of imperfection or indigence by making it pre-eminently an attribute of God.

44. See Proclus, *Commentary on the First Alcibiades* 29.15–30.3, with Riggs, "Eros as Hierarchical Principle," 86–87.

Even its pagan form, there is much to commend the Neoplatonic view. The arguments for the inscrutability of the ground of being have not lost their logical force, and were not more strongly urged in the Roman era by pagan than by Christian thinkers. Unless we cling, as few early Christians did, to a literal reading of the opening chapters of Genesis, we shall hardly dare to imagine that the universe with its millions of galaxies, all of which came into existence thousands of millions of years before the appearance of humanity on our undistinguished planet, was created solely as the theatre for our salvation; even those who persist in this belief can no longer presume, if theology is to stand at the bar of experience, to hold God to a visible tariff of penalties and rewards in the present life. Repeated postponement of the second coming of Christ has weakened popular expectation of a last judgment or a bodily resurrection; and the more resolutely we hold our earthly rulers to standards of justice and humanity that were first voiced in the New Testament, the less willing we are to concede that God has a right to punish ephemeral crimes with everlasting torment. We may complain that the One is too impersonal to furnish us with a philosophical concept of God, but the Platonists would reply that personality, as we know it, must be transcended if we are ever to break the cycle of transmigration; and if we retort that only personality as we know it is consistent with being human, we must surely concede that we cannot mean the same thing when we apply the word "person" to God and to human beings. The more readily we admit that God's ways are not our ways and that his thoughts are not as our thoughts, the more evident it will be that the problem of evil cannot be adequately formulated, let alone solved, within the nugatory orbit of human knowledge.

Epilogue

THIS BOOK HAS PROVED to be not so much a history of the problem of evil in the ancient world as a demonstration of its absence—or at least of the refusal to acknowledge it as a reason to doubt the existence of divine beings. Even where a belief in an omnipotent, omniscient, and omnibenevolent God was entertained, two conditions were yet to be fulfilled before the problem of evil became a compelling inducement to atheism. The first was that it should be possible for common hardihood to disbelieve in God, the second that it should be possible for common minds to doubt the inevitability of evil. As I shall argue in the first section of this epilogue, these conditions have not been jointly met until modern times, as our growing mastery of nature has fostered the growth of metaphysical skepticism. It remains true, of course, that if the regnant notion of the divine in the modern era had still been Homeric, or even Platonic (and one might as well say, Mosaic or Solomonic), the problem of evil could not have been formulated in the terms that are now familiar. The rest of the epilogue, therefore, will be a brief recapitulation of the narrative of the twelve foregoing chapters, at the end of which the problem will indeed emerge in a shape much like the modern one, except that we shall see that it serves Augustine and Dionysius as an argument against the existence of evil rather than against that of God.

On Justifying God

For almost a millennium, it has been a peculiarity of European (or, as we used to call it, Christian) thought that it has not held the existence of a god or gods to be unarguable. To be sure, explicit disbelief is seldom attested before the eighteenth century, and was disavowed even then by many who pass for atheists in modern historiography.[1] Anselm presents his ontological argument to the fool because only a fool would need to hear it,[2] while Aquinas assumes, triumphantly but inaccurately, that each of his five ways demonstrates the existence of that which everyone calls God. But once Descartes is driven to take as the ground of all his other beliefs the mere consciousness of self—a very different thing from knowledge of self, as Augustine and Plato would have told him—it was clear that God now lived only by the suffrage of humanity, and that if we could find some other origin for our idea of God than God himself, all theology would be at an end. Hence the repeated efforts of philosophy, from Descartes to the young Kant,[3] to prove that God is a necessary being, whose existence is entailed either by the very concept of God or by the very concept of existence. It belongs to the definition of a necessary being that all its properties are also necessary, and the test of this necessity is our own logic. In other words, we know nothing to be true of him that exceeds our own understanding; if, for example, goodness is deemed to be one of his necessary characteristics, we must either demand that his every action corresponds to our own understanding of goodness or else adjust our notion of goodness to correspond to his acts.

There can be no doubt that the dominant tendency in the modern world is to hold God accountable to our own calculus of goods. "I will call no being good," said John Stuart Mill, "who is not what I mean when I apply that epithet to my fellow-creatures."[4] And we perhaps are more inclined to identify goodness with benevolence, and benevolence with the satisfaction of all our material needs, or of desires that have now become needs. In the age of anaesthetics we can see no pedagogic virtue in the infliction of pain; when buildings can be made earthquake-proof (at least in the more affluent societies), we no longer admit God's right to chastise us with natural disasters; when we have the means of producing food enough for eight thousand million denizens of the planet, we see famine at a consequence of administrative delinquency, not as a salutary warning of divine displeasure. When nature gets the better of us we are angry, not submissive: some Christians wonder how God can allow us to suffer an epidemic that kills one in a hundred people, choosing most of its victims from those who would not have been alive in a previous generation. If our ancestors endured the Black Death more patiently, it was only because disease and early death were for

1. See further, Kors, "The Enlightenment."

2. This asseveration gives some color to the argument of Karl Barth, *Anselm*, that Anselm was not attempting a formal proof of the existence of God.

3. Kant, *The Only Possible Basis*.

4. Mill, *Examination of Sir William Hamilton's Philosophy*, 103.

them inescapable concomitants of life in this world, whereas we have heard accredited physicians predicting that soon we shall find a means of retarding cellular decay, if not an antidote to death itself.

This, we may say, is the reasoning of a society that has already ceased to believe in God and surrendered itself to the venal appetites that it was always the task of religion to curtail.[5] It has long been noted, however, that the period of discovery and scientific endeavor that taught Europe to think that nature could be made subservient to human ends was also the period in which the papacy lost that dominion that it had exercised over Christian minds in the western half of the continent for over a thousand years. Protestantism certainly originates as a theological movement, but its spread was accelerated by the rivalries of kings who wished to keep for themselves the wealth that had been brought within reach by the science of navigation and the power of killing rapidly at a distance. Protestants claimed for themselves the right to deduce from the scriptures all that was necessary for their salvation; it soon became clear, however, that the scriptures admitted of different interpretations even when the same philological tools were deployed with equal probity. Some of these tools indeed brought the integrity of the text into question: the appeal to scripture was therefore enhanced, if not replaced by, an appeal to reason, which gave birth in turn to deism, the doctrine that we should believe no more about God than we can comprehend according to our own principles of moral justice and scientific necessity.[6] Thus we argue into existence a God who is both almighty and perfectly good, since nothing less will content the enlightened self-interest that now passes for reason, and it thus becomes inexplicable that evil, as we define it, should be present in the world that this God is supposed to have created.

The Origins of Theodicy

The popular conception of the gods in the ancient world was troubled by no such difficulty because it did not expect the gods to be better than we are merely because they surpass us in longevity and power. Those who took the view that a god, to deserve the name, must be good were not afraid to accept the conclusion that we are frequently mistaken in our estimation of good and evil. The maxim of Heraclitus that all is good in the sight of God supplies a Greek rationale for Job's impetuous utterance, "We have received

5. On the rise of the "buffered self" in the early modern era, see Taylor, *A Secular Age*.

6. On natural religion as a consequence of the privatization of guilt, see Gauchet, *The Disenchantment of Society*, 169.

good from the Lord, and shall we not receive evil?" The Hebraic custom, however, is not so much to reflect on the character of God as to resign all things to his will, however inscrutable his will may be, even for a Solomon. The Book of Ecclesiastes declares expressly that we do not receive according to our deserts. In the Greek world this position, which is called the denial of providence, is held by the Epicureans, whose deities are of no use to us except as a model of passionless equanimity, and by those who take Book Lambda of the *Metaphysics* as Aristotle's final word on God. The Stoics maintain divine providence, but only by setting up an ideal of self-sufficient virtue that welcomes pain as readily as pleasure and courts adversity as a trial of moral prowess. The gods are easily justified when it lies with us to make use of the lot that falls to us either for evil or for good.

Only in Platonism is there a secure allocation of goods in the measure of our deserts,[7] because it is only in this philosophy that the gods of traditional myth and cult play a role in the economy of the human world, not according to their own whim, as in Homer, but under the sovereignty of the Good, which is placed at the summit of existence on the premiss that the only true explanations are explanations in terms of final rather than efficient causes. The Good is the final cause of all that exists, giving value even to that which would now be thought devoid of moral content: it is not, however, the omnibenevolent God of modern deism, for it has no personal attributes and is credited with no personal intervention in the affairs of beings, animate or inanimate. Creation is the activity of the Demiurge, who because he is good cannot fail to communicate his own goodness to that which he finds to be deficient in form and order. Here again the cosmogony of Plato is irreconcilable with the customary assumption of deists and Christians that God creates by his own will and out of nothing. Neoplatonism was to identify the Demiurge with *nous* or intellect, which arises after the One by the principle of superabundance and imparts form to the material world according to the same principle, by the mediation of soul. No active benevolence can be ascribed in this view either to the One or to the demiurgic intellect;[8] nor is it possible to rid matter entirely of its tendency to disorder, for that would be to impart to it permanent qualities, which matter, by definition, cannot possess. Hence, there is no appeal against the pronouncement of the *Theaetetus* that evil will never be banished from the world. The only strict reckoning of goods and evils is the one that will be applied to the soul by

7. Diogenes Laertius, *Lives of the Philosophers* 3.24, asserts that Plato was the first to treat *pronoia* or providence as a topic in philosophy. See further Burns, *Did God Care?*, 20–21. Evidence of latent belief in providence before Plato, if not of any systematic theory, is collected by Parker, "The Origins of *Pronoia*."

8. A point well made by Gurtler, "Providence."

the lesser gods after death; in the present we must learn to despise adversity and to treat it as an incentive to the cultivation of virtue. Cosmic justice is no more perspicuous under the Platonic than under the Stoic conception of providence.

Thus Plotinus smiles at the interlocutor who imagines that providence cares for the individual or that the universal dance will stop for him. Nevertheless, the belief that everything happens for a reason is deeply rooted in the human mind: the Azande, who demands to know not why a granary falls, but how this granary came to fall and kill these people,[9] has more in common than Evans-Pritchard cared to admit with the European of the twenty-first century. Perhaps in the twenty-first century we are more inclined to lay responsibility, even for the smallest accidents, at the door of some human agency that we curiously supposed to be omnipotent; but since the Roman world expected little but peculation from its magistrates, it turned instinctively to the supernatural. Philo's treatise *On Providence* is a collection of popular anecdotes that is not a typical specimen either of Old Testament piety or of the high philosophy that he exemplifies in other writings. By contrast, the pagan Platonist could reconcile the transcendence of the Good with divine intervention by postulating a lower order, or rather a lower aspect, of divinity to which Plutarch and Apuleius give the name daemon. For Plutarch they are guardians and guides of the just, yet sometimes painful physicians to sinners after death; Apuleius opines that, having like passions to ours, they can be cajoled by prayers and offerings. Both agree that one of the principal functions of the daemon is to tell us through oracles what will come to pass if we take a certain course of action. Alexander of Aphrodisias also ascribes this office to the gods, Peripatetic though he is. Of course, the faith of worshippers was often disappointed, and even Plutarch recognized that without some promise of reckoning after death one could not account for the indulgence that the gods extend to great wrongdoers. His argument that sparing them for a time is itself a punishment, or may give them a chance to employ their talents for the common good, were thrown away on Lucian of Samosata, whose skits on the popular theory of providence throw the philosophical apologists into the shade.

Theodicy and Sin in Christian Thought

Christians were bound to believe that God had intervened in history and would do so again: Theodoret's long vindication of God's dealings with the world can dispense with the agency of daemons, and Augustine in his

9. Evans-Pritchard, *Witchcraft, Oracles and Magic*, 22.

mature years renounced his view that the age of miracles was past. At the same time, it was all too obvious that the world in its current state is no place for the elect, and the writings of the New Testament exhort the believer to bear adversity, not with the unrewarded fortitude of the Stoic but in the hope of an everlasting crown in the kingdom of God. For some, it was enough that in the new world the last shall be first and the first shall be last: those who were troubled by the inequality of fortunes in the present sometimes entertained a theory of pre-existence, though it was only in Gnostic thought that this was accompanied by any doctrine of transmigration. Plato adopted this Pythagorean tenet because he held that soul, as the only source of motion, is naturally immortal, and that the function of soul is to animate a body. Origen shuns this inference because the church does not countenance it: he goes as far as the silence of the scriptures will permit, not because he subscribes to the metaphysics of Plato but because without some notion of pre-existence (which he admits to be a great mystery) he cannot exonerate God from the charge of injustice. For him, it is prerequisite of justice that God should respect the free will of his creatures, a position that he takes so far as to argue that even death cannot take away the possibility of repentance. At the same he outdoes any Christian thinker before him in the advancement and elaboration of two distinctive teachings of the New Testament: that this world is currently the preserve of Satan, and that humanity is more vulnerable to his intrigues because it has been corrupted by a fall.

The apostles had taught that the devil is the prince or the god of this world, that he tempted Christ and seduced Judas Iscariot, that he roams the world even now like a raging lion, and that to be outside the church is to be his prey. The human lords of the ambient society were tools of the principalities and powers who practised wickedness in high places; those who spoke against Jesus, whether they knew it or not, were children of the devil. Even in Athenagoras we read that, having been granted matter as his domain, the devil lures us into idolatry; Tertullian declares that all that pagans do in the name of religion is *pompa diaboli*, a pageant of the devil,[10] and when God gives over the church to persecution it is said that he lets the devil rage for a season. The Gnostic strain in Christianity, mingling Paul with Plato, imputes the very creation of the cosmos to an evil or ignorant demiurge, who makes the spirits of the elect his prisoners in a bleak simulacrum of the celestial realm. Plotinus joins their Christian detractors in asserting that the evils that abound in the physical world do not prove it evil in its inception; yet his pupil Porphyry takes an almost Christian view of pagan cults as oblations to demons, crediting these usurpers with a more

---

10. Tertullian, *Apology* 23.4; cf. Heliodorus, *Ethiopian History* 5.2.6.

efficacious malignity than any Christian would have dared to grant them. The Gnostic tendencies that appeared to be moribund in the third century were reinvigorated by Mani's fusion of Christian, Buddhist, and Zoroastrian motifs, for he no longer ascribed the world to an evil creator but represented the creation as a failed subjugation of matter, a tragic variant on the cosmogony of the *Timaeus* that is at the same time an allegory of the fall of Adam and the passion of Christ.

The dualism of primitive Christianity does not set form against matter or a beneficent against a maleficent deity, but (as Paul says) the things not seen against the things now seen, the God-given freedom of spirit in the kingdom with the present incarceration of the mind in its body of death, where it cannot escape the law of sin. To be in the flesh is to find oneself at war with the spirit and the law of Christ, and while the flesh is not synonymous with the body, it is indissociable from our present bodily condition. This is not because body is evil or its creation perverse, but because the progenitor of the human race brought sin into the world, and with it death, by wilful disobedience to his Creator. From the elliptical words of Paul we learn that the universality of sin is as certain as the universality of death, but the causal relation between the sin of Adam and our sinfulness remains obscure. In theologians of the second century it is more often a divagation than a fall from perfection, the venial error of beings who, because of their immaturity, are too easily deceived. Its chief effect is to retard the consummation of the image and likeness of God in the human race, though it also entails that when the perfect image and likeness becomes incarnate he has to die. In Lactantius and Athanasius the fall is a general forgetting of God by humanity, and society is the principal organ for the transmission of sin. From the third century onward, however, those who treat Adam as a historical figure assume that God endowed him with reason enough to avoid moral error, and hence that he bears the full responsibility for his transgression. In Gregory of Nyssa and Augustine, the fall in Eden replaces the Platonic descent of souls, while it seems in Origen to succeed and aggravate it. Both Gregory and Origen intimate that we inherit defilement by being born of sexual intercourse, but it is Augustine who clearly explains that the punishment of the fall is that we cannot control our appetites, and therefore cannot conceive without feeling lust, which is transmitted to our offspring as concupiscence or inordinate desire.

So far as Augustine offers any solution to the presence of natural evil, it is in his theory of order, which he derives from the Platonists. Absolute uniformity of value is not to be looked for in a world of heterogeneous creatures, each of which has its function and its place. Just as the notes in a piece of music are set off by the intervening silences, so that which is best in the world is seen more clearly by contrast with deficiency or privation, which for a Platonist is the definition of evil. Even sin, so long as it is punished by God, does not sully the natural order: to the sinner himself, on the other hand, it is the one unqualified evil. Sin resides in the will, and while our own wills may be less free than that of Adam to act in perfect accord with reason, let alone with the love of God, we are just as free as Adam to act upon whatever it is that we will. We are therefore bound to do evil unless we are predestined to salvation by the inscrutable will of God; worse still, as heirs to Adam, we are guilty at birth of the sin that he committed. When measured against our salvation or damnation, nothing else can be called good or evil: Augustine's criticism of the Stoics is not that they fail to recognize adversity as evil, but that in resting upon an illusion of self-sufficiency they make it their ideal to act without passion, whereas a Christian knows that the only good acts are those that God performs through us with love.

Can Theodicy Survive?

A similar contrast might be drawn between Dionysius the Areopagite and his mentor Proclus, who had given the Neoplatonic theory of order its classic form in his treatises on providence. Dionysius follows him closely enough to leave us wondering if he believes in either creation out of nothing or in a catastrophic fall. He displays his Christianity at least in making the world an object to its Creator, whereas for Platonists *eros* is almost always the yearning of the deficient for the perfect, and even when predicated of a higher power in relation to a lower one, cannot be applied in that sense to the first principle. The provision of an angelic and an ecclesiastical hierarchy as ladders to salvation also sets him apart from the pagan school of Athens. For all that, he has always been felt, by those in the Augustinian tradition, to have made too little of sin. In the modern world, which declines to accept the guilt that Augustine lays on us in the Adam, both he and Dionysius seem to make too little of evil. To hold suffering as light as they do, we feel, one has to be either an automaton or a fanatic whose conviction that all will be made well in another life is a daydream from which most of us have awakened. Augustine might tell his friends that so long as their faith remained whole, the Vandal invasion of Africa counted for nothing; we would not allow him to tell us that an earthquake or a tsunami counted for nothing so long as those who died in it were at peace with God. To take the problem of evil seriously means to accept that it is real, that we are not responsible for it, and that it cannot be palliated by some imagined remedy in another world.

Now of course Augustine accepted none of these three conditions, and the tradition of Christian thought that we call Catholic has based its teachings on his postulates that sin is the one true evil, that humanity rather than God is responsible for it, and that some form of restitution will be made for the evil of this world in the next. For many Christians these are not subterfuges to evade the problem of evil but legitimate inferences from the deposit of revelation. If they are true, however, they can hardly be irrelevant to theodicy, and the Christian cannot reasonably be expected to answer the atheist without reference to the afterlife or the disparity between what human nature now is and what it might be. If, on the other hand, these doctrines are as anachronistic and chimerical as they are now widely held to be, and if the evils of the world are therefore as real, as acute, and as overwhelming in number as our news bulletins assume, it would be best to admit that no such God as Christians imagine would have tolerated such an accumulation of unrelieved sufferings. And if we find ourselves, like John Stuart Mill,[11] still unable to shake off the remnants of belief, we may find it more logical to surmise either, with the Platonists, that the maker of this world is not strictly omnipotent, or, with the Gnostics, that he does not answer to our definition of the word "good."

11. Mill, *Three Essays on Religion*, 240–41.

Bibliography

Ancient Texts

THIS BIBLIOGRAPHY DOES NOT include pagan authors of the Classical and Hellenistic era, whose works are all available in the Loeb Classical Library (Cambridge: Harvard University Press), and in many other editions and translations. Any Christian texts that have been overlooked can probably be found in Patrologia Graeca and Patrologia Latina, available online; Corpus Scriptorumm Ecclesiasticorum Latinorum (Vienna: Tempsky), also online; Corpus Christanorum Series Latin (Turnhout: Brepols); Sources Chrétiennes (Paris: Cerf); Fontes Christiani (Freiburg im Breisgau: Herder); Griechischen Christlichen Schriftsteller (Berlin: de Gruyter; Leipzig: Hinrichs).

Acta Archelai. Edited by C. H. Beeson. Leipzig: Hirnichs, 1906. Edited by M. J. Vermes. Turnhout: Brepols, 2001.

Adamantius, Dialog des. Edited by W. H. van der Sande Bakhuysen. 1901. Reprint, Berlin: de Gruyter, 2020.

Alcinous. *Enseignement des Doctriens de Platon*. Edited by J. Whittaker. Paris: Belles Lettres, 1990.

Alexander of Aphrodisias. *Aristotelis Metaphysica Commentaria*. Edited by M. Hayducjk. Berlin: Reimer, 1891.

———. *On Fate*. Edited by R. W. Sharples. London: Duckworth, 1983.

———. *Praeter Commentaria Scripta Minora: De Anima Liber cum Mantissa*. Edited by I. Bruns. Berlin: Reimer, 1887.

———. *Praeter Commentaria Scripta Minora: Quaestiones, De Fato, De Mixtione*. Edited by I. Bruns. Berlin: Reimer, 1892.

Alexander of Lycopolis. *Contra Manichaei Opiniones Disputatio*. Edited by A. Brinkmann. Leipzig: Teubner, 1989.

Apuleius. *Apologia, Florida, De Deo Socratis*. Edited and translated by C. P. Jones Cambridge, MA: Harvard University Press, 2017.

———. *Metamorphoses*. Edited and translated by J. A. Hanson. 2 vols. Cambridge: Harvard University Press, 1989.

Bibliography

————. *De Philosophia Libri*. Edited by P. Thomas. Leipzig: Teubner, 1970.

Aristotle, all works, including those below: see Loeb Classical Library edition, various hands and dates, Cambridge: Harvard University Press.

————. *Fragmenta Selecta*. Edited by W. D. Ross. Oxford: Clarendon, 1955.

————. *Metaphysics*. Edited by W. D. Ross. Oxford: Clarendon, 1948.

————. *Physics*. Edited by W. D. Ross. Oxford: Clarendon, 1936.

[Aristotle.] *De Mundo*. In *Opera* III, edited by I. Bekker. Oxford: Oxford University Press, 1937.

Arnobius. *Adversus Nationes*. Edited by C. Tommasi. Rome: Città Nouva, 2017.

Athanasius. *Contra Gentes* and *De Incarnatione*. Edited and translated by. R. W. Thomson. Oxford: Clarendon, 1971.

Athenagoras. *Embassy* and *On the Resurrection*. Edited and translated by W. R. Schoedel. Oxford: Clarendon, 1971.

————. *Legatio pro Christianis*. Edited by Miroslav Marcovich. Patristische Texte und Studien 31. Berlin: de Gruyter, 1990.

Atticus. *Fragments*. Edited by E. Des Places. Paris: Belles Lettres, 1977.

Augustine. *De Civitate Dei*. Edited by E. Hoffmann. 2 vols. Vienna: Tempsky, 1899–1900.

————. *Confessions*. Edited with commentary by J. O'Donnell. 3 vols. Oxford: Clarendon, 1992.

————. *Contra Academicos, De Beata Vita, De Ordine, De Magistro, De Libero Arbitrio*. Edited by W. M. Green and K. D. Daur. Turnhout: Brepols, 1970.

————. *De Correptione et Gratia*. Edited by G. Folliet. Vienna: Tempsky, 2000.

————. *De Diversis Quaestionibus ad Simplicianum*. Edited by A. Mutzenbrecher. Turnhout: Brepols, 1970.

————. *De Doctrina Christiana*. Edited by R. P. H. Green. Oxford: Clarendon, 1995.

————. *Epistulae*, pars II. Edited by A Goldbacher. Vienna: Tempsky, 1895.

————. *De Genesi ad Litteram*. Edited by J. Zycha. Vienna: Tempsky, 1894.

————. *De Peccatorum Metritis, De Spiritu et Littera, De Natura et Gratia, De Natura et Origine Animae, Contra Duas Epistulas Pelagianorum*. Edited by C. Vrba and J. Zycha. Vienna: Tempsky, 1913.

————. *De Perfectione Iustitiae Hominis, De Gestis Pelagii, De Gratia Christi, De Nuptiis et Concupiscentia*. Edited by C. F. Vrba and J. F. Zycha. Vienna: Tempsky, 1902.

————. *De Trinitate*. Edited by W. J. Mountain and F. Glorie. 2 vols. Turnhout: Brepols, 1968.

Avitus. *Opera quae supersunt*. Edited by R. Peiper. Berlin: Weidmann, 1961.

Chalcidius. *Commentarium in Timaeum*. Edited by J. H. Waszink. Leiden: Brill, 1974.

Chaldaean Oracles. Edited by R. Majercik. Leiden: Brill, 2013.

Clement of Alexandria. *Werke*. Edited by O. Staehlin, L. Früchtel, and U. Treu. 4 vols. Leipzig: Hinrichs, 1905–70.

Corpus Hermeticum. Edited by and translated by W. B. Scott, as *Hermetica*. 4 vols. Oxford: Clarendon, 1925–36.

Corpus Hermeticum. Edited by A. D. Nock and A.-J. Festugière. 4 vols. Paris: Belles Lettres, 1960. Supplemented by I. Ramelli. Milan: Bompiani, 2005.

Didymus. *Ekklesiasteskommentar*. Edited by G. Binder et al. 6 vols. Bonn: Habelt, 1969–85.

————. *Hiobkommentar*. Edited by A. Henrichs, U. Hagedorn, D. Hagedorn, L. Koenen. 4 vols. Bonn: Habelt, 1968–85.

————. *Psalmenkommentar PsT.* 5 vols. Edited by L. Doutreleau, A. Gesché, and M. Gronewald. Bonn: Habelt, 1968–70.

————. *Sur la Genèse.* Edited by P. Nautin. 2 vols. Paris: Cerf, 1976–78.

————. *Sur Zacharie.* Edited by L. Doutreleau. Paris: Cerf, 1962.

Dionysius the Areopagite. *Corpus Dionysiacum* I. Edited by B. Suchla. Berlin: de Gruyter, 1990.

————. *Corpus Dionysiacum* II. Edited by G. Heil and A. M. Ritter. Berlin: de Gruyter, 1990.

Epictetus. *Discourses.* Edited and translated by W. A. Oldfather. 2 vols. Cambridge: Harvard University Press, 1926.

Epicurus. *Opere.* Edited by G. Arrighetti. Turin: Einaudi, 1960.

Epiphanius of Salamis. *Panarion.* Edited by K. Holl. 3 vols. Leipzig: Hinrichs, 1919–33.

Eusebius. *Praeparatio Evangelica.* Edited by K. Mras. 2 vols. Berlin: Akademie Verlag, 1913.

Evagrius. *De Oratione, Patrologia Graeca* 79, 1165–2000.

————. *Les Six Centuries des 'Kephalaia Gnostica d'Évagre le Pontique.* Edited by A. Guillaumont. *Patrologia Orientalis* 28.1.134, Turnhout: Brepols, 1958.

————. *Traité Pratique, ou le Moine.* Edited by A. Guillaumont. Paris: Cerf, 1971.

Gregory Nazianzen. *Tutti le Orazioni.* Edited by C. Moreschini and C. Soni. Milan: Bompiani, 2000.

GNO = *Gregorii Nysseni Opera Omnia.* Edited by W. Jaeger et al. Leiden: Brill, 1960–present.

Gregory of Nyssa. *De Hominis Opificio. The Fourteenth-Century Slavonic Translation. A Critical Edition, with Greek Parallels and Commentary.* Edited by L. Sels. Vienna: Böhlau, 2009.

————. *Sull' anima e la resurrezione.* Edited by I. Ramelli. Milan: Bompiani, 2007.

Hesiod. See Loeb Classical Library and Oxford Classical Texts, with annotated editions listed below under name of M. L. West.

[Hippolytus.] *Refutation of All Heresies.* Edited and translated by D. Litwa. Atlanta: Society of Biblical Literature 2016.

Homer. See Loeb Classical Library and Oxford Classical Texts.

Iamblichus. *De anima: Text, Translation, and Commentary.* Edited by J. Finamore and J. Dillon. Leiden: Brill, 2002.

————. *On the Mysteries.* Translated with introduction and notes by E. C. Clarke, J. M. Dillon, and J. P. Hershbell. Atlanta: Society of Biblical Literature, 2003.

Irenaeus. *Contre les hérésies.* Edited by A. Rousseau and L. Doutreleau. 5 vols. Paris: Cerf, 1965–82.

Justin Martyr. *Apologies.* Edited by D. Minns and P. Parvis. Oxford: Oxford University Press, 2009.

————. *Apologies.* Edited by Miroslav Marcovich. *Iustini Martyris Apologiae pro Christianis.* Patristische Texte und Studien 38. Berlin: de Gruyter, 1994.

————. *Dialogue with Trypho.* Edited by Miroslav Marcovich. *Iustini Martyris Dialogus cum Tryphone.* Patristische Texte und Studien 47. Berlin: de Gruyter, 1997.

Lactantius. *Divinarum Institutionum Libiri Septem.* Edited by A. Wlosok and E. Heck. Berlin: de Gruyter, 2005–11.

————. *Opera Omnia.* Edited by S. Brandt. Vienna: Tempsky, 1890–93.

Lucian of Samosata. *Opera.* Edited by M. D. Macleod. 4 vols. Oxford: Clarendon, 1972–87. For translations see the eight volumes in see Loeb Classical Library, Cambridge: Harvard University Press.

Lucretius. *De Rerum Natura*. Edited and translated by C. Bailey. Oxford: Clarendon, 1986.

Marcus Aurelius. *Ad se ipsum*. Edited by J. Dalfen. Leipzig: Teubner, 1979.

Maximus of Tyre. *Dissertationes*. Edited by M. B. Trapp. Berlin: de Gruyter, 1994.

Methodius. *Werke*. Edited by N. P. Bonwetsch. Leipzig: Hinrichs, 1917.

Nemesius of Emesa. *De Natura Hominis*. Edited by M. Morani. Leipzig: Teubner, 1987.

NHC = *Nag Hammadi Codices*. Edited by J. M. Robinson. *The Coptic Gnostic Library*. 5 vols. Leiden: Brill, 2000.

Numenius. *Fragments*. Edited by E. Des Places. Paris: Belles Lettres, 1973.

Origen. *Commentaire sur saint Jean*. Edited by C. Blanc. Paris: Cerf, 1966–92.

———. *Commento al vangelo di Giovanni*. Edited by V. Limone. Milan: Bompiani, 2012.

———. *First Principles*. Edited and translated by John Behr. Oxford: Oxford University Press, 2017.

———. *Gegen Celsus/Die Schrift vom Gebiet*. Edited by P. Koetschau. 2 vols. Leipzig: Hinrichs, 1897–99.

———. *Homilien zum Hexateuch*. Edited by W. Baehrens. Leipzig: Hinrichs, 1920.

———. *Jeremiahomilien*. Edited by E. Klostermann. Leipzig: Hinrichs, 1901.

———. *Kommentar zu Samuel, zum Hohelied etc*. Edited by W. A Baehrens. Leipzig: Hinrichs, 1925.

———. *Philocalia*. Edited by J. Armitage Robinson. Cambridge: Cambridge University Press, 1893.

———. *Philocalie 21–27*. Edited by E. Junod. Paris: Cerf, 1976.

———. *Philokalie*. Edited by M. Harl and E. Junod. Paris: Cerf, 1976, 1983.

———. *De Principiis*. Edited by P. Koetschau. Leipzig: Hinrichs, 1913.

———. *Römerbriefkommentar*. Edited by C. Hammond Bammel. 3 vols. Freiburg im Breisgau: Herder, 1990–97.

Origen/Gregory of Nyssa. *Sul Cantico dei Cantici*. Edited by V. Limone and C. Moreschini. Milan: Bompiani, 2016.

Orphicorum et Orphicis Similium Fragmenta. Edited by A. Bernabé. Leipzig: Saur, 2005.

Philo of Alexandria. *Opera quae supersunt*. Edited by L. Cohn and P. Wendland. Berlin: Reimer 1896–1906. See also Loeb Classical Library edition, various hands and dates, Cambridge: Harvard University Press.

Plato. See Oxford Classical Texts editions, various hands and dates Oxford: Clarendon, and Loeb Classical Library editions, various hands and dates, Cambridge: Harvard University Press.

Plotinus. *Enneads*. Edited and translated by A. H. Armstrong. 7 vols. Cambridge: Harvard University Press, 1966–88.

Plutarch. *Plutarch's De Iside et Osiride*. Edited with an introduction and commentary by J. Gwyn Griffiths. Cardiff: University of Wales, 1970.

———. For other texts by Plutarch, see Loeb Classical Library edition, various hands and dates, Cambridge: Harvard University Press.

Porphyry. *De l'abstinence*. Edited by J. Bouffartigue and M. Patillon. 2 vols, Paris: Belles Lettres, 2003.

———. *L'Antre des Nymphes de Porphyre*. Edited by T. Dorandi. Paris: Vrin, 2019.

———. *Epistula ad Anebonem*. Edited by A. R. Sodano. Naples: L'arte tipografica, 1958.

———. *Fragmenta*. Edited by A. Smith. Leipzig: Teubner, 1993.

———. *Lettre à Anebon*. Edited by H-D. Saffrey. Paris: Belles Lettres, 2012.

————. *Life of Plotinus*. Appears as introduction to editions of Plotinus.

————. *Opuscula Selecta*. Edited by A. Nauck. Leipzig: Teubner, 1886. Includes *History of Philosophy, Life of Pythagoras, On Abstinence, Cave of the Nymphs, Letter to Marcella*.

————. *In Platonis Timaeum commentarium fragmenta*. Edited by A. R. Sodano. Naples: L'arte tipografica, 1964.

————. [*To Gaurus*], *Sur la manière dont l'embryon reçoît l'âme*. Edited by L. Brisson. Paris: Vrin, 2012.

————. *Vie de Pythagore. Lettre à Marcella*. Edited by E. Des Places with appendix by 'A.-Ph. Segonds. Paris: Belles Lettres, 2010.

Proclus. *Elements of Theology*. Edited and translated by E. R. Dodds. 2nd ed. Oxford: Clarendon, 1963.

————. *In Platonis Parmenidem commentaria*. Edited by C. Steel; tomus I: libros I-III, edited by C. Steel, P. Macé, P. d'Hoine; tomus II: libros IV-V, edited by C. Steel, A. Gribomont, P. d'Hoine; tomus III: libros VI-VII, edited by C. Steel, L. Van Campe. Oxford: Oxford University Press, 2007-9.

————. *In Platonis Rem Publicam*. Edited by W. Kroll. 2 vols. Leipzig: Teubner, 1899.

————. *In Platonis Timaeum Commentaria*. Edited by H. Diehl. 3 vols. Leipzig: Teubner 1903-6.

————. *On the Eternity of the World*. Edited and translated by H. S. Long and A. D. Macro. Berkeley: University of California Press, 2001.

————. *Sur le Premier Alcibiade de Platon*. Edited by A.-P. Segonds. 2 vols. Paris: Belles Lettres, 2003.

————. *Théologie platonicienne*. Edited by and trans. H. D. Saffrey et L. G. Westerink. 6 vols. Paris: Belles Lettres, 1968-97.

————. *Tria Opuscula De providential, libertate, malo. Latine Guilemo de Moerbeka vertente et graece ex Isaacii Sebastocratoris aliorumque scriptis collecta*. Edited by H. Boesse. Berlin: de Gruyter, 1960. Containing *To Theodore on Fate, Ten Doubts concerning Providence* and *On the Existence of Evils*.

Prudentius. *Prudentius*. Edited and translated by H. J. Thomson. 2 vols. Cambridge: Harvard University Press, 2014.

Seneca. Translations can be found in Loeb Classical Library editions. Cambridge: Harvard University Press.

————. *Dialogorum Loibri Duodecim*. Edited by L. D. Reynolds. Oxford: Clarendon, 1977.

————. *Letters to Lucilius*. Edited by R. M. Gummere. Cambridge: Harvard University Press, 1917-25.

————. *Tragoediae*. Edited by O. Zwierlein. Oxford: Clarendon, 1986.

Tatian. *Oration to the Greeks*. Edited and translated by M. Whittaker. Oxford: Clarendon, 1982.

————. *Oratio ad Graecos. Rede an die Griechen*. Edited by J. Trelenberg. Tübingen: Mohr Siebeck, 2012.

Tertullian. *Adversus Marcionem*. Edited by E. Evans. 2 vols. Oxford: Clarendon, 1972.

————. *Opera*. Edited by A. Gerlo. 2 vols. Turnhout: Brepols, 1954.

Theodoret of Cyrrhus. For works, see *Patrologia Graeca* 80-84.

————. *Graecarum Affectionum Curatio*. Edited by H. Raeder. Leipzig: Hinrichs, 1904.

————. *De Providentia*. In *Patrologia Graeca* 88, 555-774.

————. *Questions on the Octateuch*. Edited by J. Petruccione. Washington, DC: Catholic University of America Press, 2007.

Bibliography

Theophilus of Antioch. *Ad Autolycum*. Edited by R. M. Grant. Oxford: Clarendon, 1970.

———. *Ad Autolycum*. Edited by M. Marcovich. Patristische Texte und Studien 44. Berlin: de Gruyter 1995.

Secondary Literature, Including Commentaries

Adamson, P. "Plotinus on Astrology." *Oxford Studies in Ancient Philosophy* 35 (2008) 265–91.

Addey, C. *Divination and Theurgy in Neoplatonism*. Farnham, UK: Ashgate, 2014.

Adkins, A. W. H. *Merit and Responsibility: A Study in Greek Values*. Chicago: Chicago University Press, 1960.

Aitken, J., with H. Patmore, and I. Rosen-Zvi, eds. *The Evil Inclination in Early Judaism and Christianity*. Cambridge: Cambridge University Press, 2021.

Allan, W. "Divine Justice and Cosmic Order in Early Greek Epic." *Journal of Hellenic Studies* 126 (2006) 1–35.

Alviar, J. *Klesis: The Theology of the Christian Vocation According to Origen*. Dublin: Four Courts, 1993.

Anatolios, K. *Athanasius: The Coherence of His Thought*. London: Routledge, 1998.

———. "*Creatio ex nihilo* in Athanasius' *Against the Greeks/On the Incarnation*." In *Creation ex Nihilo: Origins, Development, Contemporary Challenges*, edited by G. A. Anderson and M. Bockmuehl, 119–50. Notre Dame, IN: University of Notre Dame Press, 2018.

Andersen, R. "The Elihu Speeches: Their Place and Sense in the Book of Job." *Tyndale Bulletin* 66 (2015) 75–94.

Anderson, G. *Philostratus: Biography and Belles Lettres in the Third Century A.D.* Beckenham, UK: Croom Helm, 1986.

Annas, A., and A. Lenzi. *Ludlul bēl nēmeqi: The Standard Babylonian Poem of the Righteous Sufferer*. Helsinki: Neo-Assyrian Text Corpus Project, 2010.

Armstrong, A. H. "The Background of the Doctrine That the Ideas Are Not outside the Intellect." In *Entretiens Hardt V: Les Sources de Plotin*, 391–425. Geneva: Vandoeuvres, 1960.

Arnim, H. von, ed. *Stoicorum Veterum Fragmenta*. Stuttgart: Teubner, 1964.

Arruzza, C. "Le refus du bonheur: négligence et chute dans la pensée d' Origène." *Revue de Théologie et de Philosophie* 141 (2009) 261–72.

Ashwin-Siejkowski, P. *Clement of Alexandria: A Project of Christian Perfection*. London: T. & T. Clark, 2008.

———. *Clement of Alexandria on Trial: The Evidence of Heresy from Photius' Bibliotheca*. Leiden: Brill, 2010.

Asmis, E., "Lucretius' Venus and Stoic Zeus." *Hermes* 110 (1982) 458–70.

Athanassiadi, P. "Antiquité Tardive: Construction et déconstruction d'un modèle historiographique." *Antiquité Tardive* 14 (2006) 211–24.

Athanassiadi, P. "Numenius: Portrait of a Platonicus." In *Brill's Companion to the Reception of Plato in Antiquity*, edited by H. Tarrant, D. A. Layne, D. Baltzly, and F. Renaud, 183–205. Leiden: Brill, 2018.

Aulen, G. *Christus Victor: An Historical Study of the Three Main Types of the Idea of the Atonement*. Translated by A. G. Hebert. London: SPCK, 1931.

Bakhouche, B. "Le dualime en question dans le commentaire au *Timée* de Calcidius." *Chora* 13 (2015) 247–58.

Bammel, C. P. "Adam in Origen." In *The Making of Orthodoxy: Essays in Honour of Henry Chadwick*, edited by R. D. Williams, 62–93. Cambridge: Cambridge University Press, 1989.

———, ed. *Der Römerbriefkommentar des Origenes*. Freiburg: Herder, 1997.

Bardy, G. "Théodoret." In *Dictionnaire de la Théologie Catholique*, 299–325. Paris: Letouzey and Ane, 1946.

Barnes, T. D. *Constantine and Eusebius*. Cambridge: Harvard University Press, 1981.

———. "Methodius, Maximus and Valentinus." *Journal of Theological Studies* 30 (1979) 47–55.

Barr, J. "The Book of Job and Its Modern Interpreters." *Bulletin of the John Rylands Library* 54 (1971) 28–46.

———. *The Garden of Eden and the Hope of Immortality*. London: SCM, 1992.

Barth, K. *Anselm: Fides Quarens Intellectum. Anselm's Proof the Existence of God in the Light of His Theological Scheme*. London: SCM, 1960.

Barton, J. *Amos's Oracles against the Nations*. Cambridge: Cambridge University Press, 1980.

Baumgarten, A. I. *The Phoenician History of Philo of Byblos*. Leiden: Brill, 1981.

Bayliss, G. *The Vision of Didymus the Blind*. Oxford: Oxford University Press, 2015.

Beasley-Murray, G. R. *Jesus and the Kingdom of God*. Grand Rapids: Eerdmans, 1986.

Beatrice, P. F. "*Quesodam Platonicorum Libros*: The Platonic Readings of Augustine in Milan." *Vigiliae Christianae* 43 (1989) 248–81.

———. *The Transmission of Sin*. Translated by A. Kamesar. Oxford: Oxford University Press, 2013.

BeDuhn, J. *Augustine's Manichaean Dilemma*. Philadelphia: Pennsylvania University Press, 2013.

———. *The Manichaean Body: Its Discipline and Ritual*. Baltimore: Johns Hopkins University Press, 2000.

BeDuhn, J., and P. Mirecki. "Placing the Acts of Archelaus." In *Frontiers of Faith: The Christian Encounter with Manichaeism in the Acts of Archelaus*, 1–22. Leiden: Brill, 2007.

Behr, J. *Asceticism and Anthropology in Irenaeus and Clement*. Oxford: Oxford University Press, 2000.

———, ed. *Origen: On First Principles*. Vol. 1. Oxford: Oxford University Press, 2017.

———. "'Since the Saviour Exists': A Reconsideration of Irenaeus' *Adversus Haereses* III.22–23." *Studia Patristica* 109 (2021) 43–54.

Berno, F. "Rethinking Valentinianism: Some Remarks on the *Tripartite Tractate* with Special Reference to Plotinus, *Enneads* II,9." *Augustinianum* 56 (2016) 331–45.

Bianchi, U. "Mithraism and Gnosticism." In *Gnostic Studies*, vol. 2, edited by J. B. Hinnells, 457–65. Manchester: Manchester University Press, 1975.

———. "Plutarch und der dualismus." In *Aufstieg und Niedergang der römischen Welt* II.36.1, edited by W. Haase and H. Temporini, 350–65. Berlin: de Gruyter 1987.

Bidez, J. *Vie de Porphyre*. Ghent: Van G iethem, 1913.

Bigg, C. H. *The Christian Platonists of Alexandria*. Oxford: Clarendon, 1913.

Blosser, B. *Become like the Angels: Origen's Doctrine of the Soul*. Washington, DC: Catholic University of America Press, 2012.

Boas, G. *Primitivism and Related Ideas in the Middle Ages*. Baltimore: Johns Hopkins University, 1948.

Bibliography

Bobzien, S. *Determinism and Freedom in Stoic Philosophy.* Oxford: Clarendon, 1998.

―――. "The Late Conception and Inadvertent Birth of the Freewill Problem." *Phronesis* 43 (1998) 134–77.

Boehme, J. *Signatura Rerum.* London: Dent, 1912.

Bonner, A. *The Myth of Pelagianism.* Oxford: Oxford University Press, 2018.

Boot, P. "Plotinus, *On Providence* (*Enneads* III 2–3): Three Interpretations." *Mnemosyne* 36 (1983) 311–15.

Bordy, M. "Why Aristotle's God Is Not the Unmoved Mover." *Oxford Studies in Ancient Philosophy* 40 (2011) 91–109.

Boring, E. "The Unforgivable Sin Logion Mark XIII.28–29/Matt XII 31–32/Luke XII 10: Formal Analysis and History of the Tradition." *Novum Testamentum* 18 (1976) 258–79.

Bos, A. P. "Aristotle on 'People in a Cave.' De Philosophia, Fr. 13A Ross." In *Cosmic and Metacosmic Theology in Aristotle's Lost Dialogues,* edited by A. P. Bos, 14–184. Leiden: Brill, 1989.

Boys-Stones, G. *Post-Hellenic Philosophy: A Study of Its Development from the Stoics to Origen.* Oxford: Oxford University Press, 2011.

Brakke, D. *The Gnostics: Myth, Ritual and Diversity in Early Christianity.* Cambridge: Harvard University Press, 2011.

Braun, R. *Deus Christianorum. Recherches sur le vocabulaire doctrinal de Tertullien.* Paris: Études Augustiniennes, 1977.

Bréhier, E. *The Philosophy of Plotinus.* Chicago: Chicago University Press, 1958.

Bremer. J. M. *Harmatia: Tragic Error in Aristotle and in Greek Tragedy.* Amsterdam: Hakkert, 1968.

Bremmer, J. *The Rise and Fall of the Afterlife.* London: Routledge, 2002.

Brenk, F. "An Imperial Heritage: The Religious Spirit of Plutarch." In *Aufstieg und Niedergang der römischen Welt* II.36.1, edited by W. Haase and Hildegard Temporini, 249–349. Berlin: de Gruyter, 1987.

Breyfogle, T. "Memory and Imagination in Augustine's *Confessions.*" *New Blackfriars* 75 (1994) 210–23.

Breytenbach, C. L., and P. L. Day. "Satan." In *Dictionary of Deities and Demons in the Bible,* edited by K. van den Toorn, B. Becking and P. W. van der Horst, 1369–80. Leiden: Brill, 1995.

Brigmann, A. *God and Christ in Irenaeus.* Oxford: Oxford University Press, 2019.

Brisson, L. "D'où vient le mal chez Platon?" *Chora* 13 (2015) 15–31.

Brown, A. L. "Wretched Tales of Poets: Euripides, *Heracles* 1340–46." *Proceedings of the Cambridge Philological Society* 24 (1978) 22–30.

Brown, P. R. L. *The Body and Society: Men, Women and Sexual Renunciation in Early Christianity.* New York: Columbia University Press, 1988.

―――. *The Making of Late Antiquity.* Cambridge: Harvard University Press, 1976.

Burkitt, F. C. *Church and Gnosis.* Cambridge: Cambridge University Press, 1932.

Burns, D. M. *Apocalypse of the Alien God: Platonism and the Exile of Sethian Gnosticism.* Philadelphia: Penn State University Press, 2014.

―――. *Did God Care? Providence, Dualism and Will in Later Greek and Early Christian Philosophy.* Leiden: Brill, 2020.

Butler, E. P. "Polytheism and Individuality in the Henadic Manifold." *Dionysius* 23 (2005) 83–104.

Callard, A. G. "Ignorance and Akrasia-Denial in the Protagoras." *Oxford Studies in Ancient Philosophy* 47 (2014) 31–80.

Calma, D., ed. *Reading Proclus and the Book of Causes*, vol. 3, *On Causes and the Noetic Triad*. Leiden: Brill, 2022.

Caluori, D. "The Embodied Soul." In *The New Cambridge Companion to Plotinus*, edited by L. Gerson, 219–40. Cambridge: Cambridge University Press, 2022.

Campbell, J. *The Masks of God*. Vol. 4, *Creative Mythology*. New York: Viking, 1969.

Carter, J. W. "Augustine on Time, Time Numbers, and Enduring Objects." *Vivarium* 49 (2011) 301–23.

Cartwright, S. "Soul and Body in Early Christianity: An Old and New Conundrum." In *A History of Mind and Body in Late Antiquity*, edited by A. Marmodoro and S. Cartwright, 173–90. Cambridge: Cambridge University Press, 2018.

Casey, R. P. "Naassenes and Ophites." *Journal of Theological Studies* 27 (1926), 374–87.

Catevaro, L. G. "The Clash of the Sexes in Hesiod's *Works and Days*." *Greece and Rome* 60 (2013) 185–202.

Chappell, T. D. *Aristotle and Augustine on Freedom*. New York: Springer, 1995.

Cheon, S. *The Exodus Story in the Wisdom of Solomon*. Sheffield, UK: Sheffield Academic, 1997.

Cherniss, H. *Aristotle's Criticism of Plato and the Academy*. Baltimore: Johns Hopkins University Press, 1944.

———, ed. and trans. *Plutarch: Moralia* XIII.1. Cambridge: Harvard University Press, 1976.

Chiaradonna, R. "Iamblichus." In *The Stanford Encyclopedia of Philosophy* (online).

Cilento, V. *Paideia Antignostica*. Florence: Le Monnier, 1971.

Clark, E. A. "Vitiated Seeds and Holy Vessels: Augustine's Manichaean Past." In *Ascetic Piety and Women's Faith*, edited by E. A. Clark, 291–394. Lewiston, NY: Mellen, 1986.

Clark, S. R. L. "Plotinus: Remembering and Forgetting." In *Greek Memories: Theories and Practices*, edited by L. Castagnoli and P. Caccarelli, 325–42. Cambridge: Cambridge University Press, 2019.

Clarke, E. C., with J. M. Dillon, and J. P. Hershbell, trans. *Iamblichus On the Mysteries*. Atlanta: Society of Biblical Studies, 2003.

Clarke, M. *Flesh and Spirit in the Songs of Homer*. Oxford: Clarendon, 1999.

Clifford, R. J. "*Creatio ex nihilo* in the Old Testament/Hebrew Bible." In *Creation ex Nihilo: Origins, Development, Contemporary Challenges*, edited by G. W. Anderson and M. Bockmuehl, 55–66. Notre Dame, IN: University of Notre Dame Press, 2018.

Coenen, J., ed. *Lukian: Zeus Tragodos*. Meisenheim am Glan: Hain, 1977.

Cole, T. *Democritus and the Sources of Greek Anthropology*. Cleveland, OH: American Philological Association, 1967.

Coleman, A. P. *Lactantius the Theologian: Lactantius' Doctrine of Providence*. Piscataway, NJ: Gorgias, 2017.

Collingwood, R. G. *An Essay on Metaphysics*. Oxford: Clarendon, 1940.

Colot, B. *Lactance: Penser la conversion de Rome au temps de Constantin*. Florence: Olschki, 2016.

Coope, U. *Freedom and Responsibility in Neoplatonist Thought*. Oxford: Oxford University Press, 2020.

Copenhaver, B. *Hermetica*. Cambridge: Cambridge University Press, 1992.

Corcoran, S. P. *The Empire of the Tetrarchs*. Oxford: Clarendon, 2000.

Corrigan, K. *Evagrius and Gregory: Mind, Soul and Body in the Fourth Century*. Farnham, UK: Ashgate, 2009.

Bibliography

Corsini, E. *Il trattato* De Divinis Nominibus *dello Psuedo-Dionigi e I commenti neoplatonici al* Parmenide. Turin: Giapichelli, 1962.

Courcelle, P. "Les sages de Porphyre et les *viri novi* d'Arnobe." *Revue des Études Latines* 31 (1953) 257–71.

Crabbe, K. "The Generation of Iron and the Final Stumbling-Block: The Present Time in Hesiod's *Works and Days* 106–21 and Barnabas 4." In *Four Kingdom Motifs in and beyond the Book of Daniel*, edited by A. Perrin and L. T. Stuckenbruck, 141–66. Leiden: Brill, 2020.

Crislip, A. "Envy and Anger at the World's Creation and Destruction in the *Treatise without Title On the Origin of the World* NHC II, 5." *Vigiliae Christianae* 63 (2011) 285–310.

Croke, B., and J. B. Harries. *Religious Conflict in Fourth-Century Rome*. Sydney: Sydney University Press, 1982.

Cumont, F. "Lucrèce et le symbolisme pythagoricien des enfers." *Revue de Philologie* 44 (1920) 229–340.

———. *The Oriental Religions in Roman Paganism*. Translation by G. Showerman. Chicago: Open Court, 2011.

Currie, B. "*Cypria.*" In *The Epic Cycle and Its Ancient Reception*, edited by M. Fantuzzi and C. Tsagalis, 281–305. Cambridge: Cambridge University Press, 2015.

Daniélou, J. *The Origins of Latin Christianity*. Translated by J. A. Baker. London: Darton, Longman and Todd, 1977.

Darkus, S. M. "Daimon Parallels the Holy *Phrên* in Empedocles." *Phronesis* 22 (1977) 175–90.

Davies, M. "The Judgment of Paris and *Iliad* book xxiv." *Journal of Hellenic Studies* 101 (1981) 56–62.

Dawson, D. *Allegorical Readers and Cultural Revision in Ancient Alexandria*. Berkeley: University of California Press, 1992.

Deakle, D. W. "Harnack and Cerdo: A Re-examination of the Patristic Evidence for Marcion's Mentor." In *Marcion und seine kirchengeschichtliche Wirkung*, edited by G. May, K. Greschat, and M. Meiser, 177–90. Berlin: de Gruyter, 2002.

Dechow, J. *Dogma and Mysticism in Early Christianity: Epiphanius of Cyrprus and the Legacy of Origen*. Macon, GA: Mercer University Press, 1988.

Deck, A. N. *Nature, Contemplation and the One*. Toronto: University of Toronto Press, 1967.

Deissman, A. *Bible Studies*. Edinburgh: T. & T. Clark, 1909.

Des Places, E., ed. *Numénius: Fragments*. Paris: Belles Lettres, 1973.

Deuse, W. "Plutarch's Eschatological Myths." In *Plutarch on the daimonion of Socrates*, edited by H.-G. Nesselrath, 169–97. Tübingen: Mohr Siebeck, 2010.

Diels, H., and W. Kranz. *Die Fragmente der Vorsokratiker*. Berlin: Weidmann, 1951–52.

Digeser, E. D. "Lactantius and Constantine's Letter to Arles." *Journal of Early Christian Studies* 2 (1994) 33–52.

———. *A Threat to Public Piety: Christians, Platonists and the Great Persecution*. Ithaca, NY: Cornell University Press, 2012.

Dillon, J. M. *Alcinous: The Handbook of Platonism*. Oxford: Clarendon, 1992.

———. "The Early History of the Noetic Triad." In *Reading Proclus and the Book of Causes*, vol. 3, 391–405. Leiden: Brill, 2022.

———, ed. *Iamblichi Chalcidensis Commentaria*. Leiden: Brill, 1973.

———. *The Middle Platonists*. London: Duckworth, 1977.

———. "Monotheism in the Gnostic Tradition." In *Pagan Monotheism in Late Antiquity*, edited by P. Athanassiadi and M. Frede, 69–79. Oxford: Clarendon, 1999.

———. "'Orthodoxy' and 'Eclecticism': Middle Platonists and Neo-Pythagoreans." In *The Question of "Eclecticism*," edited by J. M. Dillon and A. A. Long, 103–25. Berkeley: University of California Press, 1988.

Dodd, C. H. *The Bible and the Greeks*. London: Hodder, 1935.

———. *Parables of the Kingdom*. London: Collins, 1938.

Dodds, E. R., ed. *Euripides: Bacchae*. Oxford: Clarendon, 1944.

———. *The Greeks and the Irrational*. Berkeley: University of California Press, 1951.

———. "On Misunderstanding the Oedipus Rex." *Greece and Rome* 13 (1966) 37–49.

———. *Pagan and Christian in an Age of Anxiety: Some Aspects of Religious Experience from Marcus Aurelius to Constantine*. Cambridge: Cambridge University Press, 1965.

———. "The *Parmenides* of Plato and the Origin of the Neoplatonic One." *Classical Quarterly* 22 (1928) 129–42.

Donas, P. "Pleasure and Human Good in Epicurus." *Oxford Studies in Ancient Philosophy* 57 (2019) 301–40.

Dorival G., and D. Pralo, eds. *Nier Dieu, nier les dieux*. Aix-en-Provence: Publications de l'Université de Provence, 2002.

Dörrie, H. *Porphyrius' Symmikta Zetemeta*. Munich: Beck 1959.

Dorter, K. *Plato's Phaedo: An Interpretation*. Toronto: University of Toronto Press, 1982.

Dowden, K. "Cupid and Psyche: A Question of the Vision of Apuleius." In *Aspects of Apuleius' Golden Ass*, vol. 2, *Cupid and Psyche*, edited by M. Zimmerman et al., 1–22. Groningen: Forsten, 1998.

Drachmann, A. B. *Atheism in Classical Antiquity*. London: Gyldendat, 1922.

Drijvers, H. J. W. *Bardaisan of Edessa*. Piscataway, NJ: Gorgias, 2016.

———, ed. and trans. *The Book of the Laws of Countries: Dialogue on Fate of Bardaisan of Edessa*. Piscataway, NJ: Gorgias, 2007.

Drozdek, A. *Greek Philosophers as Theologians*. London: Taylor and Francis, 2016.

Dryden, J. de Waal. "Revisiting Romans 7: Law, Self and Spirit." *Journal for the Study of Paul and His Letters* 5 (2015) 129–51.

Dykes, A. *Reading Sin in the World: The Hamartigenia of Prudentius and the Vocation of the Responsible Reader*. New York: Cambridge University Press, 2017.

Edmonds, R. G., III. "The 'Orphic Gold Tablets. Texts and Translations, with Critical Apparatus and Tables." In *"Orphic" Gold Tablets and Greek Religion*, edited by R. G. Edmonds, 22–34. Oxford: Oxford University Press, 2011.

Edwards, M. J. "*Aidos* in Plotinus: *Enneads* II.9.10." *Classical Quarterly* 40 (1989) 228–32.

———. *Aristotle and Early Christian Thought*. London: Routledge, 2019.

———. "Astrology and Freedom: The Case of Firmicus Maternus." In *Individuality in Late Antiquity*, edited by J. Zachhuber and A. Torrance, 29–45. Farnham, UK: Ashgate, 2014.

———. "Atticizing Moses? Numenius, the Fathers and the Jews." *Vigiliae Christianae* 44 (1990) 64–75.

———. "Augustine and His Christian Predecessors." In *A Companion to Augustine*, edited by M. Vessey, 316–27. Chichester, UK: Wiley Blackwell, 2012.

————. "Augustine and Pelagius on the Epistle to the Romans." In *The Oxford Handbook to the Reception History of the Bible*, edited by C. C. Rowland and M. Lieb, 609–20. Oxford: Oxford University Press, 2011.

————. "Christians against Matter: A Bouquet for Bishop Berkeley." In *Gnosticism, Platonism and the Late Ancient World*, edited by K. Corrigan and T. Rasimus, 569–80. Leiden: Brill, 2013.

————. "Didymus the Blind and Evagrius of Pontus." In *Handbook of Early Christian Philosophy*, edited by M. J. Edwards, 516–27. London: Routledge, 2021.

————. "The Donatist Schism and Theology." In *The Donatist Schism*, edited by R. Miles, 101–19. Liverpool: Liverpool University Press, 2016.

————. "From Justin to Athenagoras." In *Intertextuality in the Second Century*, edited by J. Bingham and C. N. Jefford, 150–62. Leiden: Brill, 2016.

————. "The Gnostic Myth." In *Christianity in the Second Century*, edited by J. Carleton Paget and J. Lieu, 137–50. Cambridge: Cambridge University Press, 2017.

————. "Greeks and Demons in the Great Persecution." In *Politiche religose nel mondo antico e tardoantico*, edited by A. Cecconi and C. Gabrielli, 217–34. Bari, Italy: Edipuglia, 2011.

————. "Ignatius and the Second Century: An Answer to R. Hübner." *Zeitschrift für Antikes Christentum* 2 (1998) 214–26.

————. "Lucretius, Empedocles and Epicurean Polemics." *Antike und Abendland* 35 (1989) 104–15.

————. "Neglected Texts in the Study of Gnosticism." *Journal of Theological Studies* 41 (1990) 26–49.

————. "Numenius." In *A History of Mind and Body in Late Antiquity*, edited by A. Marmodoro and S. Cartwright, 52–66. Cambridge: Cambridge University Press, 2018.

————. "Numenius Fr. 13: A Note on Interpretation." *Mnemosyne* 42 (1989) 478–82.

————. *Origen against Plato*. Aldershot, UK: Ashgate, 2002.

————. "Origen in Paradise: A Response to Peter Martens." *Zeitschrift für Antikes und Christentum* 23 (2019) 163–85.

————. "Origen, Plato and the Afterlife." *International Journal of Platonic Studies* 15 (2021) 160–83.

————. "Origen's Platonism: Questions and Caveats." *Zeitschrift fur Antikes Christentum* 12 (2008) 20–38.

————. "Pauline Platonsm: The Myth of Valentinus." *Studia Patristica* 35 (2001) 205–21.

————. "Porphyrius." In *Philosophie der Kaiserzeit und der Spätantike* 5.2, edited by C. Riedweg, C. Horn and D. Wyrwa, 1327–49. Basel: Schwabe, 2018.

————. "Porphyry's Egyptian: *De Abstinentia* II.47." *Hermes* 123 (1995) 126–28.

————. "Providence, Freewill and Predestination in Origen." In *Fate, Providence and Freewill: Philosophy and Religion in Dialogue in the Early Imperial Age*, edited by R. Brouwer and E. Vimercati, 292–308. Leiden: Brill, 2020.

————. *Religions of the Constantinian Empire*. Oxford: Oxford University Press, 2015.

————. "Scripture in the North African Apologists: Arnobius and Lactantius." In *The Bible in Christian North Africa I*, edited by D. Yates and A. Dupont, 168–88. Berlin: de Gruyter, 2020.

————. "Some Theories on the Dating of Arnobius." *Ephemerides Theologicae Lovanienses* 92 (2016) 671–84.

————. "Two Episodes in Porphyry's *Life of Plotinus*." *Historia* 44 (1991) 456–64.

———. "Was Lucian a Despiser of Religion?" In *International Symposium on Lucianus of Samosata*, edited by M. Cevik, 145–54. Adiyaman, Turkey: University of Adiyaman, 2009.

———. "Willed Causes and Causal Willing in Augustine." In *Causation and Creation in Late Antiquity*, edited by A. Marmodoro and B. D. Prince, 237–52. Cambridge: Cambridge University Press, 2015.

Else, G. F. *Aristotle's Poetics: The Argument*. Cambridge. Harvard University Press, 1957.

Emilsson, E. "Remarks on the Relation between the One and Intellect in Plotinus." In *Traditions of Platonism: Essays in Honour of John Dillon*, edited by J. J. Cleary, 271–90. Aldershot, UK: Ashgate, 1999.

Engberg-Pedersen, T. *Paul and the Stoics*. London: T. & T. Clark, 2000.

———. "Stoic Freedom in Paul's Letter to the Romans 6.1–8.30 and Epictetus, *Dissertation* 4.1." In *Fate, Providence and Freewill: Philosophy and Religion in Dialogue in the Early Imperial Age*, edited by R. Brouwer and E. Vimercati, 97–119. Leiden: Brill, 2020.

Englert, W. G. *Epicurus on the Swerve and Voluntary Action*. Oxford: Clarendon, 1987.

Estes, D., ed. *The Tree of Life*. Leiden: Brill, 2020.

Evans E. , ed. and trans. *Tertullian: Adversus Marcionem*. Oxford: Clarendon, 1972.

Evans, G. R. *Augustine on Evil*. Cambridge: Cambridge University Press, 1990.

Evans-Pritchard, E. *Witchcraft, Oracles and Magic among the Azande*. Oxford: Clarendon, 1937.

Festugière, A.-J. "La doctrine des *viri novi* sur l'origine et le sort des âmes." In *Memorial Lagrange*, 97–132. Paris: Gabalda, 1940.

———. *Epicure et ses dieux*. Paris: Presses Universitaire de France, 1946.

———. *Personal Religion among the Greeks and Romans*. Berkeley: University of California Press, 1954.

Fitzmeyer, J. "The Consecutive Meaning of ἐφ' ᾧ in Romans 5.12." *New Testament Studies* 39 (1990) 321–39.

Fowden, G. *The Egyptian Hermes: A Historical Approach to the Late Pagan Mind*. Cambridge: Cambridge University Press, 1993.

Francis, J. *Adults as Children: Images of Childhood in the Ancient World*. Oxford: Lang, 2006.

Fränkel, H. *Early Greek Poetry and Philosophy*. Translated by M. Hadas and J. Willis. Oxford: Blackwell, 1975.

Franzmann, M. *Jesus in the Manichaean Writings*. London: Bloomsbury, 2003.

Frede, M. *A Free Will: Origins of the Notion in Ancient Thought*. Berkeley: University of California Press, 2011.

Frye, N. *The Great Code*. London: Routledge, 1982.

Fuhrer, T. "Ille intus magister: On Augustine's Didactic Concept of Interiority." In *Teachers in Antiquity*, edited by P. Gemeinhardt, O. Lorgeoux, and M. L. Munkolt Christensen, 129–46. Tübingen: Mohr Siebeck, 2018.

Furley, D. *Creationism and Its Critics in Antiquity*. Berkeley: University of California Press, 2007.

Gardner, I. "Dualism in Mani and Manichaeism." *Chora* 13 (2015) 417–36.

———. *The Founder of Manichaeism: Rethinking the Life of Mani*. Cambridge: Cambridge University Press, 2020.

Gaskin, R. *The Sea Battle and the Master Argument: Aristotle and Diodorus Cronus on the Metaphysics of the Future*. Berlin: de Gruyter, 1985.

Bibliography

Gassman, M. "Arnobius' Scythians and the Dating of *Adversus Nationes.*" *Journal of Theological Studies* 72 (2021) 832–42.

Gauchet, M. *The Disenchantment of Society: A Political History of Religion.* Princeton: Princeton University Press, 1997.

Gentz, G. "A Reconsideration of the Date of St. Athanasius' *Contra Gentes* and *De Incarnatione.*" *Studia Patristica* 3 (1961) 263–68.

George, A. *The Epic of Gilgamesh.* London: Penguin, 1999.

Gerson, L. "Plotinus' Metaphysics: Emanation or Creation?" *Review of Metaphysics* 46 (1993) 559–74.

———. "The Unity of Intellect in Aristotle's *De Anima.*" *Phronesis* 49 (2004) 348–73.

Ginunchi, M. "*Dunamis* et *taxis* dans la conception trinitaire d'Athénagore." In *Les apologistes chrétiens et la cultue grecque*, edited by B. Pouderon and J. Doré, 121–34. Paris: Beauchesne 1998.

Girard, R. *Job, the Victim of his People.* Translated by Y. Freccero. London: Athlone, 1987.

———. *Violence and the Sacred.* Translated by P. Gregory. Baltimore: Johns Hopkins Press, 1979.

Girardet, K. *Konstantins Rede an die Versammlung der Heiligen.* Freiburg: Herder, 2013.

Girgenti, G. "Dell' ira de Achille all' ira dell' Angello." In *Lattanzio: La collera di Dio*, edited by L. Gasparri, 435–53. Milan: Bompianai, 2011.

Gnoli, G. *Il Manicheismo. Vol. i: Mani e il Manichiesmo.* Milan: Mondadori, 2001.

Golitzin, A. *Mystagogy: A Monastic Reading of Dionysius Areopagita.* Collegeville, MN: Liturgical, 2014.

Graf, F. "Text and Ritual: The Corpus Eschatologicum of the Orphics." In *"Orphic" Gold Tablets and Greek Religion*, edited by R. G. Edmonds, 53–68. Oxford: Oxford University Press, 2011.

Graham, D. *The Texts of Early Greek Philosophy.* 2 vols. Cambridge: Cambridge University Press, 2010.

Grant, M. *The Climax of Rome.* London: Weidenfeld and Nicholson, 1967.

Grant, R. M. *Gnosticism and Early Christianity.* New York: Columbia University Press, 1976.

Greer, R., and M. Mitchell, eds. *The Belly-Myther of Endor.* Atlanta: Society of Biblical Literature, 2007.

Griffin, M. "Proclus on Place as the Luminous Vehicle of the Soul." *Dionysius* 30 (2012) 160–86.

Griffin, M. T. "*Imago Vitae Suae.*" In *Seneca*, edited by C. D. M. Costa, 1–38. London: Routledge and Kegan Paul, 1974.

Griffiths, J. G. *Apuleius of Madauros: The Isis-Book (Metamorphoses XI).* Leiden: Brill, 1975.

Grube, G. M. A. *The Drama of Euripides.* London: Methuen, 1941.

Guillaumont, A. A. "Évagre et les anathémathismes antiorigéniste de 553." *Studia Patristica* 3 (1961) = Texte und Untersuchungen 78, 219–26.

———. *Les Kephalaia Gnostica d'Évagre le Pontique et l'histoire de l'origénisme chez les grecs et chez les syriens.* Paris: Seuil, 1962.

Gurtler, G. M. "Providence: The Platonic Demiurge and Hellenistic Causality." In *Neoplatonism and Nature: Studies in Plotinus' Enneads*, edited by R. Wagner, 99–124. New York: State University of New York Press, 2002.

Gwyn Griffiths, J. *Apuleius of Madauros: The Isis Book.* Leiden: Brill, 1975.

———. *Plutarch's De iside et Osiride.* Cardiff: University of Wales Press, 1972.

Bibliography

Gwynn, D. *The Eusebians: The Polemic of Athanasius of Alexandria and the Construction of the "Arian Controversy."* Oxford: Oxford University Press, 2007.

Hadot, P. "Être, vie, pensée chez Plotin et avant Plotin." In *Entretiens Hardt: Les Sources de Plotin,* 107–57. Vandoeuvres-Geneva: Fondation Hardt, 1960.

———. "La métaphysique de Porphyre." In *Entretiens Hardt 12: Porphyre,* 127–43. Geneva: Foundation Hardt, 1965.

Halfwassen, J. *Der Aufstieg zum Einen: Unteruchungen zu Platon und Plotin.* Tübingen: de Gruyter, 1992.

Hall, C. *Origen and Prophecy.* Oxford: Oxford University Press, 2021.

Halliwell, S. *Greek Laughter: A Study of Cultural Psychology from Homer to Early Christianity.* Cambridge: Cambridge University Press, 2008.

———. "Plato and Aristotle on the Denial of Tragedy." *Proceedings of the Cambridge Philological Society* 30 (1984) 49–71.

Halton, T., trans. *Theodoret of Cyrus on Divine Providence.* New York: Newman, 1988.

Hankey, W. "Denys and Aquinas: Antimodern Cold and Postmodern Hot." In *Christian Origins: Tradition, Rhetoric and Community,* edited by L. Ayres and G. Jones, 139–84. London: Routledge, 1998.

Harder, P. R. "Eine neue Schrift Plotins." *Hermes* 71 (1936) 1–10.

Harl, M. "La préexistence des âmes dans l'oeuvre d'Origène." In *Origeniana Quarta,* edited by L. Lies, 238–58. Innsbruck: Tyrolia, 1985.

Harrison, S. J. *Apuleius: A Latin Sophist.* Oxford: Oxford University Press, 2000.

———. "On the God of Socrates: Introduction." In *Apuleius: Rhetorical Works,* edited by S. J. Harrison, J. Hilton, and V. Hunink, 185–216. Oxford: Oxford University Press, 2001.

Heard, C. "The Tree of Life in Genesis." In *Tree of Life,* edited by D. Estes, 74–99. Leiden: Brill, 2020.

Heine, R. *Origen: An Introduction to His Life and Thought.* Eugene, OR: Cascade, 2019.

Helleman-Elgersma, W. *Soul-Sisters: A Commentary on Enneads IV.3.1–8.* Amsterdam: Rodopi, 1980.

Helm, R. *Lucian und Menipp.* Leipzig: Teubner, 1906.

Helmig, C. "Porphyry and Plutarch of Chaeronea on Transmigration: Who Is the Author of Stobaeus I.44514–448.3W.-H?" *Classical Quarterly* 58 (2008) 250–55.

Hengel, M. *Judaism and Hellenism: Studies in Their Encounter in Palestine during the Early Hellenistic Period.* Translated by J. Bowden. Minneapolis: Fortress, 1974.

Henrichs, A., and L. Koenen. "Der Kölner Mani-Codex." *Zeitschrift für Papyrologie und Epigraphik* 5 (1970) 97–216.

Hill, C. *The Johannine Corpus in the Early Church.* New York: Oxford University Press, 2004.

Hofreiter, C. *Making Sense of Old Testament Genocide.* Oxford: Oxford University Press, 2018.

Hubler, J. N. "Moderatus, E. R. Dodds and the Development of Neoplatonist Emanation." In *Plato's Parmenides and Its Heritage,* edited by J. D. Turner and K. Corrigan, 115–30. Atlanta: Society of Biblical Literature, 2010.

Hunink, V. "Apuleius and the *Asclepius.*" *Vigiliae Christianae* 50 (1996) 288–308.

Inwood, M. "Plato's Eschatologial Myths." In *Plato's Myths,* edited by C. Partenie, 28–50. Cambridge: Cambridge University Press, 2009.

Bibliography

Ivanovic, F. "Eros as a Divine Name according to Dionysius the Areopagite." In *The Ways of Byzantine Philosophy*, edited by M. Knežević, 123–41. Alhambra, CA: Sebastian, 2015.

Jackson, H. M. "The Seer Nikotheus and His Lost Apocalypse in the Light of Sethian Apocalypses and the Apocalypse of Elchasai." *Noveum Testamentum* 32 (1990) 250–77.

Jaeger, W. *Paideia: The Ideals of Greek Culture*. Vol. 1. Translated by G. Highet. New York: Oxford University Press, 1945.

Johnston, P. S. *Shades of Sheol: Death and the Afterlife in the Old Testament*. Chicago: Chicago University Press, 2002.

Johnstone, M. A. "Logos in Heraclitus." *Oxford Studies in Ancient Philosophy* 47 (2014) 1–30.

Jonas, H. *The Gnostic Religion: The Message of the Alien God and the Beginnings of Christianity*. Boston: Beacon, 1958.

Jones, C. P. *Culture and Society in Lucian*. Cambridge: Harvard University Press, 1986.

Jones, F. S. "The Astrological Trajectory in Ancient Syriac-Speaking Christianity Elchasai, Bardaisan, Mani." In *Atti del terzo congesso internazionaledi studi 'Manicheismo e oriente cristiano antico'*, edited by L. Cirillo and A. von Tongerloo, 183–200. Louvain: Brepols, 1997.

Jones, J. *On Aristotle and Greek Tragedy*. London: Chatto and Windus, 1971.

Jong, A. de. "*A quodam Persa exsisterunt*: Re-Orienting Manichean Origins." In *Empsychoi Logoi—Religious Innovations in Antiquity. Studies in Honour of Pieter Willem van der Horst*, edited by A. Houtman, A. de Jong and M. Missez-Van de Weg, 81–106. Leiden: Brill 2008.

Jónsson, G. A. *The Image of God: Genesis 1.26–28 in a Century of Old Testament Research*. Stockholm: Almqvist and Wiksell, 1988.

Jung, C. G. *Alchemical Studies*. Princeton: Princeton University Press, 1967.

Kannengiesser, C. "Le témoignage des *Lettres Festales* de Saint Athanase sur la date de l'Apologie contre les Païens." *Recherches de Science Religieuse* 52 (1964) 91–100.

Kant, I. *The Only Possible Basis for a Demonstration of the Existence of God* (1763). Translated by G. Treash. New York: Abaris, 1979.

Käsemann, E. *Commentary on Romans*. Translated by G. Bromiley. London: SCM, 1980.

Katos, D. S. *Palladius of Helenopolis: The Origenist Advocate*. Oxford: Oxford University Press, 2011.

Keech, D. *The Anti-Pelagian Christology of Augustine of Hippo*. Oxford: Oxford University Press, 2012.

Kelley, N. "Astrology in the Pseudo-Clementine Recognitions." *Journal of Ecclesiastical History* 59 (2008) 607–29.

Kennedy, G. *Greek Rhetoric under Christian Emperors*. Princeton: Princeton University Press, 1983.

King, D. "Ancient Philosophy Transformed: The Religious Turn in Philosophy." In *A Companion to Religion in Late Antiquity*, edited by J. Lössl and N. Baker-Brian, 411–31. London: Wiley Blackwell, 2018.

Kingsley, P. *Ancient Philosophy, Mystery and Magic: Empedocles and Pythagorean Tradition*. Oxford: Clarendon, 1995.

———. "Poimandres: The Etymology of the Name and the Origins of the Hermetica." *Journal of the Warburg and Courtauld Institutes* 56 (1993) 1–24.

Kirk, G. S., and J. E. Raven. *The Presocratic Philosophers*. Cambridge: Cambridge University Press, 1957.

Knepper, T. *Negating Negation: Against the Apophatic Abandonment of the Dionysian Corpus*. Eugene, OR: Cascade, 2013.

Köckert, C. *Christliche Kosmologie und Kaiserzeitliche Philosophie*. Tübingen: Mohr Siebeck, 2009.

Koenen, L., and C. Römer. *Der Kölner Mani-Kodex: Über das Werden seines Leibes*. Opladen: Westdeutscher Verlag, 1988.

Koning, H. H. "The Hesiodic Question." In *The Oxford Handbook of Hesiod*, edited by A. C. Loney and S. Scully, 18–29. Oxford: Oxford University Press, 2018.

Konstan, D. *The Origin of Sin: Greece and Rome, Early Judaism and Christianity*. London: Bloomsbury, 2022.

Konstantinovsky, J. *Evagrius of Pontus: The Making of a Christian Gnostic*. Farnham, UK: Ashgate, 2009.

Kors, A C. "The Enlightenment." In *The Oxford Handbook of Atheism*, edited by S. Bullivant and M. Ruse, 195–211. Oxford: Oxford University Press, 2013.

Kotzé, A. *Augustine's Confessions: Communicative Purpose and Audience*. Leiden: Brill, 2004.

Kraeling, C. H. *Anthropos and Son of Man*. Eugene, OR: Wipf and Stock, 2008.

Kraus, T. *Prudentius' Contra Symmachum, Vergil und Rom*. Wiesbaden: Reichert, 2022.

Lamberigts, M. "Was Augustine a Manichaean? The Assessment of Julian of Aeclanum." In *Augustine and Manichaeanism in the Latin West*, edited by J. Van Oort, O. Wemelinger, and G. Wurst, 113–16. Leiden: Brill, 2001.

Lamberton, R. *Homer the Theologian*. Berkeley: University of California Press, 1986.

Lankila, T. "The Corpus Areopagiticum as a Crypto-Pagan Project." *Journal for Late Antique Religion and Culture* 5 (2011) 14–40.

Laporte, J. *Théologie liturgique chez Philon d' Alexandrie at Origène*. Paris: Cerf, 1995.

Law, T. M. *When God Spoke Greek: The Septuagint and the Making of the Christian Bible*. Oxford: Oxford University Press, 2013.

Layton, R. A. *Didymus the Blind and His Circle in Late Antique Alexandria*. Champaign: University of Illinois Press, 2004.

Leeming, B. "Augustine, Ambrosiaster and the *Masas Perditionis*." *Gregorianum* 11 (1930) 58–91.

Leo, P. di. "Plotinus and the Young Augustine on the Fall of the Soul." *Augustiniana* 63 (2013) 257–88.

Leroux, G. *Plotin: Traité sur l'unité et la volonté de l'Un*. Paris: Vrin, 1990.

Lettieri, G. "Il νοῦς mistico: Il superamento orogeniano dello gnotsicismo." In *Il Commento a Giovanni di Origene. Il testo e suoi contesti*, edited by E. Prinzivalli, 177–275. Rome: Pazzini 2005.

Lévêque, P. *Homeri Catena Aurea: Une étude sur l'allégorie grecque*. Paris: Belles Lettres, 1958.

Lieu, J. *Marcion and the Making of a Heretic*. Cambridge: Cambridge University Press, 2015.

Lieu, S. N. C. *Manichaeism in Central Asia and China*. Leiden: Brill, 1998.

———. "The Self-Identity of the Manichaeans in the Roman East." *Mediterranean Archaeology* 11 (2008) 205–27.

Linforth, I. M. *The Arts of Orpheus*. New York: Arno, 1973.

Litwa, D., ed. and trans. *Refutation of All Heresies*. Atlanta: Society of Biblical Literature, 2016.

Lloyd-Jones, H. *The Justice of Zeus*. Berkeley: University of California Press, 1971.

Löhr, W. *Basilides und seine Schüle*. Tübingen: Mohr Siebeck, 1996.

———. "Did Marcion Distinguish between a Just God and a Good God?" In *Marcion und seine Kirchengeschichtliche Wirkung*, edited by G. May and K. Greschat, 131–46. Berlin: de Gruyter, 2002.

Loney, A. C. "Hesiod's Temporaliies." In *The Oxford Handbook of Hesiod*, edited by A. C. Loney and S. Scully, 109–24. Oxford: Oxford University Press, 2018.

Long, A. A. *Epictetus: A Stoic and Socratic Guide to Life*. Oxford: Clarendon, 2000.

———. "Heraclitus and Stoicism." *Filosofia* 5 (1975) 133–56.

———. "What Is the Matter with Matter, according to Plotinus?" *Royal Institute of Philosophy Supplements* 78 (2016) 37–54.

Long, J. "The Wolf and the Lion: Synesius' Egyptian Sources." *Greek, Roman and Byzantine Studies* 28 (2004) 103–15.

Louth, A. *Denys the Areopagite*. London: Continuum, 1989.

———. "Individual and Liturgical Piety in Dionysius the Areopagite." *Vigiliae Christianae* supplement 16 (2020) 308–24.

Lovejoy, A. O., and G. Boas. *Primitivism and Related Ideas in Antiquity*. Baltimore: Johns Hopkins University Press, 1935.

Luca, L. de. "Providence and Cosmology in Philo of Alexandria." In *Fate, Providence and Free Will: Philosophy and Religion in Dialogue in the Early Imperial Age*, edited by R. Brouwer and E. Vimercati, 64–79. Leiden: Brill, 2020.

Ludlow, M. A. *Art, Craft and Theology in Fourth-Century Christian Authors*. Oxford: Oxford University Press, 2020.

———. *Universal Salvation: Eschatology in the Thought of Gregory of Nyssa and Karl Rahner*. Oxford: Oxford University Press, 2000.

Macdonald, D. B. *The Hebrew Philosophical Genius: A Vindication*. Princeton: Princeton University Press, 1936.

MacGregor, A. "Was Manilius Really a Stoic?" *Illinois Classical Studies* 30 (2005) 41–65.

Mackenna, S. *The Enneads of Plotinus*. London: Faber, 1917–30.

Mackenzie, T. "Empedocles, Personal Identity and the Narrative of the Fallen Soul." *Phoenix* 74 (2020) 111–30.

———. *Poetry and Poetics in the Presocratic Philosophers*. Cambridge: Cambridge University Press, 2021.

Macleod, C. W. "Politics and the *Oresteia*." *Journal of Hellenic Studies* 102 (1982) 124–44.

Macmullen, R. *Paganism in the Roman Empire*. New Haven, CT: Yale University Press, 1981.

Macrae, G. "The Jewish Background of the Gnostic Sophia Myth." *Novum Testamentum* 12 (1970) 80–101.

Mahé, J.-P. "La création dans les Hermetica." *Recherches Augustiniennes* 21 (1986) 3–53.

———. "Remarques d'un latiniste sur l'*Asclepius* Copte de Nag Hammadi." *Revue des sciences religieuses* 48 (1974) 136–55.

Majercik, R. "Chaldean Triads in Neoplatonic Exegesis." *Classical Quarterly* 51 (2001) 265–96.

———. "The Existence-Life-Intellect Triad in Gnosticism and Neoplatonism." *Classical Quarterly* 42 (1992) 475–88.

Bibliography

Manchester, P. "The Noetic Triad in Plotinus, Marius Victorinus and Augustine." In *Neoplatonism and Gnosticism*, edited by R. Wallis and J. Bregman, 207–22. Albany: State University of New York Press 1992.

Marcovich, M. *Studies in Greco-Roman Myth and Gnosticism.* Leiden: Brill, 1988.

Markschies, C. "New Research on Ptolemaeus Gnosticus." *Zeitschrift für Antikes Christentum* 4 (2000) 225–54.

Martens, P. W. "Embodiment, Heresy and the Hellenization of Christianity." *Harvard Theological Review* 108 (2015) 594–620.

———. *Origen and Scripture: The Contours of the Exegetical Life.* Oxford: Oxford University Press, 2012.

———. "Response to Edwards." *Zeitschrift fur Antikes Christentum* 23 (2019) 185–200.

Martin, A., and O. Primavesi. *L'Empédocle de Strasbourg.* Berlin: de Gruyter, 1999.

Marx-Wolf, H. *Spiritual Taxonomies and Ritual Authority: Platonists, Priests and Gnostics in the Third century C.E.* Philadelphia: University of Pennsylvania Press, 2016.

Mastandrea, P. *Cornelio Labeone: Un Neoplatonico Latino.* Leiden: Brill, 1979.

May, G. *Creatio ex Nihilo: The Doctrine of Creation Out of Nothing in Early Christian Thought.* Translated by A. S. Worrall. Edinburgh: T. & T. Clark, 1994.

Mazzuchi, C. M. "Damascio, autore del Corpus Dionysiacum." *Aevum* 80 (2006) 299–33.

McCashen, G. "The *Apocryphon of John's* Father Discourse as Christian Theology." *Journal of Theological Studies* 73 (2022) 439–73.

Meier, P. A. *Plotinus on the Good or the One Enneads VI.9. An Analytical Commentary.* Amsterdam: Gieben, 1992.

Meijering, E. P. *Orthodoxy and Platonism in Athanasius: Synthesis or Antithesis?* Leiden: Brill, 1968.

Mill, J. S. *Examination of Sir William Hamilton's Philosophy.* London: Longmans, 1865.

———. *Three Essays on Religion.* London: Longmans, 1878.

Miller, E. L. "The Logos of Heraclitus: Updating the Report." *Harvard Theological Review* 74 (1981) 161–76.

Mitchell, S., and P. van Nuffelen. "Introduction: The Debate about Pagan Monotheism." In *One God: Pagan Monotheism in the Roman Empire*, edited by S. Mitchell and P. van Nuffelen, 1–15. Cambridge: Cambridge University Press, 2010.

Moltmann, J. *The Crucified God.* Translated by R. A. Wilson and J. Bowden. London: SCM, 1976.

———. *The Way of Jesus Christ: Christology in Messianic Dimensions.* Translated by M. Kohl. London: SCM, 1990.

Morgan, T. "*Pagans and Christians*: Fifty Years of Anxiety." In *Rediscovering E. R. Dodds: Scholarship, Education, Poetry and the Paranormal*, edited by C. Stray, C. Pelling, and S. Harrison, 182–97. Oxford: Oxford University Press, 2019.

Moses, R. "Physical and/or Spritual Exclusion? Ecclesial Discipline in 1 Corinthians 5." *New Testament Studies* 59 (2013) 172–91.

Morrison, J. V. "Kerostasia, the Dictates of Fate and the Will of Zeus in the *Iliad*." *Arethusa* 30 (1997) 276–96.

Nadaff, R. A. *Exiling the Poets: The Production of Censorship in Plato's Republic.* Chicago: University of Chicago Press, 2002.

Narbonne, J.-M. *Plotinus in Dialogue with the Gnostics.* Leiden: Brill, 2011.

Nicholson, E. *God and His People: Covenant and Theology in the Old Testament.* Oxford: Clarendon, 1988.

————. *The Pentateuch in the Twentieth Century.* Oxford: Clarendon, 1998.

Nickelsburg, E. W., trans. *1 Enoch.* Minneapolis: Fortress, 2012.

Nikulin, D. *Neoplatonism in Late Antiquity.* Oxford: Oxford University Press, 2016.

Noble, C. I. "Plotinus' Unaffectable Matter." *Phronesis* 58 (2013) 249–79.

Nock, A. D. Review of *Sobria Ebrietas*, by H. Lewy. *Journal of Theological Studies* 31 (1930) 308–13.

Norden, E. *Agnostoc Theos: Untersuchungen zur Formengeschichte religiöser Rede.* Leipzig: Teubner, 1913.

Nótári, T. "The Scales as the Symbol of Justice in the *Iliad.*" *Acta Juridica Hungarica* 46 (2005) 249–59.

Obbink, D. "The Stoic Sage in the Cosmic City." In *Topics in Stoic Philosophy*, edited by K. Ieradiakonou, 178–95. Oxford: Clarendon, 1999.

O'Brien, C. S. *The Demiurge in Ancient Thought: Secondary Gods and Divine Mediators.* Cambridge: Cambridge University Press, 2015.

O'Brien, D. *Plotinus on the Origin of Matter: An Exercise in the Interpretation of the Enneads.* Naples: Bibliopolis, 1992.

O'Brien, M. "'For every tatter in its mortal dress': Love, the Soul and her Sisters." In *Aspects of Apuelius' Golden Ass*, vol. 2, *Cupid and Psyche*, edited by M. Zimmerman et al., 23–34. Groningen: Forsten, 1998.

O'Connell, R. J. *St Augustine' Early Theory of Man, A.D. 386–391.* Cambridge: Harvard University Press, 1968.

O'Donnell J., ed. *The Confessions of Augustine.* 3 vols. Oxford: Clarendon, 1992.

O'Donovan, O. "'Usus' and 'Fruitio' in Augustine's *De Doctrina Christiana* I." *Journal of Theological Studies* 33 (1982) 361–97.

O'Neill, J. C. "How Early Is the Doctrine of *Creatio ex Nihilo*?" *Journal of Theological Studies* 53 (2002) 449–65.

Opsomer, J. "Is Plutarch Really Hostile to the Stoics?" In *From Stoicism to Platonism: The Development of Philosophy 100 BCE to 100 CE*, edited by T. Engberg-Pedersen, 296–321. Cambridge: Cambridge University Press, 2017.

————. "The Middle Platonic Doctrine of Conditional Fate." In *Fate, Providence and Moral Responsibility in Ancient, Medieval and Early Modern Thought. Studies in Honour of Carlos Steel*, edited by P. D'Hoine and G. Van Riel, 137–67. Leuven: Leuven University Press, 2014.

————. "Proclus vs Plotinus on Matter." *Phronesis* 46 (2001) 154–88.

Opsomer, J., and C. Steel, trans. *Proclus: Ten Problems Concerning Providence.* London: Bloomsbury, 2012.

Orbe, A. *Antropologia di S. Ireneo.* Madrid: Editorial Catolica, 1969.

Osborn, E. F. "Arguments for Faith in Clement of Alexandria." *Vigliiae Christianae* 48 (1994) 1–24.

————. *Clement of Alexandria.* Cambridge: Cambridge University Press, 2005.

Osborne, C. "Empedocles Recycled." *Classical Quarterly* 37 (1987) 24–50.

————. *Eros Unveiled: Plato and the God of Love.* Oxford: Clarendon, 1996.

————. *Rethinking Early Greek Philosophy.* Ithaca, NY: Cornell University Press, 1987.

Pagels, E. H. "The Demiurge and His Archons: A Gnostic View of the Bishops and Presbyters." *Harvard Theological Review* 69 (1976) 301–24.

————. *The Gnostic Paul: Gnostic Exegesis of the Pauline Letters.* London: Bloomsbury, 1992.

Papadogiannakis, Y. *Christianity and Hellenism in the Fifth-Century Greek East: Theodoret's Apologtics against the Greeks in Context*. Washington, DC: Center for Hellenic Studies, 2012.

Paparella, F. D., ed. *Proclo: Tria Opuscula. Povidenza, Libertà, Male*. Milan: Bompiani, 2014.

Parker, R. "The Origins of *Pronoia*: A Mystery." In *Apodosis: Essays Presented to Dr W. W. Cruichsank to Mark His Eightieth Birthday*, edited by H. C. Nutting, 84–94. London: St Paul's School, 1992.

Partenie, C., ed. *Plato's Myths*. Cambridge: Cambridge University Press, 2009.

Patterson, L. G. *Methodius of Olympus: Divine Sovereignty, Human Freedom and Life in Christ*. Washington, DC: Catholic University of America Press, 1997.

———. "Who Are the Opponents in Origen's *De Resurrectione*?" *Studia Patristica* 19 (1989) 221–29.

Pearson, B. *Ancient Gnosticism: Traditions and Literature*. Minneapolis: Fortress, 2007.

Pavlos, P. "Theurgy in Dionysius the Areopagite." In *Platonism and Christian Thought in Late Antiquity*, edited by P. G. Pavlos, L. F. Janby, E. Emilsson, and T. T. Tollefsen, 150–80. London: Routledge, 2019.

Peradotto, J. "The Omen of the Eagles and the ΕΘΟΣ of Agamemnon." *Phoenix* 23 (1969) 237–63.

Perczel, I. "Dionysius the Areopagite." In *The Wiley Blackwell Companion to Patristics*, edited by K. Parry, 211–25. London: Wiley-Blackwell, 2014.

Perl, E. *Theophany: The Neoplatonic Philosophy of Dionysius the Areopagite*. Albany: State University of New York Press, 2007.

Perone, G. R. "Reversing the Myth of the *Politicus*." *Classical Quarterly* 54 (2004) 88–108.

Petersen, A. R. *Royal God: Enthronement Festivals in Ancient Israel and Ugarit?* Sheffield, UK: Sheffield University Press, 1998.

Pétrement, S. *A Separate God: The Christian Origins of Gnosticism*. Translated by C. Harrison. New York: HarperCollins, 1993.

Pierris, A. L. *The Empedoclean Kosmos: Structure, Process and the Question of Cyclicity*. Patras, Greece: Institute for Philosophical Research, 2005.

Pittenger, N. *After Death: Life in God*. London: SCM, 1980.

Pohlenz, M. *Vom Zorne Gottes*. Göttingengen: Vandenhocek and Ruprecht, 1909.

Pourkier, A. *L'hérésiologie chez Epiphane de Salamis*. Paris: Beauchesne, 1992.

Prinzivalli, E. "L'uomo e il suo destino nel *Commento a Giovanni*." In *Il Commento a Giovanni di Origene: Il testo e suoi contesti*, edited by E. Prinzivalli, 360–82. Rome: Pazzini, 2005.

Proctor T. W. *Demonic Bodies and the Dark Ecologies of Early Christian Culture*. Oxford: Oxford University Press, 2022.

Puech, H.-C. "Les Nouveaux écrits d'Origène et de Didyme découverts à Toura." *Revue d' Histoire et de Philosophie Religieuses* 31 (1951) 293–329.

Quispel, G. "Gnostic Man: The Doctrine of Basilides." In *The Mystic Vision: Papers from the Eranos Yearbook*, edited by J. Campbell, 210–46. Princeton: Princeton University Press, 1968.

Ramelli, I. *Bardaisan of Edessa: A Reassessment of the Evidence and a New Interpretation*. Piscataway, NJ: Gorgias, 2009.

———. *The Christian Doctrine of Apokatastasis: A Critical Assessment from the New Testament to Eriugena*. Leiden: Brill, 2013.

———. "The Dialogue of Adamantius: Preparing the Critical Edition and a Reappraisal." *Rheinisches Museum* 163 (2020) 40–88.

———, ed. *Gregorio di Nissa sull'anima e la resurrezione*. Milan: Bompiani, 2007.

———. "Gregory of Nyssa's Purported Criticism of Origen's Purported Doctrine of the Preexistence of Souls." In *Lovers of the Soul, Lovers of the Body*, edited by I. Ramelli and S. Slaveva-Griffin, 277–308. Cambridge: Harvard University Press, 2022.

———. *Social justice and the Legitimacy of Slavery: The Role of Philosophical Asceticism from Ancient Judaism to Late Antiquity*. Oxford: Oxford University Press, 2016.

———. "Some Overlooked Sources of the *Elements of Theology*." In *Reading Proclus and the Book of Causes*, vol. 3, edited by D. Calma, 406–75. Leiden: Brill, 2022.

Rankin, D. *Athenagoras: Philosopher and Theologian*. Farnham, UK: Ashgate, 2009.

Rasimus, T. *Paradise Reconsidered in Gnostic Mythmaking*. Leiden: Brill, 2009.

———. "Porphyry and the Gnostics: Reassessing Pierre Hadot's Thesis in the Light of Second- and Third-Century Sethian Treatises." In *Plato's Parmenides and Its Heritage*, edited by J. D. Turner and K. Corrigan, 81–111. Atlanta: Society of Biblical Literature, 2010.

———. "The Sethians and the Gnostics of Plotinus." In *Handbook of Early Christian Philosophy*, edited by M. J. Edwards, 426–37. London: Routledge, 2021.

Reale, G., and C. Cassanmagnago, eds. and trans. *Epitteto: Tutte le opere*. Milan: Bompiani, 2017.

Reed, A. Y. *Fallen Angels and the History of Judaism and Christianity: The Reception of Enochic Literature*. Cambridge: Cambridge University Press, 2005.

Reed, D. "Bodily Desires and Afterlife Punishment in the *Phaedo*." *Oxford Studies in Ancient Philosophy* 59 (2021) 46–77.

Reitzenstein, R. *Poimandres: Studien zur Griechisch, Agyptisch und Fruhchristlichen Literatur*. Leipzig: Teubner, 1904.

Reydams-Schils, G. "Calcidius Christianus?" In *Metaphysik and Religion*, edited by T. Kobusch, M. Erler, and I. Männlein-Robert, 193–211. Leipzig: Teubner, 2002.

———. "Calcidius on Matter: A Minimalist Dualism." *Chora* 13 (2015) 241–45.

———. *Calcidius on Plato's Timseus*. Cambridge: Cambridge University Press, 2020.

———. "Maximus of Tyre on God and Providence." In *Selfhood and the Soul: Essays on Ancient Thought and Literature in Honour of Christopher Gill*, edited by R. Seaford, J. Wilkins, and M. Wright, 125–38. Oxford: Oxford University Press, 2017.

Riggs T. "Eros as Hierarchical Principle: A Revaluation of Dionysius' Neoplatonism." *Dionysius* 27 (2009) 71–96.

Rist, J. M. "The Indefinite Dyad and Intelligible Matter in Plotinus." *Classical Quarterly* 12 (1962) 99–107.

———. "Monism: Plotinus and Some Predecessors." *Harvard Studies in Classical Philology* 69 (1965) 329–44.

———. "Plotinus on Matter and Evil." *Phronesis* 6 (1961) 154–66.

Robinson, J. A. T. *The Body: A Study in Pauline Theology*. London: SCM, 1962.

———. *In the End God . . . : A Study in the Christian Doctrine of the Last Things*. 2nd ed. London: Collins, 1968.

Robinson, J. M., ed. *The Coptic Gnostic Library*. Vol. 1. Leiden: Brill, 2000.

Rombs, R. "A Note on the Status of Origen's *De Principiis* in English." *Vigiliae Christianae* 61 (2007) 21–29.

Roots, P. A. "The *De Opificio Dei*: The Workmanship of God and Lactantius." *Classical Quarterly* 67 (1987) 466–86.

Roslem, G. "Apollon, est-il vraiment le dieu du soleil?" In *Plutarque, E de Delphes*, edited by J. Boulogne, M. Brize, and L. Couloubaristis, 178–85. Paris: Vrin, 2006.

Rowley, H. H. *Darius the Mede and the Four World Empires in the Book of Daniel.* Cardiff: University of Wales Press, 1935.

Runia, D. "From Stoicism to Platonism: The Difficult Case of Philo of Alexandria's *De Providentia* I". In *From Stoicism to Platonism*, edited by T. Engberg-Pedersen, 159–78. Cambridge: Cambridge University Press, 2017.

———. "Philo's *De Aeternitate Mundi*: The Problem of Its Interpretation." *Vigiliae Christianae* 33 (1981) 105–51.

Russell, D. A., ed. *Longinus: On the Sublime.* Oxford: Clarendon, 1964.

Russell, N. *The Doctrine of Deification in the Greek Patristic Tradition.* Oxford: Oxford University Press, 2006.

Russell, P. "Hume's Lengthy Digression: Free Will in the *Treatise*." In *The Cambridge Companion to Hume's Treatise*, edited by A. Butler and D. Ainslie, 230–51. Cambridge: Cambridge University Press, 2015.

Rutherford, R. B. *The Meditations of Marcus Aurelius.* Oxford: Clarendon, 1989.

———. "The Philosophy of the *Odyssey*." *Journal of Hellenic Studies* 106 (1986) 145–62.

———. "Voices of Resistance." In *Ancient Historiography and Its Contexts: Studies in Honour of A. B. Woodman*, edited by C. S. Kraus, J. Marincola and C. B. R. Pelling, 312–20. Oxford: Oxford University Press, 2010.

Sanders, E. P. *Jesus and Judaism.* London: SCM, 1985.

Schäfer, J. "Hugo Koch and Josef Stiglmayr on Dionysius and Proclus." In *The Oxford Handbook of Dionysius the Areopagite*, edited by M. J. Edwards, G. Steiris, and D. Pallis, 568–82. Oxford: Oxford University Press, 2022.

Schiavone, M. *Neoplatonesimo e cristianesimo nello Pseudo-Dionigi.* Milan: Marzorati, 1963.

Schibli, H. "Hierocles of Alexandria on the Vehicle of the Soul." *Hermes* 121 (1993) 109–17.

Schlam, C. *The Metamorphoses of Apuleius: On Making an Ass of Oneself.* London: Duckworth, 1992.

———. "Platonica in the *Metamorphoses* of Apuleius." *Transactions and Proceedings of the American Philological Association* 101 (1970) 477–87.

Schröder, S. "Plutarch on Oracles and Divine Inspiration." In *Plutarch on the daimonion of Socrates*, edited by H.-G. Nesselrath, 145–68. Tübingen: Mohr Siebeck, 2010.

Sciesaro, A. *The Passions in Play: Thyestes and the Dynamics of Senecan Drama.* New York: Cambridge University Press, 2003.

Scott, D. A. "Manichaean Views of Buddhism." *History of Religions* 25 (1985) 99–115.

Scott, G. A., ed. *Does Socrates Have a Method? Rethinking the Elenchus in Plato's Dialogues and Beyond.* University Park, PA: Penn State University Press, 2022.

Scott, W. B. *Hermetica.* Vol. IV. Oxford: Oxford University Press, 1936.

Scotti, M. Hirsfall. "The *Asclepius*: Thoughts on a Reopened Debate." *Vigiliae Christianae* 54 (2000) 396–415.

Sedley, D. *Lucretius and the Transformation of Greek Wisdom.* Cambridge: Cambridge University Press, 1998.

———. "The *Timaeus* as Vehicle for Platonic Doctrine." *Oxford Studies in Ancient Philosophy* 56 (2019) 45–72.

Segev, M. *Aristotle on Religion.* Cambridge: Cambridge University Press, 2017.

Bibliography

Shaked, S. *Dualism in Transformation: Varieties of Religion in Sasanian Iran*. London: School of Oriental and African Studies, 1994.

Sharples, R. W. "Alexander of Aphrodisias on Providence: Two Problems." *Classical Quarterly* 32 (1982) 198–211.

———. "The Stoic Background to the Middle Platonist Discussion of Fate." In *Platonic Stoicism-Stoic Platonism: The Dialogue between Platonism and Stoicism in Antiquity*, edited by M. Bonazzi and C. Helmig, 169–87. Leuven: Leuven University Press, 2007.

———. "Threefold Providence: The History and Background of a Doctrine." In *Ancient Approaches to Plato's Timaeus*, edited by R. W. Sharples and A. D. R. Sheppard, 107–27. London: University of London, 2003.

Sharples, R. W., ed. and trans. *Alexander of Aphrodisias on Fate*. London: Duckworth, 1983.

Shaw, G. "Neoplatonic Theurgy and Dionysius the Areopagite." *Journal of Early Christian Studies* 7 (1999) 573–99.

———. *Theurgy and the Soul: The Neoplatonism of Iamblichus*. University Park, PA: Penn State University Press, 1995.

Shea, G. *The Poems of Alcimus Ecdicius Avitus*. Tempe, AZ: Arizona State University Press, 1997.

Simmons, M. B. *Arnobius of Sicca: Religious Conflict and Competition in the Age of Diocletian*. Oxford: Clarendon, 1995.

———. *Universal Salvation in Late Antiquity: Porphyry of Tyre and the Pagan-Christian Debate*. Oxford: Oxford University Press, 2015.

Simonetti, M. "Alcune osservazioni sull' interpretazione origeniana di 'Genesi' 2.7 e 3.21." *Aevum* 36 (1962) 370–81.

Smith, A. "Porphyrian Studies since 1913." In *Auftstieg und Niedergang der Römischen Welt* II.36.2, edited by W. Haase and H. Temporin, 717–73. Vienna: Tempsky, 1992.

———. "The Significance of 'Physics' in Porphyry: The Problem of Body and Matter." In *Neoplatonism an the Philosophy of Nature*, edited by J. Wilberding and C. Horn, 30–43. Oxford: Oxford University Press, 2012.

Smith, M. S. "Before Human Sin and Evil: Desire and Fear in the Garden of God." *Catholic Biblical Quarterly* 80 (2018) 215–30

Smith, R. "What Augustine Did Not Find in the Books of the Platonists." *Logos* 23.4 (2020) 1–33.

Snell, B. *The Discovery of the Mind in Greek Philosophy and Literature*. Translated by T. G. Rosenmeyer. New York: Harper, 1960.

Sodano, A., ed. *Porfirio, Lettera ad Anebo*. Naples: L'arte tipografica, 1958.

———, ed. *Porphyrii in Platonis Timeeum Commentarorium Fragmenta*. Naples: L'arte tipografica, 1964.

Sorabji, R. *Emotion and Peace of Mind: From Stoic Agitation to Christian Temptation*. Oxford: Oxford University Press, 2000.

———. "A Neglected Chapter of the Aristotelian Alexander on Necessity and Responsibility." In *Rereading Ancient Philosophy: Old Chestnuts and Sacred Cows*, edited by V. Harte and R. Woolf, 240–56. Cambridge: Cambridge University Press, 2017.

———. *Time, Creation and the Continuum*. London: Duckworth, 1983.

Sparks, H. F. D., ed. *The Apocryphal Old Testament*. Oxford: Clarendon, 1984.

Spanu, N. *Plotinus, Ennead II.9 [33] "Against the Gnostics."* Leuven: Peeters, 2012.

Spat, E. "The Teachers of Mani in the *Acta Archelai* and Simon Magus." *Vigiliae Christianae* 58 (2004) 1–23.

Squires, S. "Augustine's Changing Thought on Sinlessness." *Augustinianum* 54 (2014) 447–66.

Stackpole, R. *The Incarnation: Rediscovering Kenotic Christology.* British Columbia: Chartwell, 2021.

Staley, G. A. *Seneca and the Idea of Tragedy.* Oxford: Oxford University Press, 2010.

Stamatellos, G. "Plotinus on Transmigration: A Reconsideration." *Journal of Ancient Philosophy* 7 (2013) 49–64.

Stang, C. M. *Apophasis and Pseudonymity in Dionysius the Areopagite.* New York: Oxford University Press, 2012.

Stead, G. C. *Divine Substance.* Oxford: Clarendon, 1977.

Steel, C. *Proclus: On Proividence.* London: Duckworth, 2007.

Steenberg, M. C. "Children in Paradise: Adam and Eve as 'Infants' in Irenaeus of Lyons." *Journal of Early Christian Studies* 12 (2004) 1–22.

———. *Of God and Man: Theological Anthropology from Irenaeus to Athanasius.* Farnham, UK: Ashgate, 2009.

Sterling, G. E. "'The Most Perfect Work': The Role of Matter in Philo of Alexandria." In *Creation ex Nihilo: Origins, Development and Contemporary Challenges*, edited by G. A. Anderson and M. Bockmuehl, 99–109. Notre Dame, IN: University of Notre Dame Press, 2018.

Storey, D. "What Is *Eikasia*?" *Oxford Studies in Ancient Philosophy* 58 (2020) 19–57.

Stratton, B. J. *Out of Eden: Reading, Rhetoric and Ideology in Genesis 2–3.* Sheffield, UK: Sheffield Academic Press, 1995.

Sundermann, W. "Mani." In *Encyclopedia Iranica*, online edition 2009: http://iranicaonlone.org/articles/mani-founder-manicheism.

———. "Mani's Revelations in the Cologne Mani Codex and Other Sources." *Manichaica Iranica: Ausgewählte Schriften* I–II, 83–93. Rome: Istituto italiano per l'Africa e l'Oriente, 2001.

Tarn, W. W. "Alexander Helios and the Golden Age." *Journal of Roman Studies* 22 (1932) 135–60.

Taylor, C. *A Secular Age.* Cambridge: Harvard University Press, 2007.

Taylor, J. V. *The Go-Between God: The Holy Spirit and Christian Mission.* London: SCM, 1972.

Tennant, F. R. *The Sources of the Doctrines of the Fall and Original Sin.* Cambridge: Cambridge University Press, 1903.

Teske, R. J. "St Augustine on the Incorporeality of the Soul in Letter 166." *The Modern Schoolman* 60 (1983) 220–35.

Thiselton, A. *Life after Death: A New Approach to the Last Things.* Grand Rapids: Eerdmans, 2012.

Thom, J. "The Problem of Evil in Cleanthes' Hymn to Zeus." *Acta Classica* 41 (1998) 42–57.

Thomassen, E. *The Coherence of Gnosticism.* Berlin: de Gruyter, 2021.

———. *The Spiritual Seed: The Church of the "Valentinians."* Leiden: Brill, 2008.

Timmins, W. N. *Romans 7 and Christian Identity: A Study of the "I" in Its Literary Context.* Cambridge: Cambridge University Press, 2017.

Todd, R. B. *Alexander of Aphrodisias on Stoic Physics.* Leiden: Brill, 1976.

Tommasi, C., ed. *Arnobio contro I pagani.* Rome: Città Nuova, 2017.

Bibliography

Torchia, J. *Creation and Contingency in Early Patristic Thought.* New York: Lexington, 2019.

Tornau, C. "Intelligible Matter and the Genesis of Intellect: The Metamorphosis of a Plotinian Theme in *Confessions* 12–13." In *Augustine's* Confessions: *Philosophy in Autobiography*, edited by W. F. Mann, 181–214. Oxford: Oxford University Press, 2014.

Trapp, M. B. *Maximus of Tyre: The Philosophical Orations.* Oxford: Clarendon, 1997.

Trelenberg, J. *Tatianos: Oratio ad Graecos. Rede an die Griechen.* Tübingen: Mohr Siebeck, 2012.

Trouillard, J. *La Mystagogie de Proclus.* Paris: Belles Lettres, 1982.

Turner, J. D. "The Platonizing Sethian Treatises, Marius Victorinus's Philosophical Sources and Pre-Plotinian Parmenides Commentaries." In *Plato's Parmenides and Its Heritage*, vol. 1, edited by J. D. Turner and K. Corrigan, 130–70. Atlanta: Society of Biblical Literature, 2010.

Turner, J. D., and K. Corrigan, eds. *Plato's Parmenides and Its Heritage.* 2 vols. Atlanta: Society of Biblical Literature, 2010.

Tzamalikos, P. *Origen and Hellenism.* Bern: Lang, 2022.

———. *Origen: Philosophy of History and Eschatology.* Leiden: Brill, 2007.

Vaillant, A. "Le De Autexousio de Methode d'Olympe: Version Slave et Texte Grec edités et raduits en Français." *Patrologia Orientalis* 22, 631–888. Paris: Firmin Didot, 1930.

Valgiglio, E., ed. *Plutarco: Il fato.* Naples: D'Auria, 1993.

Van den Berg, R. "Proclus in *Platonis Timaeum Commentarii* 2.333.28ff.: The Myth of the Winged Charioteer according to Iamblichus ad Proclus." *Syllecta Classica* 8 (1997) 149–62.

Van der Horst, P. W., and J. Mansfeld. *An Alexandrian Platonist against Dualism.* Leiden: Brill, 1974.

Van der Lof, J. "Mani as the Danger from Persia in the Roman Empire." *Augustinana* 24 (1974) 75–84.

Van der Waerdt, P. A. "Zeno's *Republic* and the Origins of Natural Law." In *The Socratic Movement*, edited by P. A. Van der Waerdt, 272–308. Ithaca, NY: Cornell University Press, 1994.

Van Winden, M. C. *Calcidius on Matter: His Doctrine and Sources. A Chapter on the History of Platonism.* Leiden: Brill, 1959.

Vickers, B. *Towards Greek Tragedy: Drama, Myth, Society.* London: Longmans, 1973.

Viltanioti, I.-F. "Cult Statues in Porphyry of Tyre and Macarius Magnes: Porph. Chr. fr. 76 and fr. 77." *Journal of Late Antiquity* 10 (2017) 187–220.

Vinzent, M. *Marcion and the Dating of the Synoptic Gospels.* Leuven: Peeters, 2014.

Vlad, M. "L'Être premier—entre Proclus et Denys l'Aréopagite." In *Reading Proclus and the Book of Causes*, vol. 3, edited by D. Calma, 89–116. Leiden: Brill, 2022.

Vogel, C. de. "Who Is God in Plato?" In *Philosophia*, by C. de Vogel, 210–43. Amsterdam: Assen, 1970.

Volk, K. "Manilian Self-Contradiction." In *Forgotten Stars: Rediscovering Manilius' Astronomica*, edited by S. Green and K. Volk, 104–19. Oxford: Oxford University Press, 2011.

Waldstein, M., and F. Wisse. *The Apocryphon of John.* In *The Coptic Gnostic Library*, vol. 2, edited by J. M. Robinson, 12–244. Leiden: Brill 2000.

Ward, H. C. *Clement and Scriptural Exegesis: The Making of a Commentarial Theologian.* Oxford: Oxford University Press, 2022.

Waszink, J. H., ed. *Plato Latinus IV: Chalcidius, Commentarium in Timaeum.* Leiden: Brill, 1974.

———. "Le rapport de Calcidius sur le doctrine platonicienne sur la métampsychose." In *Mélanges d'histoire des religions offerts à Henri-Charles Puech,* 315–22. Paris: Presses Universitaires de France, 1974.

Wear, S. K., and J. M. Dillon. *Dionysius the Areopagite and the Neoplatonist Tradition: Despoiling the Hellenes.* Farnham, UK: Ashgate, 2011.

Weissner, S. "Why Does Philo Criticise the Stoic Ideal of Apatheia in *On Abraham* 257: Philo and Consolatory Literature?" *Classical Quarterly* 62 (2012) 242–59.

West, M. L. *The East Face of Helicon: West Asiatic Elements in Greek Poetry and Myth.* Oxford: Clarendon, 1997.

———, ed. *Hesiod: Works and Days.* Oxford: Clarendon, 1978.

———. *The Orphic Poems.* Oxford: Clarendon, 1983.

———. "Towards a Chronology of Early Greek Epic." In *Relative Chronology in Early Greek Epic Poetry,* edited by O. Andersen and D. D. Haug, 224–41. Cambridge: Cambridge University Press, 2012.

Westerink, L. G., trans. *Anonymous Prolegomena to Platonic Philosophy.* Amsterdam: North Holland, 1962.

Westra, L. "Freedom and Providence in Plotinus." In *Neoplatonism and Nature: Studies in the Enneads of Plotinus,* edited by R. Wagner, 125–48. Albany: State University of New York Press, 2002.

White, F. C. "Love and Beauty in Plato's *Symposium.*" *Journal of Hellenic Studies* 109 (1989) 149–57.

Whitmarsh, T. *Battling the Gods: Atheism in the Ancient World.* New York: Knopf, 2016.

Whitney, W. *Two Strange Beasts: Leviathan and Behemoth in Second Temple and Early Rabbinic Judaism.* Leiden: Brill, 2006.

Whittaker, J. "*Epekeina nou kai ousias.*" *Vigiliae Christianae* 23 (1969) 91–104.

———. "Moses Atticizing." *Phoenix* 21 (1967) 196–202.

———. "Self-Generating Principles in Second-Century Gnostic Systems." In *The Rediscovery of Gnosticism,* vol. 1, edited by B. Layton, 176–93. Leiden: Brill, 1980.

Wetzel, J. "Pelagius Anticipated: Grace and Election in Augustine's *Ad Simplicianum.*" In *Augustine from Rhetor to Theologian,* edited by J. McWilliam, 121–32. Waterloo, ON: Wilfrid Laurier University Press, 1992.

Williams, N. P. *The Ideas of the Fall and of Original Sin: A Historical Study.* London: Longmans, 1927.

Wilson, K. *Augustine's Conversion from Traditional Free Choice to "Non-Free Free Will."* Tübingen: Mohr Siebeck, 2018.

Winiarczyk, M. *The "Sacred History" of Euhemerus of Messene.* Berlin: de Gruyter, 2013.

Winkler, J. J. *Auctor and Actor: A Narratological Reading of Apuleius' Golden Ass.* Berkeley: University of California Press, 1985.

Winterbottom, M. "Speaking of the Gods." *Greece and Rome* 36 (1989) 33–41.

Wittgenstein, L. *Philosophical Investigations.* Translated by P. M. S. Hacker and J. Schulte. London: Wiley-Blackwell, 2009.

Wolfson, H. A. *Philo: Foundations of Religious Philosophy in Judaism.* Cambridge: Harvard University Press, 1952.

Bibliography

Woschitz, K. "Der Mythos des Lichts und der Finsternis." In *Das manichäische Urdrama des Lichts. Studien zu koptischen, mitteliranischen und arabien texte*, edited by K. Woschitz, M. Hunter, K. Prenner, 105–8. Vienna: Herder, 1989.

Yoder, R. "Ezekiel 29.3 and Its Ancient Near Eastern Context." *Vetus Testamentum* 63 (2013) 386–96.

Zachhuber, J. *Human Nature in Gregory of Nyssa*. Leiden: Brill, 2000.

———. "Luther on Dionysius." In *The Oxford Handbook of Dionysius the Areopagite*, edited by M. J. Edwards, G. Steiris, and D. Pallis, 516–32. Oxford: Oxford University Press, 2022.

———. "Stoic Substance, Non-Existent Matter? Some Passages in Basil of Caesarea Reconsidered." *Studia Patristica* 41 (2006) 425–31.

Zanker, A. T. "The Golden Age." In *Handbook to the Reception of Classical Mythology*, edited by V. Zajko and H. Hoyle, 197–211. London: Wiley-Blackwell, 2017.

Ziesler, P. *Paul's Letter to the Romans*. London: SCM, 1989.

Zuntz, G. "Zum Cleanthes-Hymnus." *Harvard Studies in Classical Philology* 65 (1958) 297–308.

Index

Index

Index

idolatry, 57, 70, 101, 128, 135, 139, 147, 228, 229, 233, 302

Ignatius of Antioch, 94, 99, 195

image of God, 206
    and polytheism, 19, 39, 111, 126, 128, 131, 190, 231
    as primal man, 91, 92, 209
    body participates in, 132–33
    contrasted with likeness, 56, 133, 234
    in Christ, 135–36, 215, 235, 303
    in future state, 69, 166, 234, 283, 303
    in human race, 55–56, 63, 64, 71, 138, 146, 210, 215–16, 230–32, 235–38, 240, 248, 266
    in Wisdom, 63, 98
    in world, 23, 121, 279
    loss of, 160, 165, 234
    seductive, 90, 98, 204, 211

immortality, 174, 263
    in Heraclitus, 8, 18
    of Adam and his posterity, 10, 69, 78, 132–33, 152, 198, 225, 231, 234
    of angels and daemons, 66, 108, 197
    of God, 43, 233
    of gods, 1, 34, 127
    of soul, 10, 18, 37, 63, 88, 130, 156–57, 170, 172, 196, 214, 234, 245, 290–91, 302

India, 139

innocence, 13, 60, 69, 83, 128, 262–64, 275, 294
    primaeval (in classical thought), 5, 22, 30, 134
    primaeval (in Christian thought), 152, 165, 172, 228, 232, 234, 244

Iphigeneia, 14–15, 36

Irenaeus, 139, 152–53, 179–80, 183, 198
    as heresiologist, 90, 94–95, 217
    on protology, 132–36, 210, 225, 234, 262, 270–271

Isaiah, Book of, 55, 57–58, 67, 68, 163, 293

Isis, 102, 106–7, 122

Israel, xiii, xiv, 75, 144
    as chosen people, 54–57, 59, 63, 67, 68, 72, 81
    in Christian thought, 78, 131, 226

scriptures of, 71, 93, 218, 239
oppression of, 70, 79, 89, 125, 161
remnant of, 80, 86
vindication of, 56, 61, 164

Jacob, 55, 58, 72
    in Christian thought, 85, 155, 164, 170, 219, 245, 269

James, letter of, 84

jealousy, 14, 23, 65, 89, 152, 211, 217, 295

Jeremiah, 85, 131, 170

Jerome, 168–69, 195, 273

Jerusalem, 61, 65, 72, 76, 161, 169

Jesus Christ, xi, 174, 207, 216, 233, 270, 275, 296
    and demonic powers, 124, 128–29, 135, 210, 241, 302
    as Savior, xi, 82–83, 86, 90, 92–93, 95, 97–98, 125, 133, 135–36, 150, 157, 165, 167, 218, 232, 228, 270
    body/flesh of, 78, 86, 94, 133, 145–46, 156, 206, 209, 219, 238
    death of, 81, 84, 96–97, 125,127, 135–36, 150, 165–67, 232, 234, 241, 295, 302
    divine character or commission of, xiii, 91, 125, 132, 152, 154, 158–59, 161, 171, 235, 246, 273
    in Gnostic thought, 88, 90–91, 94–99, 144–45, 202–3, 208
    in human soul, 165, 263–64, 268, 275, 303
    preparation for, 68, 96, 135, 163–65, 208, 215, 226, 234–35, 239, 246, 248
    resurrection of, 81–82, 84, 133
    teachings of, 70, 79–81, 85–86, 97, 100, 143, 150, 161–62, 165, 201, 207, 210, 218, 226–28, 231, 248, 282

Jews, 23, 28, 125, 165, 229
    beliefs and customs of, 65, 73–74, 84, 139, 146, 155, 269
    history of, 58, 76, 86, 89, 246
    in Greco-Roman world, 53–54, 59, 68, 70–71, 75–76, 78